The Origin of Speech

OXFORD STUDIES IN THE EVOLUTION OF LANGUAGE

General Editors
Kathleen R. Gibson, *University of Texas at Houston*,
and James R. Hurford, *University of Edinburgh*

PUBLISHED

[For a list of books in preparation for the series, see p 390]

The Origin of Speech

Peter F. MacNeilage

OXFORD
UNIVERSITY PRESS

OXFORD

UNIVERSITY PRESS

Great Clarendon Street, Oxford OX2 6DP

Oxford University Press is a department of the University of Oxford.
It furthers the University's objective of excellence in research, scholarship,
and education by publishing worldwide in

Oxford New York

Auckland Cape Town Dar es Salaam Hong Kong Karachi
Kuala Lumpur Madrid Melbourne Mexico City Nairobi
New Delhi Shanghai Taipei Toronto

With offices in

Argentina Austria Brazil Chile Czech Republic France Greece
Guatemala Hungary Italy Japan Poland Portugal Singapore
South Korea Switzerland Thailand Turkey Ukraine Vietnam

Oxford is a registered trade mark of Oxford University Press
in the UK and in certain other countries

Published in the United States
by Oxford University Press Inc., New York

British Library Cataloguing in Publication Data

Data available

Library of Congress Cataloging in Publication Data

Data available

Typeset by SPI Publisher Services, Pondicherry, India
Printed in Great Britain
on acid-free paper by
CPI Antony Rowe, Chippenham, Wiltshire

ISBN 978–0–19–958158–0

1 3 5 7 9 10 8 6 4 2

Contents

Part VI
A perspective on speech from manual evolution

Part VII
Last things

Figures

Tables

Acknowledgments

This book has been a long time in the making, and I have benefited from a rich and complex support network, which I am supremely grateful for. My first thanks must go to Gardner Lindzey, long-time mentor, friend, tennis partner, and master of repartee, particularly for his support in having Bjorn Lindblom, Michael Studdert-Kennedy, and me together at Stanford's Center for Advanced Study in the Behavioral Sciences to consider our early ideas about the evolution of speech in an idyllic yet intellectually stimulating setting.

An enormous thank-you goes to my close friend and personal editor, John Trimble, for heroic midwifery, and for his enthusiastic belief in the project. He and his wife, Jan, provided convivial conversation and boundless hospitality, making the task of expressing myself more lucidly a pleasurable one.

Particular thanks goes to Babs Davis, former student, friend, and colleague, for harmonious collaboration in our long-term project on speech acquisition, the results of which form the empirical core of the book. I am really grateful for what we were able to accomplish together. And we could not have done what we did without the help of another former student, Chris Matyear, the cornerstone of lab operations. Thanks also to Babs and Krisztina Zajdó for editing the book *The Syllable in Speech Production: Perspectives on the Frame/Content Theory*.

I am grateful to Randy Diehl for his willingness to share his expertise on speech perception, and to Richard Meier for his patient assistance in helping me to understand the nature of sign language, as well as for sharing his viewpoint on sign language, a perspective I am particularly sympathetic to. I am fortunate enough to have had Bjorn Lindblom to share ideas with since 1963, and his presence at the University of Texas for prolonged periods of time has been a continued source of inspiration and conviviality . I have fond memories of the many dinners that he and his wife Ann Marie have kindly afforded me.

Wendy Sandler, another colleague I proudly claim as a former student, also helped initiate me into the world of sign language, and has continued to be a friend and a source of correction and enlightenment on issues concerning sign language. Another former student, Greg Whitemore, facilitated my sign language immersion well beyond providing the knowledge that signers solve the problem of communication in the dark by turning the light on. One source of pride for me is that Kim Oller was my very first graduate student, and I have deeply enjoyed my personal and intellectual contact with him over the years.

Many thanks go to my two most recent students, Lisa Redford and Ashlynn Kinney, for their dedication and contagious enthusiasm, which I credit with helping to keep me young. I am delighted that Lisa has continued to pursue the frame/content perspective. As a long-time teaching assistant, Ashlynn provided an endless supply of much-needed computer literacy band-aids. Many other students, both graduates and undergraduates, have been a pleasure to work with over the years. With a freshness of outlook, as well as a spirit of inquisitiveness and a willingness to challenge established dogma, they have contributed to the sharpening of a number of my own ideas.

France has been an intellectual home away from home for me for many years. In 1992 I spent a very fruitful semester with Benedict de Boysson-Bardies at the Maison l'Homme in Paris. I am grateful to the group at Institut de la Communication Parlée, Grenoble, particularly Christian Abry, Jean Louis Boe, and Jean-Luc Schwartz, for their repeated hospitality, and for their sympathy toward my way of looking at things. At Dynamique du Langage in Lyon, Jean-Marie Hombert and Sophie Kern have provided an ongoing base of hospitality and intellectual stimulation.

I am someone who hates to ask for help, and so I am especially indebted to John Dennis and Sialia Reike, both of whom made this as painless as possible in matters regarding tables and figures, construction of the index, and the task of seeking permissions. John is another of the people whose enthusiasm about my project helped to inspire me, while Sialia's attention to detail never failed to astonish me.

Bobbie Alford deserves a special kind of credit for making her lake cottage available to me as a place of refuge, where I could work on the manuscript without distractions. It turned out to also be a place where one can see canyon wrens using the frame/content mode of organization in their songs.

Most recently, my two OUP editors, John Davey and Chloe Plummer, deserve very special recognition and thanks for all their work, patience, support, and particularly for their unconditional positive regard. Thanks also to series editors Kathleen Gibson and Jim Hurford for their constructive comments, and to one particular reviewer for an exhaustive and extremely helpful critique.

One contribution lay behind all the others. My wife, Linda, has always been there for me, and her unshakable belief that I had something important to contribute at the level of conceptual synthesis made continuing effort possible. I am a better person in this and other ways than I would have been without her love, support, and encouragement.

PART I

Introduction

1 Background: the intellectual context

1.1 Introduction

> In the distant future I see open fields for far more important researches. Psychology will be based on the foundation . . . of the necessary acquirement of each mental power and capacity by gradation. Light will be thrown on the origin of man and his history.
> Charles Darwin, *The Origin of Species* (1859/1952), p. 243

> You can't just assume that because something's there it is functional, or has been adapted for. . . . It could be just there.
> Noam Chomsky, cited by MacFarquhar, 2003, p. 71

"The possession of speech," T. H. Huxley once remarked, "is the grand distinctive character of man" (1871). And indeed it dwarfs most other evolutionary achievements. It involved not just the invention of words but, more remarkable still, the development of the ability to speak them, understand them, and think with them. All of these things are quite unprecedented in the animal kingdom.

Consider speaking. We speak at the rate of some fifteen consonants and vowels per second, and we manage to neatly organize these utterances into larger output chunks called "syllables" by surrounding our vowels with consonants in various ways. In ordinary conversation, the typical number of different consonants and vowels that we produce per second is at least an order of magnitude greater than the unit output rate of any other behavior, or "output complex," either our own or that of any other living form. And we don't simply produce monotone sequences of consonants and vowels, either. We'll invariably give certain syllables more stress than others, and each of our sentences will follow a melodic line whereby the pitch of our voice varies in rule-governed ways, eventually signaling to the listener, by a descending pitch, that the end is approaching. Though the world currently numbers over 6,000 different languages (Grimes, 1998), virtually everybody in every language community—a total of several billion people—can somehow learn and do any commonly occurring patterns of speech acceptably.

The topic of this book is how we *do* speech—specifically, how we produce it—and how, as a species, we came to be able to produce it. I won't also be trying to focus on the other side of the coin, speech perception, simply because I need to keep the enterprise within reasonable bounds.

What exactly *do* we do when we produce speech? The individual consonants and vowels—in English, about forty of them—are each produced by a unique complex of movements that modulate the flow of air coming out of the mouth in such a way as to produce a unique acoustic pattern. Thus each consonant and vowel will sound different from all the others—a necessity if words are to signal their separate meanings. Were I to work on it long enough, I could probably come up with a sentence in which all forty of these sounds would be produced at least once. That sentence would not take much more than three seconds to produce, and, leaving aside tongue-twisters, one would produce it as easily as any other sentence, though most other possible sentences would involve many fewer different sounds per unit of time. The number of different muscles in the speech apparatus—the chest, larynx, throat, mouth, and face—totals about forty. Not all these muscles work for all sounds, of course, but even assuming that just fifteen have to change what they are doing for each successive sound, this would mean that about 225 different muscle activations would occur *in each second of speech.* That averages one event every 5 milliseconds! And add to this the fact that we can't simply think of the same set of about fifteen muscle actions for each individual consonant and vowel whenever they are produced. The muscles used will vary depending not only on what sound comes before the consonant or vowel in question, but also on what sound comes after it, too.

Yet it's something we readily take for granted. Not one person in a thousand would suspect how far speech exceeds in complexity any other kind of action in the animal kingdom. And why? Because speech is mostly *hidden.* We see the lips and the jaw moving, yes, but as even the best lip-reader will tell you, these two components don't come close to conveying all the required information. The key player is the tongue. And we can't see it flipping around in the mouth at its characteristic rate of over a dozen positions per second.

We don't even really *feel* our own tongue moving, either. None of my undergraduate students know, until I ask them, which of the two variants of vocal tract constriction they use to make the "s" sound—the one with the tongue tip, or the one with the tongue blade. The visual equivalent of this would be having to knock on a door to see whether we do it with our finger tips or our knuckles. In speech, we just hear a single acoustical consequence that represents the sum of the movements for a given consonant or vowel. Thus every pattern of fifteen or so muscle actions boils down to one sound. Consequently, the astounding versatility of the speech action system, which is in a league of its own in the animal kingdom, doesn't begin to get the respect it deserves, either in science or in the world in general. It is, in effect, an invisible miracle.

But to truly understand ourselves, we must ask how this miracle was bestowed on us. The two statements at the beginning of the chapter define our central issue here. Did speech evolve "by gradation"—that is, in Darwin's much-quoted phrase, by "descent with modification"—or is it one of those things that is "just there," as Chomsky and many other linguists seem to believe.

Darwin made his hopeful statement on the last page of his 1859 monograph *The Origin of Species*, certainly one of the most important books in the history of science. But surprisingly, though we can agree on the importance of the development he foresaw, a century and a half later we are not there yet. We don't have an agreed-upon descent-with-modification scenario for a single human mental characteristic. Despite the general acceptance of Darwin's theory of evolution by natural selection, and despite an increasing emphasis on evolution in cognitive science, including cognitive neuroscience, and despite the recent advent of the new subdiscipline of Evolutionary Psychology, the notion that even human mental powers evolved by descent with modification has not yet been widely accepted. Instead, many continue to adhere to a still-robust tradition of what I will call "classical" Western philosophy bestowed on us particularly by Plato and Descartes, and, most germane to the topic at hand, enthusiastically embraced within linguistics by its most prominent practitioner, Noam Chomsky (1966). In this tradition, called "generative linguistics," forms are considered to exist a priori, that is, in advance of their use. Moreover, they have no antecedents. For Plato, it was forms in the world and in the mind; for Descartes, it was forms in the mind in particular; for Chomsky, it is language forms in the mind.

My aim here is to help realize Darwin's dream by focusing on one key human mental attribute—speech. I take the standpoint of an evolutionary biologist who, according to Mayr (1982), "studies the forces that bring about changes in faunas and floras ... [and] studies the steps by which have evolved the miraculous adaptations so characteristic of every aspect of the organic world" (pp. 69–70). I will present descent-with-modification scenarios for two aspects of one particular miracle: the evolution of speech itself and the left-cerebral-hemispheric specialization that typically goes with it. And, in parallel, I will argue that the classical structure of Chomskyan linguistic theory, with its anthropocentric claim of linguistic forms originating completely and virtually instantaneously in the *human* mind, and available to the infant prior to use, is inimical to a descent-with-modification approach to the evolution of speech.

In short, I will try to deconstruct the miracle that is speech in the way in which all miracles in nature should be deconstructed—in terms of their history of natural selection. And in the course of doing this I will try to make it clear that the generative approach to speech simply explains one miracle in terms of another.

(A brief clarification is in order here. Most of Chomsky's work has been done in the field of syntax—the study of sentence structures—not in phonology—the study of sound patterns. I will not deal directly with syntax in this book, and I will not claim that syntax evolved directly from phonology. However, Chomsky's conceptual innovation, "generative grammar," and its central construct, "universal grammar," were applied explicitly to phonology as well as syntax, and the book that Chomsky wrote with Halle in 1968, *The Sound Pattern of English*, ushered in an era of dominance of the generative approach to speech which has not yet been transcended. That is one reason why Chomsky's views are a primary concern here.)

To return to the main theme, what we seek for speech is what Mayr calls "ultimate causes" (p. 67). I share Mayr's view that Darwin's theory of evolution by natural selection offers the only framework for understanding how life forms evolved their various traits. But what exactly *is* natural selection? Darwin hypothesized that the survival of any important aspect of body form or behavior depends on successful use. The behavioral component boils down to the production of successful movement complexes, which, collectively, we'll call "action." Think of a predator catching its prey. Success for the predator depends on its having evolved effective movements of capture—an action routine—just as success for its prey involves effective movements of evasion, also an action routine.

If one believes Darwin, as virtually everyone in modern science does, the capacity to speak must have evolved by natural selection. But here the criterion for selection, we may suppose, was effective social communication. Most directly, speech had to have initially involved certain movement patterns (which I will call "action patterns") of the lungs, larynx, and mouth that generated early sound patterns. Each action/sound pattern signaled to the listener, by mutual agreement, a particular concept. Each pairing of a concept with a sound pattern made up what linguists would now call a "morpheme"—a meaning unit. But it was also a word in those simple days, before there were words which could have more than one morpheme.

Now, as we will see, there is a complex mental apparatus underlying our five-per-second delivery of the syllables that make up our typically un-broken sequences of words/sentences. But at the outset we had no such complex mental structure. All we had were some pre-existing movement-generation capacities of what would later be dubbed the "speech appar-atus." It was these successful initial action patterns, and whatever patterns followed them as speech evolved, that dictated the mental apparatus that eventually came to more or less directly underlie speech. Think of a mental dictionary in which every concept is paired with instructions as to how you speak the vocal symbol that goes with it. The action patterns involved in these words were subject to natural selection. They had to be both producible and understandable. The mental representations that devel-oped to provide the instructions were inevitably influenced in their form by the nature of the patterns. In this regard, then, the body influenced the evolution of the structure of the mind.

This contention perhaps becomes more plausible if we note both the final sentence in Darwin's book *The Descent of Man* (1871/1952) and his choice of the word "Descent" rather than "Ascent" in its title: "Man still bears in his bodily frame the indelible stamp of his lowly origins" (p. 597). The bodily components of the speech production apparatus are hundreds of millions of years old, and therefore none of them initially evolved for speech purposes. For example, the respiratory system (basically the lungs), which we use as a power source for speech, originally served as a flotation device in fish, and came to be a life-supporting system of gas exchange in animals using terrestrial habitats. The vocal folds, the component of the larynx that we set into vibration to produce phonation/voicing, were originally part of a valve preventing water from entering the lungs. The airway above the larynx that we now configure in various ways to shape sounds began life as a food-ingestion device. Doesn't it stand to reason that because we modified the control of these devices to produce speech, their heritage influenced the evolution of what we might call the mental overlay of this miraculous system, by which I mean the algorithms that came into use specifically for speaking. Isn't this just as obviously true as the proposition that as different vertebrates developed different oral food-processing strategies, the concurrently developing neural control systems were influenced by what those strategies were?

This book is about what these movement patterns—action patterns—were, and the role they played in the evolution of the mental structures that came to underlie them. But first I ask the reader a favor. *Don't take the movement patterns of speech for granted.* They are the key to our understanding the evolution of speech, including the mental patterns that eventually came to underlie its production. The alternative view, common in modern linguistics, is that speech, from the outset, was essentially a *mental* phenomenon and that its movement patterns are of scant interest. I aim to rebut that view by providing a plausible descent-with-modification account of the natural selection of the motor patterns. Those who believe that speech began as mental patterns have not—and, in my opinion, cannot—provide such an account. And their motivation to try to do so is limited. They are inclined, with Chomsky, to regard the patterns as being "just there."

In taking this body-to-mind stance I ally myself with the Nobel Prize-winning neurobiologist Roger Sperry. In a paper written half a century ago entitled "Neurology and the mind–brain problem," Sperry contended that the best way to fathom the structure of the mind is to start with the body's observable movements and then try to reason backwards, so to speak, to the brain processes—and, by implication, the mental processes—that underlie these movements:

the unknown cerebral events in psychic experience must necessarily involve excitation patterns so designed that they intermesh in intimate fashion with the motor and premotor patterns. . . . The more we learn about the motor and premotor mechanisms, the more restrictions we add to our working picture of the unknown mental patterns and hence the closer our speculation will be forced to converge towards an accurate description of their true nature. (Sperry, 1952, p. 300)

Sperry's approach, anticipating what is now known as the "Embodiment" perspective (see Clark, 1997 and later discussion), holds that mental activity cannot be understood outside of the context of bodily activities. It lets us start out precisely where we have the most readily available observable data—from the movements themselves, including those made visible by X-ray movies and other modern imaging devices; from relatively direct inferences we can otherwise make about the movements based on the acoustic patterns they produce; and from well-accepted methods of phonetic transcription of words observed in the field or supplied in dictionaries. The phonetic alphabet used in these transcriptions gives us a vocabulary for talking about speech—something that is absent in, for example, the study of hand movements.

Beyond my belief in the primacy of the movement patterns in the evolution of speech, I have another perspective guiding my approach to the question.

I first became interested in speech as an undergraduate, when a professor gave me a landmark paper he thought I'd appreciate. It was by the famous neuropsychologist Karl Lashley, and it was called "The problem of serial order in behavior" (Lashley, 1951). How, Lashley wanted to know, is any action sequence *organized*? It's a fascinating question, and far-reaching, since it potentially applies to all living creatures and to all the activities they engage in. Lashley's main focus, though, was on speech. How, he wondered, do we humans make the sequence of words in phrases and sentences, or the sequence of sounds in individual words, even syllables—anything, in short, that involves more than one event in the time domain? Although he proffered a number of valuable suggestions as to how to solve the serial-order problem in speech, which I will summarize later, he didn't lay out a coherent theory about it. But he offered me an enormously rich field of study and a valuable point of departure. In the subsequent half-century, I developed the theoretical perspective on this particular question regarding speech that you will be exploring with me here.

Some readers might think that trying to study the mind by inferring its properties from the movements it directs seems so commonsensical as to be unarguable. But, in fact, there has been virtually no attempt to implement it. Why? Because Western philosophical thought has long focused on the mind–world relationship (i.e., the question of how the mind relates to its input), not on the mind–body relationship (i.e., how the mind controls the body). A central issue in epistemology—the study of the nature and grounds of knowledge—has been whether knowledge or mental structure is *innate* or whether it comes solely from experience of the world—in particular, *perceptual experience*. The dominant classical view, initiated by Plato and reinforced by Descartes, holds that knowledge exists in the human mind a priori. Noam Chomsky, the dominant force in modern linguistics, subscribes to this assumption and bases his linguistic theories on it. He believes our innate knowledge includes both the syntactic aspect of language (sentence structure) and its phonological aspect (sound structures underlying speech). An opposing intellectual tradition is that of Empiricism, associated particularly with the British philosophers Locke and Hume. They held that knowledge isn't innate at all; rather, all of it comes from life experience.

But, curiously, even Empiricists didn't ascribe an important role to *action* in the development of our mental capacities. Consequently, action does not even figure in the usual dictionary definitions of "mind," such as this one from *Merriam-Webster's Collegiate Dictionary*, eleventh edition: "the element or complex of elements in an individual that feels, perceives, thinks, wills, and esp. reasons." Perhaps this neglect has occurred because actions seem, in a way, to be a property of neither the mind nor the world. We tend to act automatically, without conscious awareness, and have little memory of actual actions themselves. Movements tend, literally, not to come to mind. In contrast, both our thoughts and what we apprehend in the external world are available for conscious reflection, with the aid of memory. Thus knowledge holds the stage. But regardless of why action has been neglected in Western philosophy, the effects of its neglect show up dramatically, not only in the history of scientific thought about speech but in its relative absence from modern science's concern with mind/brain relationships. To cite but one example of the neglect of speech as an action, *The New Cognitive Neurosciences* (Gazzaniga, 2000), a 1,400-page encyclopedic text generally considered the authoritative source on its subject, has no section on speech production.

My own discipline, psychology, has also historically neglected the study of action. Rosenbaum (2005) recently called motor control the "Cinderella of psychology" (p. 308). Psychology even went through a phase when the mind itself wasn't deemed an appropriate subject of study. The behaviorists, back in the first half of the twentieth century, felt that psychology should be restricted to the study of observable stimulus–response relationships. Why? Because, in their view, the mind was not accessible to science. It might appear that by emphasizing the importance of responses, which are actions, they were bringing the study of action into the fold. But they were actually only using them as a means to an end, namely, as an indicant of what was happening in the learning process. They weren't interested in the understanding of actions as such.

The cognitive-science movement of the last half of the twentieth century brought mind back into our purview. But cognitive scientists continued to be influenced by philosophy's indifference to action. The influential volume *Foundations of Cognitive Science* (Posner, 1989) includes only two chapters on motor control—just 68 pages out of 900, with no coverage of speech production whatsoever! Jordan and Rosenbaum (1989), who authored one of those chapters, found it necessary to provide a reason for even considering motor control in a volume on cognitive science: "Thus cognitive science, insofar as it regards perception as one of its core problems, cannot afford to ignore action" (p. 727). True. Yet, one may reasonably ask, why not make action just as important a part of cognitive science as perception? Indeed, which statement is more accurate: that perception is in the service of action, or that action is in the service of perception? Both statements obviously have some truth to them, but surely we use perception in order to help us get something done more than we do something in order to get certain perceptions. Jordan and Rosenbaum even implied that action may not be a part of cognition proper but instead be relevant only to transmitting cognitive information: "For cognitions to be communicated, they must be physically enacted" (p. 727).

Action is equally neglected in psycholinguistics, the area of the cognitive science of language most related to traditional psychology. For every contribution on language production, we'll see perhaps two dozen on comprehension. Levelt said it well: "Language production is the stepchild of psycholinguistics" (W. Levelt, 1989). But if language production is a stepchild, speech production seems positively feral. Even the 1,200-page *Handbook of Psycholinguistics* (Gernsbacher, 1994) contains no chapter on speech production. Speech perception, yes (four chapters). Eye movements in reading, yes (one chapter). Speech production or writing, no.

More surprising still, only a tiny fraction of the limited concern with speech has focused on its evolution. The main body of work comes from Lieberman (e.g., 1984), who explored the inference that evolutionary increases in speech-signal diversity have resulted from anatomical changes in the speech apparatus. But it bears very little on what I see as the central question of speech evolution, namely, Lashley's serial-order question: *"How did we evolve our ability to organize the movement sequences of speech?"*

So here we must try to do better. But in order to understand the basic nature of the questions we must ask, we must first flesh out the two major perspectives forming the intellectual context in which the questions reside—the

Neodarwinian perspective, which in principle accords a central role to successful actions in the evolution of the mind, and the classical perspective, which accords prior status to mental functions.

1.2 The Neodarwinian perspective

The last century and a half has seen a revolution in our knowledge of ourselves and all other living forms. That revolution was launched in 1859 when Darwin published his theory of evolution by natural selection. He based it on an idea that is quite straightforward but often misunderstood. In its simplest form it can be described by Herbert Spenser's phrase "survival of the fittest."

Darwin's approach began with the contention, now generally accepted, that members of a given species will vary in their biological attributes. (In humans, for example, such variation would include differences in height, weight, and susceptibility to diseases.) Darwin surmised that in the presence of life-threatening pressures, such as a limited availability of food or exposure to predators, individuals possessing more of certain attributes are better able to withstand these pressures, and consequently have more offspring. This will tend to skew the distribution of the relevant attribute in the population in the next generation slightly more towards the values possessed by those members who had more offspring. If such pressures—selection pressures—and the pattern of response to them extend over many generations, the result is a significant shift in the nature of the population. In the extreme case, the shift will result in an entirely new species. Hence the first part of the original title of Darwin's book: *On the Origin of Species by Means of Natural Selection* (1859).

In broad compass, the sequence of events in the history of life forms had two stages, Darwin theorized. The first was a stage of formation of living entities out of inorganic materials, a stage of self-sustaining reactions that might have occurred, in his view, just once, or a few times. The second involved the ramifications of this event, shaped by natural selection into the entire *single* family tree of life forms.

With this theory, says Francis Crick, Darwin gave us "the secret of life" (Crick, 1988, p. 25). During the entire history of life forms, any major change in form or action capabilities, called an "adaptation," was, according to this view, selected for by the same single mechanism.

In recent years, increasing numbers of scholars have stressed the role in evolution of a factor not known to Darwin—self-organization. A classic example of self-organization in biology concerns the cells in a beehive. When first laid down, they are round. But when a cell is surrounded by six others, as it always is if it isn't on the hive's periphery, the pressure of all those surrounding cells results in a flattening of the cell's margin into six straight lines. Voilà, a hexagon (Thompson, 1917)! Darwin was fooled by this phenomenon. He thought it showed that the bee possessed an instinct that allowed it to manufacture these hexagons. But the organization simply results from the interaction of local causal factors. The six surrounding cells all exert pressure on the central cell, giving it six more or less flat facets. The organization is not handed down by some external agent. Calvin and Bickerton (2000) show a photograph of piles of what were circular bales of hay in the English countryside that have taken on a similar hexagonal configuration (p. 134).

Thompson and many others have thought that self-organization is an alternative to natural selection. But things aren't so simple. Natural selection is still needed to determine whether the results of self-organizational processes survive. If, for example, the hexagonal shape of bees' cells should possess a fatal survival disadvantage—if, say, the six interstices of the bees' cells remained open after a circular bee larva occupied the cell, and if these interstices should provide a home for parasites fatal to the host—then bees that make hives would not survive *because* of self-organization. Thus, *survival* remains the ultimate arbiter in the choice of forms, and the results of self-organization in living forms are only preserved if they are not inconsistent with survival.

A common complaint about evolutionary approaches is that evolution happened in the past, so it isn't directly observable; hence, evolutionary ideas may be no more useful than Kipling's *Just So Stories*—in other words, fanciful post-hoc accounts of, for example, how the elephant got its trunk. To such skeptics, Neodarwinism is personified by the character of Pangloss, in Voltaire's *Candide,* who believed that the bridge of the nose came into being in order to support spectacles. Two things may be said about this. First, evolutionary biology does not have a corner on vacuous speculation. It can be found in any branch of science. Consequently, evolutionary biology should not be singled out for special blame when instances of such speculation are found. Second, contrary even to the belief of Darwin, who thought that natural selection always acted very slowly, an increasing number of studies have shown natural selection operating over *directly observable* time spans—even spans as short as one generation.

Among the best of such studies are those of Peter and Rosemary Grant and their colleagues (e.g., Grant, 1986). Interestingly, the subject of their observations has been the finches of the Galapagos Islands—the very birds that were crucial in leading Darwin to conclude that natural selection occurred in the first place. At the time that Darwin made his famous journey on the *Beagle*, the predominant view about the nature of living forms was the essentialistic view of Plato—namely, that all life forms have a single fixed essence that has remained fixed ever since their divine origin. But when Darwin reached the Galapagos Islands, he found that while some species of finch resembled those on the mainland, others were substantially different. Since the Galapagos Islands had only recently been formed by volcanic upthrust, the ancestors of all these birds had to have originated on the mainland. So the only reason they could be different from mainland birds was that they were modifications of ancestral birds. Darwin eventually reasoned that if such modifications leading to new species could happen on those islands, they could happen as a general case.

The Grants have shown that the forces of natural selection that Darwin surmised to be working on these birds are still working on them. For many years the Grants have been keeping an annual count of the various species. On two occasions they observed a marked change in the size of the population of one species of finch following a climatic anomaly. As described by Weiner:

Back in 1977, they and their team witnessed a terrible drought in the archipelago. It was a year that highlighted Darwin's "struggle for existence." Flocks of *Geospiza fortis*, the most common finch on Daphne, were reduced from more than 1,000 that January to less than 200 by December. And the birds evolved. The beaks of the next generation were bigger, and proportionately narrower and deeper, which made them better instruments for opening the last tough seeds on the desert island.

A few years later, in 1983, the Grants witnessed a flood: the wettest year of the century in the Galapagos. Thunderstorms turned Daphne from desert to jungle almost overnight. In the upheaval many finches died while others multiplied. This time the beaks of the next generation of *fortis* were smaller, which made them better adapted to the wealth of tiny seeds that covered their new green island. Again the birds had evolved, and again the Grants had seen their evolution and recorded it in hard numbers. (Weiner, 1994a. See also Weiner, 1994b)

1.3 Evolution as a tinker

At this point we need a good metaphor to help us firm up our grip on the evolutionary process. Metaphors play an indispensable explanatory role in science, just as in ordinary life, letting us characterize one thing in terms of some analogous thing that's more familiar to us. Jacob (1977) has given us an extraordinarily useful metaphor for evolution: evolution is a *tinker*—that is, a tinkerer. Traditionally, a tinker was someone who traveled the countryside in a horse-drawn cart, offering to fix broken domestic articles, like kitchen utensils. In his cart he'd have stockpiled various materials for this purpose, obtained from diverse sources. Pieces of a tin can, for example, might be used for patching. My father used to cook up kitchen scraps with grains and make a mash for our chickens. He used a leaky old kitchen pot that he had mended by thrusting a bolt upwards through the leak-hole in the bottom of the pot, and then securing it with a nut from the inside. This is tinkering.

An important connotation of the tinkering metaphor, for Jacob, is that adaptations exploit whatever is available in order to respond successfully to selection pressures, whether or not they originally evolved for the use they're now put to. Gould and Vrba (1982) have coined the term "exaptation" to describe the particular case in which there is a borrowing of the results of prior adaptations for *new* uses. The concept is of great importance for us because, as already mentioned, nothing in the speech-production apparatus originally evolved for speech purposes. So part of the explanation of speech must involve an understanding of how early humans co-opted this apparatus for linguistic communication.

It should be emphasized that, according to our tinkering metaphor, *anything* that works can be adopted in support of an adaptation. One result is messiness. The human nervous system, for example, is an engineer's nightmare because its development wasn't constrained by the necessities of elegant design. An engineer builds things from scratch to solve a particular problem. Evolution doesn't. Consequently a phenomenon such as exaptation can lead to problems in our understanding because the course of historical events is not readily accessible to rational thought in retrospect. It is difficult to retrace the path followed by tinkering. Imagine someone from Mars trying to figure out why my father put a nut and bolt into his cooking pot from an engineer's perspective. But if we are ever to understand evolution, we must try to think like tinkers.

Darwin gave us the basic tenet of descent with modification to emphasize his contention that if we think that some biological attribute has evolved entirely de novo, as an engineer's solution typically does, we are wrong. He said, "We should be extremely cautious in concluding that an organ could not have been formed by transitional gradations of some kind" (1859/1952, p. 87). Novel forms or behaviors don't suddenly appear out of nowhere. They are always modifications of pre-existing forms or behaviors. And these novel forms or behaviors evolve as a result of successful use. The crucial role of use in these outcomes is conveyed in Mayr's assertion that "Behavior...[is]...the pacemaker of evolutionary change" (Mayr, 1982, p. 612).

Jacob has proposed two ways in which descent with modification can occur by tinkering. One is by *transforming* an existing attribute into something different. The other is by *combining* two existing attributes into something that is more than their simple sum. Assuming Jacob is right, the task of Neodarwinians is to fathom what changes of these two types occurred in the evolution of the function they are interested in, and how selection pressures could have evoked them. But again, in retrospect, it isn't always easy to see that one of these two things has happened, especially when there are gaps in the phylogenetic record.

Perhaps the most difficult part of Darwin's theory for many people to accept is that it applies to humans no less than to all other species. Recall, once again, the last sentence of *The Descent of Man* (1871/1952): "Man still bears in his bodily frame the indelible stamp of his lowly origins" (p. 597). Ironically, even Alfred Russell Wallace, co-discoverer of the principle of natural selection, wanted it to apply to every species *except* humans!

There are at least two good reasons for such anthropocentrism. First, we certainly *are* very different from any other species—including even our closest living relatives—particularly in our possession of culture and language. Second, we have been encouraged to view ourselves as a breed apart by Western religion, which tells us that only *we* commune with the deity, and that our role is to preside over the rest of the animal kingdom. Unfortunately, this anthropocentrism has introduced a bias into our thinking regarding human evolution, even when we otherwise agree on the importance of natural selection and its tenet of descent with modification. Cartmill, Pilbeam, and Isaac (1986) eloquently spell out that bias:

since the time of Darwin humans have, for the most part, taken their task to be the documentation of the ways in which humans are special. In accepting this persistently pre-Darwinian definition of their problem, scientists who study evolution have saddled themselves with the paradoxical job of explaining how causes operating throughout nature have in the case of *Homo sapiens* produced an effect that is radically unlike anything else in nature. (p. 410)

In simple truth, we have not faced up to the consequences of Darwinian theory, with its cornerstones of descent with modification and the lowly origins of humans. Instead, by beginning, however implicitly, with the proposition that humans are *special*, we tend to bias ourselves toward the conclusion that they always were. We tend, without proper justification, to look for causes that are as special to us as the results are. To put it in an extreme form, few people have become standard-bearers for Darwin's contention that "he who would understand baboon would do more toward metaphysics than Locke" (Darwin, cited in Gruber, 1974). But I find myself one of those few. It is my intention, in this book, to give an account of the evolution of speech that unflinchingly adheres to a Neo-darwinian perspective—that contends, in short, that speech didn't just "happen" by means of a secular miracle but, instead, evolved by descent with modification in accordance with the principle of natural selection.

Cartmill, Pilbeam, and Isaac have unearthed here what Bickerton has called the "continuity paradox" (Bickerton, 1990). If descent with mod-ification is a basic tenet, novel evolutionary outcomes can't come from nowhere. Bickerton (1990) was concerned with the continuity paradox in the context of language evolution: "Language cannot be as novel as it seems, for evolutionary adaptation does not evolve out of the blue" (p. 7).

How am I to deal with this continuity paradox in the case of speech? How can I, in effect, get from baboon to human while remaining free from an anthropocentric bias? I plan to do some reverse tinkering here. What this tinkering will give us, ultimately, is evidence supporting Stephen J. Gould's fine insight that "external discontinuity may well be inherent in underlying con-tinuity, provided that a system displays enough complexity" (1977, p. 409).

1.4 The Classical perspective

While Neodarwinism has profound implications for the nature of the human mind, just as it does for all important phenomena in nature, those implications have scarcely begun to be addressed. The attempt to understand the mind has, instead, been highly influenced throughout the history of ideas by a very different theoretical focus. The tension between the particular ancient perspective, which I am calling "Classical," and the Neodarwinian perspective is a main theme of this book. I use the term "classical" in the sense of definition 4 b (1) of *Merriam-Webster's Collegiate Dictionary* (11th ed.) to mean "of or relating to a form or system considered of first significance in earlier times."

A central early issue in Classical epistemological thought—that is, inquiries into the nature and grounds of knowledge—was that of the relative importance of permanence and change. As Bertrand Russell pointed out, "The search for something permanent is one of the deepest of the instincts leading men to philosophy" (Russell, 1945, p. 45). He gave us an obvious example: "Religion seeks permanence in two forms, God and immortality" (p. 45).

But we are faced with change in our experience: change in the state of the world from moment to moment, diurnal change, change in the seasons, change in life forms with age, and the ultimate worldly change—death. In the sixth century BC, Heraclitus saw change as all-pervasive in life. According to Guthrie (1962): "One of his most famous sayings is 'you cannot step into the same river twice'" (p. 450). Guthrie notes that "Plutarch . . . adds the explanation which may have been given by Heraclitus himself: 'for fresh waters are flowing on'" (p. 450).

Heraclitus' view was a pessimistic one because it even questioned the possibility of attaining knowledge. But it was not influential for long. By the fourth century BC, according to Toulmin and Goodfield (1965), change, rather than being regarded as the essence of all things, came to be regarded as a problem. The problem was one "of explaining the transitory flux of experience in terms of the 'unchanging realities' that lay behind it" (p. 40). We will consider some of these supposed realities later. But note here that, as Toulmin and Goodfield point out, this conceptual ascendency of permanence over change led to a downgrading of the importance of history in Greek natural philosophy. Historians such as Herodotus and Thucydides focused on contemporary history, and the latter summarily dismissed the remote past from consideration at the outset in his book on the history of the Peloponnesian War. Toulmin and Goodfield conclude that "In short, Human History had become quite detached from the History of Nature" (p. 40).

This early divorce of history from philosophy is of interest to us because history is at the center of the Darwinian perspective:

Once the axiom was accepted that all temporal changes observed by the senses were merely permutations and combinations of "eternal principles," the historical sequence of events (which formed part of the flux) lost all fundamental significance. It became interesting only to the extent that it offered clues to the nature of the enduring realities. So questions of historical change ceased to have any relevance to the central problems of philosophy, and philosophers concerned themselves instead with matters of *general principle*... (Toulmin and Goodfield, 1965, p. 40)

I will argue that this nonhistorical approach to the question of the nature of knowledge is still with us and hampers our applying Neodarwinian theory to the understanding of the mind, including the mental underpinnings of speech.

The Greeks' relegation of history to a marginal status was perhaps not surprising, given their general ignorance about their own antecedents and about the nature of the world that preceded them. But another factor—the growing sophistication and allure of mathematics—was simultaneously reinforcing the claims for eternal realities. As Toulmin and Goodfield explain it, largely following from the work of Pythagoras, mathematics became an important means by which matters of general principle could receive their initial adumbration. For example, the layout of the heavens was now considered in geometrical terms. Similarly, the forms associated with the different material elements were viewed from the standpoint of mathematics. Even the fundamental axioms of morals and politics were considered amenable to mathematical formulation.

As a result, any knowledge derived from mental application, via mathematics, became prized for its supposed purity and objective reliability, while knowledge derived from sensory experience became devalued as subjective, hence unreliable. Russell states it well:

Mathematical knowledge appeared to be certain, exact, and applicable to the real world; moreover it was obtained by mere thinking, without the need for observation. Consequently, it was thought to supply an ideal, from which everyday empirical knowledge fell short. It was supposed, on the basis of mathematics, that thought is superior to sense, intuition to observation. If the world of sense does not fit mathematics, so much the worse for the world of sense. (Russell, 1945, pp. 33–34)

This notion that thought, and specifically reason, with its mathematical basis is in itself a source of knowledge, superior to and independent of sense perception, came to be known as "Rationalism."

Within mathematics, geometry has had the most influential effects on philosophy, according to Russell, because it offered the seductive appeal of leading to seeming certitudes:

Geometry, as established by the Greeks, starts with axioms which are (or are deemed to be) self-evident, and proceeds by deductive reasoning to arrive at theorems that are very far from self-evident. The axioms and theorems are held to be true about actual space, which is something given in experience. It thus appeared to be possible to discover things about the actual world by first noticing what is self-evident and then using deduction. (Russell, 1945, p. 36)

Here, Plato was the seminal influence, especially in his elaboration of Pythagoras' formulations. Using the concept of the triangle, Plato illustrated his fundamental distinction between reality and the ephemeral states of appearances. As Mayr (1982) explains:

A triangle, no matter what combination of angles it has, always has the *form* of a triangle, and is thus discontinuously different from a quadrangle or any other polygon. For Plato, the variable world of phenomena...was nothing but a reflection of a number of fixed and unchanging forms, *eide* (as Plato called them) or *essences*. (p. 38)

The emphasis on underlying forms in general in philosophy has come to be known as "Formalism."

Plato's particular application of the Formalistic approach, which proved enormously influential, is known today as "essentialism." For a Platonist, as Ernst Mayr put it, "These essences are what is real and important in the world. As ideas, they can exist independent of any objects" (Mayr, 1982, p. 38). Bertrand Russell offers this example: "though there are many beds, there is only one 'idea' or 'form' of a bed. Just as a reflection of a bed in a mirror is only apparent and not 'real,' so the various particular beds are unreal, being only copies of the 'idea,' which is the one real bed, and is made by God" (Russell, 1945, p. 122).

Hallett (1991) defines "essences" this way: "Essences in the traditional sense are core properties or clusters of properties present, necessarily, in all and only those things that bear the common name. Knowledge is one thing; language is one thing" (p. 2). For instance, I define a triangle as "three straight lines in two-dimensional space, with each line connected at its ends to the other two, and with the internal angles summing to 180 degrees."

Since the time of Plato, one of the most important Western philosophers has undoubtedly been René Descartes, who basically elaborated Rationalistic and Formalistic philosophy in much the same way that Plato had elaborated the formulations of Pythagoras. According to B. P. Davis and R. Hersch (1986), the state of world knowledge that Descartes found himself confronting was actually a wild hodgepodge—"an uncritical mixture of fact and fancy, of legend and hearsay, of sense and nonsense, of doctrine and dogma, of experiment, conjecture and prejudice, all infused with stale and ineffective metaphysics and with chaotic and misguided procedures" (p. 7). Deeply troubled by all this, Descartes found himself wondering how the general principles of human knowledge could be "placed on new and more certain foundations" (Toulmin and Goodfield, 1965, p. 78). Consequently, he "aimed at purging the principles of human knowledge of all but 'clear and distinct ideas'" (Toulmin and Goodfield, 1965, p. 78). Following Plato, Descartes took geometry as his great clarifier and touchstone:

The long concatenations of simple and easy reasoning which geometricians use in achieving their most difficult demonstrations gave me occasion to imagine that all matters which may enter the human mind were interrelated in the same fashion. (Descartes, cited by Toulmin and Goodfield, 1965, p. 77)

In order to distinguish the intellectual wheat from the chaff, Descartes used a method we know today as "Cartesian Doubt" (Descartes, 1637). He compelled himself to doubt everything that could possibly be doubted. The end point of this method was his famous conclusion: "I think, therefore I am" (*Cogito ergo sum*). The existence of his own thought was the sole thing he couldn't deny. This conclusion had profound consequences for Descartes' view of the relation between the mind and the body. His position became: "I may have no *body*: this might be an illusion. But thought is different" (Russell, 1945, p. 564). Thus mind became more certain than matter. And a mind–body dualism was elevated to new prominence. The scorned temporal body was viewed as a mere *machine* that we share with other animals, whereas the mind was specific to humans—and synonymous with the soul.

Ideas, then, for Descartes, came only from the human mind. More wonderful still, they were *innate*. The sense experience that we share with animals played, for him, a negligible role in our knowledge. In the *Philosophical Works of Descartes*, edited by Haldane and Ross (1955), Descartes is explicit on this distinction between innate ideas and insignificant sense experience. Sense experience, he asserted, was important only for allowing us to attach an innate idea to a property of the world:

in our ideas there is nothing which was not innate in the mind, or faculty of thinking, except that only those circumstances that point to experience—the fact for instance that we judge that this or that idea, which we now have present to our thought, is to be referred to a certain extraneous thing, not that these extraneous things transmitted the ideas themselves to our minds through the organs of sense, but because they gave the mind occasion to form these ideas by means of an innate faculty, at this time rather than at another. (Haldane and Ross, 1955, vol. 1, pp. 442–443)

Descartes expresses incredulity that such things as propositions of formal logic could possibly be bestowed on us by experience: "[C]ould anything be imagined more preposterous," he exclaimed (p. 443). He challenged any critic to "instruct me as to what corporeal movement [experience] it is that can form in our mind any common notion, e.g., the notion that *things which are equal to the same thing are equal to one another* or any other he pleases" (ibid.).

Like Plato, Descartes viewed the triangle as an example of an innate idea. He tried to illustrate his notion by discussing what he believed would be involved in an infant's mentally apprehending a triangle. Descartes discusses this question in his *Reply to Objections V*:

Hence when first in infancy we see a triangular figure depicted on paper, this figure cannot show us how a real triangle ought to be conceived, in the way in which geometricians consider it, because the true triangle is contained in this figure just as the statue of Mercury is contained in a rough block of wood. But because we already possess within us the idea of a true triangle, and it can be more easily conceived by our mind than the more complex figure of the triangle drawn on paper, we, therefore, when we see that composite figure, apprehend not it itself but rather the authentic triangle. (Haldane and Ross, 1955, vol. 2, pp. 227–228)

In the simple terms in which Descartes frames this issue, the ability to apprehend a seen triangle ought to be independent of experience. But we know today that it isn't, thanks to a long series of reports of people who have had congenital cataracts removed from their eyes and are thus seeing the world for the first time. The eminent neuropsychologist Donald Hebb summarized their performance: "Investigators...are unanimous in reporting that the perception of a square, circle or triangle, or of sphere or cube is very poor" (Hebb, 1949, p. 28). Commenting on Hebb's analysis of this special population, Gregory points out that Hebb "attributed the general slowness to see after the operation as evidence that a very great deal of learning is needed," and concludes that "This indeed is now generally accepted..." (Gregory, 1989, p. 95). A fascinating modern treatment of this topic, thoroughly consistent with Hebb's conclusion, may be found on pages 108–152 of Oliver Sacks' book *An Anthropologist on Mars: Seven Paradoxical Tales* (1995).

Let's now summarize the classical view associated with Plato and Descartes. When one goes beyond mere appearances, the world consists of a set of eternal, mathematically definable forms. The human mind, unlike the animal mind, has these forms innately available to it. The forms are God-given. True, we possess a body, like other animals, but our body is finally irrelevant, no more important than a mere machine. Our sublimity, our true humanness, lies in our eternal mind.

A Neodarwinian scenario obviously can't be applied to these forms. It makes no sense to ask whether the forms resulted from modifications of pre-existing forms, given the essentialistic basis of the mathematical models used to derive them. Dennett (1995) offers an example to show us exactly why it makes no sense:

consider what your attitude would be towards a theory that purported to show how the number 7 had once been an even number, long, long ago, and had gradually acquired its oddness through an arrangement where it had exchanged some properties with the ancestors of the number 10 (which had once been a prime number). Utter nonsense of course. Inconceivable. (p. 38)

Nevertheless, as Dennett points out, "Even today Darwin's overthrow of essentialism has not been completely assimilated" (p. 39).

However interesting these historical developments, the reader might be pardoned for wondering what such philosophically cosmic concerns have to do with something as apparently mundane as the question of how humans acquired the ability to speak. The answer is that as the linguist George Lakoff says,

Philosophy matters. It matters more than most people realize, because philosophical ideas that have developed over the centuries enter our culture in the form of a world view and affect us in thousands of ways. Philosophy matters in the academic world because the conceptual frameworks on which entire academic disciplines rest usually have roots in philosophy—roots so deep and invisible that they are usually not even noticed. This is certainly true in my discipline, linguistics . . . (p. 157)

Noam Chomsky, the founder of generative linguistics, which will no doubt have a permanent place in the pantheon of ideas, has explicitly embraced the Cartesian view of the human mind. In his 1966 book *Cartesian Linguistics*, he characterizes his own invention, generative linguistics, as a reversion to ideas of a group of seventeenth-, eighteenth-, and nineteenth-century thinkers practicing what he calls "classical linguistic theory."

As Chomsky points out, language was perhaps the most important evidence Descartes used to support his conclusion that humans and other animals were incommensurate. According to Descartes, the ability to use language must not be confused with "natural movements which betray passions and may be imitated by machines as well as manifested by animals" (Haldane and Ross, 1955, vol. 1, p. 116). The crucial difference is that automata "could never use speech or other signs as we do when placing our thoughts on record for the benefit of others" (ibid). Chomsky notes that "This is a specific human ability, independent of intelligence" (Chomsky, 1966, p. 4). As Descartes himself said,

it is a very remarkable fact that there are none so depraved and stupid, without even excepting idiots, that they cannot arrange words together, forming of them a statement by which they make known their thoughts; on the other hand, there is no animal, however perfect and fortunately circumstanced it may be, which can do the same. (Haldane and Ross, 1955, vol. 1, pp. 116–117)

Chomsky goes on to emphasize Descartes' conclusion, cited below, that this distinction between man and animal cannot be based on peripheral physiological differences:

it is not the want of organs that can bring this to pass, for it is evident that magpies and parrots are able to utter words just like ourselves, and yet they cannot speak as we do, that is, so as to give evidence that they think of what they say. On the other hand, men who being born deaf and dumb, are in the same degree, or even more than the brutes, destitute of the organs which serve the others for talking, are in the habit of themselves inventing certain signs by which they make themselves understood. (Haldane and Ross, 1955, vol. 1, p. 117)

What is unique to language, according to Chomsky, is its creativity—"its property of being unbounded in scope and stimulus-free" (Chomsky, 1966, p. 5). The basis for this unique capability of humans, according to Chomsky, is their possession of a "generative grammar":

By a generative grammar I mean a description of the tacit *competence* of the speaker-hearer that underlies his actual *performance* in production and perception (understanding) of speech. A generative grammar, ideally, specifies a pairing of phonetic [sound-level] and semantic [meaning-level] representations over an infinite range; it thus constitutes a hypothesis as to how the speaker-hearer interprets utterances, abstracting away from many factors that interweave with tacit competence to determine actual performance. (p. 75)

Thus, for Chomsky, "competence" is the linguistic component of the Cartesian mind—a set of innate ideas underlying language. In contrast, "performance" has to do with what actually happens when we speak and listen. Of course we speak with one part of the body (a complex of lungs, larynx, and mouth)and listen with another (the ears). So the competence/performance distinction is, in effect, the mind/body distinction of Descartes, and the continued adherence to this distinction makes generative linguistics incompatible with Neodarwinism.

At the base of the generative grammar of any language, Chomsky posits a Universal Grammar, a set of rules and representations that, he believes, are part of the genetic endowment of every human. He places this development in a tradition that derives from Descartes (though Descartes did not speculate on the specific characteristics of the innate ideas underlying language).

He also sees his work as being in the tradition of the German scientist Wilhelm von Humboldt (1836), who is of interest here because he extended the Rationalistic view of language to include speech. As Chomsky pointed out, Humboldt argued for a fundamental difference between the perception of speech and the perception of other sounds:

But furthermore, speech perception requires an analysis of the incoming signal in terms of the underlying elements that function in the essentially creative act of speech production, and therefore it requires the activation of the generative system that plays a role in the production of speech as well, since it is only in terms of these fixed rules that the elements and their relations are defined.... It follows then that both the perceptual mechanisms and the mechanisms of speech production must make use of the underlying system of generative rules. It is because of the virtual identity of this underlying system in speaker and hearer that communication can take place, the sharing of an underlying generative system being traceable ultimately to the uniformity of human nature. (Chomsky, 1966, pp. 70–71)

While at the moment I am concerned simply with summarizing Chomsky's position, I shall argue later that generative linguistics has not established a generative rule structure that underlies actual speech. All it has done is describe certain regularities in the sound patterns of speech, and then deem these descriptions to be explanations that are couched in terms of underlying abstract rule structures.

As illustrated in Fig. 1.1, Chomsky's Universal Grammar, aka generative grammar, lies between what he has recently called the conceptual/intentional level which includes linguistic meaning (semantics), and the sensorimotor level, which includes perception and production of speech—the level of phonetics. It is described as a system for pairing meanings and sounds—a system of sound–meaning correspondences. It has two main components: (1) a *syntactic* component responsible for the basic grammatical categories, like nouns and verbs, and their organization into sentences; and (2) a *phonological* or sound component composed of abstract sound-related elements that are responsible for the sound patterns of words. Chomsky believes that both of these components have a genetic basis—i.e., they are built into all humans at their very conception.

Chomsky's idea about the mental basis of languages is of the same character as Descartes' views on mind. Both posit the existence of an underlying fixed reality (innate ideas), which stands in stark contrast to our everyday world—the world of appearances. Humans selectively assimilate key aspects of appearances during the developmental process, thanks to the guiding force of innate ideas. Chomsky cites with approval Descartes' description of how an infant perceives a triangle, and believes that an entirely analogous process occurs when infants perceive speech and, more generally, understand language: "In short, language acquisition is a matter of growth and maturation of relatively fixed capacities, under appropriate external conditions" (Chomsky, 1966, p. 64). And: "The form

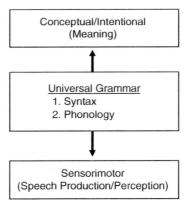

Fɪɢ. 1.1   Chomsky's Universal Grammar and its relation to other aspects of language.

of language that is acquired is largely determined by internal factors" (ibid.). Of course, as mentioned earlier, my own position here is that just as perceiving a triangle is only possible with a lot of learning, perceiving speech, as we also now know, requires a lot of learning.

Chomsky has also embraced the Classical tradition by referring to the problem of language acquisition as "Plato's problem." Chomsky cites, without a reference, Bertrand Russell's statement of the problem, rephrasing Plato: "How comes it that human beings, whose contacts with the world are brief and personal and limited, are nevertheless able to know as much as they do know?" (Chomsky, 1986, p. xxv). Thus, like his Classical predecessors, Chomsky has emphasized "poverty of the stimulus" (ibid.)—the insufficiency of experience as a basis for the formation of knowledge—and the consequent necessity for knowledge to be built in a priori.

One final point needs to be made. Although Chomsky's work has led to a revolution in linguistic theory, there is one important way in which his approach is simply the continuation of an already existing one. He and his colleagues remain structuralists. The structuralist conception, presented early in the twentieth century by the Swiss linguist Ferdinand de Saussure (1915/59), has remained the dominant one in linguistics ever since. Saussure regarded this structure as a single coherent social entity with a fixed set of properties that constitute its essence, much as Plato regarded things (e.g., triangles) as possessing "essences." These entities are, in a sense, everywhere and nowhere at the same time. An appropriate analogy in earlier biology is with the way Linnaeus described, for example, members of a particular species of flower, in terms of a single abstract category with particular parts and interconnections.

Saussure divided language into two levels: a level of linguistic form ("la langue") and a level of phonetic substance, in effect observable speech ("la parole"). The important level, to him, was the level of form, with the level of substance—actual speech—being of minor significance. We see Saussure's imprint everywhere. For example, in the foreword to the influential *Manual of Phonetics* (1978), the book's editor, Bertil Malmberg, explained that studying substance (speech) was only useful to the extent that it threw light on the nature of the underlying forms that determined the distinctions between one sound pattern and another.

Notice also that there is no place here for the consideration of the history of form. Thus in terms of the history of philosophy Saussure was an orthodox formalist—one who considered form to exist a priori. In fact, one reason that Saussure made his formulation was to relegate the hitherto central area of linguistics—historical linguistics—often presented via evolutionary metaphors, to a subordinate status in the discipline. And it is of particular interest here that the main focus of structural linguistics was phonology.

We can see that this conception does not necessarily have any consequences for function—what people actually do when they speak or listen. And not surprisingly it has no consequences for the history of function either. These problems thus make structural linguistics, still the most dominant approach to modern phonology, inappropriate for an evolutionary treatment of speech.

For the last half of the twentieth century the orthodox discipline of structural linguistics has taken a back seat to generative linguistics, the fruit of the Chomskyan revolution, and phonology has been superseded by syntax as the main object of concern. Chomsky was critical of the nonmentalistic focus of structural linguists. While Saussure placed linguistic form at the social level, which Chomsky described as E-linguistics (external linguistics), Chomsky himself placed form within the mind of the individual (I-linguistics, or individual linguistics). In Chomsky's hands the form/substance distinction became the competence/performance distinction. Despite these differences, it is absolutely crucial to note that Chomsky's work is a continuation of the structuralist tradition in linguistics. In both cases, form (langue) is central, and a priori. Chomsky could not be more explicit on this point: "The classical Saussurean assumption of the logical priority of the study of langue (and the generative grammars that describe it) seems quite inescapable" (1964, p. 52). Thus not only Chomsky's approach, but also the approach of the majority of modern phonologists, even those who were not heavily influenced by Chomsky, is therefore subject to the same problems that Saussure's structuralist approach had from the evolutionary standpoint.

We now have a general intellectual context for considering the question of the evolution of speech. In the next chapter I will go beyond this general context and focus more directly on the implications of the two main approaches for the specific questions we will need to address.

2 Getting to the explanation of speech

2.1 Comparing the Neodarwinian and Classical approaches

It should now be clear how diametrically opposed the Neodarwinian and the Classical approaches are concerning the question at hand. Their polar opposition gives us a great deal of structure for the task of understanding the evolution of speech. In this chapter, after comparing the two approaches in more detail, I will outline how I plan to evaluate their usefulness for understanding speech. Specifically, I will explore how they answer a set of four key questions that the Nobel Prize-winning ethologist Nikko Tinbergen (1952) insists are fundamental to the optimal understanding of any naturally occurring behavior. (He defines ethology as "the biological study of behavior"—p. 411). I will also elaborate on an important modern perspective on cognitive science, a perspective akin to Neodarwinism, which I have also used in my work on speech—the Embodiment perspective. Finally, I will summarize my own answers to Tinbergen's four questions and then present the plan of the book.

To Neodarwinians, the human mind, like all major aspects of all life forms since the first ones, has evolved, across the time domain, by descent with modification as a consequence of one simple mechanism—natural selection based on successful use. Neodarwinians also regard variation in all aspects of life forms as an essential principle, because without it there is no basis for selection—no modifiability. The classical view, meanwhile, contends that the human mind did not gradually emerge; it is timeless. And its structure, rather than varying from individual to individual, is fixed. It is, in short, one of Plato's essences. This view was, in fact, so widely held even in Darwin's time that he had to make a considerable effort to convince people that variation was a real property of life forms, however self-evident it seems today (Mayr, 1982). According to Mayr, "Darwin . . . was not at all understood by the contemporary philosophers (all of whom were essentialists)" (p. 38). Incidentally, he tried to get variation on the map by beginning his book with a review of the remarkable ways in which characteristics of animals can be shaped by breeding practices. The success of this artificial selection increased the plausibility of the suggestion that natural selection could produce similar results.

Much of the difference between the two approaches can be boiled down to one contrast: Neodarwinism has a time dimension with change occurring across it, while classicism has no time domain and assumes no change. The implications of this difference for the understanding of the evolution of speech can hardly be overestimated. Most importantly, from the classical standpoint there can be no evolution of speech in the sense of a gradual progression toward modern speech from a point in which we lacked speech. As I have pointed out, both Plato and Descartes believed that the capacity for human knowledge was God-given. It was of no significance to either Plato or Descartes when, or for that matter how, this disposition occurred. At the time these philosophers made their formulations, the paucity of knowledge of the past neither encouraged them to produce a scenario that included the time domain nor made their views subject to refutation on the basis of historical knowledge.

But this state of affairs had changed drastically by the time Chomsky came to formulate his views of language and its implications for the human mind. The old view of the world, which posits that there are fixed forms with no time domain, had been superseded in the attempt to understand living forms by the Neodarwinian view, which emphasizes gradual modification across the time domain. This acceptance of the importance of history forced Chomsky (1988) to deal specifically with the question of the origin of language—something his predecessors weren't required to do. He dealt with it, in one well-known instance, by explicitly denying the relevance of Neodarwinian theory to language— and by positing an instantaneous origin of language attributable to physical laws as yet undiscovered:

It may be that at some remote period a mutation took place that gave rise to the property of discrete infinity, perhaps for reasons that have to do with the biology of cells, to be explained in terms of properties of physical mechanisms now unknown. Quite possibly other aspects of its evolutionary development again reflect the operation of physical laws applying to a brain of a certain degree of complexity. (Chomsky, 1988, p. 170)

These suggestions and their implication that in this particular case physics somehow transcends the accepted processes of biology cannot be taken seriously. They betray the fact that an insoluble problem lies behind them. As Tomasello (1998a) points out, generative grammar is, in effect, a closed mathematical system. A datum is either within the system or outside of the system from the beginning. The insoluble problem is to characterize a time-dependent biological reality with timeless formal systems based on mathematics. Despite its great prestige in the history of thought, mathematics of the kind that has eternal forms, and total self-containment, must pay the cost of irrelevance where the realm of discourse includes living forms, the time domain, and change. (See Mayr, 1982, pp. 38–41.)

The question we might ask ourselves is, "Why, in the light of more than a century of Darwinism, should closed mathematical systems continue to be regarded as solutions to problems of evolution?" Bertrand Russell (1945, p. 33) suggests a reason—one all the more noteworthy given that he had built his career, with *Principia Mathematica*, by attempting to apply mathematics to philosophy. In discussing the contributions of Pythagoras, he points to the allure of mathematics in its role as the subject of "passionate sympathetic contemplation"—which was, incidentally, the original connotation of the word "theory." He notes that although the term "theory" later took on a different meaning,

for all who were inspired by Pythagoras, it retained an element of ecstatic revelation. To those who have reluctantly learned a little mathematics in school this may seem strange; but to those who have experienced the intoxicating delight of sudden understanding that mathematics gives from time to time, to those who love it, the Pythagorean view will seem completely natural even if untrue. It might seem that the empirical philosopher is the slave of his material, but the pure mathematician, like the musician, is a free creator of his world of ordered beauty. (ibid., p. 33)

This is perhaps one reason why mathematics-based paradigms, with their baggage of timelessness, are still with us more than a century after Darwin established their irrelevance to biology. One does not lightly abandon mathematics-based models, or even realize their defects, if working with them has this enthralling quality. But the fact remains that much of the content of mathematics is antithetical to a time-domain explanation, which is the only source of understanding of ultimate causes in modern biology.

Russell considered the role of mathematics in the history of philosophy to be unfortunate:

Most sciences, at their inception, have been connected with some form of false belief, which gave them fictitious value. Astronomy was connected with Astrology, Chemistry with Alchemy. Mathematics was associated with a more refined source of error. (ibid., p. 34)

I cited Russell's discussion of this error earlier. It was basically the belief that mathematics could be substituted for empirical observation because it was a superior form of knowledge. The result, according to Russell, was disastrous: "In various ways, methods of approaching nearer to the mathematician's ideal were sought, and the resulting suggestions were the source of much that was mistaken in the metaphysics and theory of knowledge" (ibid., p. 35).

Another reason that the mathematics-based paradigms that have eternal connotations are still with us in biology stems from their success in the physical sciences. Consideration of the time domain is obviously important in understanding the physical world, just as it is for understanding the natural world. But as Nobel Laureate Francis Crick (1988) notes: "The basic laws of physics can usually be expressed in exact mathematical form, and they are probably the same throughout the universe. The 'laws' of biology, by contrast, are often only broad generalizations" (p. 5). Crick, who was trained as a physicist, speaks from experience when he says:

All this can make it difficult for a physicist to contribute to biological research. Elegance and a deep simplicity, often expressed in very abstract mathematical form, are useful guides in physics, but in biology such intellectual tools can be very misleading. For this reason, a theorist in biology has to receive much more guidance from the experimental evidence (however cloudy and confused) than is usually necessary in physics. (p. 6)

Crick's analysis is useful to us for understanding another part of the intellectual background we need to consider before taking up the question of the evolution of speech. Just as mathematics had a deleterious effect on biology, it had an equally pernicious effect on psychology. The reason stems from psychology's roots in physiology. As Plotkin (1998) points out, nineteenth-century physiology was heavily influenced by physics, incorporating both its mathematical orientation and what Plotkin calls a "now and forever [essentialistic] attitude towards its subject matter" (Plotkin,

1998, p. 23). Psychology was founded in part on psychophysics, the study of the relationship between simple physical stimuli (e.g., light intensity) and human bodily responses to them. The relation between dimensions of the physical attribute and the bodily response could be specified mathematically. For example, Weber's Law, as stated by Plotkin, stipulated that

the smallest perceptible difference between the two sensations was related to the ratio between the stimulus energies leading to the sensations. That is, for a stimulus of magnitude 100 one has to have an increase of 1 per cent to 101 to notice the difference; for a stimulus of magnitude 300 a change will only be detected if it is increased to at least 303 magnitude. (Plotkin, 1998, pp. 21–22)

The physical component of the equation was obviously assumed to have a now-and-forever status, and psychological response was assumed to have it, too. This perhaps helps explain why psychology, as a discipline, has only recently begun to explicitly incorporate evolutionary thinking, in the form of a new subdiscipline called "Evolutionary Psychology" (Buss, 2005).

2.2 Tinbergen's four questions

So far we have dealt with the general problem arising from the fact that the Classical view of the nature of mind excludes the time domain. We have seen how its exclusion is antithetical to our understanding of evolution, that is, the understanding of phylogeny. Additional issues arise when we consider, more specifically, what is necessary to explain speech. To consider these issues, I have adopted four core perspectives from which to approach communication in general. First formulated by the Nobel Laureate Nikko Tinbergen (1952), as already mentioned, they were later adopted by Hauser (1996) in his monograph on *The Evolution of Communication*. Said Hauser, "These perspectives...provide the only fully encompassing and explanatory approach to communication in the animal kingdom including human language" (p. 2). I agree. Here are the four perspectives, with some additions to Hauser's description of them and with his ordering of perspectives #2 and #3 reversed in order to better fit the narrative that follows:

1. Mechanistic: *"How does it work?"* That is, what are the mechanisms (neural, physiological, psychological, etc.) underlying the expression of a trait? (A trait is an attribute that is reasonably consistent over time.)

2. Functional: *"What does it do for the organism?"* How does any supposed adaptation affect the organism's capabilities—that is, its survival and reproduction?

3. Ontogenetic: *"How does it get that way in development?"* That is, what genetic and postgenetic/environmental factors guide the development of a trait?

4. Phylogenetic: *"How did it get that way in evolution?"* That is, how does the evolutionary history of the species help us understand the structure of the trait in light of ancestral features?

Note that the time domain is important to all four of these questions. Question #1 deals with "real time"—the actual moment-to-moment distribution of communicative actions and their consequences. Question #2 deals with why key changes occur over time. Question #3 involves the "shallow time" of individual life spans. Question #4 involves the "deep time" of history. We have just considered the fourth question—the evolutionary question—in general terms, and concluded that the Classical approach cannot deal with it for speech or anything else. Let's now also take up the other three questions with particular regard to speech before returning to the fourth question, the most fundamental one. We'll start with Question #1, which gives us a place to explore the insights of the neuropsychologist Karl Lashley—insights fundamental to this book.

2.3 Question #1: Karl Lashley and the problem of serial order

Question #1—"How does speech work?"—concerns the actual observable phenomenon of speech as it exists today. If we hope to figure out how speech evolved, we must begin with an agreed-upon characterization of what it is that we have to explain, namely, the present-day end product—that is, how it currently works. Speech consists of rapid streams of sounds, extended in time, that we produce with the vocal apparatus. But how are these rapid sound sequences produced? And what orders them?

Karl Lashley considered the question of the serial organization of spoken language to be "both the most important and the most neglected problem of cerebral Physiology" (Lashley, 1951, p. 113). And why? Because it "presents in most striking form the integrative functions that are characteristic of the cerebral cortex and reach their highest development in human thought processes" (ibid.). Lashley sought to determine what is involved in the serial order of language production—an attempt that he made a full decade before the birth of psycholinguistics (Miller, 1962). He concluded that, in producing language and other skilled behaviors, "The order must... be imposed upon the motor elements by some organization other than direct associative connections between them" (Lashley, 1951, p. 115).

To understand the logic of that conclusion, not to mention its profundity (it foreshadowed Chomsky's similar, much-celebrated conclusion in linguistics, 1957), one needs to note the view of serial-ordered behavior that had prevailed since the inception of behaviorism (Watson, 1913). It was that this behavior was produced by a stimulus–response (S-R) arrangement of "chains of reflexes in which the performance of each element of the series provides the excitation of the next" (Lashley, 1951, p. 114). John Watson, the founder of behaviorism, wrote a paper in which he hypothesized that thought was simply talking to oneself using this kind of arrangement (Watson, 1920).

Part of Lashley's argument against the reflex-chaining view of language production was that there wasn't enough time in fast, serially ordered behaviors such as piano playing—which could reach rates of 16 strokes per second—for feedback from the previous response to influence the next. Bruce (1994), however, has cited recent research that proves Lashley wrong here. He has pointed out that sensorimotor linkages can in fact work fast enough for a response to influence the next one at these rates. But the more important part of Lashley's argument remains uncontested, namely, that the choice of a subsequent response cannot be determined by the previous response because a particular response is preceded by different responses on different occasions. Lashley offered a witty illustration of this point, focusing on the response pronounced "right": "The millwright on my right thinks it right that some conventional rite should symbolize the right of every man to write as he pleases" (1951, p. 116). Here, Lashley noted, "word arrangement is obviously not due to any direct associations of the word 'right' itself with other words, but to meanings that are determined separately" (p. 116). He made a similar point about the organization of individual words, noting that words like "right" and "tire" involve making the same motor elements in reverse order, the order being determined from above, so to speak. In writing, meanwhile, he noted that "No single letter invariably follows *g*, and whether *gh*, *ga* or *gu* is written depends upon a set for a larger unit of action, the word" (p. 116).

So where, Lashley wondered, does the order come from? He concluded that it comes from a level which is not only relatively independent of the output units (be they words or sounds), as we have seen, but also of the thought structure. To argue for the independence of this other, serial-ordering level, sandwiched between thought and observed output, from the thought structure that it serves, he noted that bilinguals can express the same thought with two different sentence structures in the two languages. And as further evidence of the need for a serial-ordering level independent from the output units, he cited a certain class of error in typing. When we type *t-h-s-e-s* for *these*, for example, or *l-o-k-k* for *look*, or *i-i-l* for *ill*, it's clear that the part of the mechanism controlling the repetition of a letter is separate from the part controlling the choice of that letter.

What Lashley was obviously trying to do here, though he did not explicitly say so, was to formulate a unified model of language production, a model that would take us all the way from the mental level of intentions to the transient temporal flux of output. When Bruce asked Chomsky what influence Lashley's paper had on his linguistic theories as expressed in the book *Syntactic Structures* (1957), Chomsky replied, "I don't think there was any" (Bruce, 1994, p. 99). He said he didn't know about the paper at the time. (He does credit Lashley in his 1968 book *Language and Mind* but only for his critique of behaviorism.) Chomsky set himself a task that was much more limited than Lashley's. He was only concerned with an abstract linguistic knowledge component (Universal Grammar) independent of both the meaning level that motivates its use on particular occasions and its implementation at the sound level.

Chomsky's approach is in some ways reminiscent of that of the psychologist Tolman (1932), who tried to get cognition into S-R behaviorism by arguing that maze learning was based on the formation of abstract cognitive maps, and involved the formation of idealized concepts such as "Sign Gestalt Expectations." But as Guthrie (1935) pointed out, "Signs, in Tolman's theory, occasion in the rat realization, or cognition, or judgement, or hypothesis, or abstraction, but they do not occasion action.... So far as the theory is concerned, the rat is left buried in thought" (p. 172). For Lashley, as for Guthrie, an acceptable theory must contain a link between cognition and action. Whatever the defects of orthodox Behaviorism, the Stimulus–Response (S-R) paradigm always had consequences for action. By analogy with Guthrie's point about Tolman, Chomsky's hominid, though endowed with a genetically determined Universal Grammar (roughly the middle level of Lashley's schema), can neither link it upwards to thought, nor downwards to actual movements. Lashley was trying to solve the problem that S-R behaviorism had with the existence of complex mental processes independent of stimuli, while retaining its capacity to give an account of action. In Chomsky's terms, Lashley was trying to get from competence to performance, something that the Chomskyan tradition has never attempted to do. (See Levelt, 1989, for a contemporary attempt to conceptualize the entire sequence of events in language from idea to action.)

Lashley made two other important contributions to our understanding of how language is produced in real time. First, he anticipated not only the concept of "working memory"—a concept that has become central to cognitive science (Baddeley, 1986)—but also the need for such a memory to include a subvocal speech component, which Baddeley called the "Phonological Loop" (p. 120). In Chapter 8, I will consider the consequences of adding a working-memory component to the Classical conception of language organization in the brain formulated by the nineteenth-century neurologists Paul Broca and Carl Wernicke. Second, at the level of actual movement control, he suggested that timing mechanisms, such as rhythm generators, may play an important role in serially ordered behaviors because of their capacity to integrate widely separated strands of central neural activity. In this book, I will argue that the rhythmic, biphasic mouth-close/mouth-open cycle associated with the syllable—closed for consonants, open for vowels—is the most fundamental component of the serial ordering of not only speech (Chapters 3–7) but also birdsong (Chapter 14).

None of these fundamental issues regarding real-time speech—the overall organization responsible for the sequencing (from intention to movement), the necessity of a working-memory component, and the moment-to-moment control of the actual output—are of any relevance in the Classical approach to language. In particular, Chomsky has often used memory limitations as an example of performance constraints, with which he is not concerned. And he has stressed the abstract nature of the underlying phonological elements of generative linguistics and their independence from both perception and production. Consequently, there is no realistic modern end point for a Classically based theory of evolution to explain. Thus we are left with the problem raised by Thelen and Smith

(1994): "If competence in the Chomskyan sense is part of our biology, then it must be embodied in living real-time process" (p. 27). But Chomsky rejects this conclusion. For him, competence is an abstract, timeless entity. In this regard, then, the Chomskyan conception is not a biological conception.

Answering Tinbergen's "How does it work?" question successfully will tell us something important about what evolution has wrought. I am going to use Lashley's serial-order problem as a basis for answering this question for speech production. And, of course, to the degree that the answer is correct, it will have important implications for the other three questions, because the present behavior is the adaptational outcome of both phylogeny and ontogeny.

2.4 Question #2: speech as an adaptation

Tinbergen's second question is "What does it do for the organism?" My answer to this question is that speech enables humans to send and receive an enormous set of messages, and that this ability has aided survival to the point where we are now the dominant species on earth. I acknowledge that I don't say much here about how it aids survival, but it is crucial to note that the role of speech is to provide the material that allows listeners to distinguish between the words of a language. At the most detailed level, this is best illustrated by the concept of "Minimal Pair." For example, the two words "pill" and "bill" are distinguished from each other at the message level by a difference at their beginnings. The two forms constitute a minimal pair in the sense that any smaller difference between their first parts would make them indistinguishable from each other, which would decrease the number of messages that the signaling system had at its disposal. The two forms are said to participate in a sound "contrast." All languages develop their own repertoire of meaning-differentiating capabilities in order to make the necessary contrasts. This capability is embodied in the consonants and vowels of the language. English has about forty of them. In my view, speech is an adaptation that made the rich message-sending capacity of spoken language possible. That is what it did for the organism. And there is survival value in this richness of communication. Basically, group knowledge is power. Any theory of evolution of speech needs to explain how the adaptation that enabled this richness of communication occurred by descent with modification guided by natural selection.

In contrast, Chomsky does not believe that Universal Grammar (UG) evolved for communication at all. He believes that it originally functioned as what he called a set of "linguistic expressions" (Chomsky, 2000, p. 8) which allowed the possessor to, in some sense, talk to herself. Chomsky does not believe in the power of adaptation to produce new forms and functions. But from the present standpoint we must raise the question of what would have been the adaptive benefits of talking to ourselves via UG. One problem is that without the incorporation of meaning into UG, which consists only of syntactic and phonological components, what could have been talked about? In addition, what would the phonological component have been for if there was initially no transmission of linguistic information to others?

At the level of everyday practice, linguists have always put the issue of distinguishable messages at the heart of their concern with speech. Their most basic conceptual unit is the "distinctive feature," which is used in an attempt to make a general classification of aspects of the sound system that participate in contrasts (distinctions between consonants or vowels) in languages in general. I will argue that although such an enterprise is useful at the descriptive level, the currently accepted conclusion that a finite small number of innate mental distinctive features underlies the input analysis and output organization of all languages is unfounded. In fact, I don't think that this unit can exist in the sense of being an independent entity used when speakers speak and listeners listen. It is simply a taxonomic convenience. It is therefore not a human adaptation.

To understand the issues involved here, we need to say a bit more about speech. Speech works both as an output system and as an input system. The formation of speech has involved an agreement between senders and receivers on a common code. Transmission of a part of this code between sender and receiver in what is called an "utterance" (a stretch of speech between pauses) is the basic speech event. As Jakobson, Fant and Halle (1963) said, "We speak to be heard in order to be understood" (p. 13). The existence of a speaker-listener dyad, however, places crucial constraints on speech. Most phoneticians (scientists who consider speech directly) follow the suggestion of Martinet (1955) that the design of the speech component of a language stems from an ongoing contest between the demands of the production system and the demands of the perception system (e.g., Lindblom, 1998). The production system is not infinitely versatile. So it presumably works best when the demands on it are ones that can be more readily met. An important issue in this book is what its preferences and aversions are. The perception system's task is to differentiate between messages, and it rewards the production system's endeavors by engendering successful communication when that system manages to provide signals properly shaped to succeed in this. Conversely, it punishes the production system by propagating a miscommunication when the production system fails to produce a sound that could be appropriately distinguished from other possible sounds.

The contributions of productive ease and perceptual distinctiveness must have been important from the origin of speech onward. From the beginning, hominids needed to use sounds/sound complexes easy enough to be produced reliably, and each must have been perceptually distinct from the others, as far as the listener was concerned, in order for vocal communication to occur. Thus the same mechanism that created the adaptive property of allowing rich communication—the contest between productive ease and perceptual distinctiveness—serves today to maintain that property.

The separate but interactive roles of productive ease and perceptual distinctiveness are not a part of the Classical conception of speech. Both production and perception are aspects of performance, whereas competence is what the Classical view is about. But it turns out that productive and perceptual contingencies are important in the formulation of distinctive-feature theory even though the theory is ostensibly about mental units separate from production and perception but in some way linking them.

2.5 Question #3: the ontogeny (development) of speech

As with the first question, how speech works, the time domain is also absent in the Classical view when we come to Tinbergen's third question, "How did it get that way in ontogeny?"—in shallow time. This would seem paradoxical because the main proving ground for Universal Grammar has been language acquisition (Jackendoff, 2002), which is quintessentially a time-domain phenomenon. There has been no attempt to understand why the main things that happen in language acquisition, either syntactic or phonological, tend to occur in a particular order. Instead, ever since Chomsky formulated the problem of language learnability as "Plato's problem," the approach has been to first identify properties of early language that don't seem to have been learnable according to concepts of learning theory current in the heyday of neobehavioristic learning theory—the 1950s—and then attribute these properties to an innate Universal Grammar.

A favorite example that supporters of the Chomskyan approach like to cite concerns what is in fact a fascinating question: How does an infant manage to correct his own grammar errors even when nobody tells her that they are errors? Where does the infant get the knowledge she needs to make those corrections? From Universal Grammar, these supporters argue. In other words, from innate ideas. But as Tomasello (1998a) points out, "the argument from the poverty of the stimulus has recently been found to be inadequate in a number of ways when the stimulus—the language that learners actually hear—is examined empirically" (p. xi). Furthermore, a number of lines of research are showing that while the input to the child often lacks single unequivocal pieces of information regarding, for instance, where a word stops and another one starts in the continuous speech signal, or what grammatical category a given word belongs to, there often exist multiple sources of information about these questions that allow an infant to take a probabilistic approach, which in turn can produce good guesses (Seidenberg, 1997).

Another important point is that however much poverty of the stimulus exists for language in general, there is none of it in the domain of the structure of words, the unit of communication I am most concerned with. Infants hear all the words they are expected to produce. Thus, the main proving ground for UG does not include phonology.

In his conceptual approach to language acquisition, Chomsky favors growth metaphors and bodily-organ metaphors to support his claim for the dominant status of innate ideas. For example, he quotes with evident approval a botanical growth metaphor of the eighteenth-century philosopher James Harris: "The growth of knowledge . . . [rather resembles] . . . the growth of fruit: however external sources may in some degree cooperate, it is the internal vigor, and virtue of the tree that must ripen the juices to their just maturity" (Chomsky, 1966, p. 111). Chomsky then adds: "Applied to language, this essentially Platonic conception would suggest that knowledge of a particular language grows and matures along a course that is in part intrinsically determined, with modifications reflecting observed usage, rather in the manner of the visual system or other bodily 'organs.' " Elsewhere he has indicated that the heart, the liver, the eye, the arm, and even the sexual organs have a basically similar ontogeny to language, and concludes:

There is every reason to suppose that this mental organ, human language, develops in accordance with its genetically determined characteristics with some minor modifications that give one language or another, depending on experience. But then one would say the same about any bodily organ, as far as I can see. (Chomsky, 1976, p. 57)

Certainly there is a good deal of justification for Chomsky's conclusion that the speaker's "normal linguistic behavior cannot possibly be accounted for simply in terms of 'stimulus control,' 'conditioning,' 'generalization and analogy,' 'patterns' and 'habit structures,' or 'dispositions to respond,' in any reasonably clear sense of these much abused terms" (Chomsky, 1966, p. 73). But this conclusion certainly does not mandate the implication, made explicit by Chomsky sympathizers, that "there is no such thing as learning" (e.g., Piatelli-Palmarini, 1989). Neither does the failure of conventional learning theory of the mid-twentieth century mandate Chomsky's own conclusion that all important aspects of language are genetically specified. (Incidentally, the impression that Chomsky has softened his stance on the dominance of a species-specific genetic contribution to language, conveyed by a recent jointly authored paper, Hauser, Chomsky, and Fitch, 2002, is belied by a still more recent paper, Chomsky, 2006.)

How does Chomsky's idea that there is a genetically specified Universal Grammar fit with current thinking in the biological sciences? We find consensus in the diverse fields of evolutionary biology (Dawkins, 1986), molecular biology (Stent, 1981), neurobiology (Damasio, 1994), neurophysiology (Singer, 1989), and neurology of language development itself (Elman et al., 1996) that the human genes contain insufficient information to specify the structure of the human nervous system, which comprises several billion cells, each having, on average, several hundred connections with other cells. In addition to the informational poverty of the genes, Stent (1981) also emphasizes what could be called the enormous causal distance between genes and the eventual structure of the nervous system in particular:

the role of the genes ... is at too many removes from the processes that actually "build nerve cells and specify neural circuits that underlie behavior" to provide an appropriate conceptual structure for posing the developmental questions that need to be answered. (Stent, 1981, pp. 186–187)

Damasio (1994) offers a somewhat less conservative view of how genes contribute to brain organization but still one that falls well short of the possibility of specification of brain organization for language. He suggests that they assist in establishing the most primitive survival-related circuits in the vertebrate nervous system but not circuits related to high-level cognition.

But if Universal Grammar cannot be directly genetically specified in the nervous system, how should we understand the relation between the genes and developmental outcomes? Dawkins (1986) asks us to consider two contrasting metaphors—blueprint and recipe. As to blueprints, take, for example, my colleague who is having a house built in Colorado. He has a blueprint that specifies the existence and location of all the main structural components of that house. For every door, for instance, there is currently a little penciled-in arc protruding from a wall. In effect, then, *essentially the entire structure is specified in advance.* Universal Grammar is an example of this metaphor. But the fact of the matter is that while every cell in the body contains genetic instructions of some sort, body parts and brain parts differentiate in a context-dependent manner that is related to local cell growth in a multistage interactive process, the complexity of which still evades systematic description. There is therefore no 1:1 relation between genes and outcome of the kind that would result from a genetic blueprint.

Instead, Dawkins suggests the recipe metaphor. A recipe for making a cake, Dawkins says, "is a set of instructions which, if obeyed in the right order, will result in a cake" (p. 295). Unlike a blueprint, which ignores issues of process, a recipe focuses on both the raw materials and, equally important, the order in which they are properly assembled. Also, a recipe takes into account that properties of the final product emerge only during the cooking. For example, when you add yeast at the right time, and subject it to the right temperature, your product will expand. But of course you can't see that expansion in the initial block of yeast. It only emerges in the correct context of the product's assemblage. So it makes no sense to look for a straightforward relation between the parts of the finished product and particular ingredients—to ask, for example, "Where's the egg yolk?"

But to Dawkins, even this metaphor for development is too simple: "To simulate the 'baking' of a baby, we should imagine not a single process in a single oven, but a tangle of conveyor belts, passing different parts of the dish through 10,000,000 different miniaturized ovens in series and in parallel, each oven bringing out a different combination of flavors from 10,000 basic ingredients" (p. 297). In short, even if Universal Grammar managed to get into the genes (which is a big enough problem in itself), there is at present no plausible scenario for how it could get out in the relatively direct manner suggested by the hypothesis.

Often, we'll find linguists using a less extreme word than "genetic" when talking about the causes of language. They'll use "innate." On the face of it, the word sounds pretty innocuous, and certainly unproblematic. But as Elman et al. (1996) point out, actually the word suggests a simplistic view of how development unfolds:

> To say that a behavior is innate is often taken to mean—in the extreme case—that there is a single genetic locus or set of genes that have the specific function of producing the behavior in question, and only that behavior. To say that a behavior is innate is thus seen as tantamount to explaining the ontogeny of that behavior. In fact, nothing has been explained. And when "innate" is used more reasonably to refer in general to our genetic endowment, the term ends up being almost vacuous, given the enormous complexity of interactions that are involved in the expression of that endowment. (p. 357)

But do we really have to choose between learning as currently defined and genetic prespecification in trying to understand language acquisition? A number of people have noted the logical problem with Chomsky's line of reasoning here, which is, basically, *If not A, then necessarily B*. It has been dubbed an example of "the argument from incredulity" by Deacon (1997, p 104). Chomsky is in effect saying, "Because I cannot believe that there is any other possibility, the solution must be genetic."

A story recounted in the introduction to the *Norton History of Chemistry* (Brock, 1993) may have a moral for us. In 1784 the eminent Dutch botanist von Helmont reported growing a tree from a small plant to a 162-pound mature form under controlled conditions in which only water was made available to it. He concluded that trees grow by water alone. Subsequently, of course, other botanists identified two other causal factors: air and sunlight.

Could Chomsky be missing the *mental* equivalents of air and sunlight in his analysis of language learning? There is an increasing consensus that he is. (See Knight et al., 2000.) What he is missing is the importance of sociocultural factors. Language must have been a sociocultural invention. The first word only became a word when a receiver and a sender—a sociocultural dyad—came to treat a particular sound complex as standing for a particular concept. From that momentous occasion onward, every word of every language came into being in this way. Thus in any of the

6,000 or so language environments that an infant happens to be born into, her task is to internalize the linguistic conventions of the culture by finding out what these thousands of instances of social consensus are. Without access to these social agreements the infant will not speak at all. As Donald has said, "Language does not self-install" (Donald, 2001, p. 280). The huge role of sociocultural factors from the dawn of language onward makes Chomsky's physical growth metaphors for language acquisition inappropriate. Sociocultural input is not something that the heart and liver require.

Knight, Studdert-Kennedy, and Hurford (2000) suggest that due recognition of the importance of social function in both language evolution and language development "has perhaps been hindered by Chomsky's (1986) proscription of externalized language (E-language), the Saussurean language of the community, as a coherent unit of linguistic and psychological study" (p. 11). (Saussure, a Swiss linguist of the early twentieth century, regarded language as a social entity.) Knight et al. contend that researchers "have instead chosen as their proper object of study Chomsky's internalized language (I-Language), a structural property of an individual mind-brain" (p. 11).

To clarify what is at stake here, we need to make a brief digression into the subject of culture. Although, depending on one's definition, a number of species can be said to have culture, there is little question that humans have undergone a quantum jump with regard to this attribute, particularly in their possession of shared symbolic systems and beliefs. (See Gibson, 2002, for background.) The only other thing that competes with language as a momentous human evolutionary development is human culture. The evolution of culture has had ramifications that are just as dramatic as the evolution of language—dramatic enough, in fact, to induce Maynard-Smith and Szathmary (1999) to include both in their list of the eight major evolutionary transitions in the history of life forms in general. By analogy with genes, Dawkins (1976) has given a name to those aspects of culture that lie within the memory of its users. He calls them "memes." Because every culture includes a set of memes for its particular language, the manifestation of these memes in speech provides an indispensable source of information for an infant learning its own language. I will argue this point in more detail in Chapter 14.

Culture has evolved as a major human attribute, just like language; thus, logically speaking, it has just as much claim to a genetic basis as language does, though as in the case of language the claim has yet to be cashed out for higher mental functions. Not only language but other aspects of culture manifest themselves to the developing infant *in the environment.* So in both cases it could be said that the genes are in the environment. Indeed, the same claim about the genes could be made for organisms without language and culture, because the evolutionary process involves adaptation to a particular niche. Consequently, under typical conditions a given animal's niche is preordained by its evolutionary history, just as its genes are. As Tooby and Cosmides (1992) have put it:

So, step by step, as natural selection constructs the species gene set (chosen from the available mutations), it constructs, in tandem, the species' developmentally relevant environment (selected from the set of all properties of the world). *Thus both genes and the developmentally relevant environment are the product of evolution.* (p. 84)

The preceding discussion makes it clear that Chomsky's dichotomy between a genetic component that is totally in the organism and a basically independent set of trivial environmental contingencies is an inappropriate one for an organism that has evolved to put culture—including the memes for a particular culture-specific language—in the environment. Hence, as Plotkin points out, this state of affairs makes it necessary to throw out the simple nature-vs.-nurture (organism-vs.-environment) dichotomy because, in his words, "Nurture has nature":

As an amplification and extension of human cognitive processes, culture is at the center of any nature–nurture question. As a highly salient part of the environment of every human being, it enters as a powerful causal force of nurture. At the same time, because it is an evolved consequence of evolved cognitive processes, it is also, like those processes, a part of our nature. (p. 241)

Plotkin's conclusion is a cornerstone of my approach here. Current evidence that the genes are effectively in the environment no less than in the individual makes it inappropriate for Chomsky and other generativists to place the effects of genes solely within an individual organism. In choosing the organ-growth metaphors that he uses to explain language acquisition, Chomsky has clearly not credited this important external source of variance in his Universal Grammar.

Fig. 2.1 shows the relation between the Classical conception of language acquisition and my own Neodarwinian approach with regard to the nature/nurture question. Fig. 2.1a shows how, in the Classical view, the

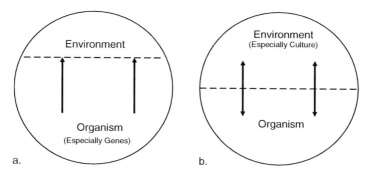

FIG. 2.1   Comparison of the generative view (left) and the present Neodarwinian view (right) of the relation between nature (organism) and nurture (environment) for language.

explanatory burden for language is shouldered almost entirely by the organism—meaning, in this case, the genes. In this illustration, I have estimated the actual proportions given to the genetic and environmental contributions on the basis of the relative emphasis put on the two in the generativist literature. The arrows indicate that the direction of causality is entirely unidirectional—the genes impose themselves on the organism. Fig. 2.1b differs from Fig. 2.1a in three respects. First, nature and nurture (organism and environment) are given roughly comparable importance, not because we know this to be the case, but because there is currently no reason to assign them unequal roles. (Note that in this context, "organism" is best taken to include both genetic and prenatal factors.) Second, culture is given a specific role in the environmental component, though again the size of this role cannot currently be estimated. Third, causality is bidirectional rather than unidirectional—the organism acts on its environment, and the environment acts on the organism, even on its genes. A major recent discovery, important enough to have already made it into introductory textbooks (e.g., Gazzaniga and Heatherton, 2003), is that environmental input influences the expression of genes; that is, it can cause genes to become active. Thus, just as the genes influence how the organism will act on the environment, the environment will influence how the genes act on the organism.

Let us return now to the specific question of the time domain's role in generative linguistic theory. Chomsky developed his concept of Universal Grammar from studies of adult languages. But the theory had nothing to say about the actual sequence of events that occurs when people acquire language or speech. So there is no predictive component to Universal Grammar regarding what structures should develop first and what should follow them. Instead, it relies on a circular argument. For example, it will say something like this: "Infants speak their first words at one year of age because they have matured to the point where their innate capabilities enable them to do so." And what is the evidence that they've matured? "The evidence is that they're speaking the words at one year of age." It's ironic that generative linguists can assert that development is a central arena for their theory and that maturation is a key concept, and yet be unwilling to offer any theory as to the causes of the particular sequence of events that occur in ontogeny.

As generativists view maturation, it's like the clearing of mist in a mountainous landscape. When the landscape—the innate state—is obscured by mist, all that one sees from above is an undifferentiated sheet of white. But as the mist begins to clear, the peaks of the highest mountains (comparable to the first speech sounds and sound patterns) become visible; and as the clearing continues, smaller peaks and then just hills become visible as well. Finally, as the mist clears from the valleys, the entire landscape comes into view. In other words, everything was in some unspecified way in place, complete in its essential outline, right from the beginning. But an additional variable—maturation—operates to reveal the components of the scene in the temporal order in which it is observed. Nothing is actually being developed here; nothing is actually changing; things are only becoming manifest, visible.

The question that obviously arises here is, "What determines the topography of the landscape?" For in terms of the mist-clearing metaphor, this determinant lies behind the order of appearance of the sounds and sound structures. As their answer to this question, generative phonologists have borrowed from early twentieth-century linguistics the concept of "markedness." The most "unmarked" sounds are considered to be the most basic. They are the ones that appear first in development and are the most frequent sounds in the world's languages (Archangeli, 1997). But this line of reasoning is also circular. The term "markedness" is asked to function as both a description of infant preference patterns and patterns of sound frequencies in languages, and as an explanation of these patterns.

This circular way of proceeding is not just a minor chink in the generativist armor, for it isn't confined to the issue of speech development.

It is, in fact, the main basis for so-called "explanations" in linguistics. Here's how it works: some generalization, which includes the coining of a cover term for the observed phenomenon, is made, and this provides a simplified description of a body of knowledge. It is then said that the cover term "accounts for" the observed state of affairs. This procedure, so characteristic of modern linguistics, has been noted by no less a luminary than George Miller (1990), often considered the father of cognitive science, who said: "Linguists tend to accept simplifications as explanations. For example, a grammarian who can replace language-specific rewriting rules with X-bar theory and lexicalization feels he has explained something: the work formerly done by a vast array of specific rules can now be done by a simple schema" (p. 321). Miller contrasts this approach with the one typical in science, which is practiced by psychologists: "For a psychologist, on the other hand, an explanation is something phrased in terms of cause and effect, antecedent and consequent, stimulus and response. To an experimental psychologist, X-bar theory is not an explanation: rather, if it is true, it is something to be explained" (p. 321).

A second problem with the "markedness" concept is that it has never been sufficiently acknowledged that the sound-preference hierarchies for infants and languages are different in some major respects. Consider one example. The two main categories of consonants in the world's languages, with respect to frequency of use, are labials and coronals. Labials are sounds made with the lips, such as the first sounds in "ban," "pan," "man," "fan," and "van" in English. Coronals are sounds made with the front of the tongue, such as the first sounds of "do," "too," "new," "Sue," and "zoo" in English. While coronals are usually a good deal more frequent in languages and therefore considered more unmarked (Paradis and Prunet, 1991), labials are more common in the infant's first words (e.g., Boysson-Bardies et al., 1992; MacNeilage, Davis, and Matyear, 1997). That a linguistic concept which has been around for more than half a century has such a fundamental flaw as lack of conformity with well-known differences between developmental preferences and language-structure preferences seriously undermines the credibility of the generativist approach.

One might object here that the mist-clearing metaphor, which is mine, not theirs, oversimplifies the generativist approach to the ontogeny of speech. But generativists themselves have led the way with simplification. For example, in addressing the role of input in development, they have endorsed Chomsky's metaphors such as "triggering" and "shaping" but without referring to any specific phonological phenomenon. Thus we're left wondering: Exactly what are the triggerer and the shaper? And what are the triggeree and the shapee? And how do the two members of each pair interact? We will take up these issues in Chapters 5 and 6 where I will offer a detailed causal scenario for speech acquisition, and will include an evaluation of the metaphors considered here.

I have said that the ontogenetic component of Chomskyan theory does not have a time domain in the sense of a theory that says what should happen when. But in overall form it can be characterized as a continuity approach in that the basic structure underlying development is given in advance and, once "triggered," is subsequently shaped, without significant reversals in development. This conception is already known to be false. As we will see, the course of development in syllable organization goes from a systematic tendency to simply repeat the same syllable (e.g., "bababa") to a systematic tendency, present in languages in general, *not* to repeat the same syllable (e.g., "bodega"). But while this developmental reversal is antithetical to the Chomskyan conception, it fits perfectly with the Neo-darwinian theory that I will present.

2.6 Question #4: the phylogeny (evolution) of speech

Let's turn now to Tinbergen's question #4: *How did speech get that way in phylogeny?* Here is one thing that Chomsky has said about the origin of Universal Grammar that supposedly contained, in its phonological level, the initial mental basis for speech:

To tell a fairy story about it, it is almost as if there was some higher primate wandering around a long time ago and some random mutation took place, maybe after some strange cosmic ray shower, and it reorganized the brain, implanting a language organ in an otherwise primate brain. This is a story not to be taken literally. But it may be closer to reality than many other fairy tales that are told about evolutionary processes, including language. (Chomsky, 2000, p. 4)

What are we to make of such a statement? I believe it is best regarded as the response of a modern essentialist in the Classical tradition who is required by the Darwinian revolution to eschew deistic causality and face at least some of the facts of biology. He wants to believe Universal Grammar is "just there." His essentialistic reluctance to pay any homage to our dominant notion of biological causality is evident in his attempt to make his scenario laughable because, in his view, there is very little to evolutionary theory:

There is no known explanation for most of the complex properties of organisms. People talk about Darwinian evolution and that sort of thing, but that does not give you answers beyond simple questions. (Chomsky, 2000, p. 49)

It's very revealing that in singling out a couple of examples of unexplained phenomena he chooses two mathematical forms—for him, essences—namely, polyhedral shells of viruses, and forms, such as the sunflower, exhibiting the Fibonacci series (Chomsky, 2000). The Fibonacci series is an infinite series of integers that begin with 1 and 1, after which every subsequent integer is the sum of the previous two; for example, 2, 3, 5, 8, 13, etc. If Chomsky is right about the limitations of Darwinian evolutionary theory, people like Crick and Dawkins (e.g., 1986) and many others are very wrong in believing that Darwin gave us the secret of life.

To my knowledge, Chomsky has never explicitly come to grips with the essentialistic basis of his work. But he shows his awareness of the issue in describing with approval the psychology of some members of the post-Cartesian mentalistic tradition ("the English Platonists, Leibnitz and Kant") as "a kind of Platonism *without pre-existence*" (1966, p. 63, italics mine). But this would be a contradiction in terms. Pre-existence is fundamental to Platonism.

What exactly did Chomsky's cosmic shower bestow on us? And, given the rather generalized effects of radiation, why was it bestowed on only one half of the brain—the left half?

Chomsky goes on to say that "The language organ is inserted into a system of mind that has a certain architecture; it has interface relations with that system. It connects to them. The assumption is that there are the two interfaces that I mentioned" (Chomsky, 2000, p. 17; the "interfaces" are with the meaning and sound levels). Chomsky continues: "These interfaces impose some conditions on what the system must be like. How good a solution is language to the conditions imposed by those external assumptions?" (p. 17). And then: "So the sensorimotor system (for sound) and the conceptual-intentional system (for meaning) have to be able to access, to 'read,' the expressions; otherwise the systems wouldn't even know it is there" (p. 17).

Consider, by analogy, what we are being asked to believe regarding the sensorimotor interface in particular. In computer terms it is as if a module, destined to make a computer the most powerful that ever existed, but designed without any reference to its input/output configuration (perception and production), somehow happens to be sufficiently compatible with it to function usefully. Or, looking at it in reverse, it's as if the controls of the automobile (the machine component) were designed without reference to a radically new type of driver (the mental component), but this driver could nonetheless suddenly climb into it and get it to do something that automobiles never did before. (And it's worse than that. As we will see in Chapter 13, the new driver is supposed to be equally adept at managing spoken language and sign language.)

This is perhaps the sharpest point of contrast between Chomsky's view and mine. I am arguing that selection-induced modifications of the already working computer, consistent with its operational integrity, gave it its phonological component. In short, I am saying that the mental capacity underlying actual speech must have, from the beginning, evolved hand-in-hand with the evolution of the bodily (sensorimotor) capabilities used to actually perform it, and therefore must have been continually constrained by these capabilities. In contrast, Chomsky's stance on the role of the phylogeny of the sensorimotor system in the evolution of language is totally negative. In his view, "it is quite senseless to raise the problem of explaining the evolution of language from *more primitive systems* of communication that appear at *lower levels of intellectual capacity*" (Chomsky, 1968, p. 67, italics mine).

Finally, we may ask what is the strength of Chomsky's commitment to linguistic nativism? Judge for yourself: "To say that 'language is not innate' is to say that there is no difference between my granddaughter, a rock and a rabbit" (Chomsky, 2000, p. 50).

At this point, something needs to be said about the terminology used in the rest of the book. From now on, in talking about the modern approach to language introduced by Chomsky, I will use the word "generative" in accordance with Chomsky's reference to his grammars as generative grammars, rather than the term "classical," which applies to the historical tradition in which his work can be placed. According to Chomsky, "language generates an infinite number of expressions; that is why the theory of a language is called a 'generative grammar'" (Chomsky, 2000, p. 8). The term "generativist" is meant to apply more specifically to a linguist who believes, with Chomsky, that language has a priori form consisting of a Universal Grammar, with a syntactic and phonological component in principle separate from the rest of language. Newmeyer (1998) has written a monograph on the debate between linguists in this category whom he called "formalists"—equivalent to my use of "generativists"—and another group of linguists called "functionalists." This latter group believes that the design of language is a result of the functions it performs—a basically Darwinian perspective. For this group, meaning and grammar are integral to each other and the communicative function of language is central, rather than being an offshoot of the initial use of language for thought. (For samples of this approach see Tomasello, 1998b.) I have no quarrel with this group.

Unless otherwise stated, I will be talking about the phonological component of generative grammar, not the syntactic component. Some readers may be aware that these days there is not much of a consensus that Chomsky's own particular grammatical theories should be the wave of the future. (For a systematic alternative see Jackendoff, 2002.) Furthermore, Chomsky has not seriously concerned himself with phonology since he wrote *The Sound Pattern of English* with Morris Halle in 1968. So one might feel that it is inappropriate to tar linguists in general with the Chomskyan brush. But in one particular respect it seems, for the most part, appropriate. I am using the term "generative" to apply to those linguistic scientists who either explicitly assert, or proceed in a manner consistent with the assumption, that phonology has a priori form, and that its main conceptual entities—features, syllables, and markedness—are innate. This designation applies to the vast majority of modern phonologists, who continue to work in the structuralist tradition introduced by Saussure and espoused by Chomsky. The strength of this tradition can be judged from the fact that no phonologist has presented a gradualistic conception of the origin of phonological form or its subsequent development. The term "nativism" (meaning "innatism") is in a way a more appropriate term, but I am using "generativist" in order to focus more on the details of the theoretical structures that some of the most prominent modern phonologists have constructed, and these structures include little reference to the origins question.

2.7 An emerging intellectual context: Embodiment

Although, with the exception of Lieberman's work (e.g., Lieberman 1984), we've seen scant systematic concern with the evolution of speech in modern times (though see recent work focusing on self-organization by de Boer, 2001, Oudeyer, 2006, and Redford and van Donkelaar, 2008, the latter adopting a frame/content perspective), an intellectual context for the present endeavor has been provided by a number of researchers seeking a basically Neodarwinian alternative to the Classical view of higher functions. Instead of subscribing to a mind–body dualism, they contend that the higher functions are best understood if we recognize that mind and body are integral to each other. This point of view has, in the past decade or so, become known as the "Embodiment" perspective. It's basically Darwinian in the sense that it focuses on bodily use—and of course Darwin's whole theory of evolution was focused on the consequences of successful (adaptive) bodily use. But the proponents do not necessarily focus on phylogeny, the cornerstone of Neodarwinism.

Perhaps the father of the Embodiment perspective in the twentieth century was the Swiss biologist Jean Piaget, who contended that a child constructs her own mind from what she does (e.g., Piaget, 1954). The Embodiment work most related to my approach within linguistics is that of Lakoff (1987). He has presented a detailed critique of the generative approach and outlined an alternative perspective, which he calls "experiential realism," that focuses on how our minds create categories. Lakoff has been influential in forming the new subdiscipline of Cognitive Linguistics (e.g., Tomasello, 1998b). Troubled with Chomsky's claim that language is autonomous—that is, unrelated to any other human capacity—it seeks a linguistics based on principles common to other aspects of cognitive science in general.

Within philosophy, Mark Johnson (Johnson, 1987), with Lakoff (Lakoff and Johnson, 1980; 1999), has argued that metaphors—normally viewed as purely mental constructs—are often born out of bodily experiences in early life. For example, an infant, trapped in his crib, learns by concrete experience the in-vs.-out aspects of the concept "container." This allows him to eventually understand the metaphorical basis of the preposition "out" in the construction "leave out" and many other verb-plus-"out" constructions. Lakoff and Johnson use the term "embodied" to refer to the emergence of thought from real experience. For a related Embodiment perspective from psychology, see Varela, Thompson, and Rosch (1992).

Andy Clark gives us a combined perspective of philosophy and Artificial Intelligence. He contends, in *Being There* (1997), that not only are our mind and body integrally related but also that both are integrally related to our environment. Thus, to understand the human mind, we must focus on the organism acting in its environment. The basic thesis here, which I may or may not have read somewhere, is "I am there, therefore I think."

Within neurobiology, Antonio Damasio, in a book entitled *Descartes'*
Error: Emotion, Reason, and the Human Brain (1994), argues against the
separation of the rational from the affective components of mental function,
relying heavily on a conception of brain evolution in which these two aspects
of the mind are, in the final analysis, inseparable, and both are inseparable
from bodily function. In his words, "Mind is probably not conceivable
without some sort of embodiment..." (Damasio, 1994, p. 234). He has
presented the "somatic marker" hypothesis in an attempt to elucidate the
nature of the mind–body relationship. Another neurobiologist, the Nobel
Laureate Gerald Edelman (1992), has also weighed in against the mind–body
dichotomy. He sees a central role for neurobiology in our understanding of
the mind and has presented a "theory of neuronal group selection" as an
attempt to understand mind as a consequence of neural evolution.

Dynamical systems theory is emerging as a paradigmatic alternative to
generative objectivism and its offspring. It attempts to understand emergent phenomena in both living systems and nonliving systems. As Turvey
and Carello (1995) explain it, in this context *dynamics* refers to "the laws
of motion and change," and *dynamical systems* refers to "the time evolution of observed quantities according to law" (p. 374). Notions of nonlinearity and self-organization arise from this approach as alternatives to
preordained causality. "Nonlinearity means that change in subsystems
may not be smooth and incremental, but can occur with spurts, plateaus
and even regressions" (Thelen and Smith, 1994, p. 84). Water coming to a
boil when subject to continual heat increase would be one example of
nonlinearity; another example would be infants proceeding from babbling
to first words. "Self-organization" refers to the emergence of new states
from the interaction of variables in a complex system, in the absence of an
external controller. Hexagonal bee cells, mentioned earlier, illustrate self-
organization, though, interestingly, as I already pointed out, Darwin
thought otherwise. He attributed the geometrical outcome to "the most
wonderful of all known instincts," though of course insisting that the
instinct evolved via descent with modification (1859/1952, p. 131). In
Chapter 6, I will call on the self-organization concept in an attempt to
explain the transition from simple to more complex word structures in
earlier hominids and modern infants. Among practitioners in the area of
dynamical systems, the work of Thelen on the development of locomotion
is thematically closest to the present approach (e.g., Thelen, 1995). (See
Thelen and Smith, 1994, for a more general approach to development.)

Frank Wilson (1998), in a fascinating and original monograph, takes basically the same position with respect to the human hand as I do with respect to the mouth—that is, he tries to get from the body to the mind, at least in part via culture. He subscribes to an epigram coined by the Canadian novelist Robertson Davies (1986), which could just as easily apply to the mouth: "The hand speaks to the brain as surely as the brain speaks to the hand" (p. 336).

But the work most closely related to my own is that of the phonetician Bjorn Lindblom (e.g., Lindblom, 1984). His work has long emphasized the importance of the ongoing interaction between a production system tending toward ease, and a perception system requiring distinctiveness. He has made a number of seminal contributions to our understanding of speech as a biological system, and I will be drawing on his work at various points in this book.

In some ways my approach can be regarded as falling within the new discipline of evolutionary psychology (Buss, 2005). This discipline attempts to understand human behavior within a Neodarwinian adaptationist perspective. But I find one central tenet of evolutionary psychologists inconsistent with the Neodarwinism that they purport to espouse. Specifically, they contend that the human adaptive capacity takes the form of a number of innate special-purpose mental modules that evolved when our hominid ancestors lived on the savanna. And, according to Tooby and Cosmides (1992) and Pinker (1994), they contend that Universal Grammar is one of these modules. They fail to recognize that UG is totally antithetical to Neodarwinian descent with modification. While there is good evidence for the existence of separate brain modules controlling distinct behaviors (e.g., taste aversion) in modern human *adults*, I don't believe we have sufficient reason to believe that these modules were or are ever innately available, either in phylogeny or ontogeny. I am pleased, of course, to see evolution explicitly represented within psychology. If we are to understand the ultimate causes of human behavior, psychology must become a branch of evolutionary biology. But until I can understand how these modules got into the hominid brain by natural selection, and how they develop during ontogeny, I will continue to fear that much of evolutionary psychology is neo-essentialism in Neodarwinian clothing. (See MacNeilage and Davis, 2005a, for a critique of evolutionary psychology's approach to language evolution.) Parenthetically, this anthropocentric tendency to postulate innateness of human mental capacities without a descent-with-modification underpinning is not restricted to evolutionary psychology. It is rife in the field of cognitive psychology in general. (For a review, see Elman et al., 1996, Chapter 7.)

2.8 Plan of the book

What alternative can we provide to the Classical/Generative view of speech using the tenets of Neodarwinian theory? Here is a summary of the alternative that I suggest, in the form of tentative answers to Tinbergen's four questions:

1. How does it work? The organization of modern speech is dominated by syllables. A syllable consists minimally of a vowel, and may also contain one or more consonants on each side of that vowel. The basic movement underlying the syllable is a close–open cycle of oscillation of the mandible—closing to various degrees for the consonant, opening to various degrees for the vowel. Studies of serial-ordering errors of speech, motivated by Lashley (1951), have shown that individual vowels and consonants (called "segments") have some independence from the syllable they were intended to occur in. For example, in a spoonerism in which somebody says "meanboom" for "moonbeam" (one of my wife's best), two segments exchange places in an otherwise correct utterance. Studies of such errors show that there is a syllable-structure constraint on the misplacement of segments in speech errors. They almost always go into the same position in syllable structure that they came out of. In the above example, vowels end up in vowel positions. In other examples, consonants that were intended to precede the vowel in a syllable (called "initial consonants") end up preceding it in another syllable. And final consonants in a syllable end up in final position in another syllable. This is how modern speech works in real time, and it can be characterized by a "frame/content" metaphor: segmental "content" elements are placed into syllable-structure "frames." Explaining this frame/content mode of modern speech organization in terms of its ultimate causes is my main purpose in this book.

2. What does it do for the organism? As I said earlier, speech allows the transmission of myriad different messages. The ongoing contest between the production system, tending toward easier forms, and the perception system, demanding distinctiveness in the signal, will be a recurring theme of mine, because it has consequences that are often identifiable. Its consequence for the evolutionary process is discussed below. The key point is that this contest extending over time gives us the adaptation we call "speech."

3 and 4. How did it get that way in phylogeny and ontogeny? My basic thesis here is that in both evolution and in development, frames come first and content later. Why is it that, in speech errors, vowels and consonants never move into each other's positions in syllable structure. Probably because in the history of movement control for speech in both the species and in the individual, there was, and still is, a total mutual exclusiveness between opening movements for vowels and closing movements for consonants. As this close–open alternation has always been a part of speech, there has never been an opportunity for vowels and consonants to get mixed up with each other in output. Thus I contend that the *mental* frame constraining speech errors may have derived from a bodily precursor, the motor or movement frame.

Although it may stretch the credulity of many readers, I suggest that the motor frame cycle underlying the syllable, produced by oscillation of the mandible, may have initially been borrowed from the ingestion domain, where it is used by all mammals for chewing, sucking, and licking. (I'll supply a neurological rationale for this suggestion in Chapter 8.) But before we began to speak, there was probably an intermediate stage of visuofacial communication in the form of "smacks," involving rhythmic close/open movements of the mouth. Many other living primates use lipsmacks, tonguesmacks, and teeth-chatters as a basic form of communication, and our ancestors probably did too. Eventually, though, the mandibular cycle underlying the close/open alternation of the mouth became consistently paired with vocal-fold vibration to form the first syllables. In beginning with a language-like vocalization stage called "babbling," infants presumably recapitulate their phylogeny by producing relatively simple, often totally repetitive cycles of mandibular oscillation (e.g., *bababa*) before elaborating them by placing various different consonants and vowels in successive frame cycles (e.g., *bodega*).

The last part of my basic argument for a frame/content mode returns again to the relationship between production and perception. I propose that in the initial frame stage of speech evolution, the form of speech was dominated by a limited set of sound-producing movements that had a deep-seated heritage, with perceptual differentiation between repertoire items being a minor problem. The logic behind this suggestion is that in a system that conveys only a few meanings, as the earliest speech system must have, there is less pressure on the sending apparatus to move beyond the signaling capabilities that it is most naturally suited to. By analogy, not much pressure was put on the engineer's design capabilities to make an adequate Morse Code generator. The listener had only to distinguish between two signal lengths—the short "dot" and the long "dash." (For example, the letter "e" is a dot, the letter "t" is a dash, the letter "a" is a dot followed by a dash, etc.) It was not much of a problem for the designer to make these two signals distinguishably different. But under pressure for the evolution of a larger message-sending capability, the inherent perceptual requirement of message differentiation forced the production system out of its most comfortable mode into territory that was less readily available.

Accordingly, I propose that there were two main stages in speech evolution—a *frame stage* and a *frame/content stage*. I propose that in speech acquisition, infants also begin with a simple basic production repertoire, and in the second stage they deal with the problem of generating an increasingly large message set.

More specifically, I will present evidence that the form of babbling and early speech is dominated by the operation of a very small set of very old action capabilities (mandibular oscillation and simple tongue- and soft-palate-placement capabilities) and is influenced only slightly by a large set of characteristics of adult speech that are readily available to the listening infant. It is only after this early-speech phase that the infant makes a big move towards producing the many further aspects of the adult speech system that probably evolved later in the history of the language under pressures for increasing the message-set size.

In numerical terms, a two-stage theory of evolution of speech is not much of an advance on the generative one-stage view. What makes them so different is that there cannot be a generative two-stage view because this perspective lacks a time domain. Consequently, any evidence for a two-stage sequence is automatically evidence against the generative view.

Most of what I have described here is in the first six chapters of the book. In the remaining chapters I develop the basic thesis further in various respects and view it from a number of perspectives.

Chapter 7 presents a hypothesis as to how the sound patterns I have talked about get hooked up with concepts to form the first words. The hypothesis is that the first words were like present-day baby-talk words and evolved within the parent/infant communicative dyad.

Chapters 8 and 9 consider the evolution of brain organization for speech, usually in the left hemisphere. Chapter 8 provides some neurological background and Chapter 9 offers a view of the evolution of the left cerebral hemisphere in the service of the frame/content mode in particular. There are two key points here. The first is that Broca's area has been historically associated with the evolution of mandibular cyclicities in mammals and has also evolved as the main action site for vocal learnability based on the operation of mirror neurons. (Mirror neurons are neurons found in monkeys, which discharge when an animal makes a particular movement—e.g., grasping—and when the monkey observes another animal making the same movement. This action–observation linkage allows, in principle, the possibility of learning to make the movements of others.) The second point is that the medial premotor cortex of the supplementary motor area has evolved as the main control site of cognitive-motor frames underlying speech production. Chapter 10 presents the contrarian view, based primarily on the evolution of handedness in primates, that the specializations of the left cerebral hemisphere for speech and right-hand control were both offshoots of a specialization of the hemisphere for whole-body control under routine circumstances.

Chapters 11 and 12 offer more detailed critiques of the generative approach to sound patterns in general and to acquisition of speech in particular. These critiques are formulated in the light of the frame/content theory already presented. In particular, I say why I find the concepts of distinctive feature, markedness, and syllabic sonority—the main conceptual building blocks of generative phonology—to be of no value in the attempt to *explain* speech in a traditional cause-and-effect way. I conclude that generative phonology has not in general transcended the mind/body dichotomy of Descartes. Bodily aspects of speech are either wrongly incorporated into the mental component or ruled completely out of mental court by being relegated to the performance level.

Chapter 13 brings the perspective of sign language to bear on the generativist-vs.-Neodarwinian question. The thesis of generative linguistics regarding sign language is that because it is just as linguistic as spoken language and develops in a similar way, it is evidence for a single underlying amodal language capacity. In this chapter I review evidence for the conclusion that there is very little basis for the claim that the phonological level of language is amodal. I also dispute the thesis that the first language was a sign language, mainly on the grounds that if this were true, sign language would still be the universal language. Instead manual gesture may have always complemented spoken language in much the way it does today.

In Chapter 14, I consider the ultimate causes of speech, finding some possibility of deep-seated innateness but not speech-specific innateness. This latter conclusion is supported by recent failures to find an aspect of the genetic substrate that is specific to speech. I also conclude that, in contrast to speech, the other major instance of vertebrate vocal learnability—birdsong—does have an innate song-specific basis but is also similar to speech in having a frame/content mode of organization. I present the argument that the meme, a unit of cultural imitation, has been the main basis for the evolution and acquisition of the second, frame/content stage of speech. To more effectively explore the mimetic aspect of speech I consider the religious symbol of the cross as a metaphor for the syllable.

In a final chapter, Chapter 15, I briefly present the conclusion that while the frame/content theory, a Neodarwinian approach featuring an embodiment perspective, shows some promise in assisting our understanding of the evolution of speech, the classical/generative approach does not.

PART II

Speech and its origin: the frame/content theory

3 The nature of modern hominid speech

What exactly is speech, and what movements do we make to produce it? These questions are pertinent because, if we seek to understand how speech evolved, we need to understand the mechanics of the end product. We need, in short, an answer to Tinbergen's first question: *How does it work?* This takes us into the realm of phonetics—the science of speech sounds.

3.1 The production of speech

Speech production involves three subsystems: (1) the respiratory system, (2) the phonatory system, and (3) the articulatory system (see Fig. 3.1).

3.1.1 Respiration

The respiratory system consists of the *lungs* at the center, the *trachea* (windpipe) exiting from them, and the *rib cage*, plus other thoracic and abdominal structures that surround and act on the lungs.

The normal adult takes about four seconds for each breath—about two seconds to breathe in (inspiration), and two more seconds to breathe out (expiration). Speech occurs during expiration and, as we will see, involves maintaining constant lung pressure across an entire utterance, which might last several seconds. This creates an outflow of air that gets modulated by the other two subsystems to produce the sounds of speech.

When we breathe in, we expand the rib cage while flattening the diaphragm, a dome-shaped muscle below the lungs. Because the lungs are attached to these two structures by a vacuum, the adjacent borders of the lungs are sucked outwards and downwards, causing lung volume to increase. Simultaneously, the air pressure in the lungs decreases, causing air to rush in (inspiration) to compensate for this decrease. When we breathe out, in contrast, we needn't do anything except turn off the inspiratory muscles.

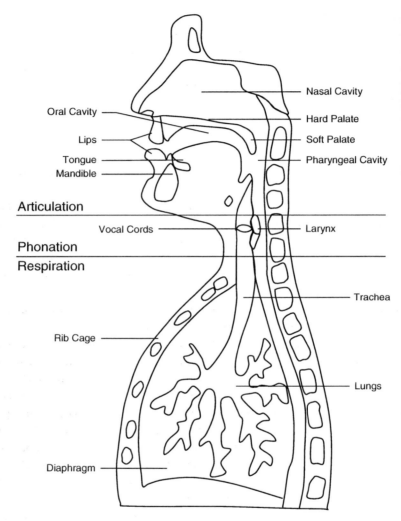

Fig. 3.1   Schematic view of the three subsystems of speech: respiratory, phonatory, and articulatory.

And when we do that, the rib cage and diaphragm simply return to their at-rest positions, thanks to elastic recoil. This leads to a decrease in lung volume, which prompts an outflow of air (expiration).

But whenever we speak, we must actively control our expiratory phase in order to keep lung pressure constant. How do we do this? After we have breathed in, we continue to contract our inspiratory muscles at lower levels to let the system down gently, by reducing its rate of elastic recoil. After the rib cage and diaphragm reach their rest position, we begin to actively squeeze the lungs to keep decreasing their volume. The two maneuvers serve to keep our lung pressure at the constant level above atmospheric levels necessary for us to make speech sounds.

3.1.2 Phonation

"Phonation" means "voicing." We voice by vibrating our vocal folds or cords (often misspelled "chords"). These folds are embedded within a system of cartilages and muscles of the larynx (often mispronounced "larnyx"), a structure at the head of the trachea. If you locate your Adam's apple, you've located your larynx. The vocal folds are a pair of parallel slivers of muscle running from the front to the back of the surrounding cartilages. When we breathe, they're drawn apart at the back while remaining together at the front. This creates a triangular slit called the "glottis." When we speak, they're brought together and caused to vibrate in response to the constant expiratory air pressure.

To understand vocal-fold vibration, let's imagine we're beginning an utterance with a vowel. We start by unconsciously instructing the folds to come together while breathing out. When this happens, it blocks the outlet of the lungs, causing lung pressure to increase. As air pressure continues to increase, the folds are eventually blown open, forming an elliptical airspace (glottis) through which a pulse of air rapidly flows. Forcing the folds into an elliptical shape has two effects on them. First, an elastic recoil force builds up in the vocal folds as they are stretched to form the ellipse, and this creates a tendency to make them return to their closed configuration. Reinforcing that tendency is a second factor, the Bernouilli effect, whereby low pressure develops in regions of high flow. Here, low pressure generated by the rapidly flowing air pulse tends to suck the folds back to the midline. The net effect of these two forces results in the folds coming together again, at which point the entire cycle is repeated and continues to be repeated, if other circumstances permit, as long as lung pressure remains sufficiently above air pressure in the mouth to initiate the cycle.

So this is how phonation, or voicing, occurs. The rate at which it occurs, computed in cycles per second, or Hertz (Hz), is called the "Fundamental

Frequency" (F0). The perceptual effect of F0 is described as "pitch." Higher F0s are heard as higher pitches. The F0 of a male adult phonating at his most comfortable level is about 125 Hz. For a female adult, the corresponding frequency is about 225 Hz. And for a 6-month-old infant, it's about 350 Hz.

Phonation is the main sound source for speech. Besides generating acoustic energy at its fundamental frequency (F0), it generates energy at all harmonics (whole numbered multiples) of F0. The patterns of modulation of the first 35 or so of these harmonics by the articulatory system are the main sources of acoustic information for most voiced sounds.

The fundamental frequency of phonation or voicing varies in a systematic way in speech, as I'll explain later. Voicing accompanies all vowels in most languages. All languages also contain some consonants that are voiced, but also contain some that are voiceless—that is, not accompanied by vocal-fold vibration.

3.1.3 The articulatory system

The articulatory system has two responsibilities. Besides modulating the just-mentioned family of harmonics coming from the vocal folds, it provides a second sound source, as we will see.

The system consists of four moveable structures bordering on the supralaryngeal vocal tract—the airspace from the larynx to the mouth and nose. These four structures are the lips, the mandible (lower jaw), the tongue, and the soft palate (velum) (see Fig. 3.2). They are brought into juxtaposition with immoveable structures—the upper teeth, hard palate, and rear wall of the pharynx (the throat area above the larynx)—and in some cases with each other, to form the great majority of speech sounds. These maneuvers create sets of continuously varying cavities, the sizes and shapes of which, when activated by voicing, give rise to families of resonances called "formants." The articulatory system also uses three of these same mouth structures (lips, mandible, tongue) to form narrow constrictions in the vocal tract. When outgoing air moves through these constrictions, it generates friction, resulting in turbulent airflow. This provides the second, or "fricative," sound source. Examples include the first and last sounds of the word "fish."

As indicated in Chapter 1, during speech, the articulators tend to alternate between a relatively closed (constricted) and open configuration of the vocal tract—closed for consonants, open for vowels. Every language

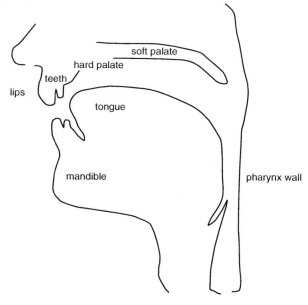

FIG. 3.2   The principal parts of the articulatory system.

includes the simplest form of this alternation—the consonant–vowel (CV) syllable—either alone, or along with one or more other syllable types (Blevins, 1995). These can include a vowel by itself, as in the vowel beginning the word "about," and one or more other combinations of a vowel and one or more consonants, either preceding or following the vowel. In subsequent discussion, following the conventions of phonetics, observable surface forms of consonants and vowels, called "phones," will be indicated by square brackets (e.g., [a]). Angled brackets will designate a supposedly underlying phonetic form or phoneme (e.g., /a/).

3.1.4 Consonants

Table 3.1 shows English consonants classified in terms of three main properties, together with examples of words in which the various consonants occur: (1) *place of articulation*—i.e., where in the vocal tract the constriction is made; (2) *manner of articulation*—i.e., the degree of constriction and how it's made; and (3) *voicing*—i.e., whether the consonant is accompanied by vocal-fold vibration. (Where there are two entries in a cell, the first is a voiced

TABLE **3.1** Phonetic symbols for English consonants and words in which they occur

	Labial		Interdental		Alveolar		Palatal		Velar	
Stops										
Voiced	b	bat			d	duck			g	goat
Voiceless	p	pat			t	tuck			k	coat
Nasals	m	mat			n	nose			ŋ	hang
Fricatives										
Voiced	v	vine	ð	this	s	bus	ʒ	azure		
Voiceless	f	fine	θ	thin	z	buzz	ʃ	shoe		
Affricatives										
Voiced							dʒ	judge		
Voiceless							tʃ	church		
Liquids					l	lash				
					r	rash				
Semivowels/ Glides	w	we			j	you				

consonant and the second is a voiceless one, except for liquids, where both sounds are voiced.) Let's look at each of these properties in turn.

3.1.5 *Place of articulation*

For present purposes, English can be considered to have consonants at five main places of articulation:

1. Labial: made with the lips.
2. Interdental: with the tongue between the upper and lower teeth.
3. Alveolar: tongue tip or blade with the alveolar ridge—a small bump immediately behind the upper incisors.
4. Palatal: front of the tongue with the hard palate.
5. Velar: back of the tongue with the soft palate or velum.

Other languages have additional places of articulation. Here are two examples:

1. Uvular: back of the tongue with the back of the soft palate, as in the consonant beginning the French word "rouge."
2. Pharyngeal: root of the tongue with the pharynx wall, as in Arabic languages.

Some sounds involve the simultaneous use of two places of articulation, as in the English semivowel "w," which involves constrictions at the lips and at the velum. When consonants are classified more globally in terms of place of articulation, the seven categories get folded into just three super-ordinate categories that we will make much use of—Labial (lips), Coronal (tongue front), and Dorsal (tongue back).

3.1.6 *Manner of articulation*

English has six manners of consonantal articulation:

1. Stop consonants: complete occlusion (closure) of the oral tract.
2. Nasals: Like stops, nasals involve complete oral-tract closure, but have an opening of the pathway between the soft palate (velum) and the pharynx wall—the pathway normally used in quiet breathing (see Fig. 3.2).
3. Fricatives: These have sufficient constriction to produce frictional effects on outgoing air resulting in turbulent air flow.
4. Affricates: These consist of a brief, stop-like period of complete occlusion followed by a brief, fricative-like constriction at the same place of articulation. English has two affricates—the voiced palato-alveolar affricate [dʒ] bounding the word "judge," on both ends, and the voiceless palato-alveolar affricate [tʃ] bounding the word "church."
5. Liquids: These have insufficient constriction to produce turbulent air flow, but also have relatively unusual tongue configurations. The lateral [l] involves a closure in the midline, but with an opening on one or both sides. The liquid [ɾ] involves the bending back or retroflexion of the tip-blade complex.
6. Semivowels (sometimes called glides): Though, like vowels, they involve relatively little constriction, they are considered consonants here because they occur in consonantal positions in syllables—i.e., on the margins of vowels.

One English consonant, [h], as in "*hair*," is omitted from the table. It can be classified as a glottal fricative. It involves a relatively open mouth, and the fricative-like noise that accompanies it is generated mostly by turbulent air flowing through the glottis.

3.1.7 Voicing

Most consonants are either voiced or voiceless during the entire period of maximal constriction. Voiceless stop consonants are further distinguished by the time lag between the release of the stop (accompanied by a brief "plosive" burst of fricative-like noise) and the onset of voicing. This property is known as "voice onset time" (VOT). If this lag lasts only a few milliseconds, the stop is called "voiceless unaspirated." If the lag is longer, the open glottis during the lag period creates an interval of *h*-like noise called "aspiration." Consequently, these stops are described as "voiceless aspirated."

3.1.8 Additional airstream mechanisms and secondary articulations

Although all complete utterances in all languages are produced on what is called the "pulmonic egressive airstream" (involving, as we have seen, a constant lung pressure), there are two additional ways in which the airstream can be manipulated within the vocal tract when producing individual consonants. In both cases, air is temporarily impounded within the tract by making an occlusion behind the consonant's place of articulation:

(1) *The glottalic airstream mechanism.* Here, the vocal folds are brought together when the tract is also closed above the folds, impounding the air in the nonnasal part of the vocal tract. Then, in sounds called "ejectives," the larynx is raised, increasing intraoral air pressure and resulting in a sharp popping sound when the anterior closure is released. In sounds called "implosives," the larynx is lowered after the vocal folds are brought together with the tract closed above them, decreasing intraoral air pressure below atmospheric levels and so resulting in an audible inflow of air at release.

(2) *The velaric airstream mechanism.* Here, the vocal tract is occluded by tongue contact with the soft palate during a consonant with a more anterior closed place of articulation. The body of the tongue between

the two obstructions is then lowered, reducing the pressure of the impounded air. Consequently, when the anterior occlusion of the air is released, air flows in. The resultant sounds are called "clicks," and they're common in many South African languages.

Some consonants are characterized by "secondary articulations." Besides the main constriction, they have a second constriction at another place of articulation, made at the same time. Depending on the place of that secondary constriction, consonants can be described as "labialized," "palatalized" (as in the "y" of Russian "*nyet*"), "velarized," or "pharyngealized."

3.1.9 Vowels

Traditionally, vowels are classified by the location of the tongue's high point in the mouth. When making speech sounds, regardless of the language, the tongue never moves to the speaker's left or right. It only moves up or down (the "height dimension") or towards the front or back (the "front-back dimension"). Table 3.2 shows American English vowels classified into three subcategories in each of these terms, together with examples of their use in words. But some vowels are made not just with the tongue but by rounding and protruding the lips as well. Examples are the high- and mid-back vowels in English—the vowels in "boot" and "boat," for example. The low-central vowel [a] requires special comment. It is a dialectal variant of the low-back vowel [a]heard in parts of the Northeastern United States. This variant, made famous by President John Kennedy, is highlighted in the sentence "Park your car in Harvard Yard," in which the "r" is not pronounced. We

TABLE 3.2 Phonetic symbols for English vowels and words in which they occur

		Front		Central		Back
High	i	beat			u	boot
	ɪ	bit			ʊ	book
Mid	e	bait	ə	about	o	boat
	ɛ	bet	ʌ	but	ɔ	bought
Low	æ	bat	a	father	ɑ	box

need to highlight it here because it's a very important vowel in babbling and early speech, as we will see later.

Most vowels can be called "monophthongs." Like most consonants, they involve a movement of the articulators to a single point in the vocal tract. Three vowels omitted in Table 3.2 are the diphthongs [aɪ] as in "bite," [oɪ] as in "joy," and [oʊ] as in "bout," all of which involve two successive movements toward two different points. The vowels [e] and [o] are sometimes called "diphthongizing vowels" because, following their initial movement, they tend to move toward a higher tongue position.

Vowels can also be nasalized, and this often results in a sound contrast in a particular language (e.g., French) between pairs of similar vowels, one being nasalized and the other not. Another variant of vowels is what are called "rhotocized vowels." In words such as "bird" in American English, the tongue is elevated in the palatal region and simultaneously retracted in the lower pharyngeal region to produce an "r"-like effect.

3.2 Distinctive features

Linguists consider that subattributes of consonants and vowels in the world's languages can be classified in terms of a supposedly finite and small set of distinctive features, a claim we will discuss later.

Fig. 3.3 shows an implementation, by Jackendoff (2002, p. 7), of one particular feature classification system for the word "star." The four segments of the word are each enclosed in brackets. I'll briefly describe the features from the top down.

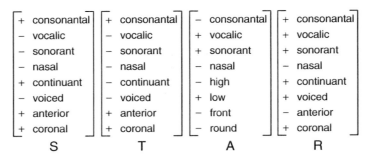

FIG. 3.3   Jackendoff's characterization of the segmental structure of the word "star" in terms of distinctive features.

The first two features indicate whether the segment is a consonant or a vowel. (The fact that the consonant "r" is classified as both consonant and vowel is not of concern here.) "Sonorant" applies to the acoustic energy level of the sound which relates in turn to how open the vocal tract is for the sound. The property of "nasality" has already been described. For the last four features there is a different classification for vowels and consonants. The classification for vowels is pretty self-explanatory. "Continuant" refers to whether there is a continuous airflow through the point of constriction, as in the fricative "s" (designated +) or whether the vocal tract is occluded, as it is for "t" (designated −). "Voicing" has already been described. "Anterior" refers to whether the consonantal constriction is made in the front portion of the mouth, as it is for labials and coronals, described earlier. "Coronal" refers to whether the front part of the tongue in particular is involved in the sound.

3.3 Patterns of occurrence of consonants and vowels in languages

3.3.1 Consonants

Table 3.3 shows, in percentage terms, how often each of the major manner classes of consonants occurs in a sample of 317 languages constituting the UCLA Phonological Segment Inventory Database (UPSID: Maddieson, 1984). Judging by the UPSID database, stop consonants are the only major manner class that is truly universal, even though the others occur at frequencies of over 90%.

TABLE 3.3 Percentages of occurrence of at least one instance of major consonant types in each one of Maddieson's (1984) 317-language sample

	%
Stops	100
Nasals	96.8
Fricatives	96.8
Liquids	95.9
Glides	90.5

3.3.2 Stop consonants

Every language has at least one stop consonant, and in terms of their place of articulation, the three stop-consonantal variants that occur in English happen to be the most popular ones—labial, alveolar, and velar (see Table 3.1). But none of these three places are completely universal. Wichita, Hupa, and Aleut have no bilabial stop consonant, Hawaiian has no alveolar stop, and Hupa and Kirghiz have no velar stop.

In terms of voicing, no particular stop-consonantal form is universal. The most frequent form, occurring in 91.8% of the world's languages, is the "plain voiceless" form—that is, a voiceless unaspirated form, as in the assumed underlying forms of English /b/, /d/, /g/ in the initial position of words. Thus, when we look at the place and voicing attributes of stops, we find that there is not a single manner-place-voicing variant that occurs in all languages. As stops are the only consonantal category that is universal, this means that there is no single consonantal sound that is universal in languages.

All the consonant classes discussed so far involve a pulmonic egressive airstream. In contrast, only 22.4% of languages have a consonant with a glottalic airstream (ejectives and implosives). Clicks, with their velaric ingressive airstream, are so rare in the UPSID database that they are not systematically analyzed.

TABLE 3.4   Percentages of occurrence of vowels in particular locations in the vowel space (From Maddieson, 1994).

	%
HF	18.9
MF	17.9
LF	3.2
HC	2.6
MC	4.2
LC	15.4
HB	17.6
MB	18.3
LB	1.9
	100

3.3.3 Vowels

As with consonants, no single vowel occurs in all languages. The most frequently occurring vowels are the high-front vowel /i/ (91.5%), the high-back vowel /u/ (88.0%), and the low-central vowel /a/ (83.9%). Table 3.4 shows in percentage terms the frequency of occurrence of different vowel types in the corpus, classified in a 3-by-3 matrix. Most vowels fall into the categories high and mid-front, high and mid-back, and low central.

Maddieson provides an exhaustive listing of the individual consonant and vowel types in the UPSID database. He found 558 different consonant types and 210 vowel types. This is an extremely large number of sounds considering that the sample includes only about 5 percent of the world's languages.

Table 3.5 lists the frequencies with which particular sound types occur in the individual languages of the corpus. The most common occurrence is for a sound to occur just once. In fact, almost 50 percent of all segments occur in only one language. Only 1.6 percent of the segments occur in more than half of the languages, and less than 10 percent of the segment types occur in more than one-eighth of the languages. Perhaps most surprising is that of the 51 different dipthongs listed, only 15 occur in more than one language, and none occur in more than six.

TABLE 3.5 Percentages representing the number of times that particular sounds occurred in the Maddieson (1994) corpus

# of times occurring	Percentage of sounds
1	47.6
2–4	22.3
5–9	11.1
10–19	6.9
20–39	4.3
40–79	3.5
80–159	2.7
160+	1.6
	100

This distribution of frequencies of usage is prima facie evidence against the existence of a small finite set of distinctive features. It would seem unnaturally uneconomical in terms of feature combinatorics that there is not a single consonant or vowel that occurs in all languages. And second, why is the modal number of occurrences of a particular subcategory of consonant and vowel only 1, a number that couldn't be any smaller? The notion that there is a small set of distinctive features implies some kind of unity in what Chomsky and Halle (1968) called "the phonetic capabilities of man," but what we find instead is diversity. This is one of several reasons why I doubt the existence of distinctive features as functional units of speech (see Chapter 11).

3.4 The acoustics of speech

Speech is primarily conveyed to the listener acoustically. The main acoustical information regarding vowels is imparted by the lowest three resonances (formants) of our vocal tract. Fig. 3.4, derived from Ladefoged

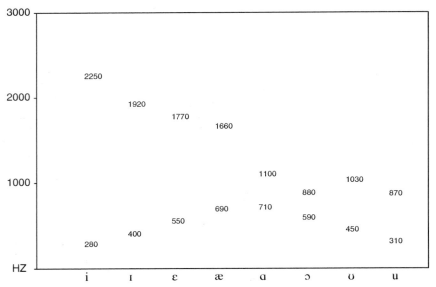

FIG. 3.4   Formant frequencies for 8 American vowels. (From Ladefoged, 1993, Fig. 8.5)

(1993, Fig. 8.5), shows formant frequencies of eight American vowels. When we compare Fig. 3.4 with Table 3.2, we find a relatively straightforward relation between the height of the vowel in articulatory terms and the value of the first formant. We also find a relation between the position of a vowel on the front-back axis and the value of the second formant. Given that tongue position isn't directly observable, it appears that an important basis used by early phoneticians to classify vowels in terms of height and front-back dimensions was formant frequencies.

3.5 Structure of the word

Fig. 3.5 is a schematic view of the English word "tomato." Its structure has two levels: suprasegmental and segmental. The segmental level, consisting of consonants and vowels, can be further divided into a number of subattributes or features, as was shown for the word "star" in Fig. 3.3. (In more behaviorally oriented treatments, subattributes of phonemes are described in terms of "gestures"—e.g., Browman and Goldstein, 1986.)

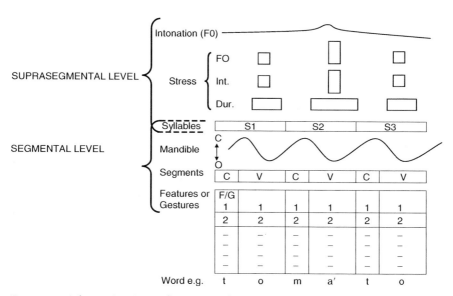

FIG. 3.5 Schematic view of aspects of speech in the word "tomato". (From MacNeilage, 1998a)

At the suprasegmental level, "stress" refers roughly to the amount of energy involved in producing a syllable, which is correlated with its perceptual prominence. In English, at least, syllables that are more stressed tend to be louder, and also have higher fundamental frequencies and longer durations. "Intonation" refers to the global pattern of fundamental frequency (rate of vocal-fold vibration). In multisyllabic words spoken in isolation, and in simple declarative sentences such as "The boy hit the ball," there is a terminal fall in fundamental frequency. The syllable lies at the interface between the suprasegmental and the segmental levels. At the suprasegmental level, the syllable has three roles. It is (1) the unit that receives the stress, (2) the unit of rhythmic organization, and (3) the unit marking any relatively abrupt change (inflection) in the intonation contour. At the segmental level, it provides an organizational superstructure for distributing consonants and vowels. (For further details, see Levelt, 1989, Chapter 8.)

From the point of view of overall linguistic structure the syllable is most commonly described in the following way: There is an Onset component and a following Rhyme component. The Rhyme component is divided into a Nucleus and a following Coda. The Onset consists of however many consonants precede the vowel. The vowel is the Nucleus. The Coda consists of however many consonants follow the vowel in the same syllable. (See Fig. 3.6.)

With minor exceptions, all syllables must contain a vowel. In syllables that contain consonants there is a sonority peak on the vowel. As will be detailed later, this means roughly that the vowel is the loudest sound in the syllable. There is also a sonority hierarchy whereby sounds on both margins of syllables successively decrease in loudness as the distance between them and the nucleus increases. Some additional properties of syllables, noted by Carstairs-McCarthy (1999), are summarized below. Some languages have no codas, though all have onsets, and "the inventory of possible codas in a

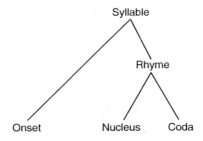

FIG. 3.6   Linguistic structure of the syllable.

language tends to be smaller than that of possible onsets" (p. 141). There is an onset maximization principle in multisyllabic sequences whereby margins tend to be assigned to onsets rather than rhymes. For example, in the word "instruction" three of the four marginal consonants [nstr] are assigned to the onset position giving [n#str] where # signifies a syllable boundary.

Part of the reason why the nucleus is considered more closely related to the consonantal coda component than the consonantal onset component is that the onset component is more free than the coda component to move independently of the vowel in speech errors. A further difference between onsets and codas is that the presence of a coda can be conducive to the placement of stress on a syllable, while the presence or absence of onsets has no influence on stress placement.

3.6 Speech errors and serial organization

For me, the most salient aspect of speech as action is that we typically produce syllables at the rate of 5–6 syllables or about 15 phonemes per second—often 15 *different* phonemes. The speed of operation here is quite phenomenal. By comparison, concert pianists are seldom required to produce individual notes with one hand at anything like this rate.

How do we achieve such an amazing performance? One way to answer this question is by studying how naturally occurring performances can go wrong—in other words, by studying speech errors. The logic behind this approach is that a system cannot malfunction in an indefinitely large number of ways. So when you look at the ways it does go wrong, you can construct hypotheses as to how it actually works. Imagine, for example, that you knew nothing about automobiles and that you were given one on the condition that you had to figure out how it worked without looking under the hood. Eventually, after much trial and error, you'd come to realize certain things. For instance, you'd find that the horn still worked even when the brakes didn't, but that same horn would sometimes not work when you couldn't get the car started, suggesting that the starting mechanism has something in common with the soundmaking one.

Lashley (1951) taught us that serial-ordering errors (i.e., producing the correct sounds but in the wrong order) reveal much about how this rapid stream of output is organized. At the level of sound structure, errors show us that individual consonants and vowels seem to constitute separate units in the organization of output. They show us this because they are often misplaced in speech errors. For instance, in a corpus collected by Shattuck-Hufnagel (1980), about two-thirds of the errors involve single segments. The other errors involve, for the most part, subsyllabic groupings of segments. For example, the "gr" part of "groupings" constitutes a consonant cluster. It could move as a whole. Another example of a subsyllabic grouping is an initial consonant and the following vowel—for instance, the "mo" in "most."

There is some agreement on the existence of five types of segmental speech error. In defining these, I will follow the terminology of Shattuck-Hufnagel in her classic 1979 paper and borrow some of her examples:

1. *Exchange* (aka "spoonerism," "reversal," and "transposition"): Two units in an intended sequence change places with each other:
   emeny (enemy)
   max welts (wax melts)

2. *Substitution*: One intended unit is replaced by another:
   It's a shallower *test* (chest)
   Anymay, I think (anyway)

3. *Shift*: A unit disappears from its intended location and appears in another location:
   State *lowned and* (owned land)
   I did it *myn ow* way (my own)

4. *Addition*: An extra unit is added to an intended sequence:
   the *plublicity* (publicity)
   spublic speaking (public)

5. *Omission*: A unit is dropped from an intended sequence:
   sonata *umber* ten (number)
   too *mentalitic* (mentalistic)

In this context, I will focus on exchange errors since they're a frequently occurring type in which you always know where the misplaced units came from. Each unit clearly comes from the space that the other one ends up occupying. But much evidence from other error types is consistent with that from exchange errors.

The central fact about exchange errors is that in virtually all segmental exchanges, the units move into a position in syllable structure like the one they vacated: syllable-initial consonants exchange with other syllable-initial consonants, vowels exchange with vowels, and syllable-final consonants with other syllable-final consonants. For example, Shattuck-Hufnagel (1979) reported that of a total of 211 segmental exchanges between words, "all but 4 take place between phonemes in similar positions in their respective syllables" (p. 307). Fromkin (1973) supplies these examples:

Initial consonants: *mell wade* (well made)
Vowels: *odd hack* (add hoc)
Final consonants: *toff shelp* (top shelf)

This result, widely attested in studies of both spontaneous and elicited errors, shows that there is a severe syllable-position constraint on the serial organization of the sound level of language.

The most remarkable thing about this constraint is that consonants and vowels never exchange with each other. What explains this superordinate structural constraint against placing consonants and vowels in each other's positions? Intuitively, one might expect serial-ordering errors such as exchanges to involve *adjacent* segments, as this would seem to be the mildest form of exchange error. There are numbers of consonant–vowel and vowel–consonant syllables in English that are mirror images of each other—for example, "eat" vs. "tea"; "no" vs. "own"; "*ab*stract" vs. "*ba*salt." Either form therefore naturally occurs as a sequence of the two opposing vocal-tract phases, but exchange errors that would turn one such form into the other are not attested. It seems that it's the order of the consonant and vowel components within the syllables of the particular intended lexical items themselves that constrains their subsequent positions in a given utterance, whether or not they finally manifest themselves in the syllables they originated in. Thus the syllable structure of the specific intended utterance is chosen before it is populated by segments, as Lashley observed long ago.

3.7 Metaphors for speech organization: slot/segment and frame/content (F/C)

For Shattuck-Hufnagel (1979), the syllable-structure constraint implies the existence of a scan–copy mechanism that scans the lexical items of the intended utterance for representations of segments, and then copies these representations into slots in a series of canonical syllable-structure matrices. The fundamental conception underlying this "slot/segment" hypothesis is that "slots in an utterance are represented in some way during the production process independent of their segmental contents" (Shattuck-Hufnagel, 1979, p. 303). This same conception also underlies the "frame/content" metaphor. The only difference lies in the choice of terms for the two components. In the present terms, *syllable-structure frames* are represented in some way during the production process independent of *segmental content elements*. This different terminology comes from Levelt (1989). I chose the frame/content metaphor over the slot/segment metaphor because the term "frame" highlights the superordinate property of the syllable as a whole in constraining the placement of the segments/content.

The speech errors that reveal the F/C mode of organization of speech production presumably occur at the stage of interfacing the lexicon or mental dictionary with the motor system. The motor system is required both to produce the overall rhythmic organization associated with syllables, basically by means of a close–open alternation of the vocal tract, and to continually modulate these cycles by producing particular consonants and vowels during closing and opening phases. Rather than there being holistic chunking of output into indissoluble motor packages, there may have developed, *in the production system,* some natural division of labor whereby the basic syllabic cycle and the individual modulations of the cycle are separately controlled. Perhaps, then, when frame modulation, by means of varying consonants and vowels, evolved as a favored way to increase the message set, the increasing load on this segmental aspect of production led to the development of a separate mechanism for its motor control.

According to the above conception, which I will amplify later, fundamental phylogenetic properties of the motor system have played the primary role in determining the F/C structure of speech. I assume that as this occurred, the consequences of the two-part division of labor then ramified into the organization of the prior stage of lexical storage. There is good evidence for an independence between lexical representation of segmental information and information about syllable structure. This evidence comes from a set of studies on the "tip of the tongue" (TOT) phenomenon, which occurs when people find themselves able to retrieve some information about the word they wish to produce, like what sound it begins with or how many syllables it has, but can't produce the whole word. Levelt (1989) concludes that "lexical form information is not all-or-none. A word's representation in memory consists of components that are relatively accessible and there can be metrical information about the number and accents of syllables without these syllables being available" (p. 321).

Viewing the syllable as the receptacle for segments during motor organization is encouraged by another body of evidence. Garrett (1988) has pointed out that there is little evidence that syllables themselves are moved about in serial-ordering errors "except where the latter are ambiguous as to their classification (i.e., they coincide with morphemes, or the segmental makeup of the error unit is ambiguous)" (p. 82). Thus "syllables appear to constrain error rather than indulge in it" (p. 82). (For a similar conclusion, see Levelt, 1989, p. 322.)

3.8 Lack of evidence for subsegmental units

This dual-component (syllable and segment) conception of speech production allows no role for the distinctive feature, the unit most favored in current phonological and phonetic conceptions of the organization of speech.

I take this stance primarily because we have little evidence from speech errors that the feature is an independent variable in the control of speech production. The fact that members of most pairs of segments involved in errors affecting two segments are similar, differing only by one feature, has sometimes been taken to mean that the feature is a functional unit in the control process. The interpretation is that similarity in feature structure potentiates errors. But the proposition that phonetic similarity is a variable in potentiating errors of serial organization can be made without invoking the feature as the unit of similarity. When two exchanged segments differ by one feature, it cannot be determined whether features or whole segments have been exchanged. In an error such as "bad debt" $\rightarrow$ "dad bet" it's impossible to decide whether there had simply been a reversal of the place feature of these consonants or of the consonants themselves, because they differ only in terms of place. But as Shattuck-Hufnagel and Klatt (1979) have noted, when the two segments participating in an exchange error differ by more than one feature, it would be simpler, from a distinctive-feature standpoint, for one feature to reverse than for two to reverse. An example of such a one-feature error would be "glear plue sky" for "clear blue sky." Here, the voicing values of the two sounds are reversed, but their places of articulation remain the same. Yet in an analysis of seventy-two exchange errors where the members of the pairs of participating segments differed by more than one feature, only three cases involved the exchange of a single feature. In other words, an error such as "blear clue sky" in which voicing and place properties move together is a much more likely error than "glear plue sky," even though Shattuck-Hufnagel and Klatt observed the latter error.

The rarity of single-feature areas when the two segments concerned differ by more than one feature is not conclusive evidence against the independence of features/gestures as units in the control process, but it does encourage a conception of production in which their independence is not required. Later on, however, I will provide more evidence that distinctive features are not independent functional units in the speech-production process.

3.9 Speech and typing

To better understand the significance of this dual-component (F/C) view of the organization of speech production, let's consider typing, another language-output behavior. There is evidence to suggest considerable commonality between spoken language and typing in *early* stages of the process of phonological output, stages in which the mental lexicon plays a role. For example, Grudin (1981) found that on eleven of fifteen occasions, typists spontaneously corrected an inadvertently misspelled word in the text that they were copying, just as an oral reader would correct such an error, showing that the typist's mental lexicon plays a role even when copying text. But typing doesn't possess an F/C mode of organization. Any typist knows that, when typing, exchange errors occur not between units with comparable positions in an independently specified superordinate syllabic frame structure, but simply between adjacent letters (MacNeilage, 1964). And this is true whether the units are in the same syllable or in different syllables. In addition, unlike in speech, there is no constraint against exchanging actions symbolizing consonants and actions symbolizing vowels. Vowel and consonant letters exchange with each other about as often as would be predicted from the relative frequency with which vowel letters and consonant letters appear in written language (MacNeilage, 1985).

In concluding this section on adult speech organization, it should be emphasized that my focusing on the frame/content dichotomy isn't just a case of deifying some marginal phenomenon. As Levelt correctly contends, "Probably the most fundamental insight from modern speech error research is that a word's skeleton or frame and its segmental content are independently generated" (1992, p. 10). In turn, speech-error data have been the most important source of information in the psycholinguistic study of language production. As a consequence of this, I am confident that it's appropriate to take the F/C mode of organization of speech as the target toward which an evolutionary explanation of speech must be directed. In the next chapter, I'll begin to sketch out the form of this explanation.

4 Speech in deep time: how speech got started

4.1 Biphasic cycles: the mandibular cycle as the motor frame

We come now to how speech actually evolved. Basically, humans produce vocalizations the way other mammals do—by producing sounds using parts of the body that initially evolved for feeding and breathing. We even use the same three subsystems—respiratory, phonatory, and articulatory. And we use them in a similar way. Most simply, we simultaneously generate and modulate *biphasic cycles*, which are sequences of two alternating movements in each of the three subsystems. In respiration (breathing), the biphasic cycle is the inspiration–expiration alternation, with the expiratory phase variously modulated to produce vocalizations. Some researchers claim that hominids developed special modulatory capabilities to produce longer vocal episodes (McLarnon and Hewitt, 1999). In the phonatory system, the biphasic cycle— the dominant contribution of this system in all mammals—involves the vocal folds alternating regularly between an open and closed position, resulting in voicing. This cycle is modulated in its frequency, in all mammals, by changes in vocal-fold tension and subglottal pressure level, which produce variations in perceived pitch. We also modulate it by briefly drawing the vocal folds out of the airway to produce voiceless consonants. This latter modulation doesn't seem to be a fundamental change in terms of operational properties of the peripheral system. Our prespeech ancestors were already capable of abducting the vocal folds at the termination of a vocalization. However abduction of the folds for one or more consonants at a time in the stream of otherwise voiced speech requires a considerable increment in skill, and this has spectacular results in almost doubling the size of our consonantal inventory.

In nonhuman mammals, the articulatory system is typically employed only in an open configuration during call production. Here, the biphasic cycle is very basic: it involves depressing the mandible to open the mouth for a single sustained vocalization and then elevating the mandible again to close the mouth after it is over. Some animals, like dogs (and, as we'll see later, some monkeys), have a vocalization variant in which they produce a rhythmic series of more or less identical close–open alternations, as in "bow wow wow." But in humans, a series of close–open alternations is the mode. Indeed, as we have seen, such a regular alternation between a relatively closed and a relatively open configuration—closed for consonants, open for vowels—is basic enough to be a definitional characteristic. Except for a few words consisting of a single vowel, virtually every utterance of every speaker of every one of the world's languages involves an alternation between the two opposite configurations of the vocal tract. As noted earlier, the syllable, a universal unit in speech, is defined in terms of a nucleus with a relatively open vocal tract, and margins with a relatively closed vocal tract. But what's new in humans, at least in human adults, is that we systematically modulate the close–open cycle by producing different basic units, consonants and vowels, collectively termed "phonemes," in successive closing and opening phases. Thus, our speech differs from other mammalian vocal communication, in movement terms, by modulating, within a single vocalization, a third level of cyclicity, an articulatory level, in addition to using the two levels of modulated cyclicity present in all other mammals.

In the last chapter, I argued that the ability of modern adults to modulate the close–open cycle by separately programming consonants and vowels probably emerged in evolution from a previous stage. In that stage, phonation was paired with the mandibular cycle and its associated sequences of mouth closing and opening, but the programming ability had not yet evolved. The modulation capacity was not yet present. Whence this initial ability to produce unmodified series of close–open alternations (the motor frames)?

Pinker and Bloom (1990) seem happy to conclude that the cyclical basis of the syllable evolved de novo in humans because the existence of other motor rhythms suggests that evolving a new one is easy to do. (See their "authors' response" to Kingston, 1990.) But we must be constrained by the extreme conservatism of evolution, and its penchant for tinkering—in François Jacob's (1977) words, its preference for combining or transforming already existing structures or capabilities in order to produce new ones. The orthodox Darwinian response is to think in terms of the modification of some existing mandibular cycle, not in terms of our capacity to come up with a de novo action form highly similar to one that already exists.

Such a cycle, as it happens, is readily available in mammalian feeding behavior. In fact, we find three cyclical activities of the mandible in feeding—chewing, licking, and sucking. These have presumably been around for as long as mammals themselves—for at least 200 million years. Sucking, of course, must have been because it is a definitional property of mammals. And all three have obvious similarities with speech, in typically involving a continuous series of cycles of mandibular oscillation. It's quite plausible, as we will see, that our hominid ancestors managed to combine the pre-existing capacity for phonation with this pre-existing capability for mandibular oscillation to produce, in effect, protosyllabic forms. In Gould and Vrba's terms (1982), this would be an example of a phenomenon mentioned earlier, namely, exaptation (borrowing). Mandibular oscillation would have been exapted from the realm of ingestion for use in vocal communication.

The use of the biphasic cycle at the articulatory level of speech as well as for respiration and phonation is hardly surprising when seen in the full context of evolutionary biology. In fact, biphasic cycles seem to be the main way that the animal kingdom performs any kind of action that requires more than a single discrete act. Examples of biphasic cycles in nature are legion. Consider locomotion in the three available media—water, land, and air. Swimming, walking, running, hopping, writhing on the ground like a snake, flying—all involve biphasic cycles. Animals also use the biphasic cycle in breathing, scratching, digging, copulating, vomiting, shaking off bodily impediments, tail-wagging—even in their heartbeat! Most of these uses reveal evolution's extreme conservatism in that they've either been around for a very long time themselves or they have been derived from cyclicities that have. For example, Cohen (1988) makes the astonishing—yet quite plausible—claim that a biphasic locomotory cycle has been present in vertebrate evolution for half a billion years. This cycle involves an alternation between flexion and extension in opposing muscles. (For example, the biceps and triceps of our upper arm consist of a flexor and an extensor, respectively.) It was originally used for swimming in fish; it was later used to help tetrapods (land-living quadrupeds) to walk.

Cohen locates the control of this biphasic cycle in a Central Pattern Generator (CPG) present in the brain stem throughout vertebrate evolution. (A Central Pattern Generator is a structure in the brain that alternately activates opposing states—in this case, opposing movements.) Thus a mechanism for fin movement continues to be used for limb movement when animals move onto the land. Cohen points out that "With the evolution of more sophisticated and versatile vertebrates, more levels of control have been added to an increasingly more sensitive and labile CPG coordinating system." Even so, she concludes, "In this view the basic locomotor CPG need change very little to accommodate the increasing demands natural selection placed on it" (Cohen, 1988, p. 161).

Ingestive oral cyclicities are similar to locomotion in also having a CPG, again located in the brain stem, with similar characteristics across a wide range of mammals. In fact, the similarity between the locomotor and ingestive CPGs is sufficiently great that Rossignol, Lund, and Drew (1988) have postulated a single neural network model that could characterize these two CPGs as well as the CPG that controls the biphasic cycle for respiration. Lund and Kolta (2006) recently proposed that brainstem circuits associated with the CPG which controls mastication "also participate in the control of human speech". In Chapter 9, I will present evidence to this effect.

But isn't something like chewing too simple for it to have been a basis for speech? Let me suggest two answers to this question. First, even a simple cycle may have been able to serve a communicative purpose early in the history of speech, with greater complexities evolving later. But second, as Luschei and Goldberg (1981) point out, the impression that chewing is simple is deceptive. They describe it as "a rhythmic activity that seems to proceed successfully in a highly 'automatic' fashion, even in the face of wide variation in the loads presented by eating different food materials" (p. 1237). They warn us that "Movements of mastication are actually quite complex and they must bring the teeth to bear on the food material in a precise way" (p. 1238). In addition, they note that "the mandible is often used in a controlled manner for a variety of tasks. For the quadrupeds, in particular, the mandible constitutes an important system for manipulation of objects in the environment" (p. 1238). The inaccessibility of the masticatory system to direct observation presumably contributes to a tendency to underestimate its prowess. It's another invisible miracle. Haven't we all experienced the surprise of biting our tongue and then wondering how it is that we don't bite it more often?

Lund and Enomoto (1988) have characterized chewing as "one of the types of rhythmical movements that are made by coordinated action of masticatory, facial, lingual, neck and supra- and infra-hyoid muscles" (p. 49). What's striking here is that this description could be a description of the articulatory control of speech. This similarity suggests that if processes related to chewing were indeed co-opted for speech, they could have made available a great deal of potential control to the speech process. The possibility that speech may have exapted not only the mandibular cycle but also a number of valuable accompanying control capabilities makes it seem more unlikely than ever that the cycle of speech was constructed from scratch. If it was constructed from scratch, so too were its subsequent modulations.

Support for the possibility of an evolutionary relation between ingestive behaviors and speech comes from studies of tongue movement in the two behaviors. On the basis of a review of these studies, Hiiemae and Palmer (2003) suggest that "the range of shapes used in feeding is the matrix for both behaviors" (p. 413).

Why has so little attention been given to the possibility that ingestive cyclicities were precursors to speech? One explanation is that this line of reasoning involves reverse tinkering, which, because of its whimsical nature, is hard to do. Also, it could be argued that because the languages of Western culture have a relatively complex structure, we're not apt to notice that speaking them involves, most basically, a close–open mouth alternation. We have to look at languages of the world in general to realize that the simple close–open alternation is the mode. But there's another element operating here: our inveterate anthropocentrism. It's easy enough to trace exaptations backwards in the case of digging and scratching in quadruped vertebrates. Though these movement complexes are for different functions than locomotion, we can readily accept the proposition that they and their associated neural control have derived from locomotor cyclicities. Here, reverse tinkering can readily be contemplated. For speech, on the other hand, we have trouble lowering ourselves to the point where we can even imagine that it has some of its origins in chewing. Consequently, we are more likely to accept proposals such as Chomsky's that speech as a mental apparatus simply appeared out of the blue, without considering what this might have involved for movement control.

But aren't we getting ahead of ourselves? If the mandibular cyclicity for ingestion was borrowed for speech, wouldn't one expect, in the light of its extreme age, to at least find signs of it in vocal communication of other primates?

Primate vocalization systems typically consist of a relatively small number of calls. For example, in a study of gelada baboon vocalizations (Aich, Moos-Heilen, and Zimmermann, 1990), "at least 22 acoustically different vocal patterns" were distinguished. But the calls in these systems are typically not similar to speech. They usually have nothing like a repeated consonant–vowel alternation involving mouth closing and opening. Instead, they tend to be holistic sound complexes produced mostly by interaction of the respiratory and phonatory systems. Their distinctively *holistic* character, lacking independently variable internal subcomponents, is indicated by the fact that they are often given names with single auditory connotations. For example, names given to gelada baboon calls by Dunbar and Dunbar (1975) include "moan," "grunt," "vocalized yawn," "vibrato moan," "yelp," "hnn pant," "staccato cough," "snarl," "scream," "aspirated pant," and "how bark." While some primate calls occur in a series, as do syllables in speech, most calls are single events. At least some calls have harmonic properties, indicating the presence of vocal-fold vibration analogous to that found in humans; others are noisy, indicating some turbulent source (presumably most often at the glottis); still others combine noisy and harmonic characteristics. Different acoustic units are not typically combined into series in other primates. Repetition of the same sound is the mode. In cases in which an animal can make a series of different sounds, and can even vary the sequence of sounds on different occasions, the different arrangements of internal subcomponents don't seem to have separate meanings in themselves (Robinson, 1979). They have no parallel to our ability to produce different meanings with different sequences of the same subset of sounds as we are able to do in, for instance, "cat," "tack," and "act."

But looking for precursors to the frame in primate *vocal* communication repertoires might be looking in the wrong place. Mandibular cyclicities, though relatively rare in nonhuman vocalization systems, are extremely common as *visuofacial* communicative gestures. "Lipsmacks," "tongue-smacks," and "teeth chatters" can be distinguished. Redican (1975) describes the most common of these, the lipsmack, this way: "The lower jaw moves up and down but the teeth do not meet. At the same time the lips open and close slightly and the tongue is brought forward and back between the teeth so that the movements are usually quite audible.... The tongue movements are often difficult to see, as the tongue rarely protrudes far beyond the lips" (p. 138). Perhaps *these* communicative events evolved from ingestive cyclicities, and their use in our ancestors may have been a step towards the evolution of protosyllables.

Even though lipsmacks are unlike speech episodes in typically not being accompanied by vocalization, it's surprising that more attention has not been drawn to the similarity between the movement dynamics of the lipsmack and the dynamics of the syllable. The up-and-down movements of the mandible are typically repeated in a rhythmic fashion in the lipsmack, just as in syllables. Besides its similarity to syllable production in motor terms, we have other reasons to believe that the lipsmack could be a precursor to speech. First, it's analogous to speech in its ubiquity of occurrence. Redican (1975) believes that it may occur in a wider variety of social circumstances than any of the other facial expressions that he reviewed. A second similarity between the lipsmack and speech is that it typically occurs in the context of positive social interactions. A third similarity is that, unlike many vocal calls of the other primates, the lipsmack is an accompaniment of one-on-one social interactions involving eye contact—and sometimes what appears to be turn-taking. The latter set of properties is likely to have been present at the very beginning of language.

Finally, in some circumstances the lipsmack *is* accompanied by phonation. Andrew (1976) identifies a class of "humanoid grunts" involving low-frequency phonation in baboons, sometimes combined with lipsmacking. In the case he studied most intensively, mandibular lowering was accompanied by tongue protrusion and mandibular elevation by tongue retraction. Green (1975) describes a category of "atonal girneys" in which phonation is modulated "by rapid tongue flickings and lipsmacks." Green particularly emphasizes the labile morphology of these events, stating that "a slightly new vocal tract configuration may be assumed after each articulation" (p. 45). Both Andrew and Green suggest that these vocal events could be precursors to speech.

If smacks evolved from ingestive cyclicities, how might they have become incorporated into the communicative repertoire in the first place? Lipsmacks occurring during grooming have often been linked with the oral actions of ingestion of various materials discovered during the grooming process, as they often precede the ingestion of such materials. In young infants, lipsmacks have been characterized as consisting of, or deriving from, nonnutritive sucking movements, and they often occur as an infant approaches its mother with the intent of suckling. It doesn't seem too far-fetched to suggest that gestures which are anticipatory to ingestion may have become incorporated into communicative repertoires. This change would have occurred at the level of actual *use*—from ingestion-related use to communication-related use. One would not have to postulate an initial mental representation with no plausible origin and then be faced with the problem of how it found some piece of phonetic substance to pair up with in order for it to be socially transmitted.

4.2 Origin of use of vocal frames: Dunbar's vocal-grooming scenario

A scenario whereby the lipsmacks associated with grooming might have become characteristically associated with phonation can be derived from the suggestion of Dunbar (1996) that speech might have first evolved in the form of vocal grooming. The background to this hypothesis includes the contention that actual grooming in other primate groups serves to enhance social bonding. Dunbar's finding that the amount of grooming increases with group size is consistent with this hypothesis. But Dunbar also found that the neocortical ratio—the ratio of neocortex size to size of the rest of the brain—also increases with group size in other primates. As Dunbar regards the neocortex as "the 'thinking' part of the brain" (p. 62) this result suggested to him that there might be strong selection pressures in favor of increased social intelligence in larger groups.

Both the characteristic group size and neocortical ratio increase considerably in hominids. A typical hominid group size is considered to be 150. Dunbar has calculated that for the relationship he found in other primates between group size, neocortical ratio, and amount of grooming to hold in humans, they would have to spend about 40 percent of their time grooming, which is about twice the maximum amount of time spent grooming in other primate groups. We obviously don't do this, and therefore according to the hypothesis should be subject to severe social-bonding problems. But we aren't. According to Dunbar, vocal grooming, which has the *present* form of gossip (defined roughly as linguistic exchange of social information), has evolved to solve the problems of social bonding that arose with increasing group size, when physical grooming became too time-inefficient.

Of course you need a real language in order to gossip in the strict sense of the word. But the initial vocal form of the communicative events that eventually took on a semantic superstructure of gossip was most likely to have been motor frames accompanied by phonation. The ability to reiterate the frames would have made it easy to spread them out across the time domain. The addition of phonation would enable the communicative event to be broadcast to recipients in close proximity regardless of whether they were looking at the sender.

To summarize, a sequence of four events may have given us the first words: (a) grooming with lipsmacking; (b) phonating while lipsmacking; (c) increasingly substituting smacking together with phonation for the actual grooming; and (d) adding specific semantic information to this vocal component.

4.3 Organization of early speech: the "particulate principle"

But if semantic information in the form of words is to be added, how does the control of the sound level develop so that different semantic concepts can be represented by different sound patterns? As I have noted, the typical nonhuman primate vocal communication system consists of only a few different calls, and each of these calls has its own relatively separate holistic structure. In contrast, modern languages have thousands of words in which each of the underlying concepts is signaled by its own sound complex. A theory of evolution of speech must account for how our ancestors got from one of these states to the other.

Studdert-Kennedy and Lane (1980) have argued that in response to selection pressures toward an increase in communication of different meanings, ancestral forms using the holistic principle of sound-meaning relationships must rapidly have run into what they call an impedance-matching problem. As additional semantic concepts were transmitted, it must have been increasingly difficult for the output system to keep each member of the increasing set of holistic signals separable from each of the others. The motor frame was initially of limited usefulness in this context because, when it first evolved, it could probably have produced only a small number of holistic structures. For example, it could perhaps have been done either entirely in a nasal mode or entirely in an oral mode. (I will argue in Chapter 7 that it might most often have been like "mama" or "baba.") It could also have been associated with a small amount of variability in basic tongue position. But if the number of discrete meanings that could be conveyed were to continue to increase as speech continued to evolve, a different principle from the holistic principle had to have been adopted in order to keep each of these new words perceptually discriminable from the others. As we now know, the principle that was adopted is called the "particulate principle."

Abler (1989) has singled out the elements of chemistry, the genes, and units of language as instances of "the particulate principle of self-diversifying systems" (p. 67). As summarized by Studdert-Kennedy: "According to this principle, elements drawn from a finite set...are repeatedly permuted and combined to yield larger units...higher in a hierarchy and more diverse in structure than their constituents. The particulate units in chemical compounding included atoms and molecules, and in biological inheritance genes and proteins" (1998, p. 203).

In modern languages, the principle is used at two levels, a state of affairs known as "duality" (Hockett, 1960). At the lower level, which presumably evolved first, sound units, probably phonemes, are combined into meaning units—monomorphemic or multimorphemic words. At the higher level, words are combined into sentences. The value of the resultant systems, as originally recognized by Humboldt (1836) in the case of language, is that they make infinite use of finite means. Thus in the case of phonology, they solve the impedance-match problem that arises from the inability of a signaling system to produce an indefinite number of holistically different signals.

A simple example makes the power of the particulate system for speech quite evident. Consider the word-making capability of New Zealand Maori, a Polynesian language with a relatively simple sound structure. It has eight consonants, five vowels, and two syllable types—"V" and "CV." With these sound-related properties, this language could in principle generate forty-five monosyllabic words, five with only vowels and forty (eight times five) composed of CV syllables. If words could also be composed of all possible two- and three-syllable strings, the number of possible words would be 91,125. Although Maori has words longer than three syllables, the number of words in my Maori dictionary (Williams, 1971) is only about 12,000. Imagine, now, computing the number of possible words with various numbers of syllables in English, which has twenty-four consonants, sixteen vowels, and syllable types ranging from V to CCVCCCC. Even if one left out the forms in which particular sound sequences occur that don't occur in the language (such as a "bn" sequence at the beginning of a syllable), the result would be an astronomically large number.

Chomsky's generative grammar, of course, incorporates the particulate principle. On the question of origins, as we have noted, Chomsky simply assumes that the principle was more or less instantaneously installed at both levels of the duality (sound and word levels) by a genetic mutation. But from my point of view, for this principle to have been adopted in speech production, an enormous increase in the versatility and skill of the production apparatus, relative to that present in other mammals including other primates, must have needed to occur. Hominids must have become capable of systematically producing, at high rates, movement complexes that had never been produced before.

There are two aspects of this development to be considered. First, a new output configuration for each new word must have been adopted by the language community. And once it was, all members of the community must have become capable of producing it, both in the generation in which it was invented and in subsequent generations. In short, words must have been coined, then learned. We need to understand how hominids evolved the remarkable skills necessary to do these things from the perspective given to us by Sperry. That is, we need to understand the origin of both the motor capabilities *and* the mental capabilities that were necessarily linked to them.

4.4 Donald: the evolution of mimesis

Merlin Donald (1991) offers us a view of what might have happened in this domain as part of his more general effort to understand the evolution of the human mind. One enormous merit of Donald's work, in my opinion, is that he has made a more comprehensive effort than anyone else to incorporate the role of the motor (i.e., action) side of humans in their mental evolution. Equally important to me is that in doing this he adopts a thoroughgoing Neodarwinian approach, attempting to replace discontinuity views with a continuity view whereby form evolved from successful use. In addition, he correctly stresses the sociocultural bases of hominid evolution without which there would never have been a language at all, because all languages are results of social agreements.

Let me summarize Donald's position on the evolution of hominid motor capabilities for speech, as given in his paper entitled "Preconditions for the evolution of protolanguages" (Donald, 1999). As his title pointedly indicates, he insists that the ability to make the sound patterns for the first words of language was a necessary precondition for making these words, rather than simply evolving with the words. In his view, the ability to make the forms for signaling the words cannot just be taken for granted as automatically following from a higher-order word-making capacity. What was needed, in advance, in his view, was a species-wide representational capacity to form symbols (such as spoken words) which stood for concepts, symbols which spontaneously gain the status of being shared by the members of the culture. Any language is a set of conventions shared by sender and receiver, for transmitting symbolic information. For this, hominids needed to evolve a capacity to invent expressive conventions in their natural environments. The question for Donald, then, is this: "What type of cognitive change would enable a group of primates to invent highly variable and culturally idiosyncratic forms of gesture and sound, and gradually develop distinctive cultures?" (p. 141). And his answer? "A generalized capacity for refining action." He explains:

All gestures and intentional vocalizations are ultimately actions of the musculature, and in order to generate greater varieties of gestures and sounds, primate motor behavior must have somehow become much more plastic, and less stereotyped, and subject to deliberate rehearsal. In other words a breakthrough in hominid motor evolution must have preceded language evolution. (p. 141)

In Donald's view, this cognitive-motor revolution required a significant advance in an aspect of motor skill commonly called "procedural learning":

To vary or refine an action—any action, not only speech—one must carry out a sequence of basic cognitive operations. These are, traditionally: Rehearse the action, observe its consequences, remember these, then alter the form of the original act, varying one or more parameters, dictated by the memory of the consequences of the previous action, or by an idealized image of the outcome. We might call an extended cognitive sequence of this sort—whose inherent complexity should not be underestimated—a "rehearsal loop." (p. 141)

Donald points out that while even human infants do this kind of thing extensively, "especially in infant babbling" (p. 142), one doesn't see it in the other great apes. He concludes, "It would be no exaggeration to say that this capacity is uniquely human, and forms the background for the whole of human culture including language" (p. 142).

One important capability that must have come with the capacity for purposive rehearsal of elaborate action patterns, according to Donald, was voluntary recall: "Hominids had to gain *access to the contents of their own memories.* You cannot rehearse what you cannot recall" (p. 143). Even babbling infants typically seem to produce babbling episodes apropos of nothing that has happened in their environment. This ability is in contrast to what appears, in the other great apes, to be the predominant dependence of memory access on environmental stimuli. Donald continues, "To be able to do this—to focus selectively on one's own action patterns—there has to be an implementable representation of action in the brain" (p. 143). Furthermore, these bodies of "kinematic imagination" can be edited in advance of use: "Without this capacity there can be no refinement of human movement, no increase in its variation within the species" (p. 143).

It is crucial to Donald's thesis that this advancement of motor skill in hominids was a *generalized* adaptation. It applied to the whole primary motor repertoire. Singing and music in general, opera, ballet, games, and sport—all involve the same general type of capacity, and all of these developments are uniquely human. And all of these capacities have been almost totally neglected in scenarios for human evolution. For Donald, the generalized nature of our creative-action capabilities raises a major problem for those who hold the more typical view that our capacity to produce the fine motor control needed for speech arose as some consequence of evolution of higher-order linguistic capabilities. Anyone who believes this must somehow explain why speech is nevertheless so much like so many other human action complexes that are generally considered to have not been subject to natural selection. Furthermore, Donald has argued, convincingly in my view, that language conferred such power on the species that had it evolved *before* these various other voluntary-action capacities, they would never have arisen in the first place.

The generalized mental status of these action capabilities is illustrated by the one-to-many relation between a particular mental conception of action in *space*, and the part/s of the body that can implement that conception. This is what Lashley (1942) had called "motor equivalence." We can write a letter of the alphabet with a series of movements of our nose, or with our tongue, or with either hand or either foot, showing that performance is based on an abstract analog representation. The generalized mental status of the action capabilities is also illustrated by the one-to-many relation between a particular conception of action in *time* and the parts of the body that can implement the conception. It is evident in our mastery of motor rhythm. We can produce a rhythmic pattern not only vocally ("dum de dum dum") but also with our fingers, our feet, or with our whole body.

Donald calls the basic capability being discussed here "mimesis"—a capability to mime or re-enact events. In Donald's opinion, this capability developed sometime in the course of evolution of Homo erectus, which first evolved about 2 million years ago. At that point, he believes,

the entire existing repertoire of primate expressive behavior would have become raw material for this new motor modeling mechanism. By "parachuting" a supra-modal device of this power on top of the primate motor hierarchy, previously stereotyped emotional expressions would have become rehearsable, refinable, and employable in intentional communication. This would have allowed a dramatic increase in the variability of facial, vocal, and whole body expressions, as well as in the range of potential interactive scenarios between pairs of individuals, or within larger groups of hominids. This is precisely what we can see in modern humans. Importantly, since a supramodal mimetic capacity would have extended to the existing vocal repertoire, it would have increased selection pressure for the early improvement of mimetic vocalization. (Donald, 1999, p. 147)

There was a considerable increase in toolmaking capacity in Homo erectus, resulting in what has been called "Acheulean culture." Donald believes that the new advances in toolmaking were supported by the use of mimesis in a pedagogical capacity, which "would have enabled widespread diffusion of new applications, and supported the underlying praxic innovations that led to new applications" (p. 147). ("Praxis" = Greek for "action.") Donald also believes:

In addition to toolmaking and emotional expression, motor mimesis would have inevitably allowed some degree of quasi-symbolic communication in the form of a very simple shared semantic environment. The "meaning" of mimed versions of perceptual events is transparent to anyone possessing the same event perception capabilities as the actor; thus mimetic representations can be shared, and constitute a cognitive mechanism for creating unique sets of socially distributed representa-tions. The expressive and social ramifications of mimetic capacity thus follow with the same inevitability as improved constructive skill. As the whole body becomes a potential tool for expression, a variety of new possibilities enter the social arena: complex games, extended competition, pedagogy through directed imitation (with a concomitant differentiation of social roles), and public action metaphor, such as intentional group displays of aggression, solidarity, joy, fear and sorrow. These would have perhaps constituted the first social "customs" and the basis of the first truly distinctive hominid cultures. This kind of mimetically transmitted custom still forms the background social "theatre" that supports and structures group behavior in modern humans. (ibid.)

How might mimesis have evolved by natural selection? Donald considers it to have been an adaptive response to pressures for social communica-tion, pressures related to the maintenance of sociocultural solidarity.

He considers all these changes discussed here to have been prelinguistic, but mimetic skill provided an essential preadaptation for speech and language because it enabled the production of the complex sound structures that came to be linked with individual lexical items—the morphophonological component of language. The other development necessary for protolanguage to occur, the one that is usually considered, was the capability of forming the conceptual side of words—the semantic and grammatical component of words. Donald argues that this is also an inherently social activity, as it won't work without the sender and receiver agreeing on the interpretation of signals. Consequently, Donald believes that the "Language Acquisition Device" (LAD) of Chomsky cannot reside solely within an individual mind.

To conclude, the most important claim of Donald, from my perspective, is that the fundamentals of articulatory gesture, from which all languages are built, were put in place when mimetic capacity emerged. Thus, in Donald's terms, the evolution, prior to language, of the aspect of mimesis that allowed us to produce vocal simulations of heard events was the basis for the later implementation of the particulate principle in word forms.

How this might have happened is explored in the next chapter.

4.5 Coda

In the present chapter, I have argued that the motor frame was the key structure in the evolution of the first true speech, and was thus the initial solution to Lashley's serial-order problem for speech. In addition, following Donald, I have argued that evolution of a general-purpose mimetic component was a necessary underpinning for the step from frames to the frame/content mode—the step that implemented the particulate principle. Our next task is to try to understand, in some detail, what the first speech was actually like, and how it proceeded to achieve the necessary increases in complexity that eventually gave rise to the frame/content mode. We will deal with this in the next two chapters, on speech acquisition, because the cornerstone of the phylogenetic argument will be that the earliest speech of hominids was very much like the babbling and early speech of modern infants, and it subsequently increased in complexity in ways very similar to the ways that speech develops in infants today.

PART III

The relation between ontogeny and phylogeny

5 Ontogeny and phylogeny 1: the frame stage

5.1 Introduction

The main proposition I have made thus far about the nature of speech is that it has evolved a "frame"—a general-purpose "carrier," which we know today as the syllable—that proved capable of containing all the subsequent segmental modulations (combinations of consonants and vowels) that have developed in the progression to modern speech. Note that this attribute had the advantage of enabling speech to extend itself in the time domain—that is, it provided, in advance, at the action level the capability for utterances to be of different lengths, depending on how many successive iterations of the syllabic, or frame cycle, were required.

The original frame was no doubt quite simple, evolving from a basic biphasic-movement capacity extending deep into our ancestry. But it eventually became programmable with "content" elements, giving us, over time, the extraordinary complexity of the myriad words of thousands of modern languages. I have also suggested, following Donald (1991), that the evolutionary progression from frames to frame/content may have rested on the prior evolution of a general-purpose mimetic capacity, making for a spectacular increase in the motor-control capability of the speech apparatus—and its ability to profit from experience.

The main proposition I will now make is that the ontogeny of speech recapitulates its phylogeny—that is, its development retraces, at least to some degree, the steps of its evolution. Making such a claim is risky, because people have become biased by the bad reputation that this concept has unfortunately incurred, thanks chiefly to the nineteenth-century biologist Ernest Haeckel (e.g., Haeckel, 1866), and are apt to dismiss it out of hand (e.g., Medicus, 1992). But as Ernst Mayr contends, "Darwin's thesis that evolutionarily new acquisitions are superimposed on the existing genetic structure, even though frequently attacked, has a correct nucleus" (1982, p. 476). The implication of Darwin's thesis is that earlier-evolving aspects of genetic causality play themselves out earlier in ontogeny. This phenomenon is evident almost everywhere in embryology—for example, in such revealing curiosities as the early development of gill arches and tails in human embryos, and the presence of vestigial hindlimb bones in whales. Where Haeckel erred was in claiming that the embyro recapitulates all the *adult* stages of its ancestry. If that were true, then fetal humans would at one stage look something like an adult version of our common ancestor with chimpanzees. But Haeckel's error gives us no reason to avoid using the recapitulationist claim when considering the evolution of motor function in general, and speech production in particular. Let us, instead, simply evaluate it on its merits.

My claim is quite specific: every human infant recapitulates the two stages I have proposed for the evolution of speech—the frame stage, then the frame/content stage. Frames without content occurred first. All that was required was for simple repetitive smacks to be paired with phonation. According to my theory, content in frames, as a phylogenetic development, presupposes the prior existence of frames. Content, meanwhile, results from frame differentiation. I will show, in this chapter, that frames are similarly available to infants in the simple forms of babbling before their internal structure can be differentiated. We will also see, in the next chapter, the seeds of differentiation of frames into separate content elements after the babbling stage. During babbling itself we find no evidence of separate control of content elements.

At the outset, however, I must emphasize that there is one respect in which ontogeny definitely does not recapitulate phylogeny. While modern infants simulate a full model of speech provided by their language community, early hominids were involved not only in simulating aspects of the model that had already been constructed but in constructing new parts of it themselves.

A good deal is at stake in making the claim that ontogeny recapitulates phylogeny. (See Gould, 1977 for background.) On the positive side, if it is true, we then have available the possibility of replaying, more or less at our leisure, a record of our evolutionary steps, thus compensating ourselves for the lack of an actual fossil record. On the negative side, if it is not true, we could be radically misled. We might end up like the proverbial drunk looking for his lost change under the lamppost, not because he lost it there but because that's where the light is brightest. How can we decide if it is true? Certainly we can't decide without exploring the possibility. I will present a number of lines of evidence that in my opinion converge on the conclusion that it *is* true. You be the judge. However it turns out, I think one thing will be clear: no other approach to the evolution of speech has anything like as much substance to it as this one does.

5.2 The nature of babbling and early speech: frame dominance

My discussion of speech acquisition is based on the results of a long-term research program I have conducted with Barbara Davis, whose contribution has been integral to my present beliefs. When I use the words "we" and "our" in this chapter, and others in which I discuss speech acquisition, I mean the two of us. We have used a novel but quite straightforward approach that we have christened "macrometric." That is, we have collected very large bodies of naturally occurring babbling and early speech (hence "macro") and have then performed statistical analyses (hence "metric") of relative frequencies of the various possible *sequences* of sounds. What has emerged has been various "macropatterns." Before we began this work there had been many large-scale counts of the frequencies of occurrence of individual sounds in infant output, but from the point of view of Lashley's serial-order problem, it is the frequency patterns of *sequences*, not just individual sounds, that need to be understood.

The first and most momentous move an infant makes towards acquiring speech-like forms is to begin babbling at about seven months of age. We view babbling as simple *motor*-frame production. There is no evidence that a babbling infant is like an adult in having the separate premotor or cognitive frame level postulated for adults in Chapter 2. In a canonical babbling episode, the infant produces a series of rhythmic alternations between closed- and open-mouth states, resulting, for example, in something that might sound like "bababa" (Oller, 1986). Van der Stelt and Koopmans-van Beinum (1986) found that babbling has a relatively sudden onset. They found that if told to listen for rhythmic, syllable-like sequences, parents have no trouble identifying its first occurrence. It appears to present itself as a fully formed rhythmic behavior; it is not gradually constructed.

Why is babbling so rhythmical from the start? It certainly seems anomalous in this respect, because skill is usually built laboriously over a long period of time, with rhythmicity—a key component of most skills—the outcome of a long history of effort. Take, for example, our learning to swing a golf club. One thing that infant speakers have that novice golfers don't have is rhythmicity from the very outset. But infants enjoy this advantage in babbling because frames, with their long history of rhythmicity, are simply evoked in an infant at this particular point in his or her history of speech mimesis. Unfortunately for golfers, we have no comparable phylogenetic leg-up on the motions of the golf swing.

It seems though, that the best way to regard babbling is not as skill but as a precursor to skill. As Thelen (1981) has noted, rather than babbling being specifically a precursor to language, as Petitto (1993) has argued, it is simply one of a wide variety of repetitive rhythmic movements characteristic of infants in the first few months of life. They include "kicking, rocking, waving, bouncing, banging, rubbing, scratching, swaying..." (Thelen, 1981, p. 238). She believes that such "rhythmic stereotypies are transition behavior between uncoordinated behavior and complex coordinated motor control." In her opinion, they are "phylogenetically available to the immature infant. In this view, rhythmical patterning originating as motor programs essential for movement control... are 'called forth' so to speak, during the long period before full voluntary control develops to serve adaptive needs later met by goal-corrected behavior" (p. 253).

Some mimetic capacity for the sounds of vowels has been shown by Kuhl and Meltzoff (1996) in infants as young as 12 weeks. But the main reason I assert that babbling, in particular, has a mimetic component is that whenever an infant happens to be born with some considerable hearing loss, babbling doesn't begin at the usual time, and when it does begin, it doesn't take a normal form (Oller and Eilers, 1988). More importantly, some infants with profound hearing loss either don't babble at all or start babbling years behind schedule (Locke, 1983).

Some details of the mimetic contribution to babbling can be gained by further consideration of infants with hearing loss. The rhythmicity of babbling is less evident in these infants, suggesting that even this basic property of frames cannot be simply regarded as endogenous (i.e., caused by factors inside the organism). Infants with hearing loss produce more labial consonants and fewer coronal consonants than hearing infants, and their vocalizations tend to have a more nasal quality (McCaffrey, Davis, and MacNeilage, 1999). The excess of labials over coronals makes sense because labial consonants are consonants that the infants can see being produced, while coronals can't be seen. Nasalization can't be seen either, but it can be heard. The relatively low incidence of nasal sounds, even at the beginning of the babbling of hearing infants, when compared with the high levels of nasality of the hearing-impaired infants, shows that hearing infants are using their mimetic capability to simulate the typically low incidence of nasal sounds of the adult language. Infants with hearing loss can't hear that languages tend to be non-nasal. So they tend to leave their soft palate in its rest position, which is the position for nasals as well as for quiet breathing, rather than elevating the palate to cut off the nasality.

Let's now consider the architecture of babbling in more detail. As I've already said, it consists basically of a rhythmic alternation between closed and open states of the mouth, powered by the mandible. Its period of occurrence is roughly from 7 to 12 months of age. The typical babbling episode begins with a consonant-like sound and ends with a vowel-like sound. I use the cautionary terms "consonant-*like*" and "vowel-*like*" (which I will immediately abandon for convenience) because the terms "consonant" and "vowel" imply independence of the two types of unit in the control process and, as I noted earlier, babbling infants lack such control.

An important difference between babbling and the comparable subsong stage that precedes birdsong is that these consonants and vowels are typically "good" sounds, totally acceptable as language-like, and not the rough messy approximations to mature song reported for the subsong stage (Stap, 2005). Only a small set of sounds is favored—voiced stops, nasals, and glides, at labial and coronal places of articulation, are the main consonants (Locke, 1983), while the vowels are concentrated in the lower left quadrant of the vowel space. That is, they tend to be either mid or low, front or central vowels (MacNeilage and Davis, 1990). The basic close–open alternation and the favored sounds change little in the first-word stage, lasting from about 12 to 18 months, during which infants typically produce only about fifty single words, one at a time.

This overall picture is very different from the one suggested earlier by the linguist Jakobson (1968), although his picture is still to be found in many introductory texts. He thought that infants babble all the sounds of the world's languages but produce only very few sounds in their subsequent first words. Actually, only the second part of this picture is correct. The severe restrictions on early preferences I have described—for stops, nasals, glides, and lower-left-quadrant vowels—are probably present in infants from all language environments from the beginning of the babbling stage and remain in place in the first-word stage.

Some two decades ago, Barbara Davis and I set out to investigate babbling and first-word patterns more closely. Our initial aim was simply to understand the acquisition of segmental independence. While studies of adult speech errors suggested independent control of segmental content elements—consonants and vowels—students of speech acquisition considered that no such independence was true of babbling and early speech. Our initial question, then, was this: "When and how did infants develop the ability to program frames with content elements?"

The then-accepted view that there was no segmental independence in babbling was based only on impressionistic observations. One particular thing stood in our way when we began to investigate this question: namely, people had tended to avoid the question of what vowels occurred in babbling, partly because it was more difficult for transcribers to agree on what vowel was being produced than on what consonant was being produced. A consequence of the lack of studies of vowels was that virtually no work had been done on the question of whether there was any relation between the "choice" of consonants and the choice of the vowels that virtually always abutted them, as one might expect there would be if successive sounds were not independent of each other. More basically, in a system alternating between consonants and vowels, if we lack information on vowels, we aren't in a good position to understand the serial-ordering process.

We began by asking the question of the consonant–vowel relationship in an intensive case study of one typical infant, Becca, beginning in the first-word period at about 14 months and continuing until 20 months, by which time she was producing a number of word combinations (Davis and MacNeilage, 1990). The particular question we asked was, "How does the frequency of occurrence of a particular consonant–vowel sequence relate to what one would expect by chance?" Chance was calculated on the basis of the frequency of that particular consonant category and that vowel category in the overall corpus of data which we collected. For example, if 40 percent of all consonants in the corpus were coronal, and 30 percent of vowels were front vowels, the chance expectation would be that $.4 \times .3 = .12$ (or 12%) of all CV pairs would involve coronals followed by front vowels.

We found three CV co-occurrence patterns. Coronal consonants tended to co-occur with front vowels, dorsal consonants with back vowels, and labial consonants with central vowels. These three patterns are illustrated in Fig. 5.1. (The vowel in the coronal front pattern is the vowel in "dad".) As we had no reason to believe at the time that the English language also had these CV

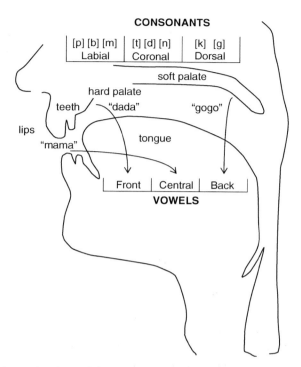

CONSONANTS

[p] [b] [m]	[t] [d] [n]	[k] [g]
Labial	Coronal	Dorsal

soft palate

hard palate

teeth / "dada"   "gogo"

lips

"mama"   tongue

Front	Central	Back

VOWELS

FIG. 5.1   Schematic view of the articulatory component of speech showing the three favored consonant–vowel (CV) co-occurrence patterns. (From MacNeilage and Davis, 2000)

co-occurrence patterns, we concluded that these patterns couldn't have resulted from the copying of language preferences. So we hypothesized that they may be present from the beginning of babbling, and may reflect a set of basic constraints against segmental independence—indeed, basic enough to continue to be present in the first-word stage, and perhaps beyond.

A further step was to study just how general these effects were in babbling infants in an English-language environment. The results of a study of six infants are summarized in Table 5.1. The three predicted effects are shown on the diagonal of the table. All six subjects showed all of the effects, and with one exception the distributions of preferences for the three classes of vowels for each consonant category in each subject were significantly beyond chance. The three patterns accounted for more than half of all the consonant–vowel sequences in the data.

TABLE 5.1 Mean observed-to-expected ratios of CV sequences in six English babbling infants (Davis and MacNeilage, 1995)

	Coronal	Labial	Dorsal
Front	1.28	0.55	1.01
Central	0.83	1.39	0.91
Back	0.72	1.23	1.34

Following the initial formulation of the hypothesis that there might be three CV co-occurrence patterns in babbling and early speech, a number of tests were made by other investigators during the babbling and the first-word periods (Boysson-Bardies, 1993; Oller and Steffans, 1994; Tyler and Langsdale, 1996; Vihman, 1992). These tests produced a complex mixture of confirmations, disconfirmations, and null results. Many of the disagreements with our findings may have resulted from methodological differences between our studies and the others. All these studies used much smaller databases than ours, and sometimes divided their databases into smaller subcategories than the ones we had used (e.g., first vs. second syllables), thus reducing the statistical power of their results. Some of the studies used different vowel categories than ours, and were therefore not true tests of our hypothesis. Some studies did not take into account the overall frequencies of both the vowel and consonant categories when computing expected frequencies.

Following our work on babbling, we did a similar study, this time of ten infants, to see whether infants in general also showed these effects in first words. We found that all three effects remained strongly present in first words (Davis, MacNeilage, and Matyear, 2002). Here are the mean observed-to-expected ratios for the three co-occurrence patterns in the babbling study (Davis and MacNeilage, 1995) and the first-word study (Davis, MacNeilage, and Matyear, 2002), respectively: Coronal–front: 1.28, 1.43; Dorsal–back: 1.34, 1.39; Labial–central: 1.39, 1.31. (Remember, any number above 1.0 is an above-chance observation.) All the effects are relatively strong. As you can see, the effects occur with a frequency nearly 30 percent higher than would be expected by chance.

A number of more recent studies suggest that these three co-occurrence effects are widely present across different language environments in both babbling and speech. We found the effects in an analysis of babbling and first words of groups of five Swedish and Japanese infants who participated in the Stanford Phonology Project (Davis and MacNeilage, 2002). (The data were made available by Marilyn Vihman.) The effects were also found in a study of seven infants in an Ecuadorian Quichua environment, in both the babbling and first-word stages (Gildersleeve-Neumann, 2000). They have been found in early and later speech of one of two infants in a Brazilian-Portuguese environment (Teixeira and Davis, 2002) and (except for the dorsal–back effect) in an Italian infant (Zmarich and Lanni, 1999). The same findings have been noted in babbling and first words of six Korean infants by Lee, Davis, and MacNeilage (in press). Finally, Kern and Davis (in press) have found a significant overall preference for the three co-occurrence patterns in groups of five infants in Dutch, French, Romanian, Tunisian Arabic, and Turkish language environments. There is little doubt that these trends are almost universally present in the babbling and first words of infants. The strength of the effects seems to be similar in babbling and first words.

Thus we and others have obtained strong evidence for a lack of intracyclical—or, roughly, intrasyllabic—segmental independence in babbling and early speech in the form of three types of interdependencies between consonants and the vowels that follow them. This result was the main reason that we concluded that babbling and early speech were characterized by "Frame Dominance" (Davis and MacNeilage, 1995). Most of the intracyclical variance was apparently due to frame production alone, with a lack of independent movements of other articulators during the transition from the consonant to the vowel. In the case of the two lingual co-occurrence patterns—coronal–front and dorsal–back—the tongue tended to stay in the same position in the mouth: front or back. We called these "fronted" and "backed" frames, respectively. But why did *central* vowels co-occur with labial consonants? Since the tongue is involved in both the consonant and the vowel in fronted and backed frames, but isn't involved in the production of a labial consonant, we argued that the central tongue position for the vowel, favored with labial consonants, was simply its rest position.

In other words, the co-occurrences of labial consonants with central vowels seemed to be instances of "pure frames," produced by mandibular oscillation alone, with no accompanying active setting of the tongue.

The labial–central pattern was the most influential one in generating our belief that the ontogeny of speech may be a recapitulation of its phylogeny. This co-occurrence pattern had never been reported before. And the pattern is the opposite of the one that might have been expected a priori. In any language, a number of different vowels are produced adjacent to any consonant. On basic biomechanical grounds, one might have expected that in a case like this, when the tongue was not required for the adjacent consonant, it would be more likely to produce a wide variety of different vowels from the outset, without any special favorites, than in situations when the tongue was also required for the consonant. The fact that this did not occur suggests an extremely fundamental role of the basic mandibular cycle alone in the formation of speech.

Additional bodies of evidence were also consistent with the frame-dominance hypothesis. The studies described so far were confined to the co-occurrences of stop consonants, nasals, and glides with vowels, because these are by far the most frequently occurring consonantal types in babbling. But a study of fricatives, affricates, and liquids, which accounted for less than 10 percent of all consonants in our studies of babbling and early speech, showed, for the most part, the same CV co-occurrence patterns (Gildersleeve-Neumann, Davis, and MacNeilage, 2000).

Two other studies provided evidence that nasalization, like tongue positioning, did not vary much during an utterance, suggesting that, to produce nasalization, the soft palate was simply preset in an open position and left there. In one study that considered the last two consonants in babbled utterances that ended in a consonant, we found that prefinal nasals were followed (after an intervening vowel) by final nasals 89 percent of the time—in other words, nearly always (Redford, MacNeilage, and Davis, 1997). We also found in an acoustical study that the vowel between two nasal consonants tended to be heavily nasalized, indicating that the soft palate tended to remain in the same open position for the vowel as for the surrounding nasal consonants (Matyear, MacNeilage, and Davis, 1998).

Our next question was this: "Are there dependencies *between* cycles—'intercyclical' or 'intersyllabic' dependencies—in babbling and early speech?" It had been thought for a long time that babbling began with a "reduplicated" phase, perhaps lasting 7 to 10 months, during which the infant tended to repeat a single syllable in utterances involving various numbers of syllables (e.g., "baba, bababa," or "dedede, dede"). This phase was then thought to be followed by a "variegated" phase in which successive syllables differed (Oller, 1980). In our terms, reduplicated babbling would simply be frame reiteration, whereas variegation would require a change in the overall structure of the frame from cycle to cycle.

This sequence of events, from reduplication to variegation, made sense intuitively, because it appeared to show that infants progressed from an initial simple phase of intersyllabic interdependence to a more complex phase with more independence. In our terms, transition from reduplication to variegation might imply a change from a simple frame stage to a stage in which the frames are independently supplied with some internal content. But a number of studies have shown that variegated babbling is common from the beginning of babbling and does not increase during the babbling stage (Davis and MacNeilage, 1995; Mitchell and Kent, 1990; Smith, Brown-Sweeney, and Stoel-Gammon, 1989). In our own study, we found that a second syllable differed from its predecessor about 50 percent of the time in the first half of the babbling stage, and that this percentage did not increase during the second half.

So apparently, contrary to established belief, babbling does not start out reduplicative and then increase in variegation. There is plenty of variegation from the start. Infants produce both simple (reduplicated) and more complex (variegated) utterances from the beginning of babbling, but do not increase in the ratio of the more complex-sounding utterances to the more simple-sounding ones across the five-month babbling period. What does this mean? Mastery of a range of complexity from the beginning of babbling, but with a lack of increase in overall complexity during the babbling period is counterintuitive in that it suggests an initial precocity, but one that does not develop further. One possibility is that the listener's impression that variegated forms involve more complex control than reduplicated forms is not accurate. What we needed to do here to resolve this question was to derive from the variegated patterns some information about what the actual movements were that were producing them. The dominant role of the mandible in producing the movement patterns observed within syllables suggested to us that the mandible might also be playing a dominant role in producing variegation across syllables. We suggested that most of the variance in variegated sequences might be in the up/down, or "vertical," dimension, produced by variations in the amplitude of the closing and/or opening phases of the mandible from cycle to cycle (MacNeilage and Davis, 1990). Most consonantal variance might be in manner of articulation, resulting from differences in amount of consonantal constriction, which might in turn be due to differences in the amplitude of the closing phase of the mandible. Similarly, most vowel variegation might be in vowel height, and might be due to variation in amplitude of the opening phase of the mandible. There might be less variation in the front/back, or "horizontal," dimension. Thus, for consonants there might be relatively few instances of changes involving a switch between labial and lingual constrictions, or between dorsals and coronals. For vowels, there might be relatively few instances of changes involving the front–central–back series.

We confirmed both of these hypotheses for both babbling (Davis and MacNeilage, 1995) and early speech (Davis, MacNeilage, and Matyear, 2002). In babbling, all six subjects showed both effects, all beyond the .001 level of significance. The mean ratio of predicted-to-unpredicted instances for the consonants was 3.6:1, with a range from 2:1 to 6:1. The mean ratio for the vowels was 1.5:1 with a range from 1.3:1 to 1.65:1. In speech a number of infants could not be tested separately for consonant variegation because they produced relatively few words that had any. A chi-square test for the group was significantly positive beyond the .001 level. A total of eight out of the nine infants who produced enough instances of vowel variegation for individual testing showed a significant excess of vowel-height changes over front–back changes.

These results raise a difficult question. Does the infant actually control the variation in amplitude of phases of mandibular movement across cycles (seemingly the main means of producing variegation)? Or does the amplitude vary randomly, and when it varies enough, the listener hears the episode as variegated? With respect to the word stage, at least, the question of what the infant intends is relatively tractable, because there her attempts can be evaluated against the hypothetical target (the word) that she may be trying to produce. But in the babbling stage we don't know what precise pattern of movement, if any, she's trying to achieve. One reason we inferred that variegated babbling was not under intentional control was that while a babbling infant often repeats a particular reduplicated pattern over and over again, she'll rarely produce a particular variegated pattern even twice in a row. In addition, remember that variegation didn't increase across the babbling period, even though language obviously demands a great deal more variegation than the infant is producing. Such an increase would have been expected if variegation capability were in fact under control. So we concluded that variegation resulted primarily from random variation in amplitude of mandibular phases, not intentional patterning of changes from cycle to cycle.

As can be seen from all these studies, "frame dominance" seems to be the best summary description of babbling and early speech. The frame is dominant in the sense that the mandible contributes almost all of the active movement, whether phase amplitude remains consistent or not, while the other three articulators—the lips, tongue, and soft palate—play a relatively passive role. Thus, the dominant state of the articulatory system during an actual utterance is one of *inertia*. In other words, apart from the mandible, the articulators tend to retain their position during an utterance. Particularly striking is the fact that the tongue, which is far and away the main contributor to the complexity of speech-sound systems, makes only a minimal active contribution to the internal structure of infant utterances. From the perspective of Lashley, serial order in infant babbling and early speech is achieved in a most economical fashion by means of the frame, with the other three parameters (lips, tongue, soft palate) either simply remaining in their rest settings or in one (soft palate–up) or two (tongue–front, back) active settings that don't vary during the utterance. So with two parameters (the mandible and lips) having only one setting, another (the soft palate) having two, and the other (the tongue) having three, there are only six possible basic output states ($1 \times 1 \times 2 \times 3 = 6$). And, importantly, the three predominant CV co-occurrence patterns simply fall out of the model as a result of tongue inertia.

5.3 The relation between early utterances and words of languages: implications for phylogeny

Let's now compare this simple model with what happens in languages, beginning with the frame itself. I have argued that the close–open alternation is basic to language. As noted earlier, this isn't obvious to speakers of English because the typical English word involves much more than a simple consonant–vowel alternation. One complication is that English has a large array of "consonant clusters," defined as two or more abutting consonants. The monosyllabic word "strengths," for example, has just one vowel but six consonants, formed into a cluster of three at the beginning of the word, and another three at the end. (We're talking about sounds here, not letters.) When an English sentence contains a number of words like this, which it often does, the fact that there's a basic alternation between a closed and open position of the mouth isn't at all obvious.

But English is quite atypical. Most languages favor a simple close–open alternation. In a recent analysis of a diverse set of thirty languages, Ian Maddieson (1999) found that twenty-one of the languages either had no consonant clusters or less than 1 percent of clusters. This suggests that the typical language involves a regular alternation between closed- and open-mouth positions. We conclude that the prevalence of simple frames in both infants and languages suggests that simple frames were the corner-stones of the first words. Thus ontogeny recapitulates phylogeny in that the first truly speech-like patterns produced by the upper articulators are, and were, frames.

When we began this work, few people had considered whether adult languages in general had CV co-occurrence constraints. Apart from some preliminary observations by Locke (1983), there were only two studies that we knew of on CV patterns. Janson (1986) had reported the two lingual patterns—coronal–front and dorsal–back—in a study of five languages. Maddieson and Precoda (1992), meanwhile, studying a different set of five languages, had failed to find any CV co-occurrences. But Maddieson and Precoda did not take consonant frequencies into account in computing expected frequencies. So we reanalyzed the combined data from both studies. Like Janson, we found the two lingual co-occurrences, but, again like him, we found no effect involving labials (MacNeilage and Davis, 1993).

We have also done an analysis of CV co-occurrence patterns in 12,360 words obtained from dictionaries of ten languages: English, Estonian, French, German, Hebrew, Japanese, Maori, Quichua, Spanish, and Swahili (MacNeilage et al., 2000). We found all three effects, although the effect sizes tended to be less than those observed in infants. Here are the mean observed-to-expected ratios and, in parentheses, the number of languages showing the trend: coronal–front, 1.16 (7); dorsal–back, 1.27 (8); labial–central, 1.10 (7). In contrast to our reanalysis of the Janson and Maddieson and Precoda data, we did typically find a labial–central effect, but it was the smallest one we found. Our finding of the existence of all three patterns has since been replicated in a diverse set of fifteen languages by Rousset (2003).

These results show that the CV co-occurrence patterns aren't simply due to a transient effect of immaturity in the infant speech-production system. The inertial effect on tongue movement, most obvious in the lingual co-occurrence patterns but also present in the labial context, may be typical in modern speech, and, being a basic biomechanical property, it is, in a sense, as old as the apparatus itself. Like the frame in which it's embedded, it must have been present from the beginning. It's presumably not a matter of adults putting these patterns into words so as to make things easier for infants. The patterns are in languages because they result from fundamental properties of the oral movement system of all hominids.

The finding of the labial–central pattern *in adults* strengthens our conviction that it is *the single most fundamental pattern in speech—indeed, perhaps the protosyllabic pattern.* I argued earlier that the occurrence of this pattern in infants is sufficient, in itself, to give it a fundamental status. The tongue, being not required for the labial consonant, is in principle equally free to make any vowel, but it nevertheless prefers the neutral, or passive, position. Why does it do this unless that position is basic to system operation? A similar argument can be made for giving it an even more fundamental status on the basis of the adult results. Given the tongue's freedom to make any vowel in this context, why in the history of languages does this pattern not go away unless it is quite fundamental to the evolution of languages?

Let me now summarize this chapter. My basic thesis is that the on-togeny of speech recapitulates its phylogeny. I have reviewed the evidence that the ontogeny of speech begins with a frame stage—a stage in which output of the articulatory system is dominated by a relatively simple alternation between closed- and open-mouth states powered by mandibu-lar oscillation. Two of the other articulators, the soft palate and the tongue, play a minimal role, while the third articulator, the lips, may be almost entirely passive. The main evidence for a minor role of the tongue, in contrast to its dominance in adult speech, is the set of three patterns of CV co-occurrence, all apparently associated with tongue inertia during babbling and early speech. These patterns may also be typical in modern languages, which testifies to their fundamental status as speech phenomena.

Because we see no reason why this simple biomechanical picture would not also have been characteristic of attempts of hominids to produce the first words, we assume that hominids began with a frame stage, just as infants do, with the exception that hominids were inventing words, not simulating already available ones. In short, my thesis is that hominids began speech as infants begin it, by adding to phonation a close–open frame cycle that can be reiterated, either alone (e.g., "mama") or accompanied by other presettings. As with infants they may also have been able to preset the soft palate in an active (closed) configuration to produce oral rather than nasal sounds ("baba"), and to preset the tongue in a front or back configuration.

6 Ontogeny and phylogeny 2: the frame/content stage

6.1 Introduction

In the last chapter, I suggested that speech began in hominids just as speech-like output does today in infants, by adding a frame—a mouth close/open alternation, produced by mandibular oscillation—to an already available capacity for phonation. But now we must ask how infants progress, and hominids progressed, from this initial stage to speech as we know it. Again, we'll begin with how infants make this progression, and see whether it is plausible that hominids made it in a similar way.

The frame/content stage—the terminus for both hominid and infant speech—is the stage observable in modern adults. We speak by inserting segmental content elements (consonants and vowels) into syllable structure frames. I described this phenomenon in Chapter 3, and pointed out that it is a widely agreed-upon conception of modern speech production. Barbara Davis and I began our work on speech acquisition with the goal of determining how and when the segmental independence necessary to the frame/content mode of adult production developed. So far, as I noted in the last chapter, there is little evidence for segmental independence in the first year of speech-like production—the babbling and first-word stages. There may not be *any* segmental independence in babbling; that is, infants may not have systematic intentional control of single segments of the kind that enables them to insert one into various contexts. But there is some evidence of the beginnings of segmental control in first words, which may be of profound importance from an evolutionary perspective.

Before considering that evidence, however, let's review what babbling and early speech have in common. The rhythmic close/open alternation of the frame dominates both babbling and early speech. Consonants tend to be labial and coronal stops and nasals; vowels tend to be in the lower-left quadrant of the vowel space. Since most consonants (the stops and nasals) involve complete oral-tract occlusion, and since most vowels are not high, the typical frame tends to have a relatively high amplitude—that is, it alternates between complete closure and relatively wide opening.

There are three types of co-occurrences between consonants and following vowels ("CV co-occurrences"): coronal–front, dorsal–back, and labial–central. Utterances usually begin with a consonant and end with a vowel. Successive syllables tend to be the same (that is, "reduplicated"); but when different ("variegated"), they tend to vary in consonant manner and vowel height. Variegation may result primarily from random variation in amplitude of mandibular oscillation phases.

6.2 From babbling to language: reduplication to variegation

As I have pointed out, two aspects of babbling structure are also characteristic of languages, leading us to believe that these aspects were characteristic of the first language. The consonant–vowel syllable form is universally present in languages, and more often than not predominates in a language. And the three consonant–vowel co-occurrence patterns of babbling are characteristically, though not universally, present in languages.

In broad outline, there are two main differences between the serial organization of speech in infants and in languages. First, many languages develop more complex syllable types, mainly by going beyond the rule that only a single consonant can occur in a syllable and that preferably at the onset of the syllable. In other words, consonants can occur in clusters. But more important than this is a difference that applies to all languages. While infants prefer to repeat (reduplicate) the same syllable, languages prefer to variegate successive syllables. We believe that this is the main thing that a babbling infant must eventually do if it is to produce any language in the world.

The tendency for languages to disfavor repetition has been formalized in linguistics as the Obligatory Contour Principle (Leben, 1973). In effect, the principle prohibits the repetition of the same consonant on each side of a vowel or the same vowel on each side of a consonant, although it's recognized that such repetition nevertheless sometimes occurs. In a ten-language analysis of consonant-place repetition involving the first two stop consonants or nasals in a word (or one of each) separated by a vowel, we found that the pre- and post-vocalic consonants had the same place of articulation only about two-thirds as often as would be expected by chance (MacNeilage et al., 2000). None of our ten languages was an exception to this below-chance trend.

Why do modern languages favor consonant variegation? Because it increases the number of possible messages that can be encoded. If variegation is allowed, the number of theoretically possible two-consonant sequences is the square of the number of consonants in an inventory, and is also the square of the number of possible sequences of the same consonant repeated. For example, in a 10-consonant system there are 10×10 possible consonant combinations, only 10 of which involve replication of the same consonant. It's easy to see that if reduplicated forms were the early mode of word structure, their frequency in the language would drop relative to variegated forms as a language becomes more complex. What is not so easy to understand is why they would get reduced to well-below-chance levels.

We believe that repetition is actively disfavored beyond chance levels in modern languages because of a problem that arises in modern high-speed speech reception and production that was not present when speech was produced at lower speeds and with smaller inventories (MacNeilage et al., 2000). The problem may lie in the confusing effect of frequent recurrence of the same sound in working (temporary) memory, probably in both the stage of analysis of an incoming utterance and of planning an outgoing utterance. A classic finding in working-memory studies is the confusability of simultaneously held items with similar pronunciation (Conrad and Hull, 1964)—for example, spelled letters with the same vowel such as "m"—[ɛm] and "f"—[ɛf] or "b"—[bi] and "d"—[di]. With respect to output, studies of speech errors show that they are potentiated by a "repeated phoneme effect" (MacKay, 1987): the occurrence of two examples of the same sound in close proximity tends to induce serial-ordering errors in speech production. Thus, in addition to a tendency to reduce the proportion of reduplicated forms in order to increase the size of the message set, there may be a tendency to reduce it to avoid confusability.

We took our usual statistical approach to the understanding of this totally foundational difference between infants, who prefer to reduplicate syllables, and languages, which prefer not to. We made statistical analyses of the serial-organization patterns shown by infants and languages with the assumption that similarities between the two sets of patterns might indicate properties of early hominid speech, while differences might be attributed to changes in languages at later stages of speech evolution.

Consider, first, another finding regarding the infant pattern. We have attributed the three CV co-occurrence patterns primarily to tongue inertia. But as the predominant intercyclical form of babbling and early speech is reduplicative, a given vowel tends to have the same consonant following it as the one that precedes it. Thus, just as tongue inertia characterizes the relation between a vowel and the preceding consonant, it should also characterize the relation between the vowel and the consonant that follows it. For the most part we found that this was the case, as is shown for words in Table 6.1. The only exception was the absence of a trend towards a dorsal–back pattern in babbling in a small subset of utterances in which C was in final position; i.e., in CVC forms. This seemed to be attributable to the very small number of observations available in this category. (Note that as utterances tend to begin with a consonant and end with a vowel, there are many fewer available VC sequences than CV sequences in general.)

To understand the differences between the reduplicative patterns of infants and the variegated patterns of languages, it's necessary to look at VC co-occurrence patterns in languages. Specifically, it's necessary to ask how much of the intersyllabic versatility of languages is achieved by the development of independence between a vowel and a preceding consonant (CV), and how much between a vowel and a following consonant (VC). We have observed that there were somewhat lower co-occurrence frequencies between vowels and the preceding consonant (CV) in languages than in either babbling or first words. What are the VC frequencies? The three mean observed-to-expected ratios in our study of ten languages were as follows: coronal–

TABLE 6.1 Mean observed-to-expected ratios of VC sequences in first words of ten English-speaking infants. (Davis, MacNeilage, and Matyear, 2002)

	Coronal	Labial	Dorsal
Front	1.36	0.65	1.07
Central	0.76	1.27	0.74
Back	1.01	0.74	1.85

front, 1.03; dorsal–back, .88; labial–central, 1.04 (MacNeilage et al., 2000). None of them are substantially above chance, and one is lower than chance.

This is an extremely surprising result. We believe it has profound significance. The implication is that in going from the infant to an adult you usually don't have to supersede your basic biomechanical propensities in one place (CV), but you do have to supersede them in the other. So the question is, why do you have to get rid, in one case, of something that comes so naturally? It perhaps relates to the fact that according to linguistic analysis, a syllable boundary is more likely to occur after a vowel than before it, even though there is no universally acceptable definition of the concept of syllable boundary. Perhaps, then, the answer is that you have to get rid of it at the VC interface because that's where languages have put the syllable boundary. So you now have a *new unit* of serial organization that has an edge there and is used to give you variegation across syllables. It allows you to make, at some level of organization, the consonant following the vowel and the rest of the syllable that follows the consonant independent of the previous one, which terminated in the preceding vowel. And the cost for developing that superordinate unit, which has obvious advantages for the serial-organization process, is that you've got to take the production system beyond its easy way of getting from V to C.

But this of course implies that the infant does not start out with syllable units. And indeed we have very good evidence that she does not. For each of eighteen infants—eight in the babbling stage and ten in the first-word stage—we first selected the most favored CV sequence for each of the main consonantal types: labial and coronal. For example, in a particular infant this might be [ba] and [di]. We then computed the total number of times each of these two syllables occurred in the corpus. Next, we determined the number of disyllable sequences in the corpus which consisted of either [badi] or [diba]. The total number of occurrences of the two favored CV sequences in the eighteen infants was 5,052. But the total number of times in which the two favored syllables were combined in a disyllabic sequence by a particular infant in either order was just five. In other words, considering that phonetic transcription of these forms is not entirely reliable, such combinations might not have occurred at all! This rather astounding fact leaves no doubt that infants are not controlling CV sequences as separate syllabic entities in sequences of two or more syllables.

Our conclusion is that although the frame is the domain of the syllable, from babbling onwards, the interframe organization that goes with syllable sequence control in adult speech only develops as an infant acquires speech. Thus we hypothesize that the syllable is a unit of speech that only evolved after the first (frame) stage of hominid evolution.

Next, let's consider the question of how infants actually go about the process of changing from a reduplicative pattern to a variegated one.

There is some consensus that the first move might be the adoption of a particular intercyclical pattern whereby the first consonant in the word is a labial and the next consonant (following the vowel) is a coronal (e.g., "bado" for "bottle"). This tendency is part of a more general tendency in early-word production that Ingram (1974) called "fronting"—the first consonant in a word tends to have a more anterior place of articulation than the second one.

As we know, consonants have three major places of articulation. But in considering this phenomenon, I will discuss only labials and coronals, since dorsals are much more rare in early speech. In a review of seven reports involving five different language communities, we found that twenty-one out of twenty-two infants preferred the labial–coronal (LC) sequence over the coronal–labial (CL) one (MacNeilage and Davis, 2000). We even found two instances in the literature of a tendency in individual infants to produce the LC sequence in attempts at words which had the opposite (CL) sequence (e.g., "top → pot") (Jaeger, 1997; Macken, 1978). C. Levelt (1994) also found that this was a favored pattern in infants learning Dutch. We sought further evidence of the tendency to favor the LC sequence in our group of ten infants at the first-word stage (MacNeilage et al., 1999). In the nine infants who showed the trend, the ratio of LC to CL productions was about 4:1, and only one-third of the infants had more than two instances of the CL pattern.

According to F/C theory, this change involves making the first syllable solely with a cycle of mandibular oscillation (a "pure frame") and then superimposing a tongue movement on the closing phase of the next mandibular cycle. Perhaps a reason why infants will favor beginning these words with the relatively easy-to-produce pure frame has to do with the problem of coordinating the articulatory system with the other two systems—respiratory and phonatory—at the point of initiation of speech. This problem may induce more frequent recourse to pure frames in the beginning of an utterance simply because, as we argued before, they're easier. But once action in the two non-articulatory systems is initiated, their main task in babbling and early speech is probably only to sustain their action for the remainder of the utterance, in the form of a constant subglottal pressure level (respiratory) and a constant configuration of the vocal folds (phonatory). The lack of an additional post-initiation demand on these two other subsystems may provide a window of opportunity to add to the pattern of articulatory activation once the utterance has begun. Justification of this line of reasoning is provided by Stager and Werker's (1997) finding of an analogous example in the domain of infant speech perception. There, they found an apparently similar simplification of operation at the phonetic level in the presence of demands associated with concurrent building of a mental lexicon. When 14-month-old infants were faced with linking spoken words with corresponding objects, the children showed less sensitivity to phonetic aspects of the spoken input than if words were not involved.

We have argued that these sequences begin with a pure frame because pure frames are easier to produce than lingual frames (MacNeilage and Davis, 2000). We have argued this not only because pure frames involve one fewer articulatory movement than lingual frames but for two other reasons as well. The first is related to the fact that frequency of labial consonants relative to coronals increases when infants go from prespeech babbling to first words. Infants typically come into the first word with more coronals than labials. For example, the mean ratio of labial to coronal consonants in our babbling infants was .77:1. But the ratio in the ten infants studied during the first-word period was 1.7:1 (Davis, MacNeilage, and Matyear, 2002). This trend has also been observed by other researchers not only in American infants but also in infants in French, Swedish, and Japanese environments (Boysson-Bardies et al., 1992). Note that this change is counterintuitive. It goes in the *opposite* direction of one which would show that the infant is assimilating to the statistical pattern of sound frequencies in the adult language. Rather than having more labials, adult languages tend to have more *coronal* sounds (Maddieson, 1984)—and to use them more often overall.

So how do we explain so curious a phenomenon? We interpret this trend toward more labials in first words as a regression to easier output forms in the face of the new demand to interface the action system with the developing mental lexicon (MacNeilage et al., 1999). As labials continue to preferentially co-occur with central vowels in first words, these words tend to involve pure frames, which, unlike lingual frames, involve only the mandible and not the tongue as well. Thus, paradoxically, first

words might even involve a major move *away* from segmental independence. The tongue is responsible for most intersegmental variation in
languages, yet here there is a trend toward using it less often.

There is one further reason to suspect that labials are easier. It emerges
from three studies of infants who, because of a medical problem involving
their larynx, needed to have a plastic breathing tube (a tracheotomy)
inserted in their trachea (windpipe) when only a few months old. This
made them unable to activate their vocal tract by phonation, so they
couldn't vocalize in the usual way. All three of these studies have found
that when the tracheotomy was removed, typically at around 2 years of
age, these infants strongly preferred labial consonants in their first attempts at speech (Bleile, Stark, and McGowan, 1993; Locke and Pearson,
1990; Vaivre-Douret, Le Normand, and Wood, 1995). Because they have
normal hearing, the infants would have heard many more coronal than
labial consonants in their first two years because there are far more
instances of coronal production than labial production in both English
and French. The fact that they nevertheless strongly favored producing
labials suggests that labials were easier for them to make.

But even if labials are easier than coronals, why would it be advantageous
to *start* with an easy action? As is well known in motor-system neurophysiology and clinical neurology (e.g., Loeb, 1987), there are relatively separable
subsystems for initiation versus continuation of movements. The independence of the movement-initiation component from the control of movement
in general can be seen in the symptoms of neurological patients. While
some patients such as those with Parkinson's Disease have difficulty initi-
ating movements for an utterance, others, such as those with Tourette's
Syndrome, have a problem in inhibiting the production of an unwanted
utterance, even a socially proscribed one, such as a swear word.

What is the possible significance of this LC pattern for the origin of
intersyllabic variegation in language? As in the case of the other infant
vocal phenomena already described, it's important to ask whether the LC
effect is characteristic only of infants or if it's also present in languages.
Statistical analysis of the relative frequencies of the LC and CL sequences in
the first and second consonants in words in our sample of ten languages
reveals the same trend (MacNeilage et al., 2000). Each of the individual
patterns is statistically significant beyond the .001 level in chi-square tests,
except for Swahili. The average ratio of occurrence of LC sequences relative
to CL sequences in the ten languages was 2.21. To our knowledge, this is the

first report of a consistent asymmetry in the intercyclical distribution of major subcategories of place of articulation, across a number of different languages, although Locke (1983) made some preliminary observations supporting this possibility. The presence of the effect in an additional corpus of fifteen languages has since been reported by Rousset (2003).

Are the infants producing their distributions of preferred and nonpreferred patterns by means of mimesis? Are they somehow internalizing the statistical properties of the ambient language that, as we have just seen, also tend to favor the LC sequence? It seems more likely that both infants and languages are revealing a basic hominid propensity. This conclusion is suggested by the fact that the ratios of LC sequences to CL sequences in the group of infants in the first fifty-word stage tended to be higher than in the sampled languages. It is also suggested by the propensity of the infants studied by Macken and Jaeger to transform CL sequences in adult target words into LC sequences in their productions of the words.

Key evidence for the non-mimetic basis of the three co-occurrence patterns comes from occasions in which infants produce the patterns when they are not present in the ambient language. One example is the labial–central effect in English. This co-occurrence was below chance levels in the dictionary count of English (MacNeilage et al., 2000). Yet it has repeatedly been observed in infants in the English language environment. More convincing evidence comes from Korean (Lee, Davis, and MacNeilage, in press). Only one of the three co-occurrence patterns predicted for infants was found in samples of adult-directed speech and infant-directed speech by adult Korean speakers. Yet all three patterns were found in babbling. And the levels of the two patterns which were not favored in the language were lower relative to babbling in the first words of the Korean infants, suggesting that the ambient language is contributing to the elimination of these preferences.

We believe that the occurrence of the LC pattern in infants and languages means that it was probably present in the early words of hominids. (It might not have been present in the very first words, because it is not present in babbling.) We believe that in both infants and early hominids the pattern can be attributed to processes of self-organization. In infants, the LC pattern probably results from the confluence of five influences:

1. Greater ease of labial production.
2. The increasing functional load of interfacing the lexicon with the output system in the first-word stage.

3. The basic neurological problem of movement initiation.
4. The problem of having to synchronously initiate action in all three components of the production apparatus.
5. A generalized pressure towards simulation of the intercyclical diversity of adult word targets.

The same factors may have operated in earlier hominids, with the exception that in phylogeny, the pressure in factor #5 was toward *creating* rather than *simulating* lexical diversity.

This result may have important implications for the "continuity paradox" mentioned earlier: "language cannot be as novel as it seems, for evolutionary adaptations do not evolve out of the blue" (Bickerton, 1990, p. 7). As we noted, a potential means of resolution of the paradox has been suggested by Gould: "external discontinuity may well be inherent in underlying continuity, provided that a system displays enough complexity" (1977, p. 409). The present case seems to be consistent with Gould's supposition. The widespread occurrence of nonlinearities in complex systems in physics and physical aspects of biology is gaining increasing attention (Prigogine and Stengers, 1984). Here we are looking at such a nonlinearity in speech acquisition. We may be looking at the way in which the nonlinear change necessary to go from reduplication to place variegation first began to occur. Starting an utterance with a pure frame, then adding tongue action, allows a quantum jump in speech-output complexity by providing a systematic basis for consonant variation within utterances where there had previously been only consonant repetition. Yet it may be an instance of continuity in that it is accomplished simply by a modification of the temporal relationship between already existing movement capacities—the capacity to do frames and the capacity to adopt a non-resting position of the tongue. While the latter may typically occur before a frame gets started in the utterances of babbling and early speech, the infant then becomes capable of introducing it *after* frame production has begun.

6.3 Conclusions: ontogeny and phylogeny

Data on ontogeny supports a recapitulatory proposition about its relationship with phylogeny that seems eminently plausible on commonsense grounds. There were probably two stages in the evolution of speech: (1) an initial frame stage in which basic, more or less pre-existing capabilities were used to build a small repertoire of words; and (2) a subsequent frame/content stage of capacity increase. The latter consists of an increase in numbers of sounds and in the complexity of serial-organization patterns, both of which, when taken together, move the production system beyond its basic capabilities. As repertoire size increased across generations, adult speakers were eventually forced into a mode of processing content independently of frames, in order to speak efficiently; present-day infants are forced into that same mode as their developing repertoire increases. In both cases, the tongue leads the way into the independent content phase because it is the organ that has been, and still is, primarily responsible for the increasing repertoire. The LC sequence pattern was probably the first step in this direction of increasing serial complexity in earlier hominids, just as it is in present-day infants.

We are now in a position to say how the particulate principle may have been implemented for speech. Our view is that the frame provided the potential for an initial cut of the speech stream into two types of particles— consonants and vowels. Initially, however, these two components were simply two phases of mandibular oscillation. The speech-related correlates of the two phases, as in babbling, were not initially under independent control. The labial–coronal sequence may have been the first discrete step towards having separate segmental particles. Even here, however, there was presumably no sudden emergence of a segmental coronal particle. The CV and VC co-occurrence patterns shown in infants suggest that coronals initially were not independent of a tendency to favor adjacent front vowels over others.

This is about all the detail about the move from frames to frame/ content that we are prepared to suggest. Beyond that, we suggest, in more general terms, that selection pressures for increases in the number of words may have interacted in many other ways with what can be called the initial "problem space" to eventually lead adult speakers at least to be able to differentiate out a repertoire of segmental particles. The problem space consisted most basically of the close/open alternation, tending to be reduplicative, and its consequences in terms of the asymmetry of words— begin with consonants and end with vowels.

Our results actually suggest that we may need to talk in terms of a duality of types of particles for speech. There may have been *segmental* particles that are formed into *syllabic* particles in modern adult speakers, but both may have needed to evolve from non-particulate states, and both develop from non-particulate states in modern infants. There seems to be an analogy here with elements combining into molecules in chemistry, but in neither case is an essentialistic notion of a priori form justifiable. Contrary to the views of most linguists, I don't believe that distinctive features ever constituted particles with a functionally independent status in speech. They are instead units invented by analysts. This stance will be elucidated in Chapter 11.

We now have a relatively well-developed picture of how the main syllabic and segmental properties of modern speech might have arisen. It's especially notable that no *speech-specific innateness* is required in this theory. This is in contrast to the generative view of Chomsky in which such innateness is responsible for everything of any importance.

I don't even like to *use* the nasty word "innate" because it so often serves simply to finesse the question of causality. However, it might provide a little structure to say that some innateness—though not *speech-specific* innateness—seems to be called for in two aspects of the theory.

First, the capacity to oscillate the mandible might safely be called "innate" under any of the many definitions of this term because it is a universal mammalian property going back a fifth of a billion years. And I have provided a causal scenario for the evolution of the mandibular oscillation capacity in a direction which terminates in speech. There would seem to be no need to invoke speech-specific innateness for mandibular oscillation nor for the pairing of such oscillation with phonation, the latter being an attribute which also goes back to mammalian origins.

Second, for the capacity for mimesis to be available in hominids but not in other primates, innateness is presumably involved, but in the absence of a descent-with-modification scenario it gains us nothing to say this. Donald (1991; 1999) has provided a possible causal scenario for the evolution of mimesis, but it does not require speech-specific innateness.

Beyond this, I see only a role for sociocultural factors in implementing the phylogeny and ontogeny of speech. The mimetic capacity presumably allowed hominids to begin to voluntarily control the invention and application of sound patterns to go with particular concepts, and thus construct the first words. We are saying that initially the resultant patterns were determined by simple motor-system "affordances," to use a term introduced by James Gibson (1977). Clark (1997) defines an affordance as "an opportunity for use or interaction which some object or state of affairs presents to a certain kind of agent" (p. 172). But at the time each word was invented by cultural agreement, it became a "meme" (for Dawkins, 1976, a memory unit externally stored in the culture). And from then on until this day, the sound pattern of every word in every language (plus its link to a particular concept) has had to be accessed from the culture. But the use of simple motor-system affordances for the early words of hominids, and even subsequently for others, has probably had the advantage of giving every new infant a leg-up in using its mimetic capabilities for speech acquisition.

A possible advantage that infants have for acquiring *mental* aspects of language has been suggested by Deacon (1997):

> One way to facilitate children's inspired "guessing" about language, and thus to spare them countless trials and errors, would be to present them with a specially designed language whose structures anticipated their spontaneous guesses.... Children's minds need not embody language structures if languages embody the predispositions of children's minds. (p. 109)

I would put it somewhat differently, for speech at least. It is the predispositions of children's *bodies* that the phonological component of language structures reflects. It is the frame, and (usually) the CV co-occurrence constraints, and (usually) the LC effect. And these are being supplied not because of the phylogeny of mind but because children's bodies are hominids' bodies, and the form of speech bestowed on the modern infant has in effect gone through the filtering effect of those bodies. Ancestral forms built their speech-related mental capabilities using the guidance of the structure provided by the output of the filter, and infants have the same structure to guide the formation of their mental representations.

But we can go one better than Deacon, not only by saying that the *body* provides affordances for the mind, and how it provides them, but also in saying how it simultaneously impedes the process of obtaining mental representations for speech. The body impedes the mind in the creation of separate syllabic representations, and therefore intersyllabic variegation in real-time output, by virtue of the biomechanical inertia that impedes the independence of vowels from the consonants that follow them across syllable boundaries.

In the last two chapters, I have just summarized the particular ways in which we believe ontogeny recapitulates phylogeny. This is our attempt to deal with Tinbergen's third and fourth questions—the questions of how a behavior gets that way in phylogeny and ontogeny. The answer is what would be expected from the Embodiment perspective. For us and our ancestors it is a matter of the body placing constraints on the structure of the mind, and the mind in turn making demands on the body.

Now that we have some conception of what early speech might have been like, we can take up a more difficult but a more important problem: how the original speech system came to be able to do words—that is, how pieces of its output got hooked up with meanings.

7 The origin of words: how frame-stage patterns acquired meanings

7.1 Introduction

How did hominids actually make their first words?

So far I have presented a theory that includes a hypothesis about what the sound patterns of the first words were like. But that is only one part of the story of speech, and, in the view of most, the less important part. The other part—the part that made vocalizations become speech, because speech is a component of *language*—was the pairing of particular sound patterns with particular concepts. When this happened, the sound pattern took on meaning, becoming a symbol for the concept to which it was paired. This pairing is what made words, and language proper began with words. I share the view of Jackendoff (2002) and many others (e.g., Deacon, 1997; Donald, 1991) who, in Jackendoff's words, see "symbol use as the most fundamental factor in language evolution" (Jackendoff, 2002, p. 239). And the origin of symbol use could well have been the most important event in the evolution of humans.

The frame/content theory is a theory about how we evolved the sound *system* we have today. It is a system whereby consonants and vowels are programmed into syllable structures. This system is what allows the production of an indefinite number of words in present-day languages. I have argued that the motor basis for this system—the frame stage of output—evolved before speech, in the service of vocal grooming, and then was pressed into service for the first words. So my task will be to present a possible scenario for the origin of words by pairing of concepts with pre-existing frame-stage patterns in particular. There might have been other pairings of concepts with sounds. I will consider some possibilities later. And these may have even preceded the pairings of concepts with frame-stage patterns. But for me, speech, and therefore language, truly began with the latter pairings because only they provided the initial groundwork for the speech sound *system* that we have today. Remember from Chapter 3 that what was required to have an open-ended vocabulary of words was an implementation of the particulate principle whereby "elements drawn from a finite set . . . are repeatedly permuted and combined to form larger units" (Studdert-Kennedy, 1998, p. 203). Both syllables and segments can be considered to have this property.

What *concepts* are is a very complex issue, one that I must necessarily gloss over here with the excuse that this book is primarily about the sound level, not the concept level. But note that the concepts that initially became associated with sound patterns must have been very simple. Certainly they must have been simple in the sense that they were available prior to the explosion in conceptual complexity made possible by the ability to pair them with sound patterns. More importantly, however simple they were, there must have been compelling reasons for them to acquire a signaling component. I will try to evaluate possible candidates for first words against this criterion.

It is relatively uncontroversial that living primates most closely related to us have concepts, by which I mean mental representations that can stand for particular aspects of the world of their experience. For example, Jackendoff (2002)

take[s] it as established by decades of primate research . . . that chimpanzees have a conceptual structure in place, adequate to deal with physical problem solving, with navigation, and above all with rich and subtle social interaction incorporating some sense of the behavior patterns and perhaps intentions of others. (p. 238)

What then was necessary for the evolution of speech was to pair pre-existing concepts with vocal patterns that symbolized them. But when we raise this issue we immediately encounter a major stumbling block, an obstacle so important that it deserves a digression into the history of thought about the origins of speech.

In the ruins of the ancient city of Babylon, in Iraq, lie the remains of what is now known as the Tower of Babel, originally an impressive seven-story, stepped-pyramid construction. According to the Bible (Genesis 1:11, or see Pinker, 1994, p. 231, depending on your affiliation), this tower was intended to reach to the sky and thus bring the residents closer to God. But, the story goes, God was incensed at the presumption behind this endeavor, and responded by assigning different languages to the different subgroups of construction workers, thus preventing them from communicating with each other. As a result, the project ground to a halt.

This is the biblical account of how humans came to have many languages. Prior to this, the story goes, there was only "adamic language," the language God provided for Adam and Eve. The implication is that in adamic language there was somehow a natural relation between concepts and sound patterns. The story of the Tower of Babel seemed to explain the lack of correlation across languages between the meaning of a word and its sound pattern. For example, the word for "tooth" in German is "zahn," in Irish it is "fiacal," in Greek it is "dhondi," in Polish it is "zab," in Finnish it is "hammas," in Hungarian it is "fog," in Basque it is "ortz," etc. How on earth could the world's languages have evolved so many different sound patterns to symbolize our various words?

Since 1859, the Tower of Babel story has fallen out of favor except perhaps among certain religious fundamentalists. But what story of the origin of words do we replace it with? Sound–meaning relationships could not have been arbitrary in the beginning. There must have been a time at which the first word was invented. And we have to assume that it came to signify an object or event which was present in the environment when the sound pattern was made. The connotation of the word "arbitrary" suggests that if the initial sound–concept pairing was arbitrary, the speaker simply consulted a table of random numbers each of which signified a particular pre-existing sound pattern, picked a number, and assigned the associated sound pattern to the concept. But there could have been no such table of random numbers. Some sound pattern must have been produced in the presence of the entity for which we had a conceptual representation leading someone, and eventually many people, to take, by convention, the sound pattern to signify the concept. The question is, what were the circumstances that led to a particular sound pattern being produced in the presence of the entity for which presumably two observers had a common conceptual structure? This occasion must, in some sense, have arisen naturally. It must have had some natural causes. So what *naturally occurring events* might have led to this original sound–meaning pairing?

To see this stumbling block of apprehending the original nature of the concept–sound pairing better in the presence of current arbitrariness, we should note that there is a way of avoiding it if we assume that the first word was a word in sign language. For example, if two people were looking at a stationary bird and one flapped her arms up and down in unison, it's not difficult to imagine that the other person might be able to realize that the flapping motion stood for, or was a symbol for, the bird. Then on the next occasion on which a bird was in common view, the flapping action could be accepted as *meaning* bird. Here there is a natural relation between the concept and the symbol for it. This is called "iconicity."

But returning to the problem of linking *vocal* symbols to concepts, you might suppose that historical linguistics would have something to say about this. Unfortunately, this field is in disarray. There is a major split within the discipline between a rather timid orthodoxy, reluctant to push their questions back much beyond about 7,000 years, or across very many languages (e.g., Campbell; Dixon; Hamp; Goddard), and a smaller group of mavericks whose more adventurous suggestions are considered by the orthodoxy to be ill-conceived (e.g., Dogolopolsky; Greenberg; Ruhlen; Shevoroshkin). (See discussion in *Nostratic: Sifting the evidence* by Salmons and Joseph, 1998).

Disappointingly, neither the orthodoxy nor the mavericks have had much to say about the actual origin of the stage of pairing sounds with meanings. In particular, as far as I can ascertain, the predominant view of phonological organization is that it did not evolve from simple to more complex but has always been the way it is today. Bengtson and Ruhlen (1994), members of the maverick group, did suggest a list of twenty-seven possible protoword roots or global etymologies—in effect, words of the first language. These words appeared to be plausible candidates from my phonetic perspective in that they primarily involved CV syllables and consonants and vowels that are relatively frequent in infants and in modern languages. Davis and I (2000) analyzed the sound patterns of these words and found that they showed a mixture of frame-stage and frame/content-stage patterns. But Boë et al. (2008), in a subsequent analysis of the methodology that Bengtson and Ruhlen used to come up with these words, showed that it was deeply flawed, to the point that the proposed sound patterns could be simply a result of chance. Boë et al. concluded that "They used too few global etymologies, too many equivalent meanings, too many languages per family, and too many phonological equivalences for a too small number of different phonological shapes."

Incidentally, the claim that language went from simple to more complex is not simply a matter of pure speculation. Lindblom and Maddieson (1988) have shown that in languages with larger consonant inventories there is a disproportionate number of consonants that are more difficult to produce. This suggests that languages have become more phonologically complex as their inventories have increased.

7.2 Baby talk and the first words

There is one remaining domain that seems to allow us to develop a story about how frame-stage patterns in particular became linked to concepts. It is the domain of *baby talk*. This genre, which allows us today to trade concepts with infants, might have originally also allowed us to begin to trade concepts with each other.

What then is "baby talk," and how can it bear the heavy theoretical burden I am putting on it? Ferguson (1964) defines baby talk as "any special form of a language which is regarded by a speech community as being primarily appropriate for talking to young children and which is generally regarded as not the normal adult use of language" (p. 103). Since baby talk is a two-way affair, we ought to expand its definition to include the vocalizations made by infants to adults. Baby talk is known to be widespread in different language communities, and it may even be universal, although it's known that in some cultures, communicative interaction between caregivers and infants is minimal. In a study of baby talk in six languages, Ferguson (1964) found that, with respect to words, the special lexical items typically number from twenty-five to sixty. They include the following categories (accompanied here with English examples using Ferguson's notations): kin terms and appellations ("mommy", "daddy"); bodily functions ("wee-wee", "poop[oo]"); certain simple qualities ("?ae?ae" [meaning "don't"—the question marks indicate glottal stops], "teenie"); and vocabulary concerning animals, nursery games, and related items ("doggie", "kitty[-cat]", "bye-bye", "peek-a-boo"). Ferguson gives us 211 examples of these terms in six languages.

The first thing needed in order to hypothesize that baby talk might contain the key to the first words is to establish that the form of baby-talk terms is indeed analogous to the form of infants' babbling and first words. Because we have provided a precise characterization of the infant patterns, we are in a position to make, for the first time, a quantitative estimate of how similar baby talk is to infant productions in general. As to sound inventory, Ferguson points out that, just as in babbling and early speech, "baby talk items consist of simple, more basic kinds of consonants, stops and nasals in particular, and only a very small selection of vowels" (p. 109). As to serial organization, as might be expected, the CV form, as in every other aspect of speech we have considered, is the most favored syllabic form. The most favored word type is CVCV, the eighty examples of which make up 38 percent of the words in Ferguson's corpus. And intersyllabically, as in babbling and early speech, reduplication is most characteristic. For example, the CVCV utterances are totally reduplicated 53 percent of the time, as compared with the 50 percent of successive pairs of CVs we found to be reduplicated in babbling (Davis and MacNeilage, 1995).

But if these forms are to be considered truly similar to babbling and first-word forms of infants, it's crucial that they also have the three CV and VC co-occurrence constraints that are characteristic of these two stages. Table 7.1a shows the co-occurrence patterns of front, central, and back vowels with coronal, labial, and dorsal consonants in the CV syllables that occur in the eighty CVCV words. Table 7.1b shows also that, as expected, the VC patterns are very similar to the CV patterns. The two individual patterns were both significantly different from chance at the .01 level.

There was also a tendency in these forms to favor the labial–coronal (LC) sequence over the coronal–labial (CL) sequence as we had found in infants' first words. There were seven instances of the LC pattern but only one instance of the CL pattern.

TABLE 7.1 The relation between observed and expected frequencies for consonant–vowel relationships in CVCV forms from Ferguson's corpus of baby talk terms

a.   Consonant–vowel co-occurrence patterns

	Coronal	Labial	Dorsal
Front	1.33	0.96	0.28
Central	0.82	1.33	0.69
Back	0.74	0.76	2.22

b.   Vowel–consonant co-occurrence patterns

	Coronal	Labial	Dorsal
Front	1.43	0.82	–
Central	0.75	1.34	1.00
Back	0.61	0.79	2.33

Of course it's not surprising that baby-talk words are, in the main, similar to forms that the infant produces during the babbling and first-word periods. Baby talk is used by both infants, starting at about the time they otherwise produce the first words of their language, and by parents, and in order for this to be possible, given the infants' vocal limitations at the time, we can assume that this special language is at least to some degree tailored to conform to these limitations. But although the parallels of baby talk with babbling and infants' first words might have been expected, it is useful to have a specific idea of what they are. And the finding of close parallels is further evidence of the robustness of the serial-organization patterns we have identified in speech acquisition.

But while the forms of baby-talk words are, in general, similar to those of babbling, baby-talk words have meaning whereas babbling doesn't. The question is whether one could nevertheless say that baby talk is a separate genre from language proper, and therefore the origin of the sound–meaning pairings found here needs to be considered separately from the origin of words in language proper.

Such a separation may be insufficiently motivated. Numerous people have suggested that there seems to be a tendency for baby-talk forms to get into language proper, especially in the case of parental terms. Here is Roman Jakobson's (1960) view of the matter:

Some of the nursery forms overstep the limits of the nurseries, enter into the general usage of the adult society, and build a specific infantile layer in standard vocabulary. In particular, adult language usually adopts the nursery forms, designating each of the mature members of the nuclear family. Very frequently these intimate, emotional, childishly tinged words coexist with more general and abstract, exclusively parental terms. (p. 125)

A possible paradigm is illustrated by the situation in English noted by Jakobson (1960). He reminds us that the often reduplicated nursery forms "mama (mamma, mammy, ma, mom, mommy) and papa (par, pappy, pa, pop, or dada, dad, daddy)" (p. 125) coexist with orthodox variegated language terms "mother" and "father." Jakobson suggests that in this particular case, words of true language could be modifications of nursery words:

In Indo-European the intellectualized parental designations *mater* and *pəter* were built from the nursery forms with the help of the suffix -ter, used for various kin terms. (p. 125)

Then, as Jakobson sees it a sound change occurred in *pəter* making the initial stop [p] and the intervocalic stop [t] into fricatives, and another such change has the same effect on the [t] of "mater." Thus we end up, in English, with the true language terms "father" and "mother."

The strength of this tendency for baby-talk terms for parents to leak into language proper can be estimated by considering the phonetic structure of parental terms across languages. This estimate can be made from data (unfortunately only on the structure of the first syllable) from a rather remarkable study of parental terms of the language proper in 474 languages by Murdock (1959).

Note that Murdock took some pains to rule out borrowings of words from European languages "due to recent missionary and other influences." Also, "Forms for *mama* and *papa* were excluded unless comparative data on related languages clearly demonstrated their indigenous origin" (p. 1). CV relationships in 881 syllables from Murdock's data are shown in Table 7.2. The vowel classification he used was different from the one we have used. But his two categories of high and mid-front vowels and high and mid-back vowels can be taken to represent front and back vowels respectively because, as we saw in Chapter 3, languages don't tend to have many low-front and low-back vowels. In addition, his low vowels can be taken to represent central vowels, because Murdock indicated that the low-central vowel [a] was the most frequent vowel in this category, as it is in languages in general.

As the table shows, all three of the usual CV co-occurrence patterns are present in this data. No other CV category exceeds chance levels. Paine (unpublished observations) has made an independent analysis of the overall syllabic structure of parental terms (not just the first syllable) in a broad sample of 211 languages. She found that, in a corpus of 141 CVCV forms involving stops and nasals, 45 percent of them involved syllabic reduplication, a level characteristic of infant babbling and first words but much higher than in languages in general, where syllabic reduplication is quite rare.

TABLE 7.2 Observed-to-expected ratios of CV sequences in Murdock's 1959 study of parental terms of 474 languages

	Coronal	Labial	Dorsal
Front	1.34	0.92	0.76
Central	0.71	1.12	0.97
Back	1.00	0.72	2.27

As Tables 7.3a and 7.3b show, she also found the expected consonant–vowel co-occurrences between coronals and front vowels, and labials and central vowels in the first and the second syllables of CVCV forms. (As there were only nine dorsal consonants and nine back vowels in the corpus, these were omitted from the overall analysis.) She also found the preferred relationship between coronals and front vowels and between labials and central vowels in VC sequences (Table 7.3c), indicating that these forms are like infant forms but unlike words of language proper. A total of 333 sequences were analyzed. All three distributions shown in Table 7.3 were statistically significant. Finally, Paine also found significantly more LC patterns (17) than CL patterns (4).

In conclusion, parental terms in language proper are highly similar to both baby-talk words and infants' babbling and first words. And in the two cases in which infant and language patterns differ, namely in reduplication versus variegation and VC co-occurrences versus their absence, parental terms in language unequivocally go with infant and baby-talk patterns rather than language patterns in general. As the simple frame-stage patterns of infants and of baby talk tend to be found in kinship terms in actual

TABLE 7.3 Observed-to-expected co-occurrence patterns in CV sequences and VC sequences in Paine's sample of parental terms in 211 languages

a. Consonant–vowel co-occurrence patterns in the first CV sequence

	Coronal	Labial
Front	1.56	0.31
Central	0.64	1.44

b. Consonant–vowel co-occurrence patterns in the second CV sequence

	Coronal	Labial
Front	1.55	0.27
Central	0.90	1.14

c. Vowel–consonant co-occurrence patterns

	Coronal	Labial
Front	1.55	0.40
Central	0.85	1.17

languages, it becomes more difficult to dismiss the baby-talk patterns as irrelevant to the structure of language proper.

7.3 Parental terms as first words

There is one further aspect of sound–meaning relationships in baby-talk terms that also carries over into languages proper, and it may provide a crucial clue as to how the sound–meaning pairings were made in the first place. It is that baby-talk words for the female parent tend to favor nasal consonants while words for the male parent tend to favor oral consonants. In fact all the words for female parent in Ferguson's six-language baby-talk corpus have nasal consonants and all the words for male parent have oral consonants.

This pattern is also present in parental terms in languages proper. Murdock (1959) found that 75 percent of the consonants in words for female parent were nasal while only 25 percent were oral consonants. In contrast, only 19 percent of the consonants in words for male parent were nasal while 81 percent were oral consonants. Paine's findings were similar. She found that 77 percent of the consonants in maternal terms were nasal while only 23 percent were oral. In contrast, only 25 percent of the consonants in paternal terms were nasals, the remainder being orals.

This is quite a remarkable fact. To my knowledge, it is the only case in which two particular different phonetic forms are regularly linked with two opposing meanings in the world's languages. Could the basis of it have been established in the first language and have been maintained as subsequent languages descended from the first one? One could argue that the necessity for phonetic terms to be simple in order for them to work in parent–infant communication preserved these forms against change. For example, Ferguson (1964) presents evidence of the persistence of baby-talk words for "food," "drink," and "sleep" for some two thousand years in the Mediterranean area: "The Roman grammarian Varro (116–27 B.C.) cites Latin *bua* and *papa* or *pappa* as baby talk for 'drink' and 'food' respectively, and the use of Latin *naenia* 'dirge', 'lament' in the baby talk meaning of lullaby is attested" (p. 104).

Are we therefore more entitled to push the origins of modern baby-talk terms and the phonetically simple modern words of the language from which they derive back in time than we are for words in general?

Perhaps not. In standard historical linguistics, one encounters a good deal of pessimism on the question of whether *any* present-day word could have been an original word. It is the consensus among historical linguists of any stripe that sound change is ubiquitous, and it goes on all the time, often in front of our very nose. We know that it can be relatively rapid. The Old English of the classic eighth-century English text *Beowulf* is virtually unintelligible. For example, its opening line is "Hwaet! We Gar Dena in Geardagum" (Allman, 1990, p. 62). As mentioned earlier, orthodox historical linguists are in general dubious as to whether we can trace any word back beyond about 7,000 years (e.g., Dixon, 1997). From this standpoint it could be argued that present-day baby-talk terms and parental terms of language couldn't possibly be very old.

Regardless of whether these words are stable across time or not, it's common in linguistics to consider these patterns to be irrelevant to the question of actual language genesis even though they occur in words of language. For example, the historical linguist Hock (1986) concludes that "words derived from the babbling-based variety of 'baby talk' are generally considered unreliable evidence in attempts to establish genetic relationships" (p. 559). He thought this was true because of "the greater possibilities of chance similarities" (p. 555). However, the maverick historical linguist Ruhlen (1994) believes that attributing to chance any similarities in baby-talk forms across language, as orthodox historical linguists do, reflects bias. He thinks the conclusion was "so readily accepted" in historical linguistics because "it explained similarities which, for want of a better explanation, would have to be attributed to common origin, thus undermining the supposed independence of many language families" (p. 41). Instead, he believes that "the supposed independent development of kinship terms like mama and papa in the world's languages has been greatly exaggerated; in most such cases we are probably dealing with historically connected forms rather than with independent creations" (p. 41).

To address this difference of opinion on the origin of parental terms we turn to a paper, available on the Internet, by a traditional historical linguist, Larry Trask, entitled "Where do mama/papa words come from?" (Trask, 2003). He begins by noting that there are a number of people (Ruhlen presumably included) who take what he calls a "Proto-World" stance according to which the characteristic nasal/oral dichotomy in parental terms originated with the first language. But Trask, like other traditional historical linguists, asserts that this is impossible because of the fact that sound change in languages is ubiquitous and continuous. To support this generally accepted contention, he first reviews evidence regarding the fate of "*gwena-*," the supposed Proto-Indo-European (PIE) word for "woman." (The asterisk here indicates a protoform, and the hyphen indicates the option of a suffix.) He concludes that one of three things has happened to it:

(1) it has disappeared completely; (2) it has changed its meaning to something quite different (as with English *queen*); or (3) it has changed its pronunciation so much that it is no longer recognizable as the same word (as with Irish *bean* or Greek *yineka* or Persian *zan*). There is, in fact, scarcely a single IE language in which the PIE word survives with a recognizable form and the same meaning. (pp. 7–8)

Trask also gives evidence that the words "boy," "girl," and "child" have undergone similar histories (pp. 8–9).

Thus, sound patterns of words in general seem to have an ability to cover up their phonetic tracks. But could it nevertheless be, as suggested earlier, that parental terms are different from other words in that they don't change because, however indirectly, they are kept on a leash by the necessity that they maintain forms accessible to infants? Apparently not. Trask reviews evidence that they are simply like other words in being subject to continual change. Not only are they continually being created but they are sometimes being lost and then recreated in similar forms.

It's worth considering some of Trask's evidence to get a feel for the issue.

In Old Japanese, for example, the word for "mother" was *papa* which, with its oral consonants, was already an exception to the general trend, but its modern equivalent is *haha*, with no articulatory consonants at all. In the virtually extinct language Manchu, the modern forms—*eme* for "mother" and *ama* for "father"—have changed from earlier forms by participating in a recently developed generalized gender-marking system whereby female words have the vowel "e" and male words the vowel "a."

Several further patterns come from Indo-European languages where the protoforms were *mater* and *pater*, which had even then acquired the kinship suffix -ter which also occurs in PIE *bhrater* "brother" and *dhugater* "daughter." The equivalent forms in Spanish are *madre* and *padre*; in English, *mother* and *father*; in Swedish, *mor* and *far*; in French, *mère* and *père*; and in Irish they are pronounced [*ma:hir*] and [*ahir*]. In other languages, the PIE words have been lost and replaced by what Trask calls other mama/papa words—by *mama* and *tata* in Romanian, for example, and by *mam* and *tad* in Welsh.

A further example comes from Turkic languages many of which still have the inherited words *ana* and *ata*. But in Turkish, *ata* is now instead an elevated term meaning "forefather" or "ancestor," as in the surname chosen by the founder of the modern Turkish republic Kemal Atatürk, meaning "Father Turk." But now there is an everyday *mama/papa* word for "father"—*baba*. Meanwhile, the language Uyghur has replaced *ata* with *dada*, and Turkmen has replaced it with *kaka*.

In many languages, inherited words that are traditional and more formal coexist with newer forms that are informal or intimate, and these new words are *mama/papa* words. For example, Modern Greek has *mitera* and *mama* for "mother" and *pateras* and *babbas* for "father." And in this case *babbas* is definitely a new word, because in the history of Greek there was a stage where /b/ was totally replaced by /v /.

Trask provides dozens of further examples, and one must agree with his conclusion that there is an "endless re-creation and recycling of *mama/papa* words" (p. 15). He takes this as evidence that language did not begin with parental terms. But his evidence shows that instances of this form are continually being recreated, apparently with a continual tendency for the nasal–non-nasal distinction to co-occur with the maternal–paternal distinction. This emphasizes the deep-seated nature of this general tendency which is consistent with it being present at the time when the first words are formed.

When Trask comes to give his own answer to the question of "where are these words coming from?" (p. 15), he suggests a scenario that is not supported by the facts. First he asserts, correctly in my opinion, that the forms of parental terms come from babbling, and singles out the shared tendency toward reduplicated CVCV forms of babbling and parental terms as evidence for this origin. But then he asserts that the details of the process of formation of parental terms are triggered by successive members of a chronological sequence of events in modern babbling, a sequence that does not exist. Ironically, he makes his claims on the basis of a conception of ease of articulation similar to the one I will use later in the chapter when talking about the *phylogeny* of speech. But his conception does not fit the facts of babbling. He asserts that the first vowel in babbling is the vowel [a] because it is the easiest vowel to produce, and the first consonants are labial because, unlike coronals, they don't require tongue activity. In addition, among labials he asserts that nasal labials come first because they are easier in not requiring the palatal elevation that oral labials require.

As a result of this supposed sequence of events, the first babbled utterances take the form "*mama*" and, according to Trask, a modern mother "happily concludes that Jenny is saying 'mother' as well as her little speech organs will allow her" (p. 17). He goes on to say, "And, of course, one of the earliest babbling sequences to follow, usually something like *papa* or *dada*, is taken to be Jenny's word for father" (p. 17).

But I know of no reports of such a sequence of events in the development of babbling. Instead, labial and coronal stops, nasals, glides, and vowels in the left quadrant of the vowel space seem to be present at the outset, and, as we have seen in Chapter 5, the vowel [a] and other central vowels are only favored in labial contexts, with front vowels favored in coronal contexts.

Many years ago, Jakobson (1960) suggested a naturalistic explanation for the prevalence of nasals in words for the female parent. He claimed that "the sucking activities of the child are accompanied by a slight nasal murmur, the only phonation to be produced when the lips are pressed to the mother's breast or to the feeding bottle and the mouth is full" (p. 130). He thought that later "this phonatory reaction to nursing is reproduced as an anticipatory signal at the mere sight of food and finally as a manifestation of a desire to eat, or more generally, as an expression of discontent and impatient longing for missing food or absent nurser, and any ungranted wish" (1960, p. 130). Then, thought Jakobson, "Since the mother is, in Grégoire's [1937] parlance *la grande dispensatrice*, most of the infant's longings are addressed to her, and children, being prompted by the extant nursery words, gradually turn the nasal interjection into a parental term, and adapt its expressive make-up to their regular phonemic pattern" (pp. 130–131).

Assuming for the moment that something like this happens, how long ago might it have begun to happen? An argument that the assignment of a vocal pattern, including nasalization, to female parental terms could possibly be of considerable antiquity has recently been made by Falk as part of a more general thesis that parent–infant vocal communicative interaction may have played a key role in prelinguistic evolution (Falk, 2004).

Falk suggests that there has been an increase in selection pressures for parent–infant communication in hominids beginning as early as the australopithecine/hominid transition over 2 million years ago. The steps that set this trend in motion were two—bipedalism and brain-size increase. Bipedalism led to changes in the design of the pelvis which made it more difficult for females to deliver large offspring just at the time that brain size was increasing. The solution to this problem, apparent from present-day facts, was to deliver infants earlier in the gestation period, resulting in smaller infants that were more helpless at birth and took longer to mature. One consequence of natal immaturity was an inability of infants to cling to their parents, thus reversing a secure early physical link between parent and offspring ubiquitous in primates up until that time. This resulted in a tendency for females to park their babies while foraging, thus decreasing energy use from holding and carrying them, and increasing the mother's foraging efficiency.

As a consequence of all this, a need arose for increasing use of a vocal communication channel for maintaining distal contact with babies—for remotely pacifying them and getting them to follow during foraging. Falk suggests that these circumstances gave rise to prosodic vocalization including the universal infant-directed genre of motherese. In this context "the meanings of certain utterances (words) became conventionalized" (p. 491). Lying behind this trend, Falk suggests, was strong selection for "mothers that attended vigilantly to infants" (ibid.).

Falk suggests a scenario for a nasalized infant vocalization becoming conventionalized as a maternal parental term that is slightly different from Jakobson's scenario whereby nasalized sucking noises became conventionalized. For the noise she chooses instead a nasalized demand vocalization, documented by Goldman (2001) in modern infants, beginning at about 2 months, and roughly translated as "mama," though not canonical babbling. This form tends to be terminated when a parent approaches an infant or in the extreme picks it up. Falk chooses this form partly because of my argument (especially MacNeilage, 2000) based on the frame/content theory that the simplicity and probable antiquity of utterances such as "mama" would have been conducive to their use in early words.

A modern infant signal that seems to have properties partly overlapping the one discussed by Goldman but is better documented has been called the "grunt" by McCune and her collaborators (1996). This is a vocalization that they consider to have phylogenetic precursors. They show that it takes on a communicative function in modern infants shortly after one year of age, following two earlier stages when it is first associated with physical efforts and then with focused attention by the infants. McCune et al. conclude that, of the various non-linguistic communicative vocalizations that infants make in the first half of their second year, "only the grunt form was observed to fulfill communicative functions in the majority of children" (p. 28). They add that "These communicative grunts were directed towards the mother and might be accompanied by infant looks at mother, extension of objects, pulling at mother or reaching toward her or other objects" (p. 32).

What are the acoustic properties of these grunts? "In humans, the grunt is defined as a vocalization that results when brief glottal closure . . . is followed by abrupt vowel-like release (i.e., a brief egressive voiced breath) occurring with open or closed lips but no other supraglottal constriction" (McCune et al., 1996, p. 27). There are two possible variants of these grunts, each favoring one of the two airways above the glottis. If the lips are closed but the nasal airway remains open, the grunt will have a *nasal* vocal quality ("-m-"). If the lips are open, the predominant airflow will be through the mouth, and the grunt will have an *oral* quality ("-uh-"). Grunts occur singly or in a repetitive series, like multisyllabic babbling episodes.

Falk's key suggestion for the semantic consequence of the association of nasality with the mother is similar to Jakobson's, namely, that the cognitive act of pairing the nasalized vocalization with the meaning "female parent" may have been done by the infant: "After all, wouldn't maturing prelinguistic infants, then as now, be inclined to put a name to a face that provided their initial experiences of warmth, love and reassuring melody?" (Falk, 2004, p. 503).

But if this was the origin, how would it spread, given that it would be associated by others only with the specific demand situation? My suggestion, following Jesperson (1922), is that the female parent, in the presence of the nasal demand vocalization made directly to her, decided that "This sound stands for me." Having undergone this realization, the mother then produces from within her pre-existing repertoire the canonical babbled form /mama/ as a self-naming vocalization, perhaps first addressed to the baby, with a meaning of the form "Yes, this is your mother." This labeling operation could then transcend the adult–infant dyad and get used by both parents as a term for the mother in a nuclear family situation, eventually becoming common currency for labeling mothers in a group.

The nasal form for female parent can be considered iconic in the somewhat specialized sense of its being a sound that is consistently associated not with the emitter but with the recipient—the mother— who I assume to be the only direct infant provider at the time this began to occur. But what could be iconic about an oral consonant for a male parent? Again following Jesperson (1922; see also Jakobson, 1960), I see operating here a step beyond iconicity—an instance, perhaps the first, of

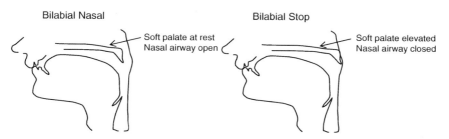

Bilabial Nasal

Soft palate at rest
Nasal airway open

Bilabial Stop

Soft palate elevated
Nasal airway closed

FIG. 7.1   Schematic views of the configuration of the soft palate for nasal sounds (a) and oral sounds (b). (Adapted from Ladefoged, 1993, Figs 1.5 and 1.6)

active use of the *fundamental linguistic concept of contrast*. Nasal and oral sounds are produced by the two possible different configurations of the upper airways. (See Fig. 7.1.) In nasals (7.1a), the nasal airway remains open, and for maximum contrastive effect the oral airway must be closed. In oral sounds (7.1b), in which the mouth is open, for maximal contrastive effect the nasal airway must be closed. It may even have been that for /mama/ both the nasal and the oral airways were originally open, giving a somewhat nasal quality, but after the oral contrast for /papa/ developed, the oral airway was closed for /mama/, making the nasality stronger and therefore more contrastive with /papa/.

What happened to the evolution of words after that? The coinage of the two parental terms must have originally occurred in a single family group. But after that the usage must have spread into the culture in general. However, two words aren't enough to be called a language. One possibility sometimes mentioned (e.g., Thong, 1999; Trask, 2003) is the generalization of words with frame-stage properties and the nasal phonetic quality of the maternal term to other aspects of the mother. A relatively modern example close to home that supports Jakobson's idea that /mama/ arose in a feeding context is "mammal." Parts of *Merriam-Webster's* (11th ed.) definition of the term are of interest: "mam-mal...*n* [NL *Mammalia*, fr. LL, neut. pl. of *mammalis* of the breast, fr. L *mamma* breast] (1826): any of a class (Mammalia) of warm-blooded higher vertebrates that nourish their young with milk secreted by mammary glands..."

But what seems necessary at some point is a flash of what McShane (1979) called, in a developmental context, "nominal insight"—*the realization that things can have names*. That such a thing can indeed happen is indicated by an incident in the remarkable life of Helen Keller, the deaf blind genius

(Keller, 2003). She suddenly realized, when a tactile signal accompanied the pouring of water on her arm, that the signal was a label for the substance, and that this was an instance of the general case that tactile signals were labels for concepts. Once the analogous insight occurred in a single earlier hominid, then the possibility of conscious assignments of signals to concepts could have arisen, and this presumably involved developments in the frame-stage *system* driven by the necessity of phonetic contrast.

Let's return to the possible initial two-word sequence of events of word invention, and consider it further in the context of what we have said about the frame stage. The frame is the constant base for all vocalizations. As Trask noted, nasalized frames require no movements in addition to the frame. The soft palate simply stays in its breathing configuration. It's possible, then, that nasalized frames were the most available frame types in ancestral hominids, and this makes it more likely that they would have been involved in the first word.

But a complication appears to arise here. From the point of view of ease alone, nasal consonants should be the dominant consonant types in *modern* languages, but they are not. However, it is well known in phonetics that nasals don't contrast very effectively with each other, either in consonants or in vowels (See Hura, Lindblom, and Diehl, 1992, regarding consonants, and Wright, 1986, regarding vowels.) So there was presumably a trend in the evolution of speech toward more oral than nasal sounds in the progression toward modern languages. But at the beginning, the simplest form, the nasal form, might have been used for the female parent. And note that the nasalization would be present for the entire utterance. The most straightforward way of producing a perceptually different utterance for a paternal form would be to close off the soft palate to produce a word entirely consisting of oral sounds. Thus the initial contrast would have been a gross and therefore unmistakable one consisting of a difference that stretches across the whole word.

An additional consideration is that both the nasal and the oral sounds would have labial consonants because these could have been produced by the frame alone, without the additional tongue movements necessary for coronal or dorsal consonants. These considerations suggest that an oral–nasal contrast between labials (basically [mama] versus [papa]) would have been the most likely initial contrast from the articulatory point of view.

The choice of place of articulation of consonants in parental terms in Ferguson's sample of six languages is consistent with the expectation that most parental terms in baby talk would be labial consonants. There are eight words with labials and four with coronals. I pointed out in Chapter 6 that coronals tend to exceed labials in babbling but that this trend is reversed in first words. However, in either case the difference is relatively small. Because of the small size of the baby-talk sample, the excess of labials is unconvincing.

But what are the relative proportions of labials and coronals in parental terms? Murdock found 430 labials and 462 coronals, while Paine recorded 69 labials and 63 coronals. The roughly 1:1 proportion of labials to coronals is much higher than would typically be found in languages in general. For example, in an analysis of the phonetic properties of conversational English, Mines, Hanson, and Shoup (1978) found a 2.5:1 ratio of coronals to labials. And in an unpublished survey of dictionary counts of Dutch, French, Romanian, and Turkish, S. Kern (Institut Dynamique du Langage, Lyon) found that the coronal/labial ratio ranged from 2.5:1 (French) to 3.5:1 for Romanian. In conclusion, there are proportionately more labials both in baby talk and in the parental terms of languages than there are in modern languages in general, and this is consistent with the prediction regarding the forms of first words arising from consideration of the frame stage.

Beyond Falk's argument for the likelihood that terms such as "mother" might have been important in the evolution of the word for ecological reasons, what else can be said about the possibility that parental terms might have been among the earliest words? It's interesting to note that while Trask talked about the "endless recycling of mama/papa words," he never considered the implication that the process might stretch a long way back in time and could therefore have given rise to the first words. It would seem that the sheer robustness and productivity of the trend can be taken as evidence for the antiquity of its origin. Thus, although Trask is apparently correct that present-day mama/papa words are not themselves living *fossils*, they are presumably *replicas* of them, because the conditions that mandate their generation remain similar to what they always were.

If there has long been this strong general propensity for the mother to regard the infant's nasal demand vocalization as a label for her, and also a tendency to then choose a simple distinctive alternative term for the male parent, then this event could, in principle, have occurred in more than one location. If it first happened in Africa before the last human migration out of Africa occurred, perhaps some 60,000 years ago, language *could* have been monogenetic in origin and then spread, notwithstanding the subsequent coming and going of particular forms. If it happened after that, a mono-genetic basis for the spread would not have been possible because language in general, and this regularity in parental terms in particular, could not have spread by contact from a single source to all other parts of the world. Nevertheless, it's conceivable that it happened more than once, either before or after the migratory Rubicon was crossed, and each time served to ignite the language process. The latter would be consistent with the orthodox historical linguistic view of independence of different language families. Unfortunately, we don't know when language began. My contention is simply that however many times the invention of the two parental terms happened in an infant–parent matrix, *the first time it happened may have marked the first step toward the invention of words with a systematic phonology.*

7.4 Other possibilities for first words

There have been a number of other candidates for first words. One well-known possibility is onomatopoeic forms. *Merriam-Webster's* eleventh edition defines *onomatopoeia* as "the naming of a thing or action by a vocal imitation of the sound associated with it." Some English examples are "cockatoo," "curlew," "swish", "bubble," "buzz," and "trickle." From the point of view of understanding their origins, these forms have the advantage that they are iconic—they contain some semblance of the noise that the entity or action being symbolized makes. It is therefore easy to see how the sound–meaning link was made by capitalizing on properties of the physical world. However this mode of sound–meaning pairing is primarily restricted to concepts related to our experience of the physical world, in particular to entities that make noises, or events that provoke them. Furthermore, from the phonetic point of view they tend to involve complex sounds and sound patterns, patterns that might not have been as easy to stabilize in a population as more simple sound patterns of the frame stage. Infants would have trouble producing any of the forms cited above. And the forms do not, in themselves, demand a systematic organization in the way that the CV syllable does.

One additional property of onomatopoeic forms that does not sit well with the possibility that they were the first words is that forms for the same acoustic event are different from language to language. Jackendoff (2002) points out that "After all, dogs go *bow-wow* in English but *gnaf, gnaf* in French, and roosters go *cockadoodledoo* in English but *kikiriki* in German" (p. 251).

There is a particular subclass of onomatopoeic forms that conforms to a "Size Principle" (Ohala, 1994). Terms for small objects tend to involve a vowel with a higher spectral center of gravity than terms for large objects. Consider the /i/ at the end of "tiny" and other "diminutive forms" that end in /i/ (e.g, "baby") versus the /u/ in "huge." Try to say each of these vowels with the same energy level and you will find that the /u/ has a lower perceived pitch.

These forms can be considered to have a deep history in communication. For simple mechanical reasons, sound frequencies vary inversely with size in animal calls and in noises that animals create when moving about the environment, and there is evidence that other animals can use these sounds as information about the size of the animal producing them—information that can be important to survival. In addition, like the parental terms, these forms lend themselves to creating a phonetic contrast, but only one, and one that is isomorphic with one basic contrast at the semantic level—the size contrast. And as they don't involve consonants, they don't contribute to the formation of a phonetic system centered on CV syllables. Another question that can be asked is, how important was it to vocally communicate information about the size dimension to others, relative to other semantic properties, at the time that hominids began to invent a symbolic system?

Jackendoff (2002) identifies a third class of forms that have some claim to a relatively early origin. He calls them "defective" lexical items, forms that have semantics and phonology but no syntax. He lists seven subclasses of these forms, "sorted approximately by semantic class", under (25) on p. 131, and I give six of them (leaving out onomatopoeia) in Table 7.4 with some of his examples, and with some added information about semantics.

Jackendoff "would like to think of such words as these as 'fossils' of the one-word stage of language evolution—single-word utterances that for some reason are not integrated into the larger combinatorial system" (p. 240). He notes that "Their semantic and pragmatic diversity suggests that they are island remnants of a larger system, superceded by true grammar" (p. 240). He notes too that "I am not suggesting that the actual 'defective' lexical items of English are historical holdovers from this stage of evolution. Rather, what is a holdover is the possibility for a language to contain such 'defective items'; those of English are realizations of this possibility" (p. 240).

Note some properties of these various forms. For the forms in group #1, it seems more likely that we first evolved head movements, such as the head nod for "yes" and the head shake for "no." Greeting forms in group #2 may not have been important enough to be the first words, and again,

TABLE 7.4 Examples of "defective" word forms given by Jackendoff, 2002 (pp. 131–2) with semantic notes added

1.	yes, no	(assent/dissent)			
2.	hello, goodbye	(greeting forms)	thanks	(gratitude)	
3.	ouch	(pain cry)	oops	(mishap label)	dammit	(swear word)	yuck	(expression of disgust)
4.	hey	(attention getter)	oo-la-la	(admiration marker)	
5.	shh	(quieting signal)	psst	(attention-getting signal)	tsk-tsk	(disapproval signal)
6.	abracadabra	(incantation)	hocus pocus	(deceptive content)	

as in the assent/dissent dichotomy, gestures such as eyebrow-raising and waving may have been early available alternatives. The affective linkages of items in group #3 may make them bad candidates for generalization into true language, which is typically defined in terms of the lack of an obligatory link between symbols and affective states. Some of these at least may be members of a second affective linguistic system, perhaps with right-hemisphere involvement, that sometimes remains present in aphasics who cannot produce lexical items of language proper (see Chapter 9). Of the forms under group #4, a form such as "hey" might have had an early nonverbal alternative that served as an early substitute for a verbal form. For example, chimpanzees are known to crinkle up leaves to get attention (Tomasello and Camaioni, 1997). The forms under group #5 are not actual words, and like many onomatopoeic words have complex phonetic properties that probably ruled out their early occurrence as part of a systematic phonology. The forms listed under group #6 can probably be ruled out as early forms because of their semantic complexity.

Considering these forms in general, one notable fact is that with the exception of onomatopoeic forms, they don't function as nouns. And it has been argued that the first words were predominantly nouns (Calvin and Bickerton, 2000). Another fact is that unlike the use of nasal and nonnasal consonants in parental terms, none of these classes of term has consistent specific phonetic properties across languages. Notwithstanding my caveats about these vocal forms as first words, I conclude that some of them could conceivably have been around at the time that the first systematic sound contrast in words was made. They could even have contributed to the eventual and presumably necessary conscious insight that concepts could be vocally symbolized. But my argument is that they were less important than the earliest parental terms because they were not as conducive to the formation of the systematic structure of the sound level as parental terms were. As I consider that the initial form of that system, the frame stage, had to have been firmly in place in a vocal-grooming mode before anything that could be called a word evolved, I consider the initial engagement of that system to provide the underpinnings of phonological protoforms of words to be the key issue in the advent of words proper. Baby-talk parental terms qualify as candidates for that initial step. To my knowledge, there is no other rationale for origin of the sound patterns of the first words that provides a base for the eventual appearance of systematic phonology.

7.5 Summary

Having theorized how the sound system of modern speech evolved, I now sought in this chapter to explain how parts of this system might have become paired with concepts to form words. The modern phenomenon of baby talk seems relevant. It involves the pairing of frame-stage patterns with concepts. The simplicity of the frame-stage patterns that accompany particular concepts might mean that modern patterns and their links with concepts closely reflect ancient ones. From an ecological perspective, the increasing importance to survival of parent–infant communication-at-a-distance, and the intimacy, stereotypy, and attention-getting properties associated with the communicative dyad were, together, presumably conducive to the invention of sound–meaning linkages. Finally, parental terms in baby talk and languages proper are not only being continually created, which suggests a robust and therefore longstanding history, but also have one particular phonetic property redolent of systematic phonology—a consistent way of implementing a phonetic *contrast* between nasalized (female) forms and oral (male) forms. Perhaps the nasalized female form was initially derived from infant nasalized demand vocalizations and the oral male form, not being iconic in a similar way, was formed specifically for contrast, perhaps the first systematic contrast. Although there may have been some other symbolic uses of the sound patterns at the time words first evolved, the advent of parental terms in the parent–infant matrix seems most likely to have led to the origin of the phonological system of present-day language.

7.6 Coda

It's a telling point regarding the intellectual orientation of generative linguists that they almost totally ignore the question of how actual events in hominid history created linkages between the semantic and the phonetic levels in the first place (though, for a recent exception see Jackendoff, 2002). One could say this is not surprising because the origin of words is, *par excellence*, a performance-level issue and therefore not within the generativists' domain of competence. Furthermore, one could hardly take the usual generative stance on causality and say that an innate tendency to pair sounds and meanings preceded the actual pairing event. The pairings must have been culturally invented.

But if indeed this event was the most important one in language evolution and therefore hominid evolution, as many people believe, it leaves generative linguistics looking a little intellectually impoverished. My attempt to explain this event, the only one specifically attempting to incorporate the origin of systematic phonology, could certainly be regarded as flimsy. But it will serve a purpose if it suggests to some that we should not really be comfortable with our understanding of ourselves until we have understood this key event in our becoming.

PART IV

Brain organization and the evolution of speech

8 Evolution of brain organization for speech: background

8.1 Introduction

We are in the midst of a neuroscientific revolution (Gazzaniga, 2000). Consequently, for a theory of evolution of speech to have any real weight today, it must accord with what we now know about the brain of modern hominids and its phylogeny. In fact, if Tinbergen were alive today, he probably would have posed a fifth question regarding any naturally occurring behavior: "How is it controlled by the brain?" So far, I have proposed a scenario at the action level for how speech might have evolved. Now I will propose a parallel scenario at the level of brain organization. In this chapter, I will review aspects of speech and manual control that form a background for considering brain organization of the F/C mode. In the next chapter, I will provide a conception of the organization itself. Then, in the final chapter in this section I will consider the evolution of the cerebral hemispheric specialization for speech in the left hemisphere.

Let's quickly recap the key points of the action-level scenario. Speech emerged as part of the evolution of a general-purpose mimetic capacity. With respect to the speech-production mechanism, the motor frame for speech appears to have originated in mandibular cyclicities (e.g., chewing). Then, after an intermediate stage of use as visuofacial communicative cyclicities (smacks), it eventually became paired with phonation to form protosyllables. Speech itself began when simple frame structures became paired with concepts. Eventually, in the final frame/content stage, hominids evolved the capacity to speak an indefinite number of time-extended utterances spontaneously by programming frames with segmental content elements—consonants and vowels.

Our task now is to pinpoint the brain organization that emerged to support these developments—basically, communicative learnability in general, and the F/C mode of speech organization in particular.

8.2 Functional anatomy of the brain

The human brain has three main structures.

First, it is dominated by a pair of *cerebral hemispheres* separated by the *longitudinal fissure*. A lateral view of the left cerebral hemisphere is shown in Fig. 8.1. The *cerebral cortex*—the outer few millimeters of these cerebral hemispheres—is packed with cell bodies of neurons, and it's the region most responsible for our higher functions. Its surface is highly convoluted. The convexity of an individual convolution in the cortex is called a *gyrus*, while a depression between convolutions is called a *sulcus*.

The second major structure of the brain—the *cerebellum* (Fig. 8.1)— comprises a pair of smaller hemispheres situated at the back of the head.

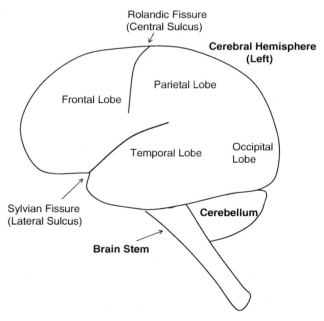

FIG. 8.1   Schematic left-lateral view of the brain, showing the main structures.

The cerebellum's main function, in the present context, is to control balance and fine movements.

The third major structure, connecting the brain with the spinal cord, is the *brain stem*. Its main functions in the present context are to conduct sensory information to the cerebral hemispheres and cerebellum and also to conduct movement-control information from these centers.

As can be seen from Fig. 8.1, three of the four lobes of each cerebral hemisphere can be roughly described in relation to its two major fissures: the *Sylvian fissure* (or lateral sulcus) and the *Rolandic fissure* (or central sulcus). The *frontal lobe* is anterior to the Rolandic fissure and superior to the Sylvian fissure. The *parietal lobe* is superior to the Sylvian fissure and posterior to the Rolandic fissure. The *temporal lobe* is inferior to the Sylvian fissure. The fourth lobe, the *occipital lobe*, occupies the posterior part of each hemisphere.

Before discussing the function of cerebral cortex, let's look at the distribution of some of its important areas and subsystems. Fig. 8.2 is another lateral view of the left hemisphere, but at the top it shows how the left hemisphere would look if the midline surface—the surface inside the longitudinal fissure—were artificially flipped upwards so that it could be viewed on top of the lateral view instead of being invisible. The figure indicates four areas of primary cortex. (Their titles are underlined.) Three of these areas, in the parietal, temporal, and occipital lobes, are where most sensory information in the cortex arrives and are thus the main basis for perceptual organization. The *post-central gyrus* receives somatic (bodily) sensory information regarding touch pressure and movement. *Heschl's gyrus*, an area in the temporal lobe within the Sylvian fissure (hence the dashed lines), receives auditory information. And the *striate cortex*, in the posterior occipital lobe, receives visual information.

The fourth area of primary cortex is the *pre-central gyrus* in the frontal lobe. It is the cortex's chief site of departure for information about motor (movement) control. I also show some other regions of frontal cortex, and use a numbering system introduced by Brodmann (1909) to distinguish between subregions with different cell types and arrangements. An area immediately in front of the primary motor cortex (area 4) is designated "area 6." This is *premotor cortex* ("pre" = "in front of"), a region more responsible for higher-order control of movement than primary cortex. The medial part of area 6 (enclosed in dashed lines) is known as the *Supplementary Motor Area* (or "SMA"). Also in medial cortex is the *anterior cingulate*

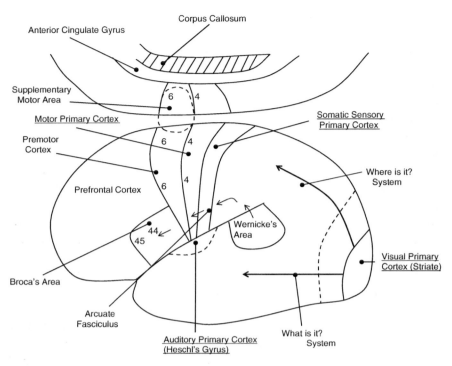

Fig. 8.2   Schematic left-lateral view of the cerebral cortex showing a number of structures and pathways (mostly) relevant to speech production.

gyrus, an old area of cortex with some motor capabilities. Brodmann's areas 44 and 45 are the *pars triangularis* and the *pars opercularis* of the *inferior frontal gyrus*. Together, they constitute *Broca's area*, an area fundamental to the production of language. Area 44 is more directly related to movement control, while area 45 is part of the *prefrontal cortex*, which is also the designation for the remainder of frontal cortex. The prefrontal cortex is the site of the highest brain functions. It has cognitive, regulatory, and executive control of the brain in general. Finally, the arc-like hatched structure seen in the medial view is the *corpus callosum*, the fiber tract that joins the two hemispheres.

In Fig. 8.2 the two major divisions of the visual system are indicated as sets of arrows originating in the visual cortex of the occipital lobe and terminating in the parietal and temporal lobes. The system terminating in the parietal lobe—the "Where is it?" system—allows the apprehension of visual space. The parietal cortex posterior to the somatic sensory primary cortex is also concerned with space—in this case, somatic (body) space. The system terminating in the temporal lobe—the "What is it?" system—allows object identification. Finally, there's *Wernicke's area*, the posterior region of the superior and middle temporal gyrus, sometimes also considered to include some inferior parietal cortex. This area is important for language comprehension. The arrows originating in Wernicke's area indicate an arcuate (arc-like) fiber tract, terminating in Broca's area and known as the *Arcuate Fasciculus*.

These major aspects of organization of the cerebral cortex are consistent with a generalization made many years ago by Pribram (1976), who observed that posterior cortex—the parietal, temporal, and occipital lobes—is primarily concerned with our perception and conceptualization of the world, while anterior (frontal) cortex is primarily concerned with action.

8.3 Neural control of mimesis

With this much knowledge of brain organization at our disposal, let's try to sketch what might be involved in a mimetic act of an ancestral hominid. Suppose he wanted to simulate a wildebeest (African antelope) pawing at the ground aggressively with its head down and then charging a threatening animal. The intention to do this routine would originate in prefrontal cortex. The developing intention would be supported by a motivational/emotional control system within the cerebral hemispheres termed the *Limbic System*. This system includes *anterior cingulate cortex* (see Fig. 8.2), which is considered to have a relatively cognitive role in selecting among motivated action alternatives and dealing in particular with relatively difficult actions. The chosen action routine would be primarily represented in premotor cortex and in a set of subcortical nuclei within the hemispheres, called the *Basal Ganglia*, while the actual actions would be executed primarily via primary motor cortex.

The posterior cortex's role in mobilizing this action complex needs to be viewed in the context of the history of the hominid's acquisition of the ability to do it. Of course, the original information regarding the animal's action comes from observing the action itself, using visual and auditory modalities. Much recent evidence supports the proposition that important aspects of our memories of observed events are laid down in those parts of posterior cortex that were used to perceive them in the first place—the visual and auditory systems. Damasio and Damasio have described the recalling of these memories as a matter of what they call "multiregional activation of originally stimulated structures" (Damasio and Damasio 1994, p. 73). And such recall would presumably be involved in any attempts to simulate the action, based, as they must be, on memorized events. Thus, visual memory would be involved in the form of visual field changes associated with simulating the head-bowed posture, the pawing of the ground, and the galloping gait of the attack. The auditory cortex, meanwhile, would be involved in the memory supporting the simulation of the snorts that accompany the aggressive display. There would also be some preserved representation of the somatic sensory information that accompanied the postures and movements. All this information would have to be used in some way for the next simulation.

8.4 The intrinsic/extrinsic dichotomy in action control

A more detailed consideration of human action capabilities that are most directly responsible for mimetic acts can begin with a recent conceptualization of motor and premotor centers and pathways in the monkey. (See Fig. 8.3, from Wise, in press.) These are considered, for the most part, to be relatively similar to those of humans. One particular aspect of this conception should be noted. In recent years a dichotomous structure of areas of premotor cortex has been observed whereby the posterior regions—SMA, PMd (dorsal premotor cortex), and PMv (ventral premotor cortex)—are more directly involved in movement control, while the areas with the prefix "pre"—preSMA, prePMd, and prePMv—have more cognitive functions. In the ventral region, PMv is considered analogous to the area 44 subcomponent of Broca's area in humans and prePMv to the area 45 component.

Although all the components in Fig. 8.3 tend to be involved in actions, their overall mode of operation can be characterized more specifically in terms of their involvement in either of two complementary subsystems. One subsystem—an "intrinsic" one in medial cortex including anterior cingulate cortex, represented by CMAs (Cingulate Motor Areas) in Fig. 8.3, and the preSMA/SMA complex—is devoted primarily to self-generated activity; the other—an "extrinsic" subsystem in lateral cortex consisting of the dorsal and ventral premotor complexes (described

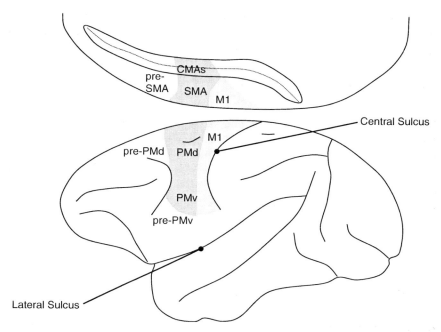

Fɪɢ. 8.3   Wise's (in press) conception of cortical regions involved in motor control in the monkey. (Adapted)

above)—is more specialized for responding to external stimulation. This dichotomy, first documented in detail by Goldberg in 1985, is now accepted enough to appear in an introductory textbook in cognitive neuroscience (Gazzaniga, Ivry, and Mangun, 2001). See also Eccles, 1982; Passingham, 1987; Rizzolatti, Matelli, and Pavesi, 1983. One basic finding in monkeys which lies behind this dichotomy is that damage to the SMA impairs the performance of tasks involving movement sequences generated from memory, but not tasks in which each successive movement is cued by an external stimulus. Monkeys with damage to ventral premotor cortex show exactly the opposite results. They are impaired in the visually guided task but not in the memory task (Tanji et al, 1995).

Recordings of motoneuronal activity in the two regions in monkeys give corresponding findings. Tanji et al. (1995) reported that "A majority of SMA cells exhibited preferential or exclusive relation to the motor task during the memory task. In contrast PM cells [cells in PMv in Wise's terminology] were more active during the visually guided task" (p. 160).

Both the intrinsic system and the extrinsic system are extensively connected to output pathways involving primary motor cortex, but it's becoming increasingly clear that they also "project" (send information) directly to subcortical centers.

The SMA is the most important motor component of the intrinsic system. I use the abbreviation "SMA" in subsequent discussion to include both preSMA and SMA proper. Earlier findings, on which I focus, involved the SMA as a single entity.

Goldberg assigns the SMA an important role in "the intentional process whereby internal context influences the *elaboration* of action" (italics mine; 1985, p. 567). He considers that "The SMA is crucial in the programming and fluent execution of extended action sequences which are projectional in that they rely on model-based prediction" (p. 567). The term "projectional" is often used in discussions of voluntary actions. It refers to the fact that such actions must be planned in advance with reference to a future goal. Watching a squirrel outside my window trying to decide where to jump from, and (apparently) whether the jump will succeed in reaching the bird feeder that I have just moved to a hopefully more squirrel-proof location, puts one in touch with the projectional capacity. Obviously, then, in these terms, the SMA would play a central role in the control of mimetic behavior and spontaneous speech.

Consistent with this intrinsic role, the SMA is not extensively connected with sensory-perceptual systems in the posterior cortex. Instead, as Gazzaniga, Ivry, and Mangun (2001) put it, "Due to their anatomical connections, these areas are in a position of allowing limbic structures to convey information related to the animal's current motivational state and internal goals" (p. 397). In contrast, lateral premotor cortex of the extrinsic system receives heavy input from posterior cortex (Pandya, 1987), as would be expected from its role in relating input to output. In particular, as Gazzaniga, Ivry, and Mangun point out, "The [ventral] premotor area is innervated extensively by the parietal cortex and the cerebellum, two areas linked not only to visuospatial function but also with rich representations extracted from other sensory channels like audition and touch" (2001, p. 471). Goldberg summarizes the role of the extrinsic system this way: "The lateral system is part of a system responsible for recognizing and associating significance with external objects, and in relation to action operates in a responsive mode in which each action is dependent on an explicit external input" (1985, p. 568). Wise (1984) has also concluded that lateral premotor cortex "is especially important in the preparation for and the execution of sensorily guided movements" (p. 549).

But in light of the conception of mimetically based actions given above, a crucial additional point must be made regarding the extrinsic system. As well as having an online role in environment-sensitive actions, this is the system that *allows mimetic actions to be learned in the first place*. That is, it allows relationships between input and output to be formed. It is therefore no coincidence that this is the system in which we find mirror neurons, neurons found in monkeys which discharge during a particular action (e.g., grasping) and when the animal observes another animal performing the same action. These neurons, to be discussed in more detail later, presumably played a crucial role in our evolving the capacity to relate observation and action as required in mimesis.

8.5 Historical views of brain/language evolution

With this brief outline of the organization of complex voluntary action control in higher primates, we are now in a position to directly consider the evolution of the brain organization underlying speech.

The main conception of present-day brain–language relations, from an historical perspective, has been one in which control of language processes is basically confined to the lateral surface of the left hemisphere of the brain, surrounding the Sylvian fissure—the so-called "perisylvian cortex" (see Fig. 8.2). In 1861 the French neurologist Paul Broca proposed that problems in *producing* speech resulted from damage to a region of left frontal perisylvian cortex now known as "Broca's area" (Brodmann's areas 44 and 45; see Fig. 8.2). In 1874 the German neurologist Carl Wernicke reported that problems in *comprehension* of speech resulted from damage to a second area of perisylvian cortex, now known as Wernicke's area (see Fig. 8.2). He then predicted the existence of a third class of aphasic patient who would have unimpaired production and comprehension but a problem in repeating others' utterances on demand. He considered that this problem would result from damage to the Arcuate Fasciculus, the fiber tract connecting Wernicke's and Broca's areas (see Fig. 8.2). Such a patient, termed a "conduction aphasic," did indeed eventually emerge, typically with damage to perisylvian cortex of the inferior parietal lobe as well as underlying white matter (Green and Howes, 1977).

Wernicke's conception of brain–language relations, has, until recently, served as the centerpiece of attempts to understand brain evolution for language. And it has generally led to the conclusion that the neural capacity for language evolved de novo. One reason for this conclusion was evidence that lateral cortex did not seem to be involved in call production in monkeys. In a classical study by Jürgens, Kirzinger, and von Cramon (1982), the monkey equivalent of the entire perisylvian language cortex on both sides was removed with no obvious effect on call production. In addition, there was evidence that *medial* cortex was involved in call generation in monkeys. For example, MacLean and Newman (1988) assign to the front region of anterior cingulate cortex (ACC) a fundamental role in the evolution of vocal communication because it was possible to elicit isolation calls in squirrel monkeys by stimulating this region. (The authors believe that the isolation call, or "isolation peep," which young animals make when out of contact with their parents, may have been the first vocalization to evolve in mammals.) A role of ACC in voluntary control of monkey vocalization is inferred from studies of a conditioned vocalization task after damage to this region (Jürgens, 1987). Monkeys were first trained to vocalize in response to a signal in order to obtain a food reward. After damage to ACC, they lost the ability to do this. Humans also have the medial centers and pathways that monkeys use in vocalization, but it is usually thought that they are used in humans, as they are in other animals, for emotional vocalizations, not for language. They *are* used for emotional vocalizations in humans, but as we will see, this is not the whole story.

In the 1970s, evidence of this kind led a number of scientists to come, rather unequivocally, to the anthropocentric conclusion that speech was an entirely new function in humans. For example, Robinson (1976) talks of the "parallel evolution" of two systems. He suggests that the system responsible for speech "did not arise from" or "out of" the old system but from "*new tissue*, namely the neocortical association area" (p. 765; italics mine). According to Lancaster (1973), the mechanisms underlying calls of other primates and human language are "entirely different" due to the use, for language, of "a uniquely human neural mechanism involving the cerebral cortex" (p. 69). Myers (1976) throws down the gauntlet in a paper entitled "Comparative neurology of vocalization and speech: Proof of a dichotomy" where he concludes:

it is apparent that the speech of man has developed not from the vocal responses of *lower* primates [italics mine] but rather speech has developed de novo in man during his evolutionary development beyond the level of monkeys or, indeed, apparently of the apes.... The separate and distinct mechanisms of the cerebrum that control emotional and instinctive behavior still remain in the human to link us phylogenetically with our lower primate forebears. For the proper study of language, however, one would do well ... to avoid speculation as to similarities between the vocal responses of animals and speech in man. (p. 755)

This discontinuity hypothesis according to which the intrinsic system does vocalization of other primates but the extrinsic system does human speech is still a part of some treatments of language evolution today (e.g., Calvin and Bickerton, 2000). The hypothesis tends to have a Cartesian flavor, according to which the medial system is seen as basically part of the body, linked to the emotional vocalizations of other animals, and human emotional cries, but not to that strictly human capstone of the rational mind, language. But this distinction is overdone. Not all primate calls can be labeled emotional, and much language use is not independent of emotion.

In this context, we must remember that, as Darwin said in *The Origin of Species* (1859/1952), "natura non facit saltum" (nature does not make jumps—p. 92). *Merriam-Webster's Collegiate Dictionary*, 11th ed., defines the modern word "saltation" this way: "the origin of a new species or a higher taxon in essentially a single evolutionary step that in some esp. former theories is held to be due to a major mutation or to unknown causes." I will now present an alternative descent-with-modification scenario which involves both the intrinsic system and the extrinsic system in the control of action in monkeys and humans, rather than leaving out the extrinsic system in monkeys and the intrinsic system in humans, as many current conceptions tend to do. The appropriate conclusion, I contend, is that the *foundation* for both mimesis and speech in humans lies in the joint role of the two systems as seen in monkeys, but that this role has expanded enormously with the evolution, in humans, of elaborate learnable action capabilities.

I will now review the roles of the two systems in monkeys and the way they have been elaborated in humans.

8.6 Phylogeny of the extrinsic system

Consider first the extrinsic system. Although electrical stimulation of ventral premotor cortex has not been shown to induce vocalization in monkeys, it is known that it controls vocal-fold movements (Hast et al,

1974) and lip and jaw movements (e.g. Wise, in press). In addition, there is an important recent finding, summarized in the title of a paper by Gil-da-costa et al: "Species-specific calls activate the homologs of Broca's and Wernicke's areas in the macaque" (2006). The homolog to Broca's area was F5 in ventral premotor cortex, considered a homolog of Brodmann's area 44. The homolog to Wernicke's area was area Tpt in the superior temporal gyrus considered a homolog of the Planum Temporale. The authors appropriately surmise that "the last common ancestor of macaques and humans, which lived 25–30 million years ago, possessed key neural mechanisms that were plausible candidates for exaptation during the evolution of language" (p. 1064).

Another important recent development in the study of auditory perception provides strong evidence of homologous organization of vocal perception capabilities of the extrinsic system in monkeys and humans. Romanski and Goldman-Rakic (2002) first identified an area of ventrolateral prefrontal cortex of the macque monkey that is responsive to "complex auditory stimuli including human and monkey vocalizations" (Romanski, Averbeck, and Diltz, 2005, p. 734). A likely human homolog with special sensitivity to voice has been identified in Brodmann's area 47 by Fecteau et al (2005) and implicated in semantic processing—decisions regarding the meaning of signals.

More indirect evidence of a role of the extrinsic system in monkey vocalization production comes from a number of studies suggesting that, as with humans, monkeys have a left-hemisphere specialization for vocal communication. In humans, the left-hemisphere language-production specialization is indicated by a tendency for right-handers to open the right side of their mouth more than the left while speaking. (Motor control of the face is predominantly crossed.) Hook-Costigan and Rogers (1998) have shown a similar tendency in affiliative vocalizations in marmosets. Although the precise locus of this lateralized production capability has not been established in monkeys, these are not emotional vocalizations and therefore are not necessarily controlled only in medial cortex. The control is likely to primarily involve lateral cortex, just as the control of affiliative vocalizations does in humans.

This finding of a left-hemispheric specialization for vocal production in monkeys complements a number of studies, reviewed in Chapter 9, showing that they also have a left-hemispheric specialization for vocal *perception*. One of the studies implicates the monkey homolog of Wernicke's area in particular

(Heffner and Heffner, 1984). Thus, as monkeys have both a human-like left-hemisphere specialization for vocal production and vocal perception, and as this specialization for both of these functions in humans is primarily vested in perisylvian cortex (part of the extrinsic system), it seems clear that there is a precursor, in nonhuman primates, to the role of the extrinsic system in language.

The fact that Broca's area, the main motor component in the extrinsic system, plays a key role in speech production fits well with a basic assumption of F/C theory, namely, that syllable frames arose from smacks, which in turn arose from ingestive mandibular cyclicities. Important evidence for this view is that the posterior inferior frontal lobe, where Broca's area is situated in humans, is the cortical site of control of ingestive movements in mammals. Thus, according to the theory, one would expect it to have had a pivotal role in the evolution of speech.

Woolsey (1958) has shown by means of electrical stimulation studies that the lateral frontal lobe is the main site of cortical ingestion-control processes in mammals in general. As to the role of this region in the three cyclical ingestive processes involved in feeding—chewing, sucking, and licking—most evidence is available for chewing. In a variety of animals—rabbits, carnivores, rodents, monkeys, and humans—stimulation of ventral lateral premotor cortex evokes "movements resembling normal well coordinated mastication" (Lund, Sasamoto, and Murakami, 1984). But Lund and Eno-moto (1988) make the important point that "When defined by electrical stimulation, the masticatory area of humans, monkeys and cats is *separate* from the jaw, face and tongue representations in area 4. It is found at the lateral end of area 6 in monkeys and *probably extends into area 44*" (p. 57; italics mine). In addition, Luschei and Goldberg (1981), in a review of the neurophysiology of mastication, note that a monkey with a bilateral lesion in ventral area 6 and the monkey homolog of human area 44 "never produced repetitive phasic biting seen in other animals" (p. 1262). Studies by Rizzolatti and his colleagues using electrical recording and microstimulation techniques have confirmed a role for ventral frontal cortex between area 4 and the arcuate sulcus (F5 in their terminology, which corresponds to PMv in Wise's termin-ology) in the control of mouth movements, as well as hand movements and hand–mouth interactions, in monkeys (Gentilucci et al., 1988: Rizzolatti et al., 1988). In fact, it was in the course of showing that neurons in this area had a one-to-one relation with particular kinds of movements that they found that some of these neurons were mirror neurons.

The involvement of ventral area 6 in ingestive processes in *humans* was first established by Foerster (1936). (Summary in *Lancet,* 1931, vol. 221, pp. 309–312.) It was reported that

electrical stimulation of ventral area 6 produces rhythmic coordinated movements of the lips, tongue, mandible, pharynx, and larynx. The area appears to be unique inasmuch as stimulation of it by continuous galvanic current produces rhythmic movements, and the effect outlasts the stimulus. *No other area of the cortex behaves in this way.* Epileptic convulsions originating from the area begin with the same type of movements—chewing, licking, swallowing and grunting movements. (p. 310, italics mine)

Lateral cortical control of these actions is superordinate to direct control in the brain stem. More direct control of the mandibular cycles in monkeys, and presumably in humans, apparently resides in a Central Pattern Generator in the pontine and medullary regions of the brain stem (Lund and Kolta, 2006).

Finally, evidence of the presence of mirror neurons in ventral premotor cortex of monkeys suggests that they served a precursor role in the evolution of mimetic capabilities, specifically speech capabilities. These neurons are found in F5 of monkey cortex (Wise's PMv), which, as explained earlier, is considered homologous with Brodmann's area 44—part of Broca's area. The initial discovery was of neurons that discharged when monkeys made a particular type of hand movement (e.g., whole-hand grasp) and also when they observed humans making a similar movement. Such neurons could have formed an initial basis for acts of visually based mimesis, although monkeys themselves show virtually no ability to imitate.

Following their discovery of these mirror neurons, Rizzolatti and his colleagues also found a region of monkey F5 more lateral to the area containing most hand-related neurons in which there are neurons associated with *mouth* movements (Gentilucci et al., 1988). This group has found, more recently, that there are mirror neurons in this region involved in both ingestive behaviors and visuofacial communicative behaviors *including lipsmacks* (Ferrari et al., 2003).

A key point here is that the finding of individual neurons with a role in *both* ingestion and visuofacial communication confirms my 1998 contention that ingestive behaviors could have been precursors to communicative behaviors (MacNeilage, 1998a). It was found that eleven of twelve "communicative mirror neurons"—neurons that responded to species-specific communicative gestures made by the experimenters—also discharged during the making of ingestive actions by the monkey. The neurons were perceptually sensitive to communicative gestures of lip-smacking, teeth chatter, lip protrusion, tongue protrusion, and lip and tongue protrusion together. Associated ingestive actions were sucking, grasping with lips, chewing, reaching with tongue, and grasping with mouth. (The twelfth neuron, which responded to the communicative gesture of lip protrusion, was active during the animal's production of another communicative gesture—lip-smacking.) The authors state, "In general there was a good correlation between the motor features of the effective observed (communicative) action and those of the effective executed (ingestive) action" (Ferrari et al., 2003, p. 1709). The group considered these findings to be consistent with the contention from F/C theory that ingestive actions may have been precursors to the subsequent oral communicative role of this region. In their own words, "Ingestive actions are the basis on which communication is built" (p. 1713).

Most recently, Rizzolatti's group has even found one mirror neuron that discharges when the monkey makes a *vocal* communicative gesture and when it *hears* the same communicative gesture (Ferrari et al., 2003). Thus there may be mirror neurons in monkeys that are direct precursors to the ones presumably operative in the vocal–auditory communication that in humans we call "speech."

Ferrari et al. (2003) come to a very important conclusion relative to their finding of oral communicative mirror neurons in F5 of the monkey. They point out, as I did earlier, that

The production of communicative signals in nonhuman primates has been traditionally associated to the activity of mesial cortical areas [i.e. intrinsic cortex] and subcortical structures...that is, to structures whose activation is correlated to emotional behavior.

But they add, with regard to communicative mirror neurons, that

their presence in an area that is not related to emotions, but to the expression/ understanding of "cold action" (not emotionally laden) may suggest that in the macaque there is an initial capacity to control and emit "voluntarily" (not emotionally) social signals mediated by the frontal lobe.

They conclude by noting that

Finally and most interestingly, this capacity develops in a cortical area that, in another primate evolutionary line, became a key for verbal communication. (p. 1713)

Additional evidence of a phylogenetic relationship between the control of ingestive cyclicities and the control of vocal communication, this time at a lower level of the output system, has been provided by Hage and Jürgens (2006). They found a large number of what they called "multipurpose" (p. 7112) motoneurons in the trigeminal motor nucleus of the brainstem in the squirrel monkey that discharged during both mastication and vocalization. These included some neurons, the activity of which was modulated in phase with the biphasic rhythmic acoustic frequency of trill and cackle types of call—a little over 10 Hz. The authors suggest that this frequency-coupled modulation of motoneuron activity "might be explained by the fact that jaw movements during vocalization serve to modulate the resonant frequencies of the vocal tract" (pp. 7112–7113). These findings suggest the existence of a deep evolutionary commonality of control of ingestive and communicative role of the mandible that the F/C theory postulates. The findings require a modification of Jürgens' conclusion, summarized in the title of an earlier peer review response to the F/C theory, that "Speech evolved from vocalization not mastication" (1998: 519).

In conclusion, there are good reasons to believe that the extrinsic system of nonhuman primates ancestral to humans possessed a number of significant precursors to the neural basis of speech in humans. It may have had a capacity for activating the larynx, which must have had some relevance to phonation. It had a left-hemisphere specialization for both the production and perception of vocal signals. And, most importantly for our present purposes, it provided the main neural basis for the proposed evolution of speech from ingestive cyclicities via smacks. Ventral premotor cortex, including the monkey homolog of Broca's area, has an evolutionary history of control of ingestive processes, and the properties of some mirror neurons are consistent with the evolution of communicative functions from ingestive functions in this area.

8.7 Phylogeny of the intrinsic system

Consider now the evidence for a role of the intrinsic system in the evolution of mimesis and speech. The key role of this system in spontaneously generated action in monkeys, already mentioned, makes it clear that its existence in primates was part of the groundwork for modern mimetic and speech capabilities. Both mimesis in general and speech in particular prototypically involve spontaneous generation.

The role of the ACC in conditioned vocalization in monkeys, described earlier, is generally considered to be at the level of control of intentional or voluntary behavior rather than involving the specifics of vocalization as such. It might be equally involved in learning to associate a manual movement with a stimulus. But the existence of motor regions in the ACC, pointed out earlier (CMAs—see Fig. 8.3), raises the possibility that this region plays some role in the actual motor control of vocalization in monkeys. Evidence from humans suggests that if this is true, it is most likely to involve *phonation.* Jürgens and von Cramon (1982) have reported that a patient with a bilateral ACC lesion had not recovered normal phonation five years after the damage was incurred.

Further evidence from humans suggests that the control of respiration, a necessary component of vocalization, is vested in the medial system. As Catrin Blank et al. (2002) have pointed out, "Functional imaging studies have implicated the SMA in both voluntary control of respiration independent of speech production (Ramsay et al., 1993) and breathing control during speech (Murphy et al., 1997)" (p. 1834). These findings are inconsistent with the claims that human speech involves an entirely new cortical system, and suggest instead that an important part of the respiratory and phonatory basis for human speech was already present in the ancestral primate medial system. And control of respiration in particular remained in the medial system as speech evolved. I am not aware of any evidence of respiratory control in the extrinsic system.

Perhaps the most straightforward evidence for a role of the intrinsic system for self-generated behavior comes from the effects of damage to it in humans. On the basis of this evidence, Damasio (1994) has proposed that "there is a particular region in the human brain where the systems concerned with emotion/feeling, attention and working memory interact so intimately that they constitute the source for the energy of external action (movement) and internal action (thought, animation, reasoning)." These patients have a condition "described as suspended animation, mental and external—the extreme variety of an impairment of reasoning and emotional expression" (p. 71). Such patients are akinetic, that is, without movement. So they are, then, obviously alinguistic as far as output is concerned. They are mute. In Damasio's terms, they have "a pervasive impairment of the drive [motivation] with which mental images and movements can be generated, and of the means by which they can be enhanced" (p. 73). Although Damasio had anterior cingulate cortex particularly in mind here, his description also applies to some extent to the SMA.

Obviously, intact perisylvian cortex is not sufficient for language production in these mute patients. Consequently, this medial cortical region plays a crucial role in language production. Yet this region has been regarded as nonlinguistic. There are three reasons. First, because patients with damage to this area suffer a lack of initiation of action in general, one can argue that the region has no specific linguistic role. Second, as such patients recover, they exhibit a lack of specifically linguistic symptomatology. Their spontaneous speech, when regained, is initially sparse and halting. But it is not agrammatic or characterized by articulatory problems. And unlike patients with lateral cortex damage, their speech is not paraphasic, that is, characterized by inappropriate phoneme substitutions. Third, their ability to repeat utterances produced by others remains good despite the rarity of spontaneous speech, suggesting that they have not lost their language capacities. Nevertheless, there is a great deal of evidence from stroke patients, and from studies involving brain imaging, electrical stimulation, and effects of irritative lesions on the SMA in particular, that interference with the normal activity of this region does have specific effects on speech, and on those grounds I wish to argue, in the next chapter, that this region has played a crucial role in the evolution of speech.

Penfield and Roberts, in their classic monograph (1959), asserted that the SMA was a *language* area on the basis of the dysphasic speech that followed its removal, even though noting that the effects of excision were transient. The transience of the effects doesn't necessarily have negative implications for the importance of the area for language. As Rubens (1975) has noted, "The relative transience of the major aphasic signs may perhaps be explained by the fact that the mesial and superior premotor areas have extensive bilateral connections with subcortical structures and with each other, and the function of one may be readily assumed by its remaining counterpart" (p. 248). In other words, damage to one hemisphere may have been compensated for by the other.

It's important to note that Damasio emphasizes both a problem in drive following medial lesions, and a problem of implementing drives by means of action. These two effects can be, to some extent, independent. Rubens (1975) describes two patients with damage to medial cortex primarily involving the SMA as being "alert and cooperative" during testing, and showing "embarrassment, frustration and anxiety when failing language tasks" (p. 246). It seems likely that drive-related effects are more likely from ACC damage, while more purely movement-related problems are more likely to accompany SMA lesions.

Because of the lack of specifically linguistic symptomatology following damage to medial premotor cortex, it has come as a surprise that, from the very beginning of the brain imaging era (see Roland, 1993, for an early summary), the SMA has consistently shown bilateral activation for linguistic tasks, sometimes with even more prominence than lateral premotor sites. In addition, the SMA is consistently activated during manual tasks in humans. In fact, it appears that if certain methodological strictures are adhered to, future studies may show SMA activation for *all* sustained motor tasks, or at least those beyond a certain minimal level of complexity. In addition, it has been shown to be consistently active even if the subject only thinks about the production of manual and vocal actions (Orgogozo and Larsen, 1979), a result that has also not been consistently observed in lateral premotor cortex. This has led to the suggestion that the SMA is a higher-order motor-control area, or a "supramotor" area (Orgogozo and Larsen, 1979).

Obviously, the fact that the SMA plays a similar role in speech and manual function does not rule out its importance in language function. But a better understanding of the role it plays in speech can be gained from first considering its role in manual function, which I will do in this chapter. Then I will compare that role with its role in speech in the next chapter.

Results of earlier studies of effects of electrical stimulation of the brain in humans in the context of operations to relieve epilepsy suggest that for the body in general, medial cortex may be the repository of what could be called "movement prototypes." For example, in stimulating the SMA, Penfield and Welch (1951) noted three classes of movements in humans: "1. assumption of postures; 2. maneuvers such as stepping; and 3. rapid incoordinate movements" (p. 310). Penfield and Jasper (1954) also report sequences of alternating finger flexion and extension. In addition, Talairach et al. (1973) observed a variety of bodily responses on stimulation of ACC in humans: "Their common feature was that all were based on several simple primitive movements such as touching, leaning, rubbing, stretching, or sucking in. . . . These movements were combined in multiple ways to yield integrated and sometimes well adapted behavior patterns, e.g., sucking, palpation or nibbling" (p. 51).

Under normal circumstances, movement complexes like these and others are self-generated and appropriately adapted to external circumstances. And it is the role of the extrinsic system to provide sensory information that allows such adaptation. Evidence for this feature of normal operation was provided by Talairach et al. (1973). They noted that the detailed structure of the responses to ACC stimulation was dependent on the externally available context. For example, they observed

rubbing the fingers and palm together reproducing either a kneading movement when the subject was holding something pliable, or a palpatory movement when the object was harder in consistency. (p. 47)

The form of hand–mouth interactions

depended on whether the subject was or was not holding something in his hand. When he was holding nothing he touched or rubbed his lips, tongue, teeth, nose or chin or else scratched his lips, sucked his fingers or tapped lightly on the tip of the tongue. If he was holding a rigid object, he sucked it, suckled on it, and chewed on it. When holding a cigarette he put it to his mouth and smoked as if it was lit. (p. 47)

The extrinsic system was presumably important in providing the information that led to an object-appropriate action when an object was present in these acts. In a study of two patients with SMA damage, Watson et al. (1986) observed severe deficits in what they called "transitive limb movements," which they defined as "movements made in relationship to an object or instrument" (p. 790). This deficit showed up most clearly in an inability to pantomime object use, less clearly in problems with imitation of demonstrations of object use, and least obviously in actual use of objects. The results suggest that the more external information was available to the patient, presumably via the extrinsic system, the more capable he or she was of doing the task.

Finally, the neurophysiologist Herbert Jasper provided a patient self-report that beautifully illustrates the fundamental role of the SMA in the generation of the intrinsic basis for action:

following excision of the SMA . . . with Dr. Bertrand, we observed a very curious effect. There was no obvious defect in testing motor function following the removal but the patient found that in the morning when he got up and read the newspaper while drinking his coffee for breakfast, he could no longer automatically drink his coffee and read the paper. He had to change and watch his hand moving from the coffee to his mouth and take his eyes off the paper, otherwise he would spill the coffee. So somehow or other, sequences of motor functions which are performed automatically were disrupted by this supplementary motor excision. (in discussion of Dinner and Lüders, 1995, p. 270)

In the absence of a normal representation of movement prototypes for spontaneous actions in the intrinsic system, the patient was forced to rely more on extrinsic information.

In summary, it may be that medial cortex, in conjunction with the basal ganglia, can generate movement "prototypes" for manual action, the connotation being that a prototype provides the basic form of the movement complex. There are two senses in which this might be true. First, from an evolutionary perspective, medial cortex may have been influential in helping to provide a sort of movement vocabulary for various basic multi-joint movement synergies underlying other bodily actions (all of course in concert with lower nervous-system structures). Second, in online control, the prototypes may provide the basis for more complex overall configurations, adjusted to their context.

In the next chapter we will see that medial cortex plays a role for speech that is highly similar to the role it plays for manual movements.

9 A dual brain system for the frame/content mode

9.1 Speech and the intrinsic system: a cognitive-motor frame

We concluded the last chapter by noting that medial cortex seems to be a site for generating manual-movement prototypes. What is the equivalent in speech to this role of medial cortex in manual function? In a meta-analysis of forty-five imaging studies of word production, Indefrey and Levelt (2000) conclude that "the SMA is in some complex way related to motor planning and imagination of articulation" (p. 860). This is consistent with the conclusion of Orgogozo and Larsen (1979) that this area is a supramotor area. But more specifically I wish to contend that while the role of the SMA (Supplementary Motor Area) for speech is like that for manual function in that it is concerned with movement prototypes, the specific role that it plays in this regard is unique to speech. I contend that *the SMA has evolved a role as a frame generator.* There is converging evidence for the existence of this particular movement prototype from studies of electrical stimulation and studies of the effects of brain damage.

As to the effects of electrical stimulation, it's unfortunate that earlier evidence regarding them wasn't presented in the influential Penfield and Roberts (1959) volume. If it had been, it wouldn't be necessary for me to be making the case half a century later that the intrinsic system played a crucial role in the phylogeny of speech. But in other sources Penfield and his colleagues make clear that one type of speech-related response to stimulation is *unique* to the SMA. For example, Penfield and Jasper (1954) state that the vocalization produced by SMA stimulation "resembles that produced by stimulation in the lower Rolandic area of either hemisphere, but it is more often *rhythmic* or interrupted. It is also more complicated and at times resembles words such as 'kata, kata' or 'wata,

wata' " (pp. 101–102, italics mine). Penfield and Welch (1951) reported fifteen instances of such vocalizations in seven patients.

The first report of this phenomenon was by Brickner (1940), before the SMA was even discovered. As Brickner describes it, this particular property of the area "was discovered accidentally during routine exploration. The patient suddenly uttered syllables resembling 'err, err, err,' in what seemed a stereotyped manner" (p. 128).

Since Brickner's study, there have been numerous other reports of this phenomenon, not only by Penfield and his colleagues but also by others. (For a summary see MacNeilage and Davis, 2001). Although specific findings in subsequent studies varied, the theme of repetition of a non-meaningful speech form in a rhythmic manner continually recurs. The most common phonetic description is of a series of consonant–vowel syllables, typically repetitions of the same syllable. It's very important to note that this particular phenomenon has not been observed in studies of stimulation in any other part of the brain—not even in the basal ganglia, a motor center closely linked to the SMA. In contrast, stimulation of Broca's area results in interference with or suppression of ongoing speech, but not in evocation of phonetically well-formed syllable sequences, either meaningful or non-meaningful (Ojemann, 1983).

In commenting on this tendency to rhythmically repeat syllables following electrical stimulation, Penfield and Welch (1951) made what I consider to be an extremely prescient remark: "these mechanisms, which we have activated by gross artificial stimuli, may, however, under different conditions, be important in the production of the varied sounds which men often use to communicate ideas" (p. 303). Unfortunately, this suggestion has been almost totally ignored.

In the context of F/C there is one notable fact about the effects of electrical stimulation on humans. It is that the only two instances of evocation of rhythmic mandibular cyclicities are mutually exclusive. Stimulation of ventral premotor cortex only evokes chewing, not CV sequences, and stimulation of the SMA evokes only CV sequences, not chewing. My hypothesis is that frames came into initial communicative use in smacks in extrinsic cortex as an exaptation from the ingestive mandibular cyclicities already controlled there. Then, in hominids, as the capacity for spontaneous generation of series of frames for spontaneous speech purposes evolved, superordinate control of frame generation for this particular purpose shifted from the extrinsic to the intrinsic system. The basic ingestive cyclicities themselves continued to be controlled in the extrinsic system because they continued to be dependent, for their successful use, on oral somatic sensory information accompanying food processing, available from adjacent primary somatosensory cortex.

One could be tempted to argue that this rhythmic syllabic-repetition phenomenon is simply an artifact of the electrical stimulation and has nothing to do with normal brain organization. But a similar phenomenon has repeatedly been observed in patients with irritative lesions affecting the SMA. An example of an irritative lesion would be an adjacent tumor exerting pressure on SMA tissue. A clinical description by Jonas (1981) gives the flavor of the phenomenon:

A 37-year-old lady... suddenly found herself saying "la, la, la, la" at 6:05 p.m. on 2/19/79. This preceded a seizure in which she became unconscious. On 2/24/79 she had a spell during which she said "da, da, da, da"; she neither could stop making this sound nor could she speak. There were some other motor signs of a seizure. The phenomena subsided in 7 or 8 minutes. (Jonas, Case 3, p. 355)

This patient proved to have a meningioma lying against the SMA.

In all, Jonas (1981) described twelve patients who produced this repetitive type of vocalization, eleven in five other studies, and the one he himself studied. (For a summary, see MacNeilage and Davis, 2005b.) The similarity between these irritative lesion effects and the electrical stimulation effects is quite striking, as was noted by some of the researchers themselves. The highly specific and speech-like nature of these phenomena suggests that they aren't examples of artificially evoked disorganization of function, but rather of release of a function normally used in speech but not normally revealed independently of meaningful speech acts in adults.

Ziegler, Kilian, and Deger (1997) have made the most comprehensive study of the speech of a patient with problems involving the SMA. They showed, in a word-repetition task, that onset latencies for speech increased as the number of syllables in the word increased, but the patient showed no effect of the complexity of the syllables involved. Their conclusion that the SMA is involved in "downloading temporarily stored multisyllabic strings" is consistent with my claim that the SMA is involved in frame generation.

When the thesis that the SMA was responsible for frame generation was first presented (MacNeilage, 1998a), three reviewers contended that both frames and content are mediated primarily by ventral premotor cortex (Abbs and de Paul, 1998; Jürgens, 1998; Lund, 1998). None of these reviewers dealt with the evidence from electrical-stimulation studies and irritative-lesion studies of the SMA summarized above. Nor did they provide any evidence for their alternative conception. But another group of reviewers did produce evidence that patients can generate frames even when Broca's area has been destroyed. Abry et al. (1998, 2002) called attention to a subclass of global aphasics that behave in that way. Global aphasics have extensive damage to the left hemisphere, leaving them unable to comprehend or produce normal speech. Many of these patients are virtually entirely mute, but some produce, as their sole vocalizations, speech automatisms called "non-meaningful recurrent utterances" (NMRUs) (Blanken et al., 1990). Like babbled utterances and the involuntary utterances of patients subject to electrical stimulation or irritative lesions of the SMA, NMRUs characteristically consist of a repetitive sequence of a single CV syllable (Blanken, Wallesch, and Papagno, 1990; Brunner, et al., 1982; Code, 1982, 1994, 2002; DeBleser and Poeck, 1985; Poeck, DeBleser, and von Keyserlingk, 1984; Wallesch, 1990). As global aphasia typically results from the destruction of the entire perisylvian language cortex, Broca's area cannot be involved in these utterances. It's of interest to note that Broca's first patient, Leborgne, suffered from this syndrome. That is, he was, in fact, a global aphasic rather than a Broca's aphasic. He was nicknamed "Tan" because the only speech he could produce was repetitions of this syllable (Abry et al., 2002). (It is actually a CV syllable because "an" in "Tan" stands for a nasal vowel in French.)

A relatively large number of specific utterances of these patients have been reported. This data allows a detailed comparison of the structure of these utterances with the structure of infant babbling. Code (1982) has presented thirty examples of utterances produced by seventeen English patients. All but two patients produced only a single form. Blanken, Wallesch, and Papagno (1990) presented utterances from twenty-seven German patients. The babbling and aphasic corpora are remarkably similar. At least three-quarters of all syllables were CV syllables in all groups. In addition, when pairs of successive syllables were compared, the two syllables were the same approximately half of the time.

Why do some global aphasics produce NMRUs while others don't? Brunner et al. (1982) found that while both subgroups were similar in having massive perisylvian damage, the group who produced NMRUs also had damage to the basal ganglia. They hypothesized, in the light of knowledge that the basal ganglia normally exert an inhibitory effect, that the basal ganglia damage resulted in a disinhibitory effect on speech. But as perisylvian cortex was unable to supply meaningful speech, the outcome was these simple stereotyped forms. The implication is that these forms are in some sense present in the normal brain, but don't manifest themselves under ordinary circumstances.

The most important recipient of the basal ganglia's contribution to movement is the SMA. Therefore, any disinhibitory effect of basal ganglia damage on movement must have its primary effect there. In patients with perisylvian and basal ganglia damage, the SMA is the only remaining intact region of the brain characteristically involved in the organization of speech production. Consequently, it must be primarily responsible for the production of NMRUs. This contention is supported by the similarity of NMRUs to the automatisms produced by electrical stimulation and irritative lesions of the SMA. The NMRUs and the SMA automatisms seem to be instances of the same phenomenon, elicited in the first case by an electrical current, and in the second by abnormal (artificial or disease-related) tissue perturbations.

How can the existence of these speech automatisms be explained? My conclusion is that the speech automatisms reveal the existence of a neural component of the mental-motor interface for speech production, and that it evolved and develops from the motor frame in the course of establishing a mental representation for speech. To support this conclusion we first need to reconsider the ontogenetic situation.

In an infant, the motor frame first appears at the onset of canonical babbling before the infant can produce any meaningful speech. A short time after the infant begins to acquire spoken words, at about 1 year, a general-purpose superstructure for their mental representation perhaps begins to crystallize out by means of self-organization. Adult speech errors show us that this mental representation eventually includes independent segmental and syllable-structure components. As we have seen earlier, the close–open alternation is a constant part of the developmental process. Consequently, this movement alternation eventually acquires a separate abstract representational status, somewhat independent of the particular close–open movements for individual words as well as the detailed syllable structure of words (such as how many consonants are in particular closing phases). In short, *the motor frame spawns a premotor frame.* The derivation of this premotor or cognitive frame structure from speech behaviors early in ontogeny allows us to understand why adult patients, in three different sets of circumstances, produce such a childlike form, so superficially unrelated to their pre-morbid speech behavior.

As befits its intermediate status between detailed movements and abstract mental structures for words, this frame is best described as a "cognitive-motor" entity. It is cognitive enough to allow elaborate modifications for particular syllables. In English, for example, detailed modifications might involve not one but several consonants (e.g., "*spring*"). The ordering of these sounds in syllables is premotor in the sense that it must be laid down before the movements needed to proceed from one segment to the next are computed. But it's still sufficiently closely related to actual movements to have its own basic rhythmic figure, resulting in a characteristic average cycle time or period, which, when varying as it does across individuals, results in their different basic speaking rates.

I see the phylogenetic derivation of this cognitive-motor frame as being similar to its ontogenetic derivation. I believe the first words were produced with *motor* frames with a predominant CV form (MacNeilage and Davis, 2000). But as words continued to accumulate, a general-purpose CV superstructure for the mental representation of this action constant must have begun to crystalize out, and the cognitive motor frame played a role in this as part of the mental-motor interface necessary for producing individual speech events required by various lexical representations. Thus in both phylogeny and ontogeny, mental structure is considered to derive from regularities in movement patterns.

9.2 A revised conception of the extrinsic system

So far I have been trying to sketch out the consequences of needing to add the intrinsic system to the classical Wernicke–Geschwind conception of brain–language relationships, a conception confined to the extrinsic system. But the extrinsic system itself must be revised to be consistent with current knowledge of brain/speech relations. One thing that makes this necessary is the existence of "working memory." According to Baddeley, that term "refers to the assumption that some kind of temporary storage of information is necessary for performing a wide range of cognitive skills including comprehension, learning and reasoning" (Baddeley, 1995, p. 755). An everyday event that indicates the existence of this temporary storage mode, requiring continuous rehearsal, is the way in which a distraction can make us forget a whole telephone number if we're inter-rupted while going from the telephone, where we heard the number, to the site of a pen and paper, where we intended to write it down.

Baddeley and Hitch (1974) have presented a tripartite model of working memory:

> This assumes an attentional controller, the *central executive*, that is aided by two slave systems, the *visuospatial sketchpad*, which is able to hold and manipulate visual and spatial images, and the *phonological loop*, which involves a speech-based system. The central executive is a limited-capacity system that is responsible for providing the link between the slave systems and the LTM (long-term memory) and which is responsible for strategy selection and planning. (Baddeley, 1995, p. 760)

The central executive is located in prefrontal cortex. Baddeley describes the phonological slave system for speech in this way: "The phonological loop appears to comprise two components—a memory store capable of holding phonological information for a period of one or two seconds, coupled with an articulatory control process" (p. 761). Memory traces can be refreshed, though, by subvocal articulation, which is what is disrupted by the interruption in the telephone-number situation described above.

The phonological-loop conception of verbal working memory must be a central one in our attempt to understand the evolution of speech. Baddeley has said that the phonological loop of working memory "has evolved, probably from more basic auditory and verbal production mechanisms, as a device for language acquisition" (Baddeley, 1995, p. 762). Brain-imaging studies have shown that the subvocal articulation capacity is in ventral premotor cortex, which is consistent with Broca's original conception that this region mediates "motor images" for speech and can therefore be included in the Wernicke–Geschwind model. But the memory-store component is in posterior parietal cortex. Given the role of the parietal lobe in somatic sensation and perception, the contribution of the parietal lobe to verbal working memory, and therefore to the production of speech in general, is presumably the provision of orosensory goals (Perkell et al., 1995) or perhaps oral-spatial targets (MacNeilage, 1970). The existence of this memory-store component in the parietal lobe makes it necessary to revise the Wernicke–Geschwind conception of the extrinsic system for language.

Three roles for working memory in speech can be distinguished. One, applicable to the child, is the temporary holding of feedback—auditory, somatosensory, and motor—from an attempt to make a word, so that the attempt can be compared with a target representation. This must be important in word-learning. The second is the holding of incoming information during the process of comprehension. The third is the holding of output information in various stages of completion during the assembly of a spoken sentence. It is in this latter process that serial-ordering errors in speech production occur. One of Lashley's signal contributions was to point out, before the concept of working memory existed, that serial-ordering errors of speech which involve two different pieces of a planned sequence of speech erroneously changing places with each other, as in spoonerisms, entail the existence of a buffer—a temporary store in which the two pieces were simultaneously activated. There must have been continual selection pressures on the size of this buffer as utterances became increasingly long.

Arboitiz and García (1997) provide us an important set of arguments for why we need to elaborate the Wernicke–Geschwind conception and include parietal cortex and working memory in a theory of evolution of speech. Let me summarize some key points of their proposal. They assert that

the neural device involved in language is embedded into a large scale neurocognitive network comprising widespread connections between temporal parietal and frontal (especially prefrontal) cortices. This network is involved in the temporal organization of behavior and motor sequences and in working (active) memory. (p. 381)

The role for prefrontal cortex envisaged here includes the operation of the central executive of working memory.

They go on to say, "In human evolution, a precondition for language was the establishment of strong cortico-cortical interactions in the postrolandic cortex that enabled the development of multimodal associations" (p. 381). Here they are apparently referring to concepts such as object concepts, which are the bases for nouns in particular. As I pointed out earlier, such concepts involve the "What is it?" system with a terminal locus in the temporal lobes. For example, a spoon is represented in the visual modality (what it looks like), in the auditory modality (what it sounds like if you drop it), and in the somatic sensory modality (what it feels like in the hand or mouth). Of course, there is also a motor representation (how you use it), though this might primarily involve prerolandic (frontal) cortex.

Then they propose that "Wernicke's area originated as a converging place in which such multimodal associations (concepts) acquired a phonological correlate" (p. 381). As Wernicke's area is auditory association cortex, the phonological representation would of course be primarily in auditory terms.

With regard to the evolution of working memory, they postulate that these phonological representations projected into inferoparietal areas, which were connected to the incipient Broca's area, thus forming a working-memory circuit for processing and learning complex vocalizations. They go on to argue that "As a result of selective pressure for learning capacity and memory storage, this device yielded a sophisticated system able to generate complicated utterances (precursors of syntax) as it became increasingly connected with other brain regions, especially in the prefrontal cortex" (p. 381).

As part of their thesis, they endeavor to indicate the extent to which the necessary circuitry for the phonological aspects of this conception is present in monkeys. They find a strong link between inferior parietal cortex and the monkey homolog of Broca's area. They point out that "The latter makes functional sense as it provides the basis for a somatosensory-motor circuit for coordination of orofacial movements" (p. 386). It also makes sense in terms of my emphasis on ingestive action capabilities as a basis for subsequent speech. They cite the failure of Cavada and Goldman-Rakic (1989) to find temporo-parietal connections homologous to human ones in monkeys. But they do find evidence for a direct temporofrontal connection, similar to the human one via the arcuate fasciculus. It tends to terminate in front of the monkey homolog of Broca's area, in prefrontal cortex, consistent with the findings of auditory sensitivity in this region mentioned earlier.

Consequently, they propose that two important developments may have occurred in the path to language evolution. The first was that "the superior temporal region (area Tpt) became increasingly connected with the inferoparietal regions" (p. 386). In their view, "This contributed to produce a strong link between the auditory system and a parieto-premotor loop involved in the generation of complex vocalizations" (p. 386). "The second process may have been the development of direct connections between the precursor of Wernicke's region and areas 44/45 and prefrontal sectors such as area 46, which served as a parallel pathway to send auditory information to the orofacial premotor region" (p. 386).

Rather spectacular support for some aspects of Arboitiz and García's conception of the evolution of the structures and pathways necessary for speech comes from some very recent findings regarding the connectivities of the various perisylvian regions in humans. Until recently, brain-imaging techniques weren't able to provide anatomical evidence regarding pathways in subcortical white matter of living subjects. But using the technique of (brace yourself) "in vivo diffusion tensor magnetic resonance imaging tractography," Catani, Jones, and ffytche (2005) found that "Beyond the classical arcuate pathway connecting Broca's and Wernicke's areas directly [there is] a previously undescribed indirect pathway passing through inferior parietal cortex. The indirect pathway runs parallel and lateral to the classical arcuate fasciculus and is composed of an anterior segment connecting Broca's territory with the inferior parietal lobe and a posterior segment connecting the inferior parietal lobe to Wernicke's territory" (p. 8). Thus they not only confirm the continued existence of the temporofrontal and parietofrontal pathways found in monkeys, but they also find the emergent temporoparietal pathway postulated by Arboitiz and García.

Besides fitting more or less perfectly with Arboitiz and García's conception, the findings of Catani et al. also seem to resolve a long-standing puzzle regarding conduction aphasia. According to Wernicke's model, there should be only one kind of conduction aphasia: the patient should have normal comprehension and spontaneous production of speech but impaired repetition. But other symptom patterns result from perisylvian damage between Wernicke's and Broca's area.

In a paper entitled "A Two-Route Model of Speech Production," McCarthy and Warrington (1984) presented two patients showing the typical pattern mentioned above with temporoparietal lesions extending into white matter. However, a third patient with a superficial lesion of parietal cortex had difficulties with spontaneous speech production but with relatively intact repetition. Warrington and McCarthy suggested that the first two patients had damage to a direct route between Wernicke's and Broca's areas subserving fast automatic word repetition, whereas the third patient had damage to an indirect pathway with a stage of verbal comprehension and semantic-to-phonological transcoding between verbal input and articulatory output.

Catani et al. see their findings as being consistent with the results of Warrington and McCarthy (1984). While their first two patients may have had damage to the classical pathway, the third patient may have had damage at and around the confluence of the temporoparietal and parietofrontal pathways.

Taken together, the work of Arboitiz and García and Catani et al. leads us to the possibility of a tripartite cognitive representation of speech in the extrinsic system, with reciprocal interconnecting pathways between each region and the two others. Thus, in addition to having separate reciprocal connections with somatosensory and motor regions, the auditory component of this system would also contain representations linked to concepts—the bases for words—which would serve the lexical access process for both comprehension and production. With regard to speech production, the direct route from auditory to motor representations via the arcuate fasciculus allows remarkably fast repetitions (called "shadowing") with little reference to semantic information (Kozhevnikov and Chistovich, 1965). The route to production via parietal cortex allows the generation of motor representations from lexical (conceptual/auditory) representations via somatosensory goals/targets in spontaneous self-generated speech. And importantly, as Catani et al. point out, "the mirror neuron system includes inferior frontal, inferior parietal, and superior temporal regions" (2005, p. 14). We can therefore think of this revised Wernicke–Geschwind system as having the mimetic capability for learning the 6,000 or so extant modern languages.

We need to note here that the syndrome resulting from medial cortical damage is, in an important way, opposite to the classical conduction-aphasia pattern. While the conduction aphasic has good spontaneous speech though often with a *difficulty of repetition*, the medial aphasic has absent or halting spontaneous speech *with good repetition*. The preserved repetition ability of medial aphasics is apparently the result of having an intact perisylvian system, particularly an intact direct temporofrontal pathway. In the light of the characterization of perisylvian cortex as *extrinsic*, it can be concluded that external stimulation from a speaking model is sufficient to overcome frame-generation limitations of the system in the medial syndrome, allowing production of acceptable repetition. In accordance with this conclusion, Passingham (1987) has suggested that in instances of good repetition in patients with little spontaneous speech, due to SMA and ACC damage, "it is Broca's area speaking" (p. 159).

9.3 Coordination of the extrinsic and intrinsic systems

It is of course necessary under normal conditions for the activity of the extrinsic system to be coordinated with the intrinsic system, especially for spontaneous speech. Though the anatomical basis for this particular connection is not clear, posterior cortical representations for words need to make contact with the SMA, perhaps primarily via parietal cortex, and the activity of the SMA needs to be coordinated with ventral premotor activity. The primary information involved here would be related to frame generation. For a spontaneously generated word it would be necessary to transmit information via this route regarding how many frames were necessary and perhaps what the lexical stress pattern of the word is (e.g., [con'tent] versus [con tent']).

A clue to how the SMA transmits information to ventral premotor cortex comes from consideration of a rather peculiar aphasic syndrome termed Transcortical Motor Aphasia (TCMA) (Rubens, 1976), or, in Luria's terms, "Dynamic Aphasia" (Luria, 1970). This syndrome is in many ways similar to the one resulting from damage to medial cortex. Its main properties are a limited ability to produce spontaneous speech, but with intact repetition ability and good auditory comprehension. However, in this case, the inability to produce spontaneous speech cannot be attributed to limbic control of affective processes since the limbic system is not involved. Neither can it be attributed to SMA damage. A study of Freedman, Alexander, and Naeser (1984) involving CT scans of 15 patients including 7 deemed to be classical TCMA patients concluded that "the essential lesion is disruption of connections at sites between the supplementary motor area and the frontal perisylvian speech zone" (p. 409). I would suggest that another name for this syndrome could be "Frame Transmission Aphasia." The primary cause of the deficit may be loss of the normal ability to transfer internally generated frame-control signals from the SMA to ventral frontal cortex for elaboration of the content component. This is in accord with Eccles' suggestion that "SMA projects to primary motor cortex largely via the [ventral] premotor area, where there can be refinement in the instructions to the motor cortex" (1989, p. 183).

Another instance in which perisylvian cortex alone is sufficient for repetition is the syndrome of "Isolation of the Speech Area" (Geschwind, Quadfasel, and Segarra, 1968). A typical patient in this class has had carbon monoxide poisoning, which can lead to the loss of all cortex except perisylvian cortex because the latter is fed most directly by the middle cerebral artery—the main blood supply to lateral cortex. The perisylvian region is therefore more likely to have retained some residual blood supply and therefore some functional cortical tissue. Consequently, the direct temporofrontal pathway via the arcuate fasciculus can still be used for repetition. In fact, repetition tends to be obligatory in these patients because they lack the normal ability to choose whether to repeat something or not. This obligatory mode of repetition seems to be a counterpart, in the extrinsic system, to the obligation of global aphasic patients to repeat only a single CV syllable, mediated by the intrinsic system, when they are presumably attempting propositional speech. In each case a normally existing capability of the speech system is disconnected from discretionary supervision.

9.4 Schematic view of brain organization for speech production

A schematic view of the organization of spontaneous speech production suggested by the foregoing discussion is shown in Fig. 9.1. The immediate activation of the system (forgetting for the moment intentional and motivational factors) begins with the activation of concept/sound linkages for particular words (especially nouns) in Wernicke's area.

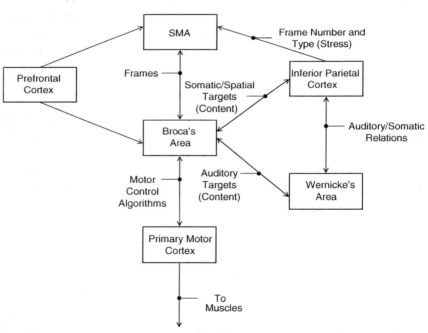

FIG. 9.1   Schematic view of the cortical organization of speech production.

At that point, there are two possible ways to obtain speech actions. One is through a direct link via the arcuate fasciculus to motor algorithms in ventral premotor cortex (Brodmann's area 44, the posterior part of Broca's area), and then to primary motor cortex and out to the muscles. This is the circuit involved in repetition. The other way is through a dual route activated in spontaneously generated propositional speech. In one of these routes, information regarding the number of frames and possibly stress-related information is sent to the SMA. From there the basis for realizing frames in terms of movement is sent to ventral premotor cortex. In the other route, content-related information regarding the types of segments and their serial ordering is sent to ventral premotor cortex from Wernicke's area via an indirect pathway, with an intermediate stage of somatic/spatial target formation in inferior parietal cortex. Frame and content information is put together in ventral premotor cortex, and the result is sent to the periphery via primary motor cortex. The concurrent activation of inferior parietal cortex and ventral premotor cortex during this process is the main basis for working memory, although Wernicke's area and the SMA are probably also involved in this to some extent.

It should be recognized that this conception of the phylogeny of brain organization for speech is oversimplified. In particular, it tends to treat each of the three lobes involved in the perisylvian component as playing single homogeneous functional roles. We know this isn't the case. For example, Indefrey and Levelt (2000) provide a much more differentiated view of temporal lobe function. In addition, Catrin Blank et al. (2002) provide evidence of a much more elaborate and nuanced pattern of brain activation during spontaneous speech than would be expected from the model presented here. But the conception might nevertheless be correct in broad outline, and it does provide us with the opportunity to raise some important evolutionary issues regarding brain/speech relationships.

9.5 The generativist approach to brain/language relations

As a footnote, let us briefly consider how the generativists would address Tinbergen's imaginary fifth question regarding speech—how is it organized in the brain? Their stance is well summarized by Caplan (1994). He states that "language processing is carried out only in perisylvian association cortex" (p. 1043). He considers this to be so because the region "contains a genetically determined system allowing the activation of abstract linguistic codes and of computational processes applying to the representations specified in these codes" (p. 1045). He correctly points out that this view "contrasts sharply with the classical connectionist theory and many other localizationist models that maintain that language functions are localized in perisylvian cortex because of the relationship of these areas to cortical structures supporting other aspects of sensory and motor functions" (p. 1045).

I have argued that the evolution of a general-purpose dichotomous (intrinsic/extrinsic) control system in which the two components have had, and still have complementary roles has been the main event in the phylogeny of neural control of speech production, and manual function as well. I contend that a response to the exigencies associated with evolving an action system that is at the same time under intentional control and dependent on extrinsic information for its acquisition and use is what has given us the neural basis of both the speech and the manual function we have today.

My stance differs from Caplan's in two major respects. His perspective includes no role for the intrinsic system, and no functional relationship between speech/language and anything else. I have shown that the intrinsic system cannot be left out of the picture, and I have provided evidence for functional parallels between vocal and manual organization.

Perhaps most importantly, the intrinsic/extrinsic dichotomy will presumably be of little interest to the generativists because it is a performance-level phenomenon. Thus while I argue that the history of speech performance is the key to understanding the present neural basis of speech, the generativists would consider the performance level to be basically irrelevant.

9.6 Summary

Let me briefly summarize the last two chapters. The existence of the same two sets of brain areas and pathways related to action in monkeys and humans—one intrinsic, the other extrinsic—suggests that these areas and pathways provided a basis for the evolution of both mimesis and speech. What has happened in the progression from ancestral monkeys to humans has been a set of further developments of the functions that they mediate.

Monkeys ancestral to humans presumably had four precursors to the human action capabilities we are considering. First, they had a medial intrinsic system, central to spontaneous action generation, whether vocal or manual. Second, in the inferior frontal cortical homolog of Broca's area and its surround, they had ingestive motor-control capabilities including mandibular oscillation, the basis for frames and for the subsequent elaboration of content. Third, they had vocal perceptual capabilities in inferior frontal cortex, capabilities presumably related to establishing input–output relations with an auditory-motor basis. Fourth, they had an extrinsic system component involving mirror neurons, providing a basis for mimetic evolution. They may even have had mirror neurons associated with lipsmacks and vocal communication.

What humans evolved, using, for the most part, the same circuitry, was a general-purpose mimetic capability. For speech, what evolved was a capability of programming frames, mediated by the intrinsic system, with content elements mediated by the extrinsic system, according to codes for sound–meaning relations laid down in a lexicon in temporal cortex. The evolution of working memory, involving a new role for parietal cortex, allowed the input–output comparisons needed for vocal learning to occur, and allowed time-extended speech to be processed online in both comprehension and production.

10 Evolution of cerebral hemispheric specialization for speech

10.1 Introduction

The question we need to ask now is at once very simple and very important: Why is speech production usually vested in the left cerebral hemisphere?

Paul Broca's discovery, in 1861, that this was the case was a momentous one, because it gave us the first inkling that *any* function could be lateralized to one hemisphere in the vertebrate brain. The species-specific nature of speech/language, together with the Cartesian view that humans are different, encouraged people to conclude from Broca's finding that hemispheric specialization itself was a uniquely human characteristic. The additional fact that the usually-favored right hand was also controlled by the left hemisphere has led to a vigorous tradition of theories of origin of hemispheric specializations that are confined to the relation between the two functions in *humans*—an anthropocentric tradition that is still very much with us, as we shall see.

The most prevalent view of the origin of the hand–mouth relationship in the latter part of the last century was that the adaptation in tool use which occurred in *Homo habilis* about 2 million years ago led to a left-hemispheric specialization for manual "praxis" (basically motor skill) and that the first language was a gestural language built on this basis. Gordon Hewes (e.g., Hewes, 1973) was the first proponent of this view, which was subsequently adopted by Doreen Kimura and Michael Corballis. In 1979, Kimura expressed the belief that "a manual system of communication may have preceded the vocal system of communication in man.... The manual system of communication could very easily have been built on manual skills already developed in association with tool use" (p 202). She states:

It seems not too farfetched to suppose that cerebral asymmetry of function developed in conjunction with the asymmetric activity of the two limbs during tool use, the left hemisphere, for reasons uncertain, becoming the hemisphere specialized for precise sequential limb positioning. When a gestural system was employed, therefore, it would presumably also be controlled primarily from the left hemisphere. If speech were indeed a later development, it is reasonable to suppose that it would also come under the direction of the hemisphere already well developed for precise motor control. (p. 203)

Kimura's theme that the left hemisphere became specialized for *sequencing* manual movements, and that it was this specialization which was taken over for speech, has been a common one.

Corballis, in his 1991 book *The Lopsided Ape*, also suggests, as one possibility, that the first language may have been gestural and also surmises that "It may have evolved first in the contexts of tool making" (p. 164). More recently, in response to the fact that many vertebrates have a left-hemisphere specialization for vocal communication, he has suggested that an initial stage of vocal language preceded gestural language, which in turn preceded modern vocal language (Corballis, 2003). I will consider the question of whether a gestural language preceded modern vocal language in Chapter 13, only noting here, as I did in response to his paper (MacNeilage, 2003), that *two* modality switches in the history of language seems rather extravagant, especially if one regards evolution as basically conservative.

The generally acknowledged specializations of the modern human right hemisphere seem to be for emotion and for spatial function. Although Corballis (1991) was unusual in conceding that the origin of these specializations may have predated humans, he nevertheless espoused the common view that they may have primarily evolved to their high levels in humans by default, when the left hemisphere had to give up its day job so to speak, as a consequence of the drastic modification of the left hemisphere for skilled hand control/language.

In short, the most well-known approaches to the evolution of cerebral hemispheric specializations have been heavily anthropocentric, and centered on an original formative left-hemisphere praxic specialization, from which language followed, and a subsequent elaboration of right-hemisphere specializations, primarily by default. But things have changed radically in the last generation or so. There is now a plethora of findings of hemispheric specializations in all major vertebrate groups. See, for example, Rogers and Andrew, 2002; Vallortigara and Rogers, 2005.

There have been two responses to this development. One is to regard the hemispheric-specialization phenomenon as sporadic—a set of scattered unrelated hemispheric specializations in various vertebrate subgroups. For example, Hiscock and Kinsbourne (1995) conclude that "the animal data fail to suggest a general principle relating brain lateralization to behavior" (p. 563). In addition to flying in the face of Darwin's tenet of descent with modification, this approach again raises the problem noted by Cartmill, Pilbeam, and Isaac (1986) in Chapter 1—a problem they say was initially identified by Scottish philosopher, David Hume. Any singularity brings with it its own equally singular explanatory problem, and the stance of Hiscock and Kinsbourne brings with it the task of explaining a number of singularities.

The other approach is to seek an integrated view of the evolution of hemispheric specializations across the vertebrate phylum, consistent with the Darwinian tenets of descent with modification and the lowly origins of higher-order adaptive properties in general. This has been my approach (see MacNeilage, 2007; see also Vallortigara and Rogers, 2005).

The context for my initial consideration of this issue brought me face-to-face with the unanimous conclusion that among the human specializations discussed above, the only one that was generally considered to have *no* precursors was right-handedness. For example, as recently as 1991 Corballis felt able to say, "Right handedness thus serves as a marker for humanity; it is both universally and uniquely human" (p. 104). Bjorn Lindblom, Michael Studdert-Kennedy, and I began our effort to find out how left-hemisphere speech fits into the picture of evolution of lateralized specializations of the brain with a reevaluation of this anthropocentric notion that handedness originated in hominids (MacNeilage, Studdert-Kennedy, and Lindblom, 1987). This inquiry eventually led to the rather surprising conclusion that, contrary to common belief, population-level handedness is common in primates and it has a highly differentiated pattern related to various ecological aspects of primate life. This led to the conclusion that the *origin* of the human left-hemispheric praxic specialization, commonly thought to be a basis for the left-hemisphere speech capacity, cannot be attributed to the tool-use adaptation in *Homo habilis* (MacNeilage, 2007).

Meanwhile, evidence had continued to accumulate establishing that a left-hemisphere *vocal*-communication specialization is not specific to humans but is instead widespread in vertebrates. This means that an anthropocentric hand-to-mouth scenario for the *origin* of the speech specialization from manual praxis doesn't work either.

In response to the consequent need to place both the vocal and manual control lateralities of humans in a broader perspective, I suggested the possibility that there have been two complementary hemispheric specializations in all vertebrates—routine and emergency (MacNeilage, 1998b; 2007). In this view, the vocal-communication specialization and the manual specialization of the right hand were separate offshoots of the left-hemisphere routine-action-control specialization.

To see how this rather radically different conclusion from the anthropocentric one was possible, we need to look in some detail at what light a generation or so of studies of primate handedness has thrown on the nature of handedness, and then we need to consider the implications of the widespread existence of a left-hemisphere specialization for vocal communication in vertebrates.

My colleagues Lindblom and Studdert-Kennedy and I originally became interested in the question of primate handedness in the context of the frame/content theory. My initial conception regarding the origin of the frame/content mode of organization (since abandoned—see MacNeilage, 1998b, for an alternative view) was that it could have evolved from a particular form of bimanual coordination—the kind in which an object, such as a plastic container full of pills, is held in one hand while its lid is removed and a pill is taken by the other hand. In such a mode, the support hand provides the frame, and operations of the preferred hand constitute content elements.

As we knew that a number of non-human primates had good bimanual coordination (see, for example, Trevarthen, 1978), we turned our attention to the primate-handedness literature, expecting that it would throw light on the phylogeny of human handedness and consequently on speech evolution. To our surprise, we found that nobody thought that primate populations had any sign of a human-like right-hand preference—that is, a tendency to prefer the right hand for manual actions. The accepted authority on this question was J. M. Warren. In a number of review papers (e.g., Warren, 1980) he concluded unequivocally that handedness in other primates differed from human handedness in two ways. First, right-handers and left-handers were about equal in number, but there were also many animals with no hand preference. Second, certain animals showed a tendency to prefer different hands for different tasks.

Primate handedness seemed, then, to be a dead issue. But in looking into this question we found that Warren's obituaries were a bit premature. We found some instances of statistically significant population-level tendencies toward hand preference that were not included in the Warren reviews. He had never reviewed more than thirteen studies at a time. We reviewed forty-five, and published our results in the peer-review journal *Behavioral and Brain Sciences* (MacNeilage, Studdert-Kennedy, and Lindblom, 1987). Before summarizing our review and the Postural Origins (PO) Theory that arose from it, I will make a few brief orienting remarks about primates. (For a primate taxonomy, see Purvis, 1995.)

A defining characteristic of the 234 species constituting the primate order (Rowe, 1996) is that, with a few exceptions (including, notably, ourselves), they are *arboreal* mammals—they live in the trees. The first primates may have begun to evolve in the explosive mammalian radiation that followed the extinction of the dinosaurs about 65 million years ago (mya). The original true primates, of which some modern "prosimians" are the closest living counterparts—evolved as early as 55 mya, descending from an animal something like a modern squirrel or marmot. In what could be described as a three-dimensional experiment, these animals came to live entirely in the trees.

Prosimians (e.g., lemurs, lorises) are visually distinguishable from other primates by their pointed, dog-like faces. Most of the fifty species of modern prosimians (Rowe, 1996) live in central Africa and Madagascar, but some live in Southeast Asia as well. About 40 mya, a distinct "simian" (monkey and ape) taxon evolved, giving rise to two major groups of monkeys—New World monkeys, living in the Americas, and Old World monkeys, living in Eurasia and Africa (Byrne, 2000). Apes perhaps began to evolve at about 30 mya, and a split between the lesser apes (gibbons and siamangs) and a line leading to the great apes—a group now comprising orangutans, gorillas, chimpanzees, and hominids—may have originated at about 20 mya.

One of the most important findings of the past couple of decades is that, according to DNA dating evidence, we and our nearest relations, chimpanzees, may have shared a common ancestor as recently as 4–6 million years ago (Byrne, 2000).

10.2 Primate handedness: the new picture

In the words of Parnell, our review of primate-handedness studies has become "widely accepted as breathing new life into this area of study" (Parnell, 2001, p. 365). It has provoked well over a hundred studies (See MacNeilage, 2007, for a detailed summary). Here is the picture that has emerged.

There have been at least a dozen studies confirming an earlier indication of a left hand preference for reaching for food in prosimians, many of which are summarized by Ward, Millikan, and Stafford (1993). This trend led us to argue that the postural demands of rapid, one-handed predatory reaching while clinging vertically in an arboreal habitat, as ancestral primates apparently did, may have given rise to this preference. And there may have been two hemispheric specializations related to it—a specialization of the left hand/right hemisphere for unimanual predatory prehension, and a specialization of the right side of the body, controlled by the left hemisphere, for postural support (MacNeilage, Studdert-Kennedy, and Lindblom, 1987).

Further examples of the left-hand preference for simple reaching in monkeys that we noted in 1987 have also been observed, for example, in marmosets (Hook-Costigan and Rogers, 1996), spider monkeys (Laska, 1996), Japanese macaques (Watanabe and Kawai, 1993), and rhesus macaques (Westergaard, Kuhn, and Suomi, 1998). There was even one study that suggested the continuation in monkeys of the rapid predatory left-hand movement specialization observed in prosimians. King and Landau (1993) found that while a group of sixteen squirrel monkeys showed no overall hand preference for quadrupedal reaching for objects on the cage floor, a significant majority of them (13 out of 16) showed a predominant left-hand preference for the extremely rapid movement necessary for catching goldfish in a bowl or in a pool.

In addition, there were many more studies confirming the previously observed trend towards right-hand preferences in monkeys for tasks requiring manipulative skill. Most relevant to the initial reason that we directed our attention to primate handedness are a number of studies that show a right-hand preference for bimanual coordination. A right-hand preference for extracting the peanut butter from one end of a PVC pipe held by the other hand was found in rhesus monkeys by Westergaard and Suomi (1996). It has also been found in cebus monkeys by Spinozzi, Castorina, and Truppa (1998), though not by Westergaard and Suomi (1996). Most recently, in a large-scale study of 104 baboons, Vauclair, Meguerditchian, and Hopkins (2005) found that although there was no overall hand preference for simple reaching, there was a significant excess of right-hand over left-hand preferences in the tube test (52:33). The finding of many right-hand preferences in species of monkeys with relatively well-developed manipulative capabilities confirms our original suspicion that because bimanual coordination in many primates is similar to that in humans, it should be accompanied by human-like right-handedness.

As we originally surmised, posture proved to be an important variable in the direction of hand preference. For example, Hook-Costigan and Rogers (1996), in a review of thirty-two studies of hand preferences in New World monkeys, concluded that "the posture adopted during hand use appears to be the most influential variable on handedness..." (p. 200). In addition, Westergaard, Kuhn, and Suomi (1998) concluded from a review of comparisons of reaching from a quadrupedal and bipedal posture in a number of nonhuman primate species that "Highly dextrous [manipulative] primates...but not less dextrous species...are predisposed towards greater use of the right hand when in bipedal posture" (p. 62).

Capuchin (cebus) monkeys are generally considered to be the most manually versatile monkeys. They use tools in captivity (Visalberghi and Fragaszy, 2002) and in the wild (e.g., Fernandes, 1991). Hook-Costigan and Rogers (1996) concluded that "like humans, capuchins [*Cebus apella*] appear to be right handed for most tasks" (p. 198). Even more importantly, they concluded that "tool use and right handedness may have evolved before bipedalism, and well before the apes and, indeed, humans evolved" (p. 195).

These various studies are broadly consistent with the hypotheses we initially presented regarding evolution of handedness in monkeys. We hypothesized that monkeys would show some legacy of the tendency to use the left hand for unimanual prehension. But in addition we hypothesized that "With the abandonment of vertical clinging and the advent of more omnivory and more invasive foraging and manual food processing in many higher primates, the right side of the body, with its greater physical strength and its postural heritage of on-line control, may have become the operative side" (MacNeilage, 1998c, p. 230).

Although there was very little evidence regarding handedness in great apes in 1987, we hypothesized that because of their intermediate evolutionary status between monkeys and humans—having evolved from ancestral monkey forms, and having shared ancestral forms with humans—they might show handedness patterns that were intermediate between those of monkeys and humans. This also proved to be correct. Great apes moved toward the human pattern in showing no evidence of a left-hand preference for simple reaching. But, like both monkeys and humans they tended to be right-handed for tasks involving manipulative skill. With respect to bimanual coordination, using the tube test, Hopkins et al. (2003) found a significant trend toward right-hand preferences in chimpanzees (replicating Hopkins' earlier [1994] finding) and a marginally significant trend in gorillas. Most recently, Hopkins and his colleagues have administered the tube test to an astonishing total of 467 chimpanzees from three captive populations (Hopkins et al., 2004). They found a significant tendency toward right-hand preferences that was relatively uniform across the three groups. There were 272 right preferences, 162 left preferences, and 33 without significant preferences. Thus, almost 60 percent of these animals had a right-hand preference, and the number of animals without preference was remarkably small.

With respect to postural influences, Westergaard, Kuhn, and Suomi (1998) noted significant trends towards right-handedness for bipedal reaching in chimpanzees and gorillas, though not for quadrupedal reaching. Trends toward greater use of the right hand were also noted for bonobos and orangutans.

In the light of this association between bipedal posture and right-handedness in both monkeys and apes, it's likely that the assumption of bipedalism as the dominant locomotory mode in hominids contributed to a strengthening of an already existing tendency toward right-handedness. It is generally agreed that this condition is extremely demanding, posturally. In the picturesque metaphor of primate locomotion specialist Alan Walker: "From an engineering perspective, bipedalism is a ridiculous answer to the need for locomotion, posing problems akin to balancing an apple on top of a moving pencil" (Walker and Shipman, 1996, p. 199). This characterization certainly suggests that bipedalism may have severely constrained the performance of tasks requiring whole-body asymmetry in hominids, perhaps forcing them into the mode of asymmetry more supported by their phylogeny, namely, preferential use of the right side/ hand. In addition, as has often been noted, the fact that habitual bipedalism leaves the hands free could also have contributed to the already existing rightward asymmetry, not only for bimanual coordination but for other acts as well.

The primate handedness findings of most direct interest from the point of view of evolution of speech involve social and communicative behavior. Chimpanzees like to throw things—especially at unsuspecting lab visitors, among other targets. Hopkins et al. (1993) have found a significant tendency toward a right-hand preference for throwing in a group of thirty-six chimpanzees. Twenty-four animals were right-preferent, nine were left-preferent, and three were ambipreferent. Importantly from the PO standpoint, bipedal throwing was significantly more strongly associated with right-hand preferences than was tripedal throwing.

With respect to communicative gestures, Hopkins and Wesley (2002) have replicated an earlier study by Hopkins and Leavens (1998) showing that the right hand is preferred significantly more often than the left for food begs in chimpanzees. Hopkins and deWaal (1995) also found a significant tendency toward use of the right hand for communicative gestures in bonobos. In addition, Hopkins and Cantero (2003) showed that the right-hand preference for gestural communication in chimpanzees is significantly enhanced when accompanied by a vocalization. The authors conclude that "the lateralization of manual and speech systems of communication may date back as far as 5 million years ago" (p. 55). In a remarkable recent finding with profound implications for the phylogeny of human communication as well as handedness, Meguerditchian and Vauclair (2006) found a significant right-hand preference for the communicative gesture of ground-patting in a group of sixty baboons. I will return to consider the implications of these findings later.

Until recently most instances of right-hand preferences in primates have been obtained in captive populations. Some researchers have concluded from this that the findings of population-level trends in captive animals are artifacts (e.g., McGrew and Marchant, 1997), although no satisfactory explanation for the nature of the artifact has been advanced. Counter-evidence to this suggestion comes from the finding of Hopkins et al. (2004), in their study of 467 chimpanzees, that the tendency toward a right-hand preference was independent of whether the chimpanzees were reared by humans or not.

However, most importantly, Lonsdorf and Hopkins (2005) pooled available data from two instances of chimpanzee tool use in the wild—nut-cracking (N = 63) and wadge-dipping (N = 16). The latter task, also called leaf-sponging, involves bunching up leaves and dipping them into cavities in tree trunks to obtain water. They found that the predominance of right-hand preference on these tasks resulted in a significantly different preference pattern from that found for termite-fishing, and that the right-hand preference tendency was significant for nut-cracking and approached significance for wadge-dipping. (They also found a significant left-hand preference for termite fishing which might have been induced by the spatial conceptualization necessary to the task of attracting unseen insects to the twig inserted in the termite mound—see MacNeilage, 2007.) Another conspicuous exception to the typical null findings in the wild was a tendency toward right-hand preference in bimanual coordination tasks in wild gorillas that would have been significant if subject to a one-tailed statistical test, a test that would have been appropriate for an evaluation of the prediction of the PO theory (Byrne and Byrne, 1991).

The finding of right-hand preference tendencies for nut-cracking, wadge-dipping, and bimanual coordination in great apes in the wild is consistent with the PO theory. All tasks involve the coordinated use of both sides of the body. Nut-cracking involves considerable manual skill as well as the postural demands of force application. It's important to crack the nut but not obliterate it. Wadge-dipping also includes whole-body postural demands.

So what we have found out about primate handedness tells us that there was probably no anthropocentric hand-to-mouth evolution for speech consequent upon an emergent right-hand/left-hemisphere specialization for tool use. Instead, the picture we see is of ancestral primates, probably already possessing cerebral hemispheric specializations for action, responding to new ecological challenges to the manual system itself by modifying manual-action lateralities presumably without regard to the left-hemisphere specializations for vocal functions that they probably also had, as we will now see.

10.3 Evolution of cerebral hemispheric specializations for vocal communication

As already noted, the left-hemisphere specialization for acoustic communication is not specific to humans. There is evidence that it exists in all major vertebrate taxonomic groups except for reptiles, which are not much given to vocalizing. Fish are a surprise member of this cohort. According to Fine et al. (1996), a number of species of catfish produce an acoustical signal ("stridulation") by rubbing a pectoral fin spine against the pectoral girdle in circumstances involving agonistic social communication and spawning. These authors found that about half of a group of fifty-two channel catfish produced this vocalization. Within this subgroup, 90 percent preferred to use the right fin.

The catfish specialization is, of course, not a vocal one. However, Bauer (1993) found that damage to the left but not the right hemisphere eliminated territorial vocalization in frogs. Hiscock and Kinsbourne (1995) conclude from a review that there is a left-hemisphere specialization for vocal production in songbirds. Concerning non-primate mammals, Holman and Hutchinson (1991) have found left-sided hypothalamic control of ultrasonic vocalizations in Mongolian gerbils. Concerning primates, as noted earlier, Hook-Costigan and Rogers (1998) have found that, as in human speech, marmosets open the right side of their mouth more during affiliative vocalizations than their left, indicating greater left-hemisphere involvement.

A number of findings also suggest that a left-hemispheric specialization for vocal *perception* is not specific to humans either. Ehret (1987) showed that female mice are more responsive to the ultrasonic distress calls of their offspring when input was available to the right ear than when it was available to the left. It has been known for a long time that monkeys have a left-hemisphere *perceptual* specialization for vocal communication (Hauser and Andersson, 1994; Heffner and Heffner, 1984; Petersen et al., 1978; Poremba et al., 2004). Recently, evidence for a left-hemisphere perceptual specialization has also been found in seals (Boye, Güntürkün, and Vauclair, 2005).

In the absence of an obvious reason why these forms of communicative *action*, in particular, would be specialized in the left hemisphere independent of any other action, I suggested that this is further evidence for a vertebrate left-hemisphere specialization for routine action control in general (MacNeilage, 1998a). Certainly any vocal-action specialization must have evolved in the context of postural configurations of the body rather than simply as a "talking head" specialization. The implication is that rather than the human specialization for vocal action being derived from the left-hemisphere manual-control specialization, as is often proposed, they are both offshoots of a more general left-hemisphere specialization for the control of the whole body under routine circumstances.

Strong evidence for this proposition comes from an unlikely source— humans. There are now four studies showing that the hemispheric specialization for speech is more closely related to the hemisphere controlling whole-body action than to the hemisphere specialized for the control of manual skill (Day and MacNeilage, 1996; Elias and Bryden, 1998; Maki, 1990; Searleman, 1980). These are all dichotic listening studies with the wildly counterintuitive finding that in the 10 percent of the human population with mixed-limb preferences (5 percent right-handed left-footers and 5 percent left-handed right-footers), *language lateralization is more closely related to the foot preference than to the hand preference.* Foot preference is obviously related to a contralateral specialization for whole-body action control, because any selective use of the foot when in a bipedal stance must involve postural control of the whole body. This fits with the finding of Spinazzola et al. (2003) of a right-hemisphere postural specialization, which would provide left-sided support for the typical human right-foot preference. A prediction arising from these findings is that even though there are some dissociations between foot preference and manual-skill lateralization in humans, foot preference for manipulative acts in monkeys and apes will tend to be concordant with right-hand preferences. Both of these are presumed indicants of a left-hemisphere specialization for routine action control.

In this context, it's now possible to provide an interpretation of the findings of right-hand preferences for gestures in baboons and chimpanzees and their link with vocalization in chimpanzees. These findings are simply what one would expect if there is indeed a left-hemisphere specialization for whole-body action control under routine circumstances. Meguerditchian and Vauclair (2006) interpreted their findings to mean that sign language may have evolved before spoken language, an outcome I will argue against in Chapter 13. Although perhaps one could question the proposition that warning pats are routine activities, I contend that the pats are part of a complex of activities controlled by the left hemisphere in circumstances that don't reach the level of emergency reactions. I would agree with Hopkins and Cantero's conclusion from the co-occurrence of right-hand gestures and vocal communicative events in chimpanzees that "the lateralization of manual and speech systems of communication may date back as far as 5 million years ago" (2003, p. 55). In Chapter 15 I will argue that this co-occurrence pattern, which was presumably initially evoked by tinkering in the face of selection pressures on successful communication, continued to evolve in hominids, eventually taking the modern form in which the manual system, typically on the right side of the body, provides an expressive complement to instances of use of the vocal linguistic system. Chimpanzee throwing behavior seems similar to the agonistic ground-patting of baboons. They are both manual communicative threat gestures, but do not necessarily imply the existence of a sign language in earlier hominids.

10.4 Human handedness/language as a saltation

Despite the steadily accumulating evidence of various vertebrate homologs to human hemispheric specializations—in particular, anthropoid primate homologs to human handedness and left-hemispheric precursors to spoken language—some theorists, notably Annett (2002) and Crow (2004), continue to see only a saltational genetic step to human handedness/language. In fact, this saltational view of human hemispheric specializations is probably still the most common view in the scientific community. For example, with respect to handedness, in their introductory text in cognitive neuroscience Gazzaniga, Ivry, and Mangun (2001) state that "Unlike humans, nonhuman primates do not show a preponderance of right handedness" (p. 442). They follow Previc (1991) in attributing the origin of right-handedness in humans to the epigenetic results of a characteristic asymmetry in the position of the fetus in *bipedal* mothers. But then how do we explain the finding that *quadrupedal* right-handed simians tend to beget right-handed offspring (Hopkins, Dahl, and Pilcher, 2001)?

One might also ask from the saltationist standpoint why language laterality is more related to foot preference than to hand preference. The saltational view of evolution common in the early twentieth century, supposedly resulting in the creation of what Goldschmidt (1940), a proponent of this view, called "hopeful monsters" (p. 183), has been passé for a long time in evolutionary biology (Mayr, 1982). And no evidence for a mutation resulting in a species-specific genetic basis for human handedness and language, together or apart, has yet been unearthed. Perhaps more disturbing is that nothing is said by Annett or Crow about *exactly* what this supposed gene actually *did* to produce handedness/language. We are simply asked to believe that whatever these theorists believe human handedness and language to consist of, a gene did it. Despite the natural human tendency to be anthropocentric, the time for this kind of conception of the evolution of human left-hemispheric specializations has surely passed.

10.5 Extension of the postural origins theory: vertebrate hemispheric specializations

In 1998 I suggested that the postural origins theory of primate-handedness evolution might be expanded into a conception of the evolution of hemispheric specializations in vertebrates in general. (See MacNeilage,

1998a, for a more detailed discussion.) I raised the possibility that there may be two complementary vertebrate-wide hemispheric specializations: a left-hemisphere specialization for whole-body control under routine circumstances, and a right-hemisphere specialization for emergency reactions under, in the extreme, life-threatening circumstances. Here I will briefly discuss these possibilities, adding some evidence that I was not aware of in 1998.

10.5.1 A left-hemisphere routine-action specialization

One implication of the origin of a left-hemisphere routine-action-control specialization in early vertebrates is that this already-existing left-hemisphere action specialization may have been put to use in the form of the right-side dominance associated with the clinging and leaping motor adaptation characteristic of everyday early prosimian life. This would have made the left hand more available for prehension of food objects. This suggestion is compatible with the recently stated hypothesis that the earliest primates may not have been predatory vertical clingers and leapers but instead quadrupedal small-branch feeders capitalizing primarily on plant life in the outer canopies of trees (Bloch and Boyer, 2002). If so, then the left-hemisphere action-control capacity favoring right-sided postural support may have triggered the asymmetric reaching adaptation favoring the hand on the side less dominant for postural support—the left hand— before the manual-predation specialization in vertical clingers and leapers, and its accompanying ballistic reaching capacity, evolved.

In arguing for a generalized role of the left hemisphere for routine body control, I am allying myself with the Russian psychologist Vsevolod Bianki (1988), who concluded that in all vertebrates "the left hemisphere mainly controls motor activity" (p. 147). He reached this conclusion after reviewing an extremely large body of evidence, mainly about rats, accumulated by numerous Russian researchers. One important basis for his conclusion was the finding that anesthetizing the left hemisphere decreased general-activity levels in rats while anesthetizing the right hemisphere increased them. He concluded that "it is the left hemisphere that dominates in activating motor function whereas the right hemisphere inhibits it" (p. 140). This conjecture regarding rats is in remarkable correspondence with the recent rather unequivocal conclusion that there is an inhibitory specialization in the right frontal cortex of humans (Aron, Robbins, and Poldrack, 2004).

Evidence supporting the existence of this left-hemisphere dominance for routine action in another major vertebrate taxon comes from work on birds, which have the convenient anatomical property of having almost entirely contralateral projections from the eyes to the brain. A number of studies (e.g., Andrew, Tommasi, and Ford, 2000) report that chickens have better visual discrimination in pecking for food when guided by their right eye (and left hemisphere) than when guided by their left eye. In a study showing the implications of this finding for activity levels, Güntürkün and Hoferichter (1985) found that cutting the *left* forebrain bundle, which is the main outflow from the forebrain, markedly reduces the activity level of the birds when pecking at a target key to obtain food, while cutting the right forebrain bundle has no such effect.

Findings in motor *development* in humans and chimpanzees support the conclusion that they share a basic right-sided posture/action preference. Hepper, Shahidullah, and White (1990) have shown that over 90% of human fetuses suck their right thumb in utero. Hepper, Wells, and Lynch (2005) recently found that all of the sixty infants who sucked their right thumb in utero turned out to be right-handed. There is also a well-known rightward supine orientation preference in human neonates, correlated with subsequent handedness (Michel, 2002). With respect to the question of neonatal action asymmetries of the *body*, Domellöf, Rönnqvist, and Hopkins (2007) have found the right leg to be more coordinated than the left. In adults, Güntürkün (2003) has found, by means of surreptitious observation of parting rituals in airport terminals, that the rightward orientation preference, in this case of the head, tends to be shared by both participants in the act of kissing.

This orientation/action bias has precursors in chimpanzees. Bard, Hopkins, and Fort (1990) have found a significant tendency for newborn chimpanzees to bring their right hand to the mouth. Hopkins and Bard (1995) have found a significant rightward orientation preference in supine neonatal chimpanzees. Fagot and Bard (1995) have shown significantly stronger grips for the right hand and foot in neonatal chimpanzees. Imitation is obviously not a factor in these human-like neonatal rightward preferences of chimpanzees.

10.5.2 A right-hemisphere affective specialization?

In a further broadening of the postural origins theory, I suggested, following the leads of a number of other investigators (e.g., Liotti and Tucker,

1995; Robinson and Downhill, 1995; Wittling, 1995), that complementary to the left-hemisphere routine action-control specialization there may have evolved a right-hemisphere specialization "for apprehension of the world in situations with survival-related risk" (MacNeilage, 1998a). A particularly clear indication of this, pointed out by Vallortigara and Rogers (2005) is that "A variety of species of different classes appear to be more reactive to predators seen in their left rather than right hemifield" (p. 575). In a similar vein, Davidson and his colleagues (e.g., Davidson, 1995) have provided evidence that the right hemisphere is specialized for avoidance, while that the left hemisphere is specialized for approach behavior as would be expected from its specialization for routine action. An early indication of the dominant role of the right hemisphere for negative emotionality in humans was the tendency of nineteenth-century patients with hysterical paralysis to be paralyzed on the left side (Harrington, 1995). A rather spectacular confirmation of Davidson's hypothesis was the recent finding, by Quaranta, Sinischalchi, and Vallortigara (2007) of both the lateralized propensities he postulated in the same animal, in the same experiment. They found that while the wagging tails of a group of thirty dogs had a rightward bias when the dogs viewed their masters, they had a leftward bias when viewing a dominant conspecific.

10.5.3 A human attentional dichotomy

Converging evidence of a phylogenetic trend toward a right-hemisphere specialization for emergency reactions comes from studies of *human* performance on laboratory tasks amenable to brain-imaging methodology. On the basis of such studies, Fox et al. (2006) conclude that there is "a right lateralized ventral attentional system involved in reorienting attention in response to salient sensory stimuli" (p. 10046). Corbetta and Shulman (2002) suggest that this system, which they describe as a "bottom-up" system, is for "the detection of behaviorally relevant stimuli, particularly when they are salient and unexpected" (p. 201).

The left hand/right hemisphere unimanual predation specialization postulated for prosimians can certainly be put in the context of (evasive) events that could be both unexpected and threatening for the organism. There is some evidence for the continued existence of such a specialized response capacity in humans under laboratory conditions. Carson et al. (1995) note that in reaction-time tasks in which "movement preparation is not permitted in advance of the imperative stimulus," a number of studies have been "remarkably consistent" in showing a manual asymmetry favoring the left hand (p. 151). Advantages cited range from 7.5 to 21ms. The possibility that these capacities reveal a residue of a formerly adaptive function is suggested by the fact that they don't seem to be useful to modern human function except perhaps for the left jab in boxing, and in fielding in baseball and cricket!

The best-known specialization of the human right hemisphere is for spatial function (De Renzi, 1982). It is most clearly revealed in the left-sided neglect that often follows right-hemisphere lesions. My colleagues and I suggested that a precursor to this specialization, perhaps used for the targeting phase preceding ballistic reaching, may have been associated with the left-hand preference for unimanual predation in prosimians (MacNeilage, Studdert-Kennedy, and Lindblom, 1987). In support of this possibility, Vallortigara and Rogers (2005) have pointed out that such a spatial specialization "has been largely documented in birds . . . and in mammals" (p. 589). Corbetta and Shulman (2002) observe that in humans the main anatomical regions of the right hemisphere that are damaged in cases of neglect (particularly the parietotemporal junction and inferior frontal cortex) are those of the ventral attentional system. Interestingly, these regions are the right-hemisphere counterparts of Wernicke's and Broca's areas. Thus it appears that the spatial and bottom-up attentional systems are functionally related in humans, and this relationship could well have already existed in prosimians.

In humans (Sergent, 1982) there is a right-hemisphere specialization for processing global aspects of stimuli and a complementary left-hemisphere specialization for processing local aspects of stimuli. This is revealed with stimuli in which the three lines of a large letter (say, "H") are formed by a series of a small letter (say, "L"). It is found in normal subjects that while the left visual field (right hemisphere) can most readily detect the (global) "H," the right visual field (left hemisphere) can more readily detect the small (local) "L" (Sergent, 1982). In a related result, patients with left-hemisphere lesions tend to successfully reproduce the global stimulus, but simply with a set of straight lines. In contrast, patients with right-hemisphere lesions tend to produce a cluster of instances of the local stimulus but without the global spatial organization called for by the large letter (Delis, Robertson, and Effron, 1986). The ability to rapidly synthesize global patterns in the right hemisphere could be an aspect of its rapid emergency-response capacity. Contrarily an ability to characterize the environment in detail, while in a top-down planning mode in the service of subsequent action, could be a valuable component of a left-hemisphere routine-action capacity.

The right-hemisphere affective specialization might also extend to vocalization. In contrast to the greater right-sided opening that Hook-Costigan and Rogers (1998) found in marmosets for affiliative vocalizations, they observed greater left-sided opening for screams. In humans, Code (1994) refers to "extensive evidence" for "significant right-hemisphere involvement" in emotional language (p. 140).

Despite the finding just discussed, you may well ask why, in a book about speech, so much attention has been paid to the evolution of the capacities of the right hemisphere, which seemingly have little to do with speech. The most direct answer to the question is that understanding right-hemisphere phylogeny turns out to be important in the understanding of handedness (particularly prosimian left-handedness and its human residue), which has been intimately implicated in the phylogeny of speech. And properties of the right hemisphere are relevant to another aspect of the evolution of speech that is important to the evaluation of the generative approach to language. Basic to the generative approach, as we have seen, is the modularity assumption—the assumption that language is an autonomous capacity and has nothing to do with any other aspect of brain evolution. The complementarity of the left- and right-hemispheric specializations belies this claim in a manner which will now be outlined.

In each of us today, the left and right hemispheres turn out *not* to be two coexisting autonomous entities, which would allow speech to be unrelated to right-hemispheric specializations, but actually to be functionally complementary. The same researchers who contributed to the discovery that language lateralization is more closely related to footedness than to handedness have also shown that there is an inverse relation between footedness and the emotional specialization of the right hemisphere in groups of modern humans (Elias, Bryden, and Bulman-Fleming, 1998). They assessed emotional laterality with the dichotic Emotional Words Test and found a significant negative relation between ear advantage on that test and foot preference—but not hand preference. In the present view, this means that the functional relation between the left-hemisphere routine-action specialization (of which footedness is an indicant and speech lateralization is a part) and the right-hemisphere emergency-reaction specialization (related to emotionality) is actively worked out in the life span of each individual. This presumably means that the relation between left- and right-hemispheric function has been worked out in the life span of individual organisms throughout vertebrate phylogeny.

10.6 Conclusion

Contrary to what has been a common belief, the left-hemispheric special-izations underlying speech and right-handedness did not first evolve in hominids, and the vocal specialization did not evolve from the manual one. In fact, today, handedness in other primates is rife—surprisingly, *left-*handedness in prosimians, closest descendents of the ancestral primate forms, and right-handedness in simians. Furthermore, a left-hemisphere specialization for routine acoustic communication, usually vocal, may be vertebrate-wide. Instead of their joint contribution to a hominid-specific hand-to-mouth scenario for speech, the common denominator underlying both speech and handedness, according to my postural origins theory, might be a vertebrate-wide specialization of the left hemisphere for control of the whole body under routine circumstances. And, complementary to this, there might be a vertebrate-wide specialization of the right hemisphere for emer-gency reactions. Further attention to the evolutionary relationship between the hominid manual and vocal specializations in language evolution will be given in Chapter 13. There we will find that rather than one specialization having given rise to the other, they may, like the two sides of the brain, have co-evolved in a complementary relationship when it came to language.

Finally, note that this scenario for the evolution of hemispheric special-izations in general and the speech specialization in particular is a strong vindication of the embodiment perspective. Even though numerous per-ceptual/cognitive specializations are invoked, they are always in the service of action. The postural origins theory is about the different contributions of the two hemispheres of the vertebrate brain to what the organism *does*. Thus we are brought back to Huxley's dictum: "The great end of life is not knowledge but action" (1863/2005).

To my knowledge, no generativist has ever asked why language is usually in the left hemisphere, or, in Chomsky's terms, why a cosmic ray shower would have affected that particular hemisphere and (presumably) not the other. This really seems to be an unanswerable question, as long as one insists on the modularity of language—its lack of relation to any other function that the brain mediates. I hope I have shown in this chapter that if you instead put speech, and therefore language, in the context of the evolutionary history of hemispheric specializations, a possible answer, or at least a framework for seeking the answer to the question of why speech is in the left hemisphere can be obtained.

PART V

The frame/content theory and generative
linguistics

11 Generative phonology and the origin of speech

11.1 Introduction

In the last several chapters I have outlined the frame/content theory of evolution of speech and a view of the evolution of brain organization for speech that is consistent with it. The basic theory is summarized in the introduction to Chapter 8. The alternative view is the view from generative phonology, a totally non-Darwinian scenario. Generative phonology is a subdiscipline of generative linguistics. The term "generative" was coined by Chomsky to denote a structure whereby a finite number of units, plus a number of laws of combination of those units, can in effect generate a large number of linguistic forms. In syntax, words are the units, and they are combined by generative rules into sentences; in phonology, distinctive features are the units, and they are combined by generative rules into words.

The generative view is diametrically opposed to mine because its units and rules are not considered to have evolved by means of the basic Neodarwinian process—descent with modification. Instead, they are treated as if they were given in advance. This is done either tacitly, by run-of-the-mill generative phonologists, who give no thought at all to the origins question, or it is done explicitly, most notably by Chomsky. In his view, as summarized back in Chapter 1, the entire generative apparatus was suddenly given to us by a single mutation.

What exactly is supposed to have been given to us? It is some kind of abstract *mental* apparatus that supposedly underlies the sound patterns of all languages. The independence of this apparatus from both input and output is fundamental to most practicing phonologists. For them, as for Chomsky, the distinction he drew between an underlying abstract competence and a more concrete level of performance applies just as much to phonology as to syntax. Phonology is some kind of structural complex, independent of function. It is regarded as "autonomous," meaning that its laws and principles have nothing to do with phenomena outside of phonology. It is the abstract "langue" of Saussure and other structuralists. As a consequence of this compartmentalized, or "modular," status, consideration is explicitly focused on "internal evidence"—that is, on facts about sound patterns of idealized adult speakers. "External evidence", namely evidence about performance and its variants in ontogeny, society, and pathology—about function—has only marginal status.

A basic concept in linguistics is "representation," which refers to some conceptual unit of speech. In phonology, the most important representational entities are distinctive features, such as plus-high for a vowel or plus-or-minus-voice for a consonant. A related concept is "derivation." Linguistic rules are said to derive lower-level (closer to the surface) representations from higher-level (more underlying) representations. For example, in American English there is a rule whereby some underlyingly voiceless stop consonants (which have a representation in terms of distinctive features) become voiced when they occur after a stressed syllable and between vowels. So the typical American, in saying the word *butter*, actually says something more like *budder*. In this situation, it can be said that the voiced consonant at the surface is derived from the underlying voiceless one by a voicing rule. Thus the direction of generation is toward a set of *output* forms.

Modern linguistics is concerned with applying its sets of grammatical rules optimally to a corpus of utterances that have been produced, or could be produced. For phonologists, the corpus of interest is a set of "phonological words." Goldsmith, in his foreword to the flagship volume of modern phonology, *The Handbook of Phonological Theory* (1995), says:

> The most basic of the traditional goals of phonological theory has been to establish the means of specifying, for any given language, just what a phonologically well-formed word in that language is. This is the question of phonotactics: in what ways can the items of phonology be put together in a sequence to make a well-formed word? We may, after all, wish to express the notion that [blɪk] is a possible word of English, while [bnɪk] is not. (p. 3)

As I have already mentioned, the fundamental "item," or unit, of generative phonology is the distinctive feature (see Fig. 3.3 and associated discussion). In the first version of generative phonology, a book called

The Sound Pattern of English by Chomsky and Halle in 1968, well-formedness was the result of the operation, on the input, of a linear series of phonological rules involving distinctive features, resulting in the output, which was specified in surface phonetic terms. As Goldsmith describes it, subsequent work has led to our realizing that numerous other elements of construction besides the distinctive features must participate in derivations in order to optimize well-formedness. Syllable structure, for example, needs to be explicitly represented. Separate "autosegmental tiers" have been introduced to deal with situations in which consonant-related or vowel-related aspects of the variance appear to be independent, as in tone languages, for example, where tone patterns apply to the vowels only. Another example is "vowel harmony" in Turkish, where there are rules whereby properties of the first vowel and the second vowel in a word are systematically related, regardless of the intervening consonant. The rules in effect "jump over" the consonant. In addition, prosodic or suprasegmental variables such as stress require separate representation.

The rest of this chapter will primarily consider two aspects of generative phonology from the standpoint of their relevance to the evolution of speech. The first aspect is the claim that the distinctive feature is the irreducible minimal unit of speech. The second is that "markedness" can explain the well-formed patterns of serial organization of speech in the languages of the world, in terms of a hierarchy of preferences of patterns.

11.2 The concept of "distinctive feature"

The "arcane game of phonology"—the apt epithet comes courtesy of the dust cover of *The Handbook of Phonological Theory* (Goldsmith, 1995)—is played primarily with "distinctive features." For Clements and Hume (1995), in Chapter 7 of that volume, "feature theory has emerged as one of the major results of linguistic science in this century" (p. 245). Just what are "distinctive features"? According to phonologists, they are not only useful taxonomic categories that help us describe sound patterns of languages but are *actual mental entities* encoded in the genes. In effect, phonologists consider them the minimal elements of speech—the atoms of speech. Individual consonants and vowels are, thus, to be thought of as bundles of distinctive features—like molecules.

I readily concede that the concept of distinctive features is a useful basis for describing aspects of sound patterns in languages. It's useful because it often allows for more economical descriptions of those patterns than descriptions in terms of the constituent consonants and vowels. Consider an example. There is a well-known tendency in languages for consonants to be voiceless in word-final position regardless of their place of articulation. Describing this fact in terms of a distinctive feature of voicing, which has a minus value in word-final position, lets us characterize this as a single phenomenon, regardless of the specific language in which it occurs or the particular consonant involved. In contrast, were we to describe it in terms of what happens to individual consonants, we'd need to have separate subcharacterizations for each consonant. That would prove extraordinarily uneconomical.

Let's now consider the conceptual basis of distinctive features in more detail. The first set of distinctive features was proposed by Jakobson and Halle in 1956. They stated that "the inherent distinctive features that have so far been discovered in the languages of the world and which, along with the prosodic features, underlie the entire lexical and morphological stock, amount to twelve oppositions" (pp. 28–29). (For example, the words "pat" and "bat" have a voicing opposition in the first sound.) The authors described these twelve features primarily in perceptual terms because their effects, in language systems, occur at the level of perceptual distinctions between one possible word form and another. For example, we perceive that the first sound of "pat" is different from the first sound of "bat." Please note how Jakobson and Halle describe these features: they're "inherent" and have simply to be "discovered," both words implying the presence of actual pre-existing forms.

The presentation of this perceptually based distinctive-feature system was an epoch-making event in phonology and quickly became its new orthodoxy. But problems soon arose with it, many of which involved its inability to characterize sound patterns in a simple way that fit the intuition of the observer. Consider, for example, those instances of "assimilation" in which a sound comes to assimilate, or take on, some phonetic quality of its neighbor. Hura, Lindblom, and Diehl (1992) consider the example in which some consonants become palatalized in the presence of a following relatively high front vowel. (An example of a palatalized consonant is the Russian word for "no"—"*nyet*"—in which the grapheme "y" denotes the palatalization of the initial [n].) As Hura, Lindblom, and Diehl point out, the distinctive feature system of Jakobson,

Fant, and Halle (1963) can only describe this in a complex way with different perceptual features for vowels and consonants, giving no clue that a relatively simple articulatory process of assimilation is involved.

A decade later, in response to such problems, Chomsky and Halle, in their monograph *The Sound Pattern of English* (1968), proposed an almost entirely different distinctive-feature system, this time in *articulatory* terms. This let them describe palatal assimilation in a simple and intuitively satisfying way—as a matter of the consonant taking on the high front tongue position of the following vowel. Like the previous universal theory, this one, too, became readily accepted. So in a quarter of a century following the first distinctive-feature orthodoxy, we had a new orthodoxy.

But, as Hura, Lindblom, and Diehl intimate, phonology's scrapping of one supposedly universal theory for another that is practically its opposite over such a short period of scientific history raises a red flag. Shouldn't we be a little suspicious about the maturity of a scientific discipline that, in a mere decade, will abandon its entire inventory of basic units and replace it with another? Imagine if Chemistry suddenly discarded the entire Periodic Table and replaced it with a new classification whereby elements were defined in different terms.

Since 1968, articulatory distinctive features have been predominant, especially for indicating the place of articulation of both vowels and consonants, and systems have become increasingly elaborate, as is reflected, for example, in the use of the term "Feature Geometry" for the currently favored hierarchical organization of place-related features (see Clements and Hume, 1995, for a recent review).

A downside of this radical change in feature systems, pointed out by Hura, Lindblom, and Diehl, was that certain sound patterns that had rather obvious perceptual motivations became difficult to describe with the current feature system. A relevant phenomenon is observed in speech acquisition where what should be [l] is often produced as [o] (e.g., "bottle" → [bado]). Such a change requires a rather elaborate conceptualization in terms of articulatory distinctive features. But velarized [l] and [o] are very perceptually similar, and it seems likely that infants are achieving a perceptual approximation of the target sound while avoiding the articulatorily difficult liquid [l].

The unexceptionable conclusion that some aspects of sound patterns of languages are articulatorily motivated while others are perceptually motivated follows naturally from the basic assumption of many phoneticians that sound systems are formed and maintained by means of a trading relation between articulatory ease and perceptual distinctiveness. However, having chosen the articulatory domain for their currently favored distinctive-feature system, phonologists can now straightforwardly describe sound patterns that are articulatorily motivated, but they can't do that with patterns that are perceptually motivated. This is a basic problem for the entire discipline of phonology, and it's not at all clear what kind of conceptual framework is necessary for its resolution.

Momentous as this problem is, it's not the most fundamental problem for the concept of distinctive features. The main problem is that, from the classical viewpoint, distinctive features are supposed to be abstract mental entities, not entities with substantive performance-related definitions. Chomsky has been unequivocal on this point:

> It seems to me that the most hopeful approach today is to describe the phenomena of language and mental activity as accurately as possible, to try to develop an abstract theoretical apparatus that will as far as possible account for these phenomena, and reveal the principles of their organization and functioning, without attempting, for the present, to relate the postulated mental structures and processes to any physiological mechanisms or to interpret mental function in terms of physical cause. (Chomsky, 1968, p. 12)

What are the implications of this stance for phonology? The generative phonologist Steven Anderson explicitly defends the Chomskyan perspective in a paper with a provocative title from the present standpoint— "Why phonology isn't natural" (1981). He wrote it in reaction to a short-lived subdiscipline of phonology called "natural phonology" (Donegan and Stampe, 1979), which argued for a central role of perceptual and articulatory causality in phonology.

Using the Venn diagram shown in Fig. 11.1, Anderson (1981, p. 494) poses the basic question: assuming that the total area inside the dotted inner circle represents "Language" in the broad sense, while the space enclosed in each of the other, overlapping circles represents facts specific to some general domain—how much (if anything) is left in the middle?

He concludes that "an adequate account of the phonological systems of natural languages must accord a central role to a set of principles that have no direct foundation in extralinguistic considerations" (p. 535). The evidence he cites for this conclusion is of sound patterns that do not at present seem explicable in terms of any of the nonlinguistic subdisciplines

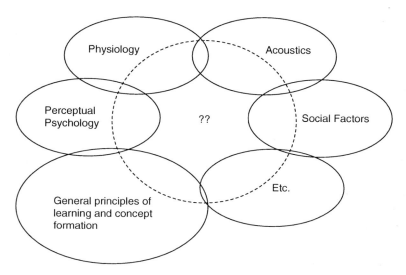

F<small>IG</small>. 11.1   Venn diagram showing Anderson's view of the relation between phonology and other subdisciplines concerned with speech. (From Anderson, 1985, diagram 1)

shown in Fig. 11.1. Anderson even makes the strong claim that "when we examine practically any phonological fact in detail, we find a certain amount of significant arbitrariness that does not appear in any serious sense to be reducible to a mechanical explanation" (p. 507).

But it is one thing to assert that there are aspects of sound patterns that don't at present appear to be explicable in phonetic terms, which is true, and another to conclude that these patterns show the existence of an "irreducible" linguistic component. The problem is that Anderson doesn't offer us any basic principles of phonology that arise from the counter-examples to phonetic determination that he presents. The purely phono-logical level thus remains formless—or, in Anderson's own words, possesses "significant arbitrariness."

It's important to note that arbitrariness is often chosen by generative linguists as a way to distinguish generative grammar from any other naturally occurring biological phenomenon. Specifically, generative gram-mar is considered to be accompanied by a lack of functional utility. For example, Newmeyer (1998), in his review of generative linguistics, talks of an "arbitrary residue of formal patterns where there is no obvious direct link to function" (p.2). One could even say that proponents of UG

(Universal Grammar) have a *fear* of function. Here is how Pesetsky (1999) puts it: "Because of the ever present possibility that a universal may have a functional explanation, researchers interested in discovering properties of language that derive from UG often focus on those universals for which functional explanations are the *least* likely" (p. 477). Nowhere is the anti-Darwinian stance of Chomskyan generative linguistics clearer than here. Darwin's theory is centered on adaptive functions.

One interesting consequence of Anderson's analysis is that generative phonology must rely on other subdisciplines to define the subject matter of its own discipline. At present, I would argue, no explanatory power arises from the body of knowledge about phonology that cannot be explained in terms of concepts from other subdisciplines. Although Anderson warns us not to conclude from his analysis that "the content of linguistic systems is intrinsically arbitrary" (p. 535), this is exactly the conclusion we are faced with. The fact is that no phenomena that can be claimed to be purely linguistic have been given an explanation in the true sense of the word.

A few years ago the phonetician John Ohala offered us a summary of what is in the middle of Anderson's Venn diagram:

phonology endlessly recycles much of the same data, trying out different labels and descriptive devices on it (markedness, abstract underlying forms, ordered rules, alpha variables, atomic rules, upside-down rules, charm, optimality, a staggering variety of conditions and principles), all of which are attributed, quite facilely, to the new theoretical deus ex machina, "universal grammar." But it does this without achieving greater insight into the mechanisms of speech. (Ohala, 1997, p. 684)

In other words, Ohala sees phonologists continually celebrating "new-and-improved" descriptive conventions without making any explanatory progress.

Anderson's claim that there is an irreducible component of autonomous phonology implies that competence and performance are unrelated, leaving competence to just float around by itself in the middle of the Venn diagram. Where, then, is the interface between competence and performance that could contribute to the answer to Tinbergen's question #1: "How does it work?" In actual operation, the interface must be crossed causally—that is, not only must specific input have specific mental consequences for the perception process, but specific pre-output mental activity must have specific consequences for the production process. Chomsky abjures attempts to relate the mental to the physical (see earlier) but at the cost of denying his approach any relevance to the actual events of speech perception and production. In other words, he remains a Cartesian dualist.

It should be obvious now that generative phonologists wish to have their cake and eat it too. On the one hand, they assert that the essential elements of sound patterns are competence-based—purely mental and abstract and unrelated to performance. On the other hand, they're happy to use perceptually-based or articulatorily-based distinctive-feature systems—systems grounded in performance. Then they claim credit for the mental level when the rules expressed in terms of these nonmental features turn out to be apt summary descriptions of patterns.

Generative phonologists talk as if they have already established that there is a finite number of distinctive features and that this set is small. (Recall Jackendoff's characterization of the word "star" in terms of eight features in Chapter 3). Finiteness is implied, for example, by Kenstowicz's statement that "phonological segments can be analyzed into complexes of *distinctive features* that cross-classify the entire inventory of possible sounds into a densely packed network" (1994, p. 19). Current proposals for sets of distinctive features do not exceed about twenty. Here is one reason to wonder whether such a small set could do such a big job. We noted in Chapter 3 that in Maddieson's survey of just 317 languages (less than 5 percent of present-day languages), there were 558 consonant types and 210 vowel types. Just from the descriptions of these 768 segment types it's clear that no existing set of distinctive features could come close to exhaustively characterizing even this small sample of the world's speech sounds. Remember, too, that Maddieson didn't find a single consonant or vowel that was present in every language, and he also found that the modal number of occurrences of a sound in his sample of languages is only one. Does this seem like the way languages would behave if they were formed by concatenations of a small set of building blocks? This possibility is also thrown into question by Mielke's (2008) finding, that the best-known feature sets fall well short of defining appropriate natural classes that operate in phonological rules in a corpus of 561 languages.

If indeed a small set of "inherent" features had been "discovered" and had in fact been shown to constitute the structure of all known phonological words of languages, this would be a great achievement for science in general. But this is far from being the case. To show what *is* the case, we must ask how linguists come up with the concept of distinctive features in the first place.

Distinctive features are established in a two-step process. First, you look for minimal pairs in individual languages. Then you compare a number of languages to see if similar minimal pairs repeatedly show up. If they do, the attribute that's responsible for the difference between the members of the pairs is called a "distinctive feature." For example, "fat" and "vat" are a minimal pair in English. They differ only in voicing: the vocal folds vibrate during the first sound of "vat" but not of "fat." Since you can find a similar distinction in many other languages, you're justified in postulating voicing as a binary (two-valued) distinctive feature that characterizes the difference between these two sounds.

I have described here a methodological aspect of phonology. But of course the claim regarding features goes well beyond the methodology required to establish them. The claim is that they are part of our innate knowledge. That's a giant inferential leap. But the justifications for it in the phonological literature are uniformly brief. For example, in Kenstowicz's textbook, *Phonology in Generative Grammar* (1994), which is about 800 pages long, we find barely half a page on this question. Let us specifically consider a similarly brief justification offered by Halle (1990). First, he notes the finding that when English speakers need to pluralize the word "Bach," which ends in a velar fricative not present in English, they correctly add /s/ rather than /əs/. (The latter form follows words ending in an /s/, e.g., "guesses".) Then he argues that this proves that we have an innate knowledge of the plural in order to make the correct choice. But one obvious alternative explanation, which he never considers, is that English speakers might well be guessing here on the basis of other knowledge they have about their own language, something they do all the time when pronouncing new words. Specifically, they could generalize from the fact that they pluralize other similar fricatives (i.e., nonstrident or low-amplitude fricatives), such as (/f/ and /θ/), with an /s/. In short, the basis for making this decision could be learned rather than genetically specified.

Let us also consider Halle's argument for a set of three innate distinctive features that are considered to be sufficient to universally specify basic vowels of languages (basic in the sense of involving something like a single standard holistic tongue configuration which can be moved about in the mouth). These features are binary; that is, they take only + (present) and − (absent) values. The features are "back", "high," and "low." Notice that this classification only allows two positions in the front–back dimension. Apparently, either front vowels or central vowels (which play a key role in frame/content theory) are impermissible. Also only three configurations are allowed in the height dimension, although languages (e.g., Danish) sometimes have more than three values in this dimension. The values are + high, − low; + low, − high; and − high, − low (mid). As Halle states: "It appears, however, that no languages utilize the feature complex [+ high, + low]" (p. 50). Halle asserts that relative to a characterization of vowels as segments, the featural specification "more accurately reflects what is going on in speakers' minds" (ibid.).

Compare this characterization with Lindblom's work on the question of how individual languages choose their vowel systems. Using a computational model, Lindblom (1986) has been able to predict, on self-organizational grounds, the favored choices of vowels within vowel systems ranging from three to nine vowels on the basis of a principle of optimal perceptual differentiation. (For example, three-vowel systems favor [i], [a], [u].) In other words, vowels behave like people entering elevators, tending to position themselves so as to distance themselves from their neighbors. In short, in real life vowels are driven by a context-sensitive principle of distinctiveness, as one might expect on communicative grounds, rather than choosing from a context-free set of innate values which is too small to characterize observed outcomes.

Perhaps the best way to decide on the present status of distinctive feature theory is to consider the conclusions of the most comprehensive monograph ever written about speech sounds, *Sounds of the World's Languages*, by Ladefoged and Maddieson (1996). One of the hopes behind this work was "that it might provide a basis for future work on phonological feature theories" (p. 369). However, they found that "The great variety of data that we have presented shows that the construction of an adequate theory of universal features is much more complex than hitherto thought" (p. 369). They began their work with the assumption that "the description of phonetic events involves establishment of parameters along which variation can be measured, and a set of categorial values along these parameters. These categorial values can be considered as labels for classifying similar distinctions in different languages." But they found that many "phonetic phenomena need to be described as variants of these categories" (p. 369):

We have shown that there is a continuous range of values within the parameters. Thus we saw that when a wide range of data from different languages is considered, it is difficult to say that there is a certain specific number of places of articulation. It is equally hard to determine a specific number of states of the glottis. Similarly we have found that there is no sharp division between ejectives and plosives accompanied by a glottal stop. We also noted that there is a gradient between one form of voiced plosive and what is clearly a voiced implosive; there are not two clearly defined classes. The same kind of notion appears throughout the book, becoming, perhaps, most apparent towards the end in the discussion of vowels. (p. 369)

To explicate the issue a little for vowels, the so-called "vowel space" is by nature an articulatory and acoustic continuum. Articulatorily, it is bounded at what could be called the consonantal end by the tongue constriction becoming sufficiently narrow that normal voicing cannot occur. At the other extreme it is bounded by the incompressibility of the tongue relative to the mandible and by how much one can conveniently open the mouth. At the terminal end of the vocal tract there is a continuum of lip rounding/retraction, and at the other end a continuum of larynx elevation/retraction. Within the boundaries, created by too much constriction, maximal compression, maximal amount of mouth opening, lip protrusion, and larynx lowering, any vowel configuration with its associated acoustic pattern is possible, though some are more straightforward than others. What Ladefoged and Maddieson encountered, even in only 305 languages, were vowels that were positioned basically everywhere in the space.

Thus when researchers like Ladefoged and Maddieson study what sounds are really like, they find virtually no basis for the postulation of discrete categories. Instead, in a number of areas they find phonetic continua within which discrete categories such as features cannot be established. This throws considerable doubt on the proposition that the distinctive feature has any comprehensive mental reality. Perhaps their realization of this induced the palpable sense of fatigue evident in the final paragraph of their monograph:

We will not attempt to turn this set of oppositions into a coherent set of universal features for use in phonological descriptions. Producing the present book has taken many years, and we are happy to let other linguists take this next step. (p. 373)

Most recently, Ladefoged (2006) has aired his doubts about whether this is even a worthwhile task. He reviews data suggesting that "the set of features necessary for describing lexical contrasts in a universal grammar is large, [and] cumbersome" (p. 10). He also notes that "any system based on our current linguistic knowledge must be incomplete" (p. 9) and gives two reasons for this. The first one is that "some distinctions permitted within the system are simply estimates of what distinctions are possible within a language. Some future language may arise that proves these estimates wrong". The second one is that "we cannot account for what is not systematic". Here he points to a number of cases in which a language has a sound that occurs in a dozen or fewer lexical items. But finally, and perhaps most importantly, Ladefoged concludes that phonological features do not have reality status as naturally occurring phenomena: "Phonological features are best regarded as artifacts that linguists have devised in order to describe linguistic systems" (p. 12).

So it seems that features cannot constitute a small set, that the set cannot be characterized as finite, and that rather than being mental entities, they are artifacts of linguistic description. On the latter point, one observation can be added. Remember from Chapter 3 that when serial-ordering errors of speech occur, the unit that seems to be affected is the *segment*, not the *feature*. For example, in exchange errors where the two segments would be described as differing by more than one feature, all the putative features "move" together even though a parsimony-based conception of feature theory would require that the typical movement pattern would involve only one feature. Thus, at this level, where there is an opportunity for the distinctive feature to show itself as an independently variable unit of function, we don't see it.

11.3 The concept of markedness

Beyond the concept of distinctive feature, one of the most central concepts in generative linguistics has been "markedness." The term refers to a continuum of units or patterns, with completely unmarked properties being those found in virtually all languages, and extremely marked properties being found very rarely. The attribute of frequency of occurrence has formed the main basis for the definition of the concept. But the concept has also been defined in other ways. It first appeared in the work of the Prague School of linguistics in the 1920s and '30s (see Anderson, 1985) in discussions of the concept of "neutralization." And what is that? In German, for example, the opposition between voiced and voiceless stop consonants, in final position, has been "neutralized" by the disappearance of voiced consonants. In this instance, voiceless was considered the unmarked form and voiced the marked form. Thus, the unmarked form is the form that remains after the neutralization occurs, and the marked form is the one that's eliminated. Another use of the markedness concept pertains to the dimension of complexity. In this domain, more unmarked forms are more simple (e.g., Paradis and Prunet, 1991), although phonologists have never given us an objective definition of complexity. In addition, markedness has sometimes been taken to be indicated by the order of acquisition of sounds and sound patterns in infants. Here, as used for example by Jakobson (1968), early-appearing sounds are considered to be relatively unmarked. But again there is a problem here because infant preferences and language preferences are not always the same. Thus, in short, markedness is not satisfactorily defined.

To see the problems of the markedness concept most clearly, it's necessary to step back and try to characterize the enterprise of generative phonology in which it is embedded in its most general terms. Stephen Anderson (1985) draws a highly useful parallel between the structural foundations of generative phonology, as provided in Chomsky and Halle's 1968 monograph, *The Sound Pattern of English* (henceforth *SPE*), and "another fundamental work of twentieth-century thought, Whitehead and Russell's (1910) *Principia Mathematica*" (p. 329). In order to make this parallel and its very important implications clear, I can do no better than to quote rather extensively from Anderson's highly informative and lucid account.

Principia Mathematica (*PM*), Anderson says, "enunciated and developed a goal of reducing all of the intellectual content of mathematics to the form of manipulation of expressions in a logistic system by means of fully explicit rules" (p. 329). Anderson observes that *SPE* does something strikingly similar:

the nature of a phonological theory as expressed in *SPE* centers on an explicit formal notation for phonological description. In common with an evaluation function for grammars defined over this notation, this would constitute a comprehensive axiomatization of the subject matter of phonology, in the sense that all problems connected with the discovery of correct (or "descriptively adequate") accounts of sound structure would thereby be reduced to the mechanical manipulation of expressions in a fully explicit notational system. (p 329)

Anderson describes the response of the philosophical community to *PM* as one that progressed from acclaim to disillusionment:

PM's account of the foundations of mathematics was initially greeted with enthusiasm, since it promised to give a full reconstruction of the traditional notion that the truth of mathematical propositions derives from logic alone, and not from contingent facts about the world. This enthusiasm soon gave way to dissatisfaction, however, as it became apparent that there were fundamental obstacles to the logicist program. In particular, the theory in its basic form was seen to give rise to a number of paradoxes that had long been troublesomely familiar to mathematicians, such as various forms of the problem of the barber who shaves everyone but who does not shave himself, and other apparent self-contradictions. In order to remedy this difficulty, Russell had proposed what is known as the theory of "types": roughly speaking a restriction on the kinds of classes that can be referred to in any given expression. (p. 329)

But, as Anderson points out, this theory of types also had several unwanted consequences:

it rendered many of the basic propositions of number theory unstatable or meaningless. It was thus necessary, in the full system of the *PM*, to appeal to an "axiom of infinity" and an "axiom of reducibility" whose plausibility and intuitive appeal are vastly less than that of the rest of the logical system. Since the theory of types seemed unavoidable in the context of the logic of the *PM*, and since it seemed to lead to such counterintuitive emendations of the system, the logicist program for the foundations of mathematics was gradually abandoned. (p. 330)

One can now see the basis for Russell's disillusionment with pure mathematics that I noted in Chapter 1.

Anderson then notes that *SPE* also had "an Achilles' heel similar to that of the classical antinomies with the framework of *PM*" (pp. 330–331). He points out that the problem was first noted by Chomsky and Halle themselves in Chapter 9, in which

it is observed that the purely formal calculus to which phonological expressions are supposed to be reduced is absolutely neutral as to the substantive content of the representations and rules appearing in particular descriptions. The notation, that is, provides a vocabulary in the form of a set of features and a formalism for rules; but within this vocabulary all expressions are essentially homogeneous with respect to the formal measure of evaluation which is intended to reconstruct the linguistic significance of generalizations embodied in particular descriptions. (Anderson, 1985, p. 331)

In other words, the theory applied equally well to "common and obviously natural" phonological states of affairs and "ridiculous and impossible ones which could never arise within a natural language" (p. 332).

For example, Anderson points out that many languages have an assimilation rule to the effect that an obstruent (a stop consonant or fricative) takes on the voicing value of a following obstruent. The presence of a [z] in the word "husband" is an example. But if one replaces the word "obstruent" in the first specification of "obstruent" with "vowel" and "voice" with "height" in the formalism, one obtains a rule whereby the height of vowels assimilates to the voicing of a following obstruent. This is of course a nonsensical rule, but one that is just as permissible within the system as the rule from which it was derived by substitution. Anderson concludes, "If the theory is so deficient in reconstructing the notion of 'possible phonological system,' the argument runs, it is obviously in need of revision" (p. 332).

Anderson observes further that

The basis for the deficiency, according to Chomsky and Halle (and all subsequent writers), is the system's principled disregard of the substantive phonetic content of phonological expressions. Only by paying attention to the phonetic interpretation of the features and relations in a phonology, they suggest, is it possible to come to terms with the evident fact that some systems are possible and natural, while others, that are formally equivalent, are less natural, or indeed impossible. (p. 332)

Chomsky and Halle's solution to this problem took the form of a theory of markedness:

In essence, the theory consists of a set of "marking conventions" or definitions of the values "marked" and "(un)marked" for phonological features in particular contexts. Thus...the unmarked value of the feature [voiced] in an obstruent followed by another obstruent is whatever value agrees with the voicing of the following one. (p. 333)

Anderson points out that "While the theory of markedness was greeted with much initial enthusiasm, it is noteworthy that no substantial analyses of phonological phenomena have appeared subsequently in which this aspect of the theory plays a significant role" (p. 334).

In Anderson's opinion, "This general lack of practical repercussions of markedness theory seems to be due at least in part to the fact that the set of marking conventions required to account for the facts of one language (or group of languages) simply do[es] not extend to comparable utility in others" (p. 334). Anderson gives an example attributed to Lass (1972): "while front rounded vowels may be unnatural in many or most of the world's languages, there is no reason to believe that they are not perfectly well integrated into the phonologies of many Germanic languages" (p. 334).

Anderson, paraphrasing Lass, observes that

these problems do not arise simply because an adequate set of marking conventions has not yet been formulated but because the role of phonetic content in a phonological system can only be analyzed relative to other properties of the system. If this is true, it's simply not possible to embody this role in a comprehensive and universal way in the definition of the notation in the way foreseen by markedness theory. The purely mechanical problems encountered here are immediately apparent to anyone attempting to formulate a description in markedness terms. (p. 334)

Anderson concludes that

the phonological importance of phonetic content reveals a fundamental inadequacy of the "logicist" program for phonology as sketched by *SPE*. ... [t]he theory of markedness seems to be an emendation with the same character as Russell's theory of types within the *PM*. In each case, the problem is that available ways of constructing a consistent formal system with the required character lead inevitably to conflicts with the subject matter for which the theories in question are intended to provide an account. (p. 334)

But the perceptive reader might note that what we are looking at here is a critique made in 1985 by Anderson of an approach to phonology put forward in 1968. Surely phonological theorists have mended their fences in the twenty or so years since then? I will let you judge for yourself.

The most recent major conceptual development in linguistic theory is "optimality theory." It is considered to apply equally to the syntactic and the phonological levels of language. To give you a flavor of this discipline, I will make use of a lead article published in *Science* in 1997 entitled "Optimality: From neural networks to universal grammar" (Prince and Smolensky, 1997). Optimality theory addresses, as it must, the most basic question of linguistic theory—the question described earlier by the phonologist Goldsmith. It is the question of well-formedness. Grammars do not allow every possible linguistic construction. (Remember /bnɪk/.) Constructions must be well-formed. From this standpoint, grammars can be regarded as statements about constraints on the well-formedness of linguistic structures.

Optimality theory, or OT, is generally considered within linguistics to be a radical advance on older attempts to characterize well-formedness that had used representations and rules that I briefly considered at the beginning of the chapter. What does this advance consist of?

Prince and Smolensky begin by noting that

Languages appear to vary widely, but the same structural themes repeat themselves over and over again, in ways that are sometimes obvious and sometimes clear only upon detailed analysis. The challenge then is to discover an architecture for grammars that both allows variation and limits its range to what is possible in human language. (p. 1604)

Prince and Smolensky note that constraints on the well-formedness of linguistic structures "are heavily in conflict, even within a single language" (p. 1604). They give the following phonological example:

In forming the past tense of "slip," spelled "slipped" but pronounced *slipt*, a general phonological constraint on voicing in final consonant sequences favors the pronunciation of *pt* over *pd*, conflicting with the requirement that the past tense marker be given its basic form *-d*; and the phonological constraint prevails. (p. 1604)

They go on to say that "a central element in the architecture of grammar is a formal means for managing the pervasive conflict between grammatical constraints" (p. 1604). According to OT there is a universal set of constraints. These constraints are considered to be "not just universally available to be chosen from, but literally present in every language" (p. 1605). The grammar of any particular language, then, "consists entirely of constraints arranged in a strict domination hierarchy, in which each constraint is strictly more important than—takes absolute priority over—all the constraints lower ranked in the hierarchy" (p. 1605). So differences between languages are considered to be simply a result of the particular hierarchy of ranked constraints that they have.

What is the fate of markedness and the phenomena that it was used to "explain" in earlier theory? The answer is that the concept itself remains exactly the same! Here's what Prince and Smolensky say about it:

One class of universal constraints in optimality theory formalizes the notion of structural complexity or markedness. Grossly speaking, an element of linguistic structure is said to be marked if it is more complex than an alternative along some dimension. The relevant dimensions may sometimes correlate with comprehension, production, memory, or related physical and cognitive functions. The word-final consonant cluster *pd* is more marked than *pt*.... Marked elements tend to be absent altogether in certain languages, restricted in their use in other languages, later acquired by children, and in other ways avoided. This cluster of properties diagnostic of marked elements is given a uniform explanation in optimality theory which follows from their formal characterization. Marked structures are those that violate structural constraints. (p. 1605)

Note that the problem for the markedness concept mentioned earlier remains unsolved. Most importantly, we do not have an objective scale of complexity, and what is favored in languages is not always favored in speech acquisition. But what has changed is the status of the concept of markedness relative to the conceptual framework in general. Whether markedness effects occur in a language now depends on how the markedness constraint is ranked relative to other constraints. So the problem of front rounded vowels in German, referred to earlier, is no longer a problem because the relevant constraint is simply ranked lower here than in other languages that don't allow them.

But this is the emperor's new clothes! What is billed as a conceptual advance is actually a conceptual retreat. A theory that was sufficiently powerful to admit of exceptions is weakened to the point where virtually any outcome is consistent with it. No explanatory power is gained. No light is thrown on why any list of constraints exists in the first place or why languages are so variable with respect to how they rank them. Now we see why Ohala listed Optimality in his list of concepts that have no explanatory power. With regard to markedness, what was true in 1968 remains just as true today.

11.4 Conclusions

Generative phonology is now about half a century old. But when we look at the conceptual apparatus of the discipline, we find no satisfactory evidence that the mental structures they propose even exist. The main structural entity that they propose, the distinctive feature, probably does not exist in the form of mental units. Furthermore, much of the descriptive utility of the concept seems to arise not from mental factors but from substantive performance consequences of motor and perceptual propensities of the language user. The concept of markedness, considered to underlie much of the spectrum of well-formed phonological patterns of languages, is not adequately defined, was not satisfactorily incorporated into earlier generative phonology, and, like the distinctive feature, has absolutely no explanatory power in the sense of telling us why any aspect of speech is the way it is.

The recent advent of optimality theory actually seems to be a conceptual step backward in the sense that it is compatible with a much larger spectrum of language patterns than earlier conceptions but only in a post-hoc manner, offering no insight into why any sets of language-specific patterns or any hierarchical ordering of them in any particular language might occur. It gives the theorist flexibility at the cost of vacuity. Not only is there a lack of well-established mental units and processes, but there is no coherent view of the way in which proposed mental entities might interface with the performance level, the level at which adaptive acts that are selected for actually occur. It is perhaps time for generative phonologists to abandon the competence/performance distinction because they don't seem to have been able to build the necessary mental superstructure independent of the performance level, and information at this level is the only thing they can use to arrest the continual conceptual recycling process noted by Ohala.

12 Generative phonology
and the acquisition of speech

12.1 Current generative phonological approaches
to speech acquisition

In the previous chapter we considered the generative approach to speech in general. Now I want to make some explicit comparisons between that approach and the aspect of F/C theory that concerns speech acquisition, the one that has been most fleshed out.

From the UG perspective, the cornerstone of modern child phonology is what Macken calls the Strong Identity Hypothesis—"the capacity of children and adults is the same" (Macken, 1995, p. 673). According to this hypothesis, the innate capacity for speech acquisition unfolds in a *continuous* fashion, without radical developmental changes. Macken contrasts this with a *discontinuity* hypothesis in the following discussion:

In nature we find two contrasting development relations. In a relation manifesting essential continuity, the young are unskilled and simpler, yet they are fundamentally like the adults of the species in key respects; in a qualitatively different kind of developmental relation (which we might call "nonlinear") there is a radical difference between the beginning and end states and a major discontinuity in development. (p. 674)

Obviously in speech acquisition, as in behavioral development in general, there must be change. The question raised by Macken is, "How are the observable changes to be interpreted?"

We are interested here in the nature of those changes: are they qualitative in the sense that the basic structures and capacities change, or quantitative in the sense that the information or knowledge of a specific domain changes? If the principles and objects of phonology are present at the outset of language learning, and thus instantiated at each stage, and in each interim grammar constructed by the learner, as in Chomsky's theory, then the developmental model is one of basic continuity. We would then look to nonqualitative factors to explain the developmental stages. If, on the other hand, some phonological principles or objects are not present at the outset, then there is no necessary relationship between a developmental stage of the child and the properties of phonological systems. The developmental model will then be one of discontinuity, and we explain the qualitative characteristics of each stage in terms of the maturation of new linguistic skills or changes in other cognitive capacities, as presented in Piaget's theories. (p. 674)

Let me give the game away at the outset because a lot of the detailed issues that we need to cover here can be somewhat difficult for the uninitiated reader, and it should therefore help to know where we are going. My contention, following from Chapters 5 and 6, is that we must have a discontinuity theory rather than a continuity theory because a developing infant makes a flip-flop between a beginning, where she repeats the same syllable, to an end, where she actively avoids this repetition. The initial frame stage of speech acquisition that we postulate is one of *syllabic reduplication*, and the frame/content stage is one of *syllabic variegation*.

This conclusion will follow the section just ahead, which is perhaps the most difficult part of the book, though perhaps the part most germane to the generativism/Neodarwinism issue. It is where I compare, in detail, the approach of F/C theory and generative phonology to the body of knowledge of speech most central to F/C theory—knowledge of babbling and the earliest speech. This is a difficult section because it requires our considering a number of diverse individual concepts constructed by various researchers to apply to different subdomains of the ontogenetic process.

Three properties of babbling and early speech are most central to F/C theory: (1) the frame itself; (2) the internal (intracyclical) organization of the frame; and (3) the intercyclical organization of frame sequences. Let's now see how generative phonology deals with these properties.

12.1.1 Frames

The core concept of the F/C approach to speech acquisition is the concept of the frame. I am not aware of any attempt to evaluate the phenomenon that led us to the concept of *motor* frames, from the generative phonological viewpoint—namely, the basic close–open alternation of the mouth. But it's relatively clear that the *acoustic* pattern produced by frames is interpretable in terms of phonological notions regarding the syllable, and, as we will see below, CV sequences in babbling are considered to be syllable sequences, at least by Blevins (1995).

In phonology, the main way the syllable is defined is in terms of a "Sonority Hierarchy" (Blevins, 1995). Sonority, roughly synonymous with the phonetic concept of "loudness," is thought to be an innate property of syllables. The syllable "nucleus" (the vowel) is considered maximally sonorous, with sonority decreasing in "onsets" (intrasyllabic prevocalic consonants) and "codas" (intrasyllabic postvocalic consonants) in a linear relation with distance from the nucleus. (See Chapter 3 for definitions of these terms.) Like loudness, sonority is a perceptually based concept. But, as with the concepts of distinctive feature and markedness, despite a heavy reliance on the level of substance or performance in the adumbration of the concept (reliance on acoustics) it is nevertheless considered an *abstract* mental component at the level of form or competence (Blevins, 1995).

As the vowels are louder than the consonants in babbling and the two forms alternate, frames can be considered to be syllables obeying the sonority principle. Again, though, as in the case of distinctive features, one might ask why only one of the two substantive domains (perception and production) is chosen to represent the abstract concept. And again it appears to be a matter of convenience rather than a necessity that arises out of a comprehensive conceptual structure. The loudness dimension is more directly available to the analyst than the attribute I find more primary because it's the *source* of the loudness variations—mandibular oscillation. I'm not aware of any discussion of the ultimate causes of the sonority principle in generative phonology. (See Chapter 13 for a further discussion of sonority.)

Aspects of syllabic patterns of babbling have been taken by Blevins to support a markedness-based conception of syllable structure, and therefore the approach is subject to the reservations about the conceptual status of markedness presented in the previous chapter. Blevins makes the following statement about syllables in babbling, which incidentally is wrong about the last two properties she cites: "In the early stages of language development (early babbling) children produce syllables in which onsets are not obligatory, there are no complex onsets; there are no codas" (p. 218). Blevins asserts that the CV form is a universal syllable type. This means that within words the syllable boundary in repeated CV alternations lies after the V. But there is no evidence that babbling infants and speakers of first words have a syllable boundary in that location. Two of our findings suggest a lack of the required independence between V's in CV syllables and the C's that follow them, in Frame sequences. The first is the one mentioned in Chapter 6. If one picks out an infant's most favored labial–central and coronal–front CV forms, which amount to hundreds of productions, and then determines how often the two forms occur successively in a CVCV sequence in either order, one finds that they almost never do. This shows that these syllable types, however often they occur, are not independent entities in the sense that they can be inserted, as units, into a string of other kinds of syllables. Second, VC co-occurrence constraints are about as great as CV co-occurrence constraints in babbling and early words, while we found evidence of CV co-occurrence constraints but not VC co-occurrences in languages. This suggests that the independence in control between a V and a following C implied by the claim that a syllable boundary lies between them is a result of *development* and not innately available to the young infant, as Blevins implies when she equates infant patterns with adult patterns. What infants have available at babbling onset seems to be primarily a capacity to produce one cycle of a particular CV alternation alone, or to produce it and then reiterate it one or more times.

The key question that Blevins doesn't address is this: "Why, when a single alternation of two sounds is made in babbling, does the first sound tend to be a consonant and the last sound tend to be a vowel?" One possible answer—namely, that these patterns aren't language-specific but rather are associated with the basic process of combining phonation with articulation in vocalization episodes surrounded by rest—is testable in other species. In brief, one would expect a tendency for phonation to begin before the mouth has opened, and to conclude while the mouth is still open, resulting in a consonant-like initiation and a vowel-like termination. In unpublished work with Kinney, we have some preliminary evidence of this in goats. They tend to go "ba" rather than "ab."

Even this would not be an explanation of the CV form in terms of ultimate causes because we would still need to know why the onset of phonation tended to precede opening and why its offset preceded closing. But it would ground the CV in more basic aspects of mammalian biology rather than leaving it to be yet another gratuitous aspect of species-specific innateness.

12.1.2 *Intracyclical organization: CV co-occurrences*

What are the consequences of the existence of the three types of CV co-occurrences that we have observed in infants and languages for generative phonology? Some distinctive-feature systems have separate places of articulation features for vowels and consonants, a configuration that does not naturally "capture" (to use a pet word in generative phonology) the close relations between consonants and vowels that we have observed. But there are other systems in which consonants and vowels are systematically paired under the same feature nodes. Whether a system with separate features for vowels and consonants or features common to both is favored is a matter of what facts the theorist is attempting to handle. For example, while joint features for vowels and consonants are useful in characterizing languages with consonant–vowel co-occurrence patterns, separate features for vowels and consonants are useful where there is "vowel harmony"— i.e., systematic patterns of vowel relationships across intervening consonants—or, as mentioned before, in tone languages.

As joint features for consonants and vowels are more compatible with our CV co-occurrence findings than separate features for each, let's consider one scenario that has them. Clements, the originator of "Feature Geometry," has presented, together with Hume (Clements and Hume, 1995), a system of feature organization in which consonants and vowels are classified into the three familiar categories *labial, coronal,* and *dorsal,* as described in their formula 41:

Labial: involving a constriction formed by the lower lip
Coronal: involving a constriction formed by the front of the tongue
Dorsal: involving a constriction formed by the back of the tongue

The three types of vowel involved in the three categories are *rounded, front,* and *back,* respectively. The second and third pairings are the same lingual co-occurrences that we observed. As to the first pairing, we did find a tendency for labial consonants to co-occur with back vowels in babbling, which we believe could be attributed to rounding (Mean observed-to-expected ratio [O/E]: 1.23), but we did not find it in first words (Mean O/E: .91).

C. Levelt (1994), in a study of the words of twelve Dutch infants from 1:4 to 2:11, found strong tendencies toward all three of these co-occurrences in the Clements–Hume formula, not only in CV but also in VC sequences. Clements and Hume justify their classification by noting instances in which these co-occurrence patterns are particularly prominent in languages, and by instances of sound change in which each major class element assimilates to the other (e.g., consonants become coronal in a front-vowel environment, or vowels become front in coronal-consonant environments). In the case of the two co-occurrences involving lingual consonants, the patterns Clements and Hume observed in languages can be regarded simply as extreme forms of the patterns that we have observed in most of our ten languages in our statistical analysis (MacNeilage et al., 2000). Levelt uses a similar feature system to the one suggested by Clements and Hume (one formulated by Lahiri and Evers, 1991) to "account for" her finding that twelve infants ranging from 1:4 to 2:11 in age showed all three of the patterns noted by Clements and Hume.

As to the lingual consonants and their tendency to co-occur with particular vowels, I noted that both we and Clements and Hume observed the same phenomenon. How are the co-occurrence preferences of lingual consonants and vowels explained from the two perspectives? Davis and I explain it as a reflection of a basic property of the speech *action* system operating at the neuromuscular level—biomechanical inertia. Clements and Hume regard it as an aspect of an innate mental distinctive-feature system. They don't say why they regard this as a mental (competence-related) phenomenon rather than as a performance-level expression of a commonplace biomechanical property of skeletal motor systems. And they make no attempt to explain why a mental subsystem would have this kind of organization.

Another question that needs to be raised is, "Where do central vowels fit in such classifications?" Levelt didn't discuss central vowels, and as she presented no quantitative data, it's not possible to determine whether central vowels co-occurred with labials in her infants as they did in ours and in the other studies we reviewed in Chapter 5. But Clements and Hume explicitly address this question for phonological theory in general by asserting that central vocoids satisfy none of the definitions in their (41) and are thus treated as "phonologically placeless" (1995, p. 277). (Their category "vocoids" consists of vowels plus glides.) They then go on to conclude that the three features given in (41) "appear sufficient to characterize all phonological relevant properties of constriction location in vocoids" (p. 277).

From the point of view of someone who is not immersed in the formalism of phonological theory, this ad hoc decision to regard central vowels as not having a place of articulation at the abstract level is extremely troubling. It makes it necessary to have a special explanation for why such vowels consistently co-occur with a particular consonantal *place* of articulation. This treatment of central vowels is an example of the double standard noted earlier: use phonetic evidence when it's useful, abandon phonetics when it isn't. The main reason articulatory terms like "place" were adopted in distinctive-feature systems since *SPE* was that, being concrete terms, they had readily available referents, in contrast to the perceptual terms of Jakobson. Constriction locations are concrete facts about articulation, so the notion of constriction can be readily understood, and that is convenient for the phonologist. But Clements and Hume don't have their phonetic facts correct. Only some front and back vowels share constriction locations with coronal and dorsal consonants, respectively. The location of the vocal-tract constriction for low *front* vowels such as [æ] is in the pharynx, not in the coronal region. The location of the major constriction for low *back* vowels is also in the pharyngeal region (MacNeilage and Sholes, 1964), while the location for the most frequent dorsal consonants, the stops [g] and [k], is in the velar region. It isn't the sharing of the same region of constriction that's responsible for the lingual co-occurrence patterns. It's the position of the tongue in the front–back axis, which can have different consequences for the place of articulatory constriction in lingual consonants and the vowels typically associated with them.

Returning to the question of feature specification for central vowels, we observe a rather complex situation. If the region of constriction is the attribute that determines feature classification of vowels, the neutral (mid-central) vowel would also have to be regarded as phonologically placeless, because it's associated with a vocal tract with a uniform cross-sectional area, and therefore has no place of constriction. But again, this is a phonetic fact, not a phonological fact, and this should not be relevant to phonologically based classification. Low central vowels, like other low vowels, have a region of constriction in the pharynx. The tongue, being an incompressible mass, bordered anteriorly by the mandibular symphysis and the lower teeth, must move back if it is actively lowered, so all low vowels—front, central, or back—have a maximal constriction in the pharynx. Thus from a phonetic point of view, low vowels should share a pharyngeal consonant feature, which would fit the tendency for some low vowels to co-occur with pharyngeal consonants (for example, in Arabic), but not the co-occurrence of low *central* vowels with *labial* consonants.

What is problematic here for distinctive-feature systems that use joint specifications of consonants and vowels based on the *phonetic* fact of anatomical propinquity (involving shared use of the anterior tongue, or the posterior tongue, or the lips) is that the co-occurrence of labial closure with a central anatomical position of the tongue isn't based on anatomical propinquity. In my opinion, it results from the most basic movement of the oral apparatus, mandibular oscillation, *and from that alone*, at least in infants, because the tongue stays in its rest position relative to the mandible. But the mandible doesn't figure at all in the discussion of vowel–consonant relations by either Clements and Hume or by Levelt. While in biomechanical and dynamic terms the mandibular frame and the other two articulators to which it is attached, the lower lip and the tongue, are inevitably interdependent, and therefore mandibular movement has consequences for both the tongue and the lips, this simple fact is not represented anywhere in phonology.

The overall function of the frame is most fundamentally related to the linguistic concept of the syllable. With few exceptions, one frame corresponds to one syllable. But, as we have seen, the application of distinctive-feature theory and syllable theory to the frame structure tends to be treated as separate areas of phonological inquiry. While distinctive features are defined articulatorily, syllables are defined perceptually. Though both are considered to have abstract innate status, the relation between them has received very little attention. Levelt (1994) explicitly treats them separately in her feature-based conception of speech acquisition, making the assumption that "universal sonority templates take care of the sequencing of segments in the word" (p. 84). There is no reference to the syllable in Clements and Hume's sixty-page chapter on distinctive features. The syllable is discussed by Blevins in terms of segments—consonants and vowels—not distinctive features.

The co-occurrence of labial consonants with central vowels is fundamental to both the concept of the syllable *and* the concept of distinctive feature. As to the syllable, it is the pure (canonical) example of the cyclicity that underlies the sonority principle. As to the application of distinctive-feature theory to frames, because of the coherence of pure frame (the labial–central form), it makes no sense to treat the labial component as part of a feature that goes with rounded vowels while at the same time regarding the central vowel as not even part of a CV-based feature system—i.e., as phonologically placeless. The failure of generative phonology to deal with the relation between labial consonants and central vowels, which I regard as the most important CV relation in speech, on both phylogenetic and ontogenetic grounds, reveals a fundamental inadequacy in the generative approach.

12.1.3 Intercyclical organization: from harmony to variegation

As we have seen, intercyclical organization develops in infants from an initial favoring of reduplication—in our terms, frame reiteration—to a favoring of variegation—frames with content. We have found that the outcome of this trend in the case of place of articulation of consonants in adults is for place reduplication to occur at only two-thirds of chance levels (MacNeilage et al., 2000). We have asserted that the first systematic step toward variegation in infants is the adoption of the labial–vowel–coronal (LC) sequence.

Let's compare our treatment of the emergence of the LC sequence preference in consonant variegation to that of Levelt and Macken (see

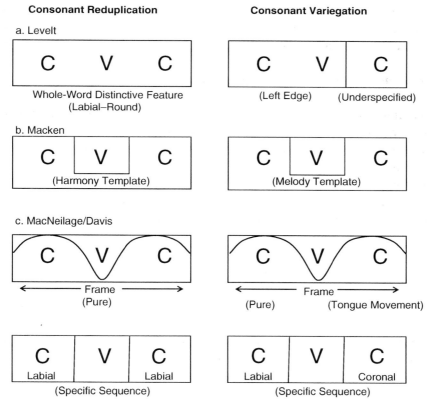

FIG. 12.1   Comparison of three conceptualizations of the development of the labial–coronal sequence effect.

Fig. 12.1) We will compare the three treatments (right side of figure) with the treatments of the characteristically favored consonant reduplication which precedes the emergence of the variegated form—the labial–labial sequence (left side of figure). Incidentally, all three models concern themselves only with place of articulation. Voicing and manner of articulation aren't separately considered.

Our view of the *facts* of early stages of intracyclical organization is reassuringly congruent with the view of Levelt (1994) based on a study of the early words of ten Dutch infants. In particular, Levelt finds that infants strongly favor consonant harmony in their first words, and then begin to develop the LC pattern. This agreement on what needs to be explained makes it particularly useful to compare our interpretation of the data with Levelt's, which is made from a generative phonological perspective.

Levelt's finding of co-occurrence constraints between vowels and adjacent consonants, together with her finding of early consonant harmony, leads her to conclude that in the initial manifestation of distinctive features in speech, they are specified for the entire phonological word. For example, when an infant produces [puf] for Dutch "poes" (cat), the joint feature of labial consonant–rounded vowel is considered to apply to the entire word, as shown in Fig. 12.1a, left side. Then when the infant subsequently produces the LC pattern [pus]—the correct phonetic rendering of Dutch "poes"—Levelt suggests that the "left edge" of the word "becomes available for place of articulation specification" (p. 75) (see Fig. 12.1a, right side). As I understand it, for this example the labial–round specification becomes restricted to the initial (left edge) consonant and the following vowel. Levelt considers that the final coronal is then produced as a result of underspecification. This assumption requires some explication.

"Underspecification" has become an extremely important concept in phonology in the last few years. What does it involve? To take a simple example, it's considered unnecessary to specify the segment /s/ in the input for English words which have three-consonant onset clusters (e.g., "screw," "splice") as all words that begin with three consonants begin with an [s] in English. Consequently, [s] can be inserted at a late stage of the derivation of such words as a default specification. Coronals are the most favored consonants for underspecification. Considered the most unmarked consonants (Paradis and Prunet, 1991), they are found to have a number of unique characteristics:

besides being more frequent, coronals are more prone to undergo assimilation processes than any other place of articulation. Conversely, coronals are the only consonants to be invisible to phonological processes such as deletion in Japanese. It has also been shown that in some languages coronals alone are transparent to vowels, and that consonant harmonies, to the exclusion of those involving laryngeal consonants, consist almost exclusively of coronal consonants. (p. 2, references omitted)

(The terms "invisible to" and "transparent to" mean that the presence of coronals in one part of a derivation doesn't interfere with—have any consequences for—patterns observable in other parts of the derivation.)

The motivation for using "underspecification" in phonology is that it increases the formal simplicity of derivations. But to the outsider, it's a counterintuitive concept, just as Clements and Hume's declaration that central vowels are placeless (unspecified for place) at the phonological level is counterintuitive. In concrete terms, it involves the existence of empty slots in the neural representation of words in the mental dictionary, and raises the question of how an infant could come by words with empty mental specifications at the most underlying level. Of course, this is not a problem for generative phonologists, who assume such empty categories are innate, hence don't concern themselves with details of the problem of origin. But it is a problem at the performance level because there is no evidence for underspecification or placelessness at the level of the control program.

Another deficiency of the concept arises when one notes that there must be two aspects to the mind/body interface: a motoric one and a perceptual one. We encounter underspecification when phonologists are attempting to give us a derivational account of *output*. But what about *input*? When a speaker produces a coronal, a listener hears acoustic correlates of a coronal. There must be some relationship between the representation of a sound as input and as output that allows an infant to learn to speak. But what would the relationship be in cases in which the representation of the output for coronals is not specified at some stage of the output derivation? Are we to believe that in the course of learning to speak, perceptual information relative to the category "coronal" is thrown away when it comes to producing speech patterns one is learning? Or do we have to believe that a veridical representation of coronals is present at a lower level of representation on the production side than on the perception side? If so, then if one is required to repeat a word with a coronal in it, does one have to go from perceptual representation to lack of specification, and then to a motor representation? This problem recalls the problem, discussed in the last chapter, of wanting to have a single set of distinctive features. Both perceptual and motor aspects of speech must eventually be understood within a single coherent framework. As we saw, if one makes distinctive features perceptual, they don't perspicuously characterize speech patterns that have articulatory motivations, and vice versa. In the case of underspecification, the desire to have a tidy output representation has negative consequences for our understanding of what an input-related representation would be like.

Levelt regards her characterization of the LC effect as preferable to the earlier assumption that it results from "a co-occurrence restriction on consonants to the effect that the first consonant in the word must have a more front place of articulation than the second one" (p. 75). This view, called "fronting," was originally formulated by Ingram (1974), who concluded that the phenomenon was an instance of markedness. But, as usual, this was only a redescription of the phenomenon and failed to consider why such a preference exists.

Let's now consider Macken's view. Her attention was drawn to the phenomenon when she found a Spanish infant with a strong tendency to prefer the labial–coronal sequence even when the word target he was attempting had a coronal–labial sequence. For example, he produced the Spanish word "sopa" (soup) as [pwæta] (Macken, 1978).

Macken characterizes consonant sequences in terms of innate C–C templates, ignoring the intervening vowel. Thus the consonant reduplications of babbling involve a "harmony template" (see Fig. 12.1b, left). However the emergence of the LC sequence preference involves a "melody template" (Fig. 12.1b, right). Both templates involve an intervening vowel slot that can be filled with *any* vowel. (In Macken's review article of 1995 she was unconvinced by the existing evidence, which has since become much stronger, that infants had co-occurrence constraints between consonants and vowels.)

In our model (Fig. 12.1c), the sine wave indicates the frame-related open–close alternation. LL sequences in our view involve one-and-a-half cycles of a pure frame, involving only mandibular oscillation with soft palate elevation (Fig. 12.1c, left). This means that the vowel called for is a central vowel. When LC structures emerge, the form is considered to still begin with a pure frame. But in the course of the open phase of the first cycle there is a tongue-fronting movement for the coronal, beginning during the vowel, and this presumably means there's a statistical tendency for the vowel to be a front vowel (see Fig. 12.1c, right). Depending on the strength of the two statistical tendencies, the actual vowel could be central (as in "but") or front (as in "bet"), but the model disfavors back vowels.

Of these three models, ours is the only model that has direct implications for performance, because it's explicitly concerned with the movements that are made. The other two models are abstract characterizations of phono-logical structure, either in featural terms (Levelt) or segmental terms (Macken). Neither model explicitly characterizes the observed rhythmic alternation between the open and closed state. Levelt's model is restricted to rounded vowels following labials, and thus, strictly speaking, is a model of "boot," not "but." Macken's model requires an abstract linkage between two temporally nonadjacent consonants, but allows the production of any vowel regardless of the articulatory configurations required for the consonants on each side of it. In Chapter 6 (see also MacNeilage and Davis, 2000), I presented an hypothesis as to *why* it's the LC sequence rather than the CL sequence that is favored. Neither of the other models has anything to say about why labials tend to precede coronals and not vice versa.

Information about what vowels actually occur in LC contexts is available from an intensive case study of one infant (MacNeilage and Davis, 1999). The observed-to-expected ratios of the three vowel types in labial–vowel–coronal environments were: front, .96; central, 1.28; back, .31. These observations, from data gathered before the hypothesis was formulated, strongly support the frame/content model which predicts either central or front vowels but not back vowels. As rounded vowels, called for in Levelt's conception, are back vowels in English, this result is a disconfirmation of Levelt's hypothesis. Macken made no predictions about vowels.

The LC effect seems to be a crucial case for distinguishing between the continuity and discontinuity options for speech development spelled out by Macken (1995). Both Levelt, and Davis and I, have found that this effect is not present earlier in development. It is therefore clearly a *surface* discontinuity. As our orientation includes a null hypothesis of assuming no difference between surface and underlying levels in early development unless there is extremely strong evidence to the contrary, we assume that it is a discontinuity, period. Note, however, that although we regard it as a discontinuity as far as the origin of speech is concerned, the elements composing it are not new. Pure frames and lingual movements were both present before the LC effect occurs/ed in ontogeny and phylogeny. It is just the relative timing of the two components that changes. In other words, in an evolutionary perspective it's a matter of "descent with modification" rather than a saltation resulting in a singularity.

Even though Levelt apparently feels she has "accounted for" the developmental sequence from consonant harmony to consonant diversity, it's worth noting that the coexistence of infant consonant harmony and an apparent constraint against consonant harmony in adult languages (termed the "infant/adult asymmetry" by Macken, 1995) has been viewed as a major problem for phonological theory *by phonologists themselves* (e.g., Drachman, 1976; Anderson, 1985) and is still viewed as a major problem in some quarters, because markedness requires only a single hierarchy of preferred forms. It is particularly notable that this asymmetry is even problematical for the new phonology, optimality theory, despite its versatility in accommodating a multiplicity of different patterns. For example, Pater (1997) observes that "chief" among the "puzzles" that "remain to be addressed" in optimality theory "is the fact that although consonant harmony is extremely common in child language, it is unattested in this form in adult languages, where primary place assimilation applies only locally, and not across intervening vowels" (p. 246). As an attempt to deal with the presence of early harmony in the context of optimality theory, in which sets of "constraints" take center stage, Pater takes the position that "the constraint *Repeat* is constructed by the child in response to the pressures imposed by the developing production system." This position "entails that at least some constraints of child phonology are inductively learned rather than innately given" (pp. 246–247). This is a peculiar stance for two reasons. First, it's difficult to see how the infant would learn harmony, when the ambient language models it is subject to tend to avoid it. Second, as consonant harmony is dominant in infants from the beginning of prespeech babbling, several months before the first words are produced, there is no evidence that the infant *constructs* it to solve problems of speech. If it were constructed, there should be a prior stage with less harmony before the construction occurs.

Pater adds a statement that, even without explication, makes it clear that the asymmetry problem goes right to the heart of optimality theory:

To explain the child/adult asymmetry it would also have to be the case that Repeat and other constraints like it are eliminated from the grammar, because if they were simply low ranked, it would be predicted by Factorial Typology that some languages would show their effects in "emergence of the unmarked" scenarios. Clearly the introduction of child-specific constraints has implications for learnability theory that cannot be taken lightly. Not only would constraint reranking have to be shown to be computationally tractable but an account would also have to be given of constraint genesis and of constraint extinction. (p. 247)

The hypothesis that harmony results from a basic hominid motor propensity that is superseded by variegation in infants, and in language evolution, because of demands for production of a large message set, is a simple alternative explanation for these findings.

There are a number of further instances in which differences between infant and adult patterns are incompatible with a single set of marking conventions across ages. These instances involve individual sound types or sound classes rather than phonotactic patterns. I'll give two examples. First, while the coronal place of articulation is considered most unmarked in languages, in terms of frequency, and other properties, labials should be considered most unmarked in first words, as labial frequencies increase to exceed coronal frequencies in the first-word period. Second, the fricative /s/ occurs in 83 percent of the languages in Maddieson's 1984 sample and therefore must be considered one of the most unmarked sounds. But, as we have seen, fricatives in general are extremely rare in first words.

Finally, there is one further problem for the markedness concept. It is the nonequivalence of two criteria of markedness: simplicity and frequency. From the point of view of simplicity, nasals should be more unmarked than oral sounds, as oral sounds require the additional movement of sealing the velopharyngeal port to block nasalization. But oral sounds are more frequent than nasals in languages, and are therefore considered more unmarked.

I shall conclude this comparison of F/C theory and developmental generative phonology, as I said I would, by asserting that a discontinuity theory of speech acquisition is more appropriate than the continuity theory favored by generativists. But a note of caution is in order here. *Continuity* and *discontinuity* are tricky words, and they can be interpreted in various ways. The developmental scientists Thelen and Smith (1994) wisely ask: "What does it mean for cognition to be 'continuous' across development? How much and in what way must the end state be contained in the organism from the beginning for development to be continuous?" (p. 30). We must also keep in mind Gould's statement, cited earlier, that discontinuity may be inherent in continuity (Gould, 1977). I am arguing for a developmental discontinuity in the context of the overall conceptual structure of F/C theory, which is considerably more well-developed than any contemporary generative conception of the nature of speech acquisition. I conclude that speech acquisition is discontinuous because I believe that the course of evolution of speech has called for such a discontinuity. I believe that the frame sequences most natural to hominids are reduplicative ones, but evolution has called for the opposite pattern—a variegated one—because it needed to expand the size of the phonological message set, and that is what such an expansion involved. An infant must telescope this progression and go from natural reduplication to unnatural variegation in a single generation. This is the nature of the discontinuity. No wonder it takes a few years to get there.

12.2 The competence–performance distinction to the rescue?

Rather than try to deal with problematical issues created by the properties of the phonetic level of speech acquisition, some phonologists in the generative tradition have tried to deal with them by ruling them out of court—by relegating them, in effect, to the performance domain. A relatively early attempt to do this was made by Moskowitz in an influential paper on language acquisition in the magazine *Scientific American* (1991). Moskowitz was influenced by Jakobson's incorrect contention that in infants, at the stage of first words, there is coexistence of phonetic versatility and phonological conservatism. Here is her argument:

There is one significant way in which the acquisition of phonology differs from the acquisition of other language systems. As a child is acquiring a phonological system, she must also learn the phonetic realization of the system: the actual details of physiological and acoustic phonetics, which call for coordination of a complex set of muscle movements. Some children complete the process of learning how to pronounce things earlier than others, but differences of this kind are not related to the learning of the phonological system. Brown had what has become a classic conversation with a child who referred to a "fis". Brown repeated "fis" and the child indignantly corrected him saying "fis". After several such exchanges Brown tried "fish", and the child, finally satisfied, replied "Yes fis." It was clear that the child was still not able to produce the distinction between the sounds "s" and "sh" though she knew such a systematic phonological distinction existed. Such *phonetic muddying of the phonological waters* complicates the study of this area of acquisition. Since the child's knowledge of the phonological system may not show up in her speech, it is not easy to determine what a child knows about the system without engaging in complex experimentation and creative hypothesizing. (1991, p. 148. Italics mine)

There is no question that infants can know things about the phonology of their language which they cannot produce. This is suggested by incorrect attempts that are in the right direction. Often, for example, place of articulation can be correct for a consonant while manner or voicing is not. It's also shown by occasions when an infant alternates between a correct and an incorrect form of the same word. Production of the correct word tells us that the infant "knows better" when she produces the incorrect version. But concluding that incorrect productions are simply phonetic-level performance problems and not part of the phonology finesses the question of how they ever become correct, and thus become an appropriate part of the phonology of the language.

This tendency to regard the phonetic level of speech as noise has a distinguished history in twentieth-century linguistics. It was favored by the structuralists before it was adopted by the generativists. For example, it led to the coining, by Hockett (1955), of perhaps the most colorful metaphor in the history of the linguistic sciences:

Imagine a row of Easter eggs carried along a moving belt; the eggs are of various sizes and variously colored, but not boiled. At a certain point, the belt carries the row of eggs between the two rollers of a wringer, which quite effectively smash them and rub them more or less into each other. The flow of eggs before the wringer represents the series of impulses from the phoneme source. The mess that emerges from the wringer represents the output of the speech transmitter. (p. 210)

What better contrast with the invisible miracle that I am trying to portray?

A more recent approach centered on the principle of phonetic muddying of the phonological waters, but a much more well-developed one, is that of Blevins (2004). Important data for her purposes are the specific kinds of speech-production errors that infants make before they succeed in producing words correctly. Four of the most common error types are shown at the bottom of Fig. 12.2. These patterns are presumably universal and therefore should play a key role in our understanding of the speech-acquisition process. Generative phonologists have generally believed that the production of these patterns results from the operation of phonological rules possessed by infants that transform correct perceptual representations of the adult lexical forms into incorrect outputs, as described at the top of Fig. 12.2. But, as usual, they don't consider why infants have these rules and not others beyond use of the flawed markedness concept. I have argued that all of these error types are articulatory simplifications. All involve the use of approximations of the required word, using aspects of the simpler, more articulatorily constrained babbling repertoire, as described on the left side of Fig. 12.2.

Blevins agrees with me that errors such as these "can all be viewed in terms of articulatory simplification" (p. 228). But, unlike me, she regards these errors as having a "superficial nature" (p. 231), by which she means they are confined to the performance level. Jakobson's (1968) designation

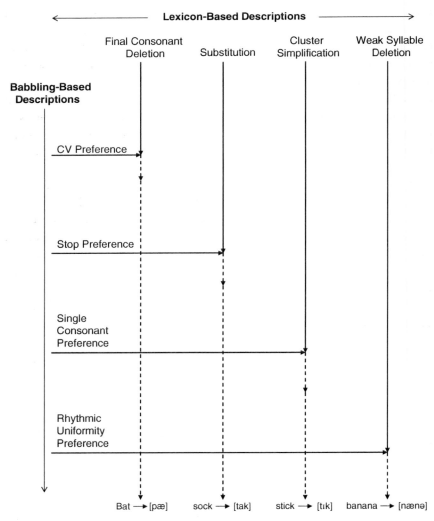

Fig. 12.2   Two alternative descriptions of infants' simplified versions of adult words.

of babbling as mere "external phonetics, predominantly articulatory in nature" (p. 27) comes to mind, but Blevins extends this characterization from babbling to the infant's incorrect word productions as well. She concludes that the "the majority of recurrent patterns in child language acquisition appear to derive from production constraints of the maturing articulatory system and do not reflect language competence" (p. 218).

There is a considerable irony in this conclusion. Blevins is unusual among modern phonologists in conceding a huge role for phonetic-level phenomena in the design of sound patterns of present-day languages. She takes a dia-chronic (historical) approach to the question, arguing that myriad present-day sound patterns result from historical sound changes formed by trade-offs between articulatory ease and perceptual distinctiveness. But once having made this case, which seems to have much merit, she proceeds to conclude that the error patterns of infants, which in many cases are reflections of patterns in languages, are not part of the grammar. Like Anderson, she believes in a remaining residue of "pure phonology." But beyond reasserting relatively well-known and debatable claims that innate perceptual capacities, distinctive features, and prosodic structures are components of this residue, she, again like Anderson, has little to say about what this pure phonology is actually like.

Obviously, Blevins and I have a fundamental difference of opinion here, despite our agreement on the articulatory basis of infant errors and on the importance of phonetic factors in the causality of sound patterns of languages. Taking the embodiment perspective, I believe the modern infant reflects the most fundamental properties of the speech-production system, and these bodily properties must therefore have been at the base of emerging mental representations of sound structures in hominids. What does Blevins believe is the origin of pure phonology? Unfortunately, though she calls her book *Evolutionary Phonology,* her conceptual structure extends back only to 7,000 years ago, which she believes is the limit of historical reconstruction. But we can assume she believes that if the first speakers indeed had the infant-like speech patterns I think they had, they must have been performance-level phenomena too, and our ancestors, like present-day infants, must somehow have risen above them from the beginning in order for pure phonology to have been the fundamental basis of speech.

Then what is to be made of serial-organization patterns of infant speech that often show up in their errors but which are characteristic of *correct* patterns of modern languages? For instance, what is to be made of errors in which infants produce one of the three types of CV syllables preferred in languages, as we have found they typically do (Davis et al., 2005) when another less preferred syllable type is called for? Do we have to put these pervasive language patterns into the performance component even though they are indistinguishable from patterns that are correctly produced at another time in an attempt at a word that also has them? What is to be made of the LC pattern—the preferred pattern in languages—when Macken's infant erroneously produces it when a CL pattern is called for? Do we have to eliminate this language pattern from the phonology, even though there is a 2:1 ratio of LC to CL patterns in languages (MacNeilage et al., 2000)? Isn't this throwing out the baby with the bathwater?

If there was any doubt that what we are looking at here is a modern reincarnation of Descartes' mind/body dualism, it is removed by Hale and Reiss' (1998) approach to child phonology. They explicitly relate the competence/performance dichotomy to the mind/body dichotomy as we will see in the following discussion. First they say that

> In order to interpret any data derived from speech behavior, the competence/performance distinction must be maintained: an explicit characterization of the boundaries should be one of the primary goals of phonological theory, since it defines the sphere of inquiry with which we must concern ourselves. It is clear that a more explicit theory of performance (or rather several theories) is a necessity; however it must be predicated on a coherent theory of grammatical competence. (p. 680)

They get their justification for this stance from Chomsky:

> Linguistic theory is concerned primarily with an ideal speaker-listener, in a completely homogeneous speech community, who knows its language perfectly and is unaffected by such grammatically irrelevant conditions as memory limitations, distractions, shifts of attention and interest and errors (random or characteristic) in applying his knowledge of the language in actual performance. This seems to me to have been the position of the founders of modern general linguistics, and no cogent reason for modifying it has been offered. (Chomsky, 1965, pp. 3–4)

Note in particular Chomsky's relegation of "characteristic errors," which must include the articulatory errors of infants, to the performance domain. For Hale and Reiss, like Moskowitz and Blevins, these articulatory errors are errors of performance, not competence. They then go on to cast this dichotomy explicitly in mind/body terms:

> An evaluation of our hypothesis involves confronting the difficult problem of distinguishing in children as we do in adults (in keeping with the Strong Identity

hypothesis) between an output of the phonology (a mental representation) and a real-time output of the body under some particular circumstances (those in effect at the time of the utterance). (Hale and Reiss, 1998, p. 672)

In other words, although they don't acknowledge their Cartesian heritage, and may not even realize it, the competence/performance distinction in the hands of Hale and Reiss *is* the Cartesian mind/body distinction. And although they don't say so, the same thing is true for Moskowitz and Blevins.

In my view, these denials of the relevance of infant articulatory patterns to our understanding of speech as a human mental phenomenon are actively preventing us from coming up with a Neodarwinian explanation of the nature of speech in terms of ultimate causes. And unfortunately we have little in the way of counterforces in the phonetic sciences that might advance the Neodarwinian perspective. Phoneticians have tended to concern themselves only with Tinbergen's "How does it work?" question.

Finally, it's only fair to say that Chomsky (2000) has recently taken a less extreme position than the above authors on the question of the implications of the competence/performance distinction for phonology. These authors tend to opt for a complete mind/body split in speech acquisition. They characterize the performance level as primarily a nuisance—a smokescreen that stops us from having a direct view of the competence level. In contrast, Chomsky recognizes that the performance level is a necessary part of language. He characterizes the situation as follows. The first event for him is the creation of the "language faculty"—UG. He notes that "this faculty includes at least a cognitive system, that is, a system that stores information" (2000, p. 4). Then he goes on to say:

There have to be systems that access that information, the performance systems. Now a factual question arises: to what extent are the performance systems language-dedicated themselves? Take, say, the sensorimotor systems, the articulatory–perceptual systems which access information that is given to them by the language faculty. Are they themselves part of the language faculty? Are they themselves language dedicated? That is not really known. The assumption is that they are dedicated to some extent, and to some extent they are not. (2000, p. 5)

So Chomsky at least recognizes that there has to be an interface between competence and performance. But the only thing he considers is a one-way adjustment—an adaptation of the performance level to the competence level. Yet this is still unsatisfactory from my embodiment perspective, because I require that the body exert a formative influence on the mind. And we have yet to see a plausible scenario for how the mental level could have gotten started on its own rather than as a response to bodily contingencies.

12.3 Explanation and the metatheory of linguistics

In these past several pages we have reviewed a number of instances in which linguists believe they have provided explanations for phenomena of speech acquisition when in fact they have not. The phonological literature is replete with the use of words like "explanation" and "accounts for," and in all these instances the terms are misused. I will go so far as to say that generative phonology has not explained a single phenomenon, if one uses "explained" in the conventional sense of pertaining to causes.

The closest that generative linguists have come to realizing that they have an explanation problem may be their vague feeling that they are not getting the respect they deserve from other disciplines. For example, in a paper entitled "Why are they saying these things about us?" Jackendoff (1988) confesses, "Often I have found myself depressed by their apparent failure to recognize the value of the sort of work my friends and I do" (p. 435).

Jackendoff asks, "What does phonology tell us about the mind, anyway?" He answers:

If there is any message that I would hope nonlinguists would derive from our work, it is the hypothesis that one's cognitive and behavioral repertoire is significantly shaped by biologically transmitted innate knowledge, and that this knowledge can be expressed by a set of formal principles. In the larger picture, the importance of phonology and syntax comes from their status as the two domains in which this hypothesis has been most extensively investigated. (p. 437)

But Jackendoff finds that "this too goes unappreciated. I have been asked by one of the major figures in cognitive science, a prominent philosopher of the Boston cognitive science community, Why do you people keep using this bogus appeal to innateness? You're getting yourselves off the hook too easily" (p. 437). The problem seems to be a lack of realization that calling something "innate" is not explaining it.

In reality, linguistics is, at bottom, a *descriptive* discipline, a discipline along the lines of classical botany, as practiced by Linnaeus. Braine (1994) has provided an extremely perceptive characterization of how the discipline operates:

The goal of linguistic theory is to *describe* human languages [italics mine]. Simplicity and generality are gained by a description that minimizes what is specific to each language; one tries to account for as much structure as possible by means of principles and facts that are universal to all languages, and one tries to account for as much variation as possible on the basis of variation along well specified parameters. The assumption that such universals have an innate basis is a natural one, and accounts for why so many linguists are nativists. (p. 14)

Chomsky (1964) has explicitly argued for the presence of an explanatory level in linguistics. He distinguishes three levels of success for grammatical description—observational adequacy, descriptive adequacy, and explanatory adequacy:

The lowest level of success [observational adequacy] is achieved if the grammar presents the observed primary data correctly. A second and higher level of success [descriptive adequacy] is achieved when the grammar gives a correct account of the intuition of the native speaker, and specifies the observed data (in particular) in terms of significant generalizations that express underlying regularities in the language. A third and still higher level of success [explanatory adequacy] is achieved when the associated linguistic theory provides a general basis for selecting a grammar that achieves the second level of success over other grammars consistent with the relevant observed data that do not achieve this level of success. In this case we can say that the linguistic theory in question suggests an explanation for the linguistic intuition of the native speaker. (p. 62–63)

But this concept of "explanation" has some grave problems.

One is the lack of an objective evaluation procedure to select what Chomsky calls the "most highly valued" (p. 65) grammar from among competing grammars.

Another problem is that we've never had several grammars offering competing descriptions of any sizeable corpus of linguistic material. Different grammars tend instead to focus on different aspects of language.

The biggest problem, though, is Chomsky's restriction of the paradigm to language-internal considerations. I contend that the linguist's conception of "explanation" is inadequate for science in the Darwinian era. To truly explain language, one must understand it in terms of its *ultimate causes,* and this ideally involves providing answers to all of Tinbergen's four questions, *especially the question of how language got that way in phylogeny.* It necessarily involves language-*external* considerations as well as language-internal considerations, because *language evolved from non-language.*

Why has generative linguistics tended to avoid language-external considerations in formulating its theories? Simply because it believes that language is a self-contained body—no less than, say, geometry and calculus. That assumption cuts off language from traditional notions of causality. Like branches of mathematics, language is considered *essentialistic*. Form is given a priori, so it isn't pertinent to ask where it comes from. There is, as I said in Chapter 2, an aesthetic component to this. Surely such a magnificent system can't have gotten there simply as a distillation of a history of communicative give-and-take between a few unwashed ancestors. But we have seen that the only attempt to provide a purely formal framework for phonology, *SPE*, has been a failure. The implications of this failure don't seem to have been assimilated.

I contend that the declaration of a Cartesian mind/body dichotomy for speech—a dichotomy between an abstract set of a priori phonological forms and a substantive phonetic level of perception and production—won't be a useful way to regard speech in the future. To declare modular status for a mental phonology is unrealistic. Generative phonologists have been able to avoid the problem of the necessary interface between the mental and the substantive level only by declaring phonology independent of the performance level, thus ducking Tinbergen's first question, "How does it work?" At the same time, they try to get us to believe that their abstract view has consequences for performance. They do this by building a conceptual apparatus much of which is actually *at* the performance level and then designating it as abstract but with consequences for performance! However, *interfaces* between any relatively abstract level and the perception and production levels with which the abstract level must cooperate in real-time speech must be part of any workable model of speech, and there are no such interfaces in phonological theory. No purely abstract level has ever been constructed by generativists for the very good reason that no such level has been constructed by the organism either.

What is the alternative? As I noted in Chapter 1, Sperry (1952) anticipated the development of an embodiment perspective on the mind when he stated the following heuristic for understanding mental organization in relation to output at the level of neural organization:

the unknown cerebral events in psychic experience must necessarily involve excitation patterns so designed that they intermesh in intimate fashion with the motor and premotor patterns. (p. 300)

Sperry's perspective assigns a central role to the study of the interfacing of the mental level with the physical because he suggests deriving the mental from the physical. Consider how this perspective applies to the LC effect. If the form of the first systematic increase in the complexity of serial organization of speech in infants (and perhaps in early hominids) is constrained by embodiment, as we have argued, the entire series of events in the achievement of modern target levels of serial complexity in ontogeny and phylogeny might be similarly constrained. If the form of the first systematic increase in serial complexity of speech in infants (and perhaps in early hominids) is constrained by the problem of interfacing the motor level with the mental level of lexical specification *in real time*, then the interfacing problem may be an important aspect of the entire process of developing a complete system. In Chapter 6, I suggested another place where the problem of interfacing of the physical with the mental components of the system seems to have important consequences. I suggested that the reason why consonant repetition might fall below chance levels in the serial ordering of speech is that repetition of the same substantive entities within a narrow time span may produce confusion effects in the processing of sequences of sounds at the level of short-term or working memory.

It is crucially important to note what Sperry goes on to say:

Once this relationship [between mental and motor patterns] is recognized as a necessary feature of the neural correlates of psychic experience, we can automatically exclude numerous forms of brain code which might otherwise seem reasonable but which fail to meet this criterion. (p. 300)

Following Sperry, we can automatically exclude structuralist characterizations which do not consider the mental/motor relationship.

Anderson (1985) has pointed out that Saussure's original distinction between "la langue" and "la parole" (form and substance), which is similar to Chomsky's competence/performance distinction, had the advantage, for linguists, that it allowed them to be "emancipated from their growing obsession with phonetic detail" (p. 42). But in the final analysis, the main thing it might have bought them was a release from reality. Again, Sperry's alternative perspective bears repeating:

the more we learn about the motor and premotor mechanisms, the more restrictions we add to the working picture of the unknown mental patterns, and hence the closer our speculation will be forced to converge toward an accurate description of their true nature. (p. 300)

Finally, as was pointed out in Chapter 1, the classical perspective has no implications for the time domain. The only comment I reviewed in this chapter that might be construed as having reference to real-time organization was Levelt's assumption that "universal sonority templates take care of the sequencing of segments in the word." However, the sonority sequencing principle applies only to the *form* of syllables, not to their real-time production. It is a structuralist conception without functional consequences.

The absence of a treatment of the time domain in generative phonology is most clearly seen when one considers the domain of shallow time—the period of speech acquisition. Jakobson's (1968) proposed perceptually based theory, which did prescribe a sequence of events, proved to be wrong, and no other one with implications for the sequence of development has become available. The question of why the sequence of events is from harmony to variegation has not even been asked. Jakobson attributed the sequence of events in sound acquisition to a markedness principle, but this concept proved to be non-viable. As the infant is considered to possess all the basic capabilities in the beginning, according to the generative phonology perspective, the question of when the various capabilities manifest themselves, and why the order of events is the way that it is, would seem to be a matter of little interest. But the order of events and the motivation for that particular order is normally a prime consideration in developmental science.

12.4 Summary

Let me recap my argument about the generative approach to speech.

This alternative to the Neodarwinian approach suffers some severe conceptual problems. First is the fancifulness of the Chomskyan biological hypothesis underlying the supposed innate universal grammar—namely, that UG originated as a saltational genetic event, a macromutation evoked by a cosmic ray shower. In current evolutionary biology, macromutations are regarded as almost universally fatal, and Stent (1981), among others, regards direct genetic specification of UG in the brain as impossible.

The implication that there was an instantaneous origin of the complete phonological component means that there is no phylogenetic time domain to accommodate a transition from simpler to more complex forms, which one might expect from a descent-with-modification perspective, and common sense. There are no time-domain consequences for ontogeny either. As

Braine (1994) points out, "nativism is ultimately unsatisfactory because it systematically neglects the...task [of] account[ing]for development, including the emergence of the postulated innate primitives" (p. 9). As I mentioned in Chapter 2, we have no principled conception of what is triggered and shaped. We only have post hoc characterizations such as the ones concerning the LC effect which we reviewed. Finally, there is no treatment of the real-time domain of online use.

No less problematical is the more detailed conceptual structure of generative phonology—specifically the notions of distinctive feature and markedness. Although distinctive features are the supposed elements of phonology, they are units invented by the analysts, not units of function. Indeed, the concept of distinctive feature is sustained by an intellectual double standard. Most if not all of the conceptual success of feature theory has resulted from defining features in perceptual or articulatory terms, but perception and articulation are at the substance (performance) level, while features are considered to be abstract concepts at the level of form (competence). The sudden radical shift, in 1968, from a perceptually defined to an articulatorily defined feature set is symptomatic of a lack of a solid basis for the feature concept.

Markedness has its own problems. A concept related to how basic our various sounds and sound patterns are, markedness is defined circularly, primarily in terms of frequency of occurrence of particular forms, and cannot be applied consistently across languages or across ontogeny.

The application of generative phonology to the main speech-acquisition phenomena addressed by the frame/content theory (frames, intrasyllabic patterns, and intersyllabic patterns) turns out to be a heterogeneous collection of ad hoc suppositions.

Notably, speech acquisition turns out to call for a *discontinuity* theory rather than the *continuity* theory required by UG. Our analysis of the generative approach to speech acquisition provides ample support for Miller's conclusion (Chapter 2) that generative linguistics is simply concerned with description, not explanation. The absence of an explanatory level results from a decision to restrict the domain of inquiry to system-internal phenomena, basically resulting in an essentialistic formulation.

PART VI

A perspective on speech from manual evolution

13 An amodal phonology? Implications of the existence of sign language

13.1 Introduction

A key development in cognitive science is the conclusion that sign languages of the deaf are true languages, differing from spoken languages only in the modality of their transmission. Perhaps the most extreme form of mentalism in generative phonology is the belief that in consequence of this equivalence of the two forms of language there is a modality-independent phonology underlying their two very different embodied surface forms: the vocal–auditory and manual–visual forms. For example, Chomsky (2006) has recently reasserted that there are "discoveries about sign languages in recent years which provide substantial evidence that externalization is modality independent."

But from the embodiment perspective that lies behind my approach there is no reason to believe that the detailed organization of the phonological components of speech and sign language would be comparable for linguistic reasons. For instance, I have argued that the evolution of speech involved taking advantage of a single pre-existing cyclicity (of the mandible) and increasing its complexity to increase message-transmission capability. There is no reason to believe that this method would have had to be adapted by the visual–manual channel in order for it to transmit language. And in fact one only needs to take a glance at the organization of sign language to see that it hasn't. Thus, in my view, the basic organization of the phonological components of spoken and sign language are modality-specific, and almost no clear amodal commonalities of the two transmission systems have been identified.

The following three sections of this chapter deal with the amodality question. In the first section, I provide a brief introduction to sign language and then consider arguments based on the structure and function of the two modalities as to whether they share a common amodal core or not. In the second section, I consider Petitto's claims that the acquisition of speech and sign are based on a single amodal process. In the third section, I evaluate the claims of Klima and Bellugi and their colleagues that amodal brain organization underlies spoken and signed languages.

Then, in the final section, I take up a more well-known claim about sign language, namely, that it was the first language. This claim is antithetical to my thesis that speech evolved first. From the point of view of action organization it would mean, if true, that the organization of speech was somehow derived from the organization of a previous very different kind of language. I don't believe there is any evidence that this was the case.

13.2 Amodality and the structure and function of sign-language phonology

So let's begin with how signs are made. Each sign has three major parameters:

(1) Location (aka "place of articulation")—the place or places in signing space to which the hand or hands are moved.

(2) Movement—the specific action associated with the sign. Path movements are relatively straight movements from the location for one sign to that of the next. Internal movements comprise handshape change, orientation change, or a combination of these.

(3) Handshape—the configuration of the fingers and thumbs.

Take, for example, the sign for "decide" in American Sign Language (ASL). The location of this sign is in front of the left and right edges of the torso (the places to which the arms move). The movement is a concurrent downward movement of both forearms. The handshape is an "O" shape made by contact between the thumb and the forefinger of each hand, with the remaining fingers splayed out. Individual signs have typically been regarded as analogous to syllables in spoken language.

The most obvious question to ask here is whether sign languages have analogous units to those of spoken language—distinctive features, segments, and syllables.

Feature systems for distinctive features of sign language have been proposed (e.g., Brentari, 2002; Sandler and Lillo-Martin, 2006, pp. 272–278), although there is no consensus on a particular set. Despite their finding a close analogy between the conceptual status of distinctive features across the two modalities, Sandler and Lillo-Martin point out that "The features themselves are of course quite different" (2006, p. 273). Thus while on the one hand we have features associated with place, manner, and voicing of consonants and tongue-position of vowels, on the other hand we have features related to location, handshape, and movement. To my knowledge, no one has tried to directly map the features of sign languages onto any proposed set for speech.

Sandler and Lillo-Martin conclude with respect to features that the "quest for a universal set of them must be conducted according to modality" (p. 273). They go on to say that

If the set of features required to describe sign languages is a function of modality, then the set of features required to describe spoken languages is also a function of modality. If each modality carves out a different set of features, then the set arrived at must be *explained*, motivated on the basis of production, perception and processing constraints, rather than assumed to be innately specified. (p. 273)

More fundamentally, if I have correctly argued in Chapter 11 that distinctive features are an artifact of linguistic description and therefore have no reality status in speech, then there is no reason to suspect that they would have reality status in sign language either.

Analogs to segments have also been proposed for sign language. Most often, locations and handshapes have been considered consonantal and movements vocalic. This has been a very complex topic, marked by conflicting criteria and evidence (see Sandler and Lillo-Martin, 2006). But from a functional standpoint, studies of signing errors (Newkirk et al., 1980; Hohenberger, Happ, and Leuninger, 2002) show there is no equivalence between the proposed segmental entities in sign language and consonantal and vocalic elements in speech. Most importantly, while speech errors are subsyllabic, involving segments serially ordered within the syllable, components of the proposed sign syllable (locations, handshapes, movement) tend to be misplaced as a whole in sign errors. And there are numerous other differences between the modalities when one considers the different contingencies associated with vowel errors and consonant errors in speech. In fact, there is no convincing argument that sign language has analogs to consonants and vowels. Facts like these and others led Hohenberger et al. (2002) to conclude, in their study of signing errors, that "Obviously the 'frame–content' metaphor cannot be transferred to signed languages straightforwardly" (p. 134). In my view, this is another way of saying that, in this aspect of function, signs cannot be regarded as analogous to syllables.

There are a number of other important ways in which signs of sign languages are different from syllables of spoken language. There is no counterpart in sign to the asymmetry in spoken syllables represented by the fact that the CV syllable is the only universal syllable type in speech. Neither is there a counterpart to the asymmetry in spoken syllables (see Ch. 3) indicated by their division into onset and rhyme whereby onset is a single component but rhyme is divided up into nucleus and coda. Furthermore, as Sandler and Lillo-Martin (2006) point out, if there was a literal analog to the sonority principle in sign language, it would be the brightness principle, and there is of course no such principle. The only reasonably well-established similarity between syllables in speech and signs is that in some instances signs seem to behave as rhythmic units. For example, temporal parameters of the implementation of a handshape and a location are coordinated with the movement for a sign (Brentari and Poizner, 1994). And Sandler (2008) notes that instances of the implementation of what could be called stress in sign language are positioned with respect to individual signs.

The sign in sign languages also differs from a spoken syllable in terms of how it relates to higher (morpho-lexical) levels of the grammar. While spoken syllables are not isomorphic with words, there is what Sandler (2008) calls a "conspiracy" in sign language for the sign, that is, the sign language word, to be monosyllabic. Further, while morphemes are typically added to the stem form of a spoken word by adding syllables, they are typically added by modifications within a single sign in sign language. This, together with the fact that spoken syllables feature sequences of segments while signs have three simultaneously available components (location, handshape, movement), has led to the common tendency to denote spoken language as sequential while sign language is simultaneous (e.g., Jakobson, 1967).

In summary, the organization of the phonological components of spoken and signed languages is radically different. Apart from the fact that they both have a level at which meaningless subcomponents are concatenated in the service of conveying meaning differences, and some indications that the syllable and the sign share aspects of rhythmic organization, there is no justification for the claim that the two components show amodality.

Brentari (2002) has made the only attempt that I know of to say what commonalities between speech and signed language are candidates for a single innate, amodal UG. Here are her two candidates that specifically relate to the phonological component (p. 60):

(1) There is a part of structure that carries most of the paradigmatic contrasts: consonants in spoken languages; handshape + place...in sign languages.
(2) There is a part of structure that comprises the medium by which the signal is carried over long distances: vowels in spoken languages; movements in signed languages.

These properties pertain to effective communication, to the performance level, but UG is not about effective communication, it is about competence.

Brentari (2002) also proposed five differences in phonological organization between speech and signed languages. Most involve technical formal claims. The only one that is intelligible in the context of the present discussion is that "Cs and Vs are realized [in sign language] at the same time rather than sequentially" (p. 60). According to the frame/content theory, there could be no more fundamental difference between speech and sign-language phonology than this.

13.3 Petitto's position: amodality revealed by acquisition of sign language

Petitto has made the widely accepted claim that language has an innate amodal core. She suggests three particular reasons. The first reason is that the structure of spoken and signed languages is "identical" from the beginning of babbling onward. The second reason is that the distribution in time of the developmental landmarks of spoken and sign language is identical. The third reason is that spoken and signed languages share an innate "structure recognition mechanism" (Petitto, 1993, p. 374). According to Petitto et al. (2004), "babies are born with a sensitivity to specific rhythmic patterns at the heart of human language, and the capacity to use them" (p. 44). This is supposedly a capacity to utilize a single one-per-second movement rhythmicity.

With respect to the first two contentions, Petitto's position is endorsed by Chomsky (2006), who states that "sign languages are structurally very much like spoken languages and follow the same developmental patterns from the babbling stage to full competence." It's not necessary to repeat the evidence that the phonological structure of sign is radically different from that of speech. In addition, it is not established that spoken and signed babbling have identical developmental schedules. The claim that time of babbling onset is identical in the two modalities comes largely from Petitto and Marentette's (1991) statement that "by age 10 months, the deaf infants were well into the syllabic manual babbling stage which occurred at the same time as in hearing infants (ages 7–10 months)" (p. 1494). This is not evidence about when sign babbling begins, and no other evidence on this matter has been presented.

Establishing a typical time of onset for a behavior requires an objective definition of the behavior, allowing its onset to be detected. In addition, as most biological attributes are normally distributed (i.e., characterized by a bell curve), a relatively sizeable group of infants needs to be studied in order to obtain a reliable estimate of typical onset time. A study of babbling onset time by van der Stelt and Koopmans-van Beinum (1986) had both of these desirable characteristics. They asked fifty-one Dutch parents to record the day on which their infant began babbling, as indicated by repetitive rhythmic close–open alternations of the mouth accompanied by phonation. This is easy for parents to do. (See also Oller, Eilers, & Bassinger, 2001.) Fig. 13.1 summarizes their results. The distribution of onset times turned out to be relatively normal, with a mean of 31 weeks (i.e., slightly into the eighth month) and a standard deviation of 3½ weeks. The latter statistic means that about two-thirds of the infants began babbling within a 7-week period centered on the mean.

Not only is there no evidence as to when sign babbling begins, but it is not clear what such evidence would consist of. There is a generally accepted criterion for spoken babbling onset provided by Oller (1986). When utterances with a relatively rhythmic alternation between a closed and open mouth (frames) account for more than 20 percent of all utterances, the infant is in the spoken babbling stage. Petitto and Marentette (1991) assert that manual babbling involves individual signs, which they equate with syllables. They state that "A well-formed syllable has a handshape, a location,

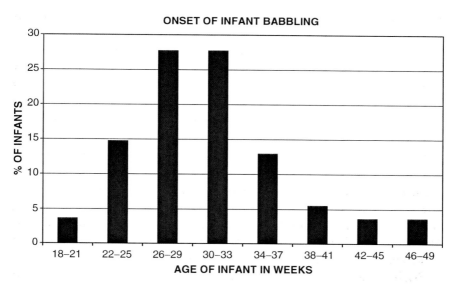

FIG. 13.1   Figure showing the distribution of spoken babbling onset times in 51 infants. (adapted from van der Stelt and Koopmans-van Beinum, 1986)

and a path movement (change of location) or secondary movement (change in handshape, or orientation)" (p. 1495). But as Meier and Willerman (1995) pointed out, "except for statically held postures, every gesture, including nonlinguistic ones, will meet these criteria" (p. 396). For example, judging from the description that Rönnqvist and von Hofsten (1994) provided of 2,530 spontaneous manual movements of newborn infants, a huge number of them qualified as signs. How do we exclude the conclusion that sign language begins at birth?

Petitto has also claimed, on the basis of unpublished observations of signed babbling, that spoken and signed babbling share two successive stages equivalent to the reduplicative and variegated stages that had been suggested for spoken babbling. As mentioned in Chapter 5, there are now a number of studies that have failed to identify a second stage within the babbling period. So if in fact Petitto has made the discovery that there are two stages of manual babbling, she has inadvertently found that manual babbling is different from spoken babbling.

Chomsky (2006) also endorses Petitto's conclusion regarding the supposed innate "structure recognition mechanism." He says that "sensitivity to phonetic-syllabic contrasts is a fundamentally linguistic (not acoustic) process and part of the baby's innate endowment." Evidence for a one-per-second rhythm comes from a study in which data from an optotrack system suggested that the sign babbling of deaf infants made manual movements at that rate while normal infants didn't (Petitto et al., 2004). This doesn't constitute evidence of a universal structure-recognition mechanism. Consider first the claim that vocal babbling occurs at a rate of one cycle per second. If true, it would be inconsistent with one of the generally accepted criteria for canonical vocal babbling (Oller, 1986), namely, that a one-second-long CV sequence is far too long to be acceptable as canonical. Also, one only has to listen to babbling to hear that the rate of CV repetition is much faster than one per second. A number of studies have put the CV repetition rate of babbling at about three per second (Levitt and Wang, 1991; Lynch et al., 1995; Nathani, Oller, and Cobo-Lewis, 2003), and we have recently replicated this finding in our laboratory (Dolata, Davis, and MacNeilage, 2008).

As to adult production rates, Bellugi and Fischer (1972) found that the adult signing rate is about 2.5 per second. And a number of studies have converged on the conclusion that the syllable-production rate of speech is about 5 per second (e.g., Arai and Greenberg, 1997; Crystal and House, 1982; Malecot, Johnson, and Kizziar, 1972). We, too, found that adults produce strings of reduplicated CV syllables at about this rate (Dolata, Davis, and MacNeilage, 2008). Thus, it has been known for a long time that there is no evidence for a ubiquitous one-per-second rate which is the supposed basis of the structure recognition mechanism.

Finally, while there is no substance to Petitto's claim that the structure of spoken and sign babbling is "identical," there are two major similarities between early vocal and manual functions. But they are not of the kind that Petitto would call "linguistic." The first is that Meier and his colleagues have found, as we have found for speech, that biomechanical constraints dominate the babbling and early-word stages of sign language (Meier, 2002; Meier et al., 2008). Easier movements and simpler handshapes are preferred, and the proximal articulators (the arms) are favored over the eventually more skilled and differentiated distal articulators (hands/fingers). The second is that vocal (babbling) and manual rhythmicities (rattle shaking) are correlated in two ways that suggest that they are part of a "broader development process" (Iverson et al., 2007) that transcends language. There is a temporal correlation between babbling onset and an increase in frequency of the manual rhythmicity

(Iverson et al., 2007), and babbling is more likely to occur with than without concurrent manual rhythmicities (Iverson and Fagan, 2004).

In summary, there is no evidence from sign babbling for claims of a structural identity between sign babbling and vocal babbling, no evidence that the two phenomena are developmentally synchronous in terms of onsets or progressive development, and no evidence that there is a single "linguistic" rhythm-based structure recognition mechanism underlying spoken and sign language acquisition.

13.4 Bellugi and Klima's position: amodality revealed by sign-language neurology

Klima, Bellugi, and their colleagues have made the claim, based on studies of sign-language aphasia and subsequent imaging studies, that "the left cerebral hemisphere in humans may have an innate predisposition for the central components of language independent of the modality" (Poizner, Klima, and Bellugi, 1987, p. 212). In this context, Chomsky (2006) cites with approval Petitto's rather unclear hypothesis that "there exists tissue in the human brain dedicated to a *function* of language *structure* independent of speech and sound" (italics mine). He asserts that "studies of brain damage among signers" and "imaging studies... lend further support to the hypothesis."

In coming to their conclusion, Poizner, Bellugi, and Klima (1987; hereafter "PKB"), despite calling their monograph *What the Hands Reveal About the Brain*, didn't consider the obvious alternative to it, namely, that sign language may be controlled by the left hemisphere because it also controls the preferred right hand. In addition, some of the symptoms of their patients, such as those suggesting problems in spatialized syntax in two patients with right-hemisphere damage, and basic manual motor problems in patient G.D. (see Whitemore, 1987), were inconsistent with their conclusion that only an amodal left-hemispheric language capacity was involved.

A second study of twenty-three sign-language users with brain damage (Hickok, Bellugi, and Klima, 1996) was also open to the interpretation that patients with right-hemisphere damage had some sign-language problems and patients with left-hemisphere damage had some nonlinguistic motor problems. In this study, the authors did not claim that the "higher order" amodal patterns that they putatively identified were "innate," but instead raised the possibility that they were not: "Whether these [higher-order properties] turn out to be domain-specific aspects of grammatical structure, or other, less specific organizational properties awaits further investigation" (p. 702).

An additional problem, not so much with PKB's own conclusions but with the interpretation of their work by others, is the claim that the relation between aphasic syndromes (Broca's, conduction, and Wernicke's) and lesion site was similar in the three left-hemisphere sign aphasics to those typical of speaking subjects. For example, in his introduction to the PKB monograph, Marshall states that "these findings do indicate broadly congruent cortical and subcortical areas committed to different aspects of modality neutral language processing" (p. xvi). This is not the case. While the lesion site of G.D. was a classical one for Broca's aphasics (even though all aspects of her symptom pattern were not), the lesion sites for K.L. and P.D., which were both mostly subcortical, were far from typical for conduction and Wernicke's aphasia, respectively.

Evidence has been accumulating that, contrary to Bellugi and Klima's belief, the right hemisphere has a considerable involvement in sign-language comprehension in native signers. In 2002, Neville and her colleagues (Newman et al., 2002) added to evidence from an earlier study (Neville et al., 1997) in showing that in language comprehension by native signers, there is mostly symmetrical activation of the left and right hemispheres, even though spoken-language comprehension primarily involves the left hemisphere. A particular problem for the claim that language is amodal was that the angular gyrus, which was activated in the right hemisphere only in native signers, possesses in Newman et al.'s words "some bias toward the processing of human biological movement generally" (p. 78).

I conclude that sign language has been a Trojan horse for the generativists whose work has been considered in the past two sections, as well as for others with a similar agenda. They have seized on sign language as an opportunity to prove that we have an innate module of the kind suggested by Chomsky—a module independent of other capabilities and, in the area of our concern, independent of the transmission modality. But they have not unearthed evidence for the amodal capacity required by UG. Instead, for these research groups the upshot of work in their fields has been, for the most part, just the opposite of what they had hoped for when they dragged this horse into their labs. Patterns of acquisition and brain organization for the phonology of sign language, like the analogous patterns for spoken language, will eventually be primarily understood not in terms of an amodal autonomous linguistic saltation but in terms of what we know about descent with modification of the relevant perceptual and action capabilities, though only the latter capabilities are considered here.

To my knowledge, generativists concerned with sign language have never raised the issue of why the putative amodal language specialization is in the left hemisphere. But their findings are consistent with my view, elaborated in Chapter 10, that language evolved and normally develops primarily in the left hemisphere because it is built upon a left-hemisphere specialization for the control of routine actions in general. In my view, both spoken-language and sign-language production are predominantly controlled in the left hemisphere for this reason. And they both have phylogenetic precursors in the form of specializations for both vocal communication and gestural communication in the left hemisphere of other hominoids (monkeys and apes). But, in addition, because of the heavy dependence of sign language on the spatial domain, comprehension of sign language, in particular, is much more dependent on the right hemisphere than spoken language is, at least in native signers.

13.5 Phylogeny of the hand/mouth relationship in language

What I believe we have established so far is that the hands and the mouth are not joint recipients of an innate amodal linguistic capability. The phono-logical organization of the two modalities is too different for that to be true. So that does not explain the concurrent presence of a universal spoken language and pockets of sign language in deaf populations. But what all the attention to sign language and its significance tends to mask is that the hands have an extremely important role today as an accompaniment to the only form of language that occurs naturally, namely, spoken language. What we should be asking is, why and how did that role evolve? The other question we should consider is, even though sign language is not the natural language of choice today, could it have been the original language of choice? My answer to this question derives from my consideration of the evolution of the left-hemispheric specializations for language and manual function in Chapter 10. I regard the hands and the mouth as having evolved in parallel, rather than the hands having laid the groundwork for the mouth in language evolution.

In the remainder of this chapter I will briefly consider how the use of the hands accompanies modern spoken-language production and elaborate on the contention that sign language did not precede spoken language in evolution. But before I do this I must note that, to my knowledge, no generative linguist has ever weighed in on the question of which of the two forms of language evolved first. This is no coincidence. If one believes that language is an amodal capacity of basically instantaneous origin, one ought to expect that both languages would be universally present since the beginning. For generativists, the issue of the preference of one over the other, either now or earlier, would have to reside in the realm of performance, and this highlights another limitation on the scope of their perspective.

David McNeill (2005) provides the most well-known conception of how the hands function in concert with spoken language today. He believes that hand gestures and speech in modern languages form an inseparable unit. In this unit, he says, the two modalities perform complementary functions. As the mouth delivers the linguistic message, using the combinatoric–sequential linguistic capability of the vocal–auditory modality, the hand simultaneously delivers an iconic imagistic message. McNeill offers this illustration:

> The following gesture, together with speech, shows an individual's thinking at a specific moment. The speaker was describing an episode from an animated cartoon that she has just seen. A character is entering a drainpipe on the side of a building and climbing up it on the inside. The speaker describes this with "and he goes **up through** it this time." Synchronously, in the bold-faced section, she raised her right hand upward, her palm up and fingers and thumb spread apart: a kind of open basket shape moving up. The gesture embodies several ideas—the character—(the hand itself) rising up (the trajectory) and interiority (the open shape). Such a combination of meanings in a single symbol is imagistic in that ideas that in speech require separation in time are concentrated and instantaneous in the gesture. (McNeill, 2005, pp. 89–90)

Three features of gesture distinguish it from the linguistic act with which it is integrated. First, gestures have a holistic or global character, whereas a linguistic event involves an integration of discrete components. Second, gestures occur more or less instantaneously. Their components are simultaneous, just as we have already noted for signs of sign language, while the speech utterance with which they co-occur is systematically sequential. Third, gestures are spontaneously created while linguistic events are constructed from a pre-existing socially constructed code. Thus, in McNeill's words, speaking with gestures involves a "dialectic," or dialog, of opposites. Why we evolved this duality rather than a single multimodal but internally coherent control structure for communication is surely one of the most important questions in modern cognitive science.

Goldin-Meadow and McNeill (1999) believe that this complementarity of a vocal linguistic channel and a manual nonlinguistic channel is as old as language itself. However, there has been a persistent belief that the first language was a sign language. (For recent conceptions to this effect, see Corballis, 2003, and Arbib, 2005). One reason given for favoring an early capacity for sign language comes from the history of attempts to teach language to the great apes. After numerous failed attempts to teach chimpanzees vocal language, the Gardners (1969) amazed the scientific world by teaching their chimpanzee, Washoe, a few hundred signs of American Sign Language. Since then, there have been many other such successes. The fact that great apes could not learn vocal language but could learn gestural language is often taken to mean that our ancestors had more of a predisposition toward gestural language. But as Tomasello and Camaioni (1997) note, these successes of great apes in learning sign languages may tell us more about the richness of the human cultural environment for stimulating communication than about early hominid sign-language capacities.

Perhaps the most convincing reason given for believing that sign language preceded spoken language is that, in conjunction with vision, the gestural system could provide a natural and thus understandable relation between concept and signal—the capacity for iconicity. Thus, for example, active verbs could be signaled by simulating an action—e.g., hands flapping could signal wings flapping. Object nouns could be signaled by movements simulating a haptic scanning of their external surfaces—e.g., the two hands moving symmetrically up and down with a space between them could signify a tree trunk. In addition, pronouns and locative prepositions could be signaled simply by pointing to the appropriate position in space, the deep-seated nature of such gestures being indicated by their early use in modern infants.

From my point of view, if earlier hominids ever had a sign communication system worthy of the term "language," it must have had a systematic phonological level. The attainment of this level was necessary to solve the impedence-matching problem pointed out by Studdert-Kennedy and Lane (1980; see Chapter 3). As the number of first words increased, it must have been harder and harder to keep them apart at the signal level. The implementation of the particulate principle (see Chapter 3)—a change to a set of discrete meaningless units which could then be combined to form an indefinite number of words—must have occurred. To me, the point at which this occurred—the point at which we implemented lexical creativity—was the point at which we had true language.

My basic thesis is that if manual gestural communication had ever evolved to this stage of systematization of phonology and the lexicon, it would have been such an important part of the hominid adaptive repertoire that it would never have been given up. I see the problem as Charles Hockett saw it many years ago: "The early hominid primarily gestural system was *only* reasonably serviceable. It could not have had the power of language or of such modern signages [meaning sign languages] as Ameslan (ASL) or the switch of channel would never have taken place" (Hockett, 1958, p. 300). But there is not even a vestige of such systematization present in the manual modality today, if one accepts McNeill's conception of the nature of modern gesture accompanying language. Thus the supposed sequence of events for the hands in a hand-to-mouth scenario, if earlier signing was indeed linguistic, is from holistic manual gestures to combinatoric manual phonology, and then, with the advent of combinatoric vocal phonology, back to holistic manual gestures. As Davis and I have argued elsewhere, in response to the gesturally based language-origins scenarios of both Corballis (MacNeilage, 2003) and Arbib (MacNeilage and Davis, 2005c, d), this does not seem plausible.

One way to evaluate the assertion that an actual sign language with combinatoric phonology would not have gone away is to consider the importance of the factors that supposedly led to its abandonment. First, signs are considered to have the disadvantage that they are not broadcast omnidirectionally. But since the modal state for the communication of early linguistic information was presumably face to face, one can question the importance of omnidirectionality. Second, signing prevents the hands from engaging in other tasks. Couldn't signing have been interspersed with other hand uses at a moment-to-moment level, as often occurs in modern sign-language use, without a deficit in responding to major selection pressures? Third, sign language does not work in the dark. I once asked a graduate student who was bilingual in English and ASL how signers cope with this problem. He said, "You turn the light on." But in the days before lights, how much pressure was there for linguistic communication to occur in the dark, and how often was it so dark that persons positioned close to each other could not see each other's movements?

Another way to evaluate the hand-to-mouth scenario is to ask what the actual process might have been for moving from a manual to a vocal language. The central supposition is that the translation was based on some natural action-based relationships between the manual and vocal systems. Hewes (1973) suggested that there may be a natural tendency to mimic with the tongue what the hands are doing, leading eventually to vocalizations that bear at least a crude relation to the gestures they accompany. But many years later Hewes conceded, "The ideas about the movement from a postulated pre-speech language to a rudimentary spoken one are admittedly the weakest part of my model" (1996, p. 489).

A fact of interest here is that modern deaf signers with basically no knowledge of a spoken language do tend to make oral expressions that are apparently outside of the phonology, and also make sounds when they sign. There is a minor subdiscipline which Woll and Sieratzki (1998) call "echo phonology" that concerns itself with linkages between signs and oral actions. They give a number of examples from British Sign Language: abrupt separation of the hands with "pa," finger or hand oscillation with "sh," movements where the hand closes and approaches the body with "up," movements where the active hand contacts the passive hand with "um," and closing hands with "thoop" (with the vowel as in "foot").

Could an analysis of such linkages be developed into a theory of the hand–mouth translation process necessary for the claim that sign language evolved into spoken language? Woll and Sieratzki note that they have been reported in other languages. But there would need to be a substantial family of universal patterns for a translation theory to have any credence. At present these linkages remain rather mysterious because, as Woll and Sieratzki point out, "The oral activities in echo phonology are not themselves iconic" (p. 532). My basic question is, How might any phonological component of sign language have metamorphosed into syllable frames, my candidate for the most basic spoken-language component? And it may not be trivial that the translation had to be from predominantly monosyllabic signs to predominantly multisyllabic words. In my opinion, we need an answer to this question of how the translation was made in order to have an appropriate hand-to-mouth evolutionary scenario at the phonological level. My conclusion is that at present this is too slender a reed on which to base the claim that a first sign language, defined as I define it in terms of lexical productivity, evolved into spoken language.

Of course I am not entitled to argue *directly* that an earlier sign language with appropriate phonology could *not* have evolved a distinct phonological organization for speech. But if it did, the best guess we can make is that it was like the phonological organization of sign languages today. We have already seen that the phonological levels of modern sign languages and spoken languages are enormously disparate, and that amodal commonalities between the two systems required by the generativists are extremely unlikely. And on the face of it, finding a set of linkages between the surface parameters of handshape, movement, and location for sign language, and the parameters of place, manner, and voicing for consonants, and tongue height and front–back positioning for vowels, seems at present to be a very uncongenial task.

In short, from my point of view, the contention that we had an earlier sign language entails two things: (1) a pre-existing manual phonology enabling lexical productivity, and (2) a subsequent implementation of a *system* of cross-modality equivalences for a hand-to-mouth translation—a system for translation from simultaneous to successive. Arguing that the translation was made before speech took on systematic form characterized by frame structure would seem to be altogether too fanciful. I myself can't find enough evidence that the required system-level equivalences could ever have existed. And McNeill's work suggests that we still have more or less instantaneous holistic gestures—plausible candidates for early gestures— and that they coexist with spoken linguistic utterances. My conclusion is that early manual communication did not have a productive phonological level, and it was therefore unnecessary for there to have been a systematic relation between the phonology of signed language and speech enabling translation from one to the other to occur. But the key argument remains: If we ever had a productive sign-language phonology, we would still have sign language as the universal choice of extended cultures (sign-language cultures being always subcultures within a culture). And of course we don't.

What, then, has been the role of the manual modality in the evolution of language? There seems to be a perfectly good option that recognizes the likelihood of a long tradition of gestural use. It entails accepting Donald's scenario for the evolution of mimetic capability and acknowledging the present role of gesture as co-occurring with language as an imagistic component of language use. The option is to argue, as Goldin-Meadow and McNeill (1999) have done, that gesture has had such a coequal role since spoken language originated because the iconicity it allows has always been an integral part of communication.

I am not so certain that a second part of Goldin-Meadow and McNeill's (1999) thesis is as plausible as the first. They say that the vocal–auditory modality ended up doing language because it was the only means left, if the iconic gestural mode of communication were to be preserved. I would like to present a more positive alternative.

Language first evolved in the vocal–auditory mode, I believe, because its prototypical structure made available a more natural solution to the problem of expanding the lexicon than was available in the manual system—a more natural way of adopting particulate structure. I suggest, as Studdert-Kennedy (e.g., 1998) has suggested, that the biphasic property of the mandibular cycle—the frame—provided an initial basis for particulate structure in the form of the first binary cut in the time domain. The two opposite movements of the cycle provide, by definition, two distinct states next to each other—free, so to speak. And because of the overall construction of the mouth, the operation of the biphasic cycle produces, again for free, a built-in *discontinuity* in the time domain that greatly increases the perceived difference between the effects of the two phases. An open mouth accompanied by phonation results in the high-amplitude acoustic output of the vowel. A closed mouth (and my thesis is that a *totally* closed mouth is the modal early form) results in a severe damping of the voiced source, and consequently a low-amplitude acoustic output. Thus the frame is *self-segmenting* at the acoustical and therefore also at the perceptual level, and so may have provided the initial basis for formation of the particulate structure of speech.

Let's consider this possibility in more detail in the context of the proposal made in Chapter 7 that the first words may have been kinship terms. The maternal term "mama" is produced by two iterations of the pure frame; that is, two cycles of mandibular oscillations without tongue movement. There are two amplitude peaks in the signal corresponding to the two vowels and two periods of relatively low frequency and low amplitude activity associated with the two lip closures for the two "m"s. The soft palate is lowered to open the nasal airway for the "m". In infants, and presumably in earlier hominids, the soft palate is left down throughout the utterance. Producing the paternal term "papa" involves the same two pure frame cycles, but as the soft palate is closed for the oral consonants—in fact closed for the entire utterance—they will sound different than the nasal ones. The vowels will be slightly different in this oral form. However, unpublished work from our lab suggests that they will not be regarded as different from vowels in the nasal context. By "self-segmenting" then, I mean the listener will hear, on the two occasions, two different consonants alternating with the "same" vowel.

Thus, in this little two-word microcosm we have the basis for particulate structure—the possibility of *independent* variation of consonants and vowels in the time domain. Two different consonants can occur, as a result of a single articulatory difference between them with (roughly) the same vowel. This is a second step—beyond the frame with phonation itself—towards a speech-specific solution of Lashley's serial-order problem. It allows the production of different sequences of what are basically the same elements. As we have seen, speech errors show that a modern adult has separate representations of consonants and vowels like these by showing that they can be misplaced independently of each other in the segmental serial-ordering process.

PART VII

Last things

14 Ultimate causes of speech: genes and memes

14.1 Introduction

Let us now try to characterize the F/C conception of evolution of speech in terms of Ernst Mayr's "ultimate causes." Or, another way of putting it, let's try to do a final accounting in terms of Tinbergen's question #4: *How did speech get there in phylogeny?*

First, though, let me recall for you the sequence of events that I think needs to be explained. As I reconstruct the process, motor frames for speech evolved from mandibular cyclicities via an intermediate stage of visuofacial communicative smacks, which eventually became paired with phonation to form protosyllables. These protosyllables initially filled a vocal-grooming role. They proved effective because they made for the omnidirectional transmission of a standard communicative signal, readily extended across time, and with sharp acoustic alternations between closed and open states of sufficient complexity to sustain a listener's interest. At some point, one of the limited sets of protosyllabic forms—a nasalized variant—became paired with a female parental concept, resulting in the form [mama]. This was a social invention—and a momentous one. It paved the way for a series of similar single events linking, one by one, additional items at two hitherto unrelated levels of function—concepts and sound patterns. Once this invention got from the infant–parent matrix into broader society, subsequent concept–sound pairings for new words got established by cultural agreement, and the history of these agreements got passed along to successive generations of language users. This led to the one-word stage of true language, which is as far as the F/C theory goes. (For a theory in which syntax evolves from the syllable, see Carstairs-McCarthy, 1999.)

14.2 The genetic substrate

So, then, what *causal* progression is involved here? A core feature of all mammals is that they use the mandibular cycle for ingestion. That is, they all chew, suck, and lick. That feature at some point got exapted for visuofacial communication (see Chapter 4), and then it got combined with another core mammalian feature, phonation. Thus the basic events behind the protosyllable—ingestive cyclicities and the basic phonatory cyclicity—are both very simple. But they may have been sufficiently important that, during a fifth of a billion years of mammalian phylogeny, some specific genetic basis for the repeated ontogeny of these two functions might have evolved. (In the following discussion one might substitute "innate" for "genetic," although I tend to find "innate" far too loose for useful discussion.) At the moment it is premature to hazard any guess as to what this genetic substrate may have been. Pressures for feeding and social communication were presumably responsible for the mandibular cyclicities and phonation, respectively. For the cyclicities, further selection pressures for social communication presumably led to the smacks and to the protosyllables.

But what about the pairing of mandibular cyclicities with phonation? Do we need to think in terms of a specific genetic basis for it? When our ancestors started inventing new signal variants to go with concepts, they needed to have in place a vocal-learning capacity because, I presume, the fine detail of the inventions that were made and the ability of listeners to apprehend them were not—and, for that matter, still aren't—coded in the genes. I have argued, following Merlin Donald (1991), that this development was part of the evolution of a general-purpose mimetic capacity. Did *that* require specific genetic changes? I'm afraid, at this point, we must uphold Stent's (1981) conclusion: the genes are at too many removes from the processes that eventually created the nervous system to form part of the basis for a research program on their specific relationships. So while it would be foolish to deny that there is *something* about the human genome that has to do with our possession of a general-purpose mimetic capacity (within which speech is subsumed), exactly what that something might be remains beyond our grasp.

But now let us ask a more specific question: what have we learned about ultimate causes from this relatively detailed conception of phylogeny and ontogeny of the mechanism of speech production?

One big lesson, I suggest, is the importance of *biomechanical inertia*, both within frames (CV co-occurrences) and across frames (VC co-occurrences and syllable reduplication) in the early babbling and speech patterns of infancy. And importantly, the former inertial effect is also typically seen in languages, whereas the latter ones are not. I argued that because the effects seen in infants are so basic, they were no doubt also obligatory for hominids when producing their first words. But I also argued that because the VC co-occurrences and syllable reduplication are found in infants but *not* languages, the basic biomechanical effects associated with them were, in this context, superseded in the history of the language, just as they are in the course of ontogeny. And I have argued that this supersession was socioculturally mediated.

This analysis has damaging consequences for the most well-known conception of speech, the *generative* conception, which posits that a genetically specified mental underpinning for speech evolved more or less instantaneously. To support their conclusion, its proponents have simply noted supposed universal properties of sound systems today and then, in a maneuver characteristic of the discipline of linguistics (Braine, 1994), in effect put the end in the beginning—that is, put the currently observable pattern regularities directly into the genes. But how likely is it, really, that the genes conveniently and neatly took advantage of basic biomechanics to get early infant (and possibly early hominid) speech patterns such as syllabic reduplication off the ground? Are we to suppose that the genes in effect said, "OK, let's go with the biomechanics"? Indeed, did they even need to say that, given that the biomechanics were there anyway? And if there were pro-biomechanics genes for early *reduplication*, did a second set of anti-biomechanical genes come along and cancel out the effects of the earlier ones in one specific phonetic context (VC) to give languages and their adult speakers their characteristic intersyllabic *variegation*? I think not. Instead, we get the biomechanics for free, and we have to learn to supersede them where necessary. This is an issue you need address only if you have built the time domain actively into your model; if you haven't, you can simply take the final pattern and, by some exercise in second-order isomorphism, put the pattern in the genetic beginning.

So we find that the facts of ontogeny trip up the generative conception of continuity of development. We saw in Chapter 6 that the required continuity of development that supposedly gets a single set of genes to gradually manifest themselves by maturation over the course of development does not exist in the data. Infants actually reverse their preferences, first preferring intersyllabic *reduplication*, which is in accordance with basic biomechanics, but finally preferring intersyllabic *variegation*, which is not.

"But wait a minute!" you might object. "Haven't actual language genes been recently found, and doesn't this make the existence of speech genes plausible?" This was certainly Pinker's tentative conclusion in *The Language Instinct* (1994): "So for now there is suggestive evidence of grammar genes, in the sense of genes whose effects seem most specific to the development of the circuits underlying parts of grammar" (p. 325). Pinker then gives us his conception of what grammar genes could do:

The grammar genes would be stretches of DNA that code for proteins, or trigger the transcription of proteins, in certain times and places in the brain, that guide, attract, or glue neurons into networks that, in combination with the synaptic tuning that takes place during learning, are necessary to compute the solution to some grammatical problem (like choosing an affix or a word). (p. 322)

Pinker's discussion is based on the work of Gopnik and her colleagues (e.g., Gopnik and Crago, 1991). They described members of an English family—identified only as "the KE family"—who consistently produced, in Pinker's words, "grammatical errors such as misuse of pronouns, and of suffixes like the plural and the past tense" (Pinker, 1994, p. 49). Here are some of his examples:

It's a flying finches they are.
She remembered when she hurts herself the other day.
The neighbors phone the ambulance because the man fall off the tree.

Gopnik and Crago conclude, "It is not unreasonable to entertain the interim hypothesis that a single dominant gene controls for those mechanisms that result in a child's ability to construct paradigms that constitute morphology"(p. 47). Pinker concurs, and asserts that "the [KE] syndrome shows that there must be some pattern of genetically guided events in the development of the brain (namely the events disrupted in this syndrome) that is specialized for the wiring in of linguistic computation" (1994, p. 324).

Not surprisingly, this conclusion was enthusiastically embraced by the generative linguistic community. Newmeyer (1998), for example, in his review of the status of generative linguistics, concludes, on the basis of Gopnik and Crago's reports, that "there *are* recent findings which I feel provide incontrovertible evidence that . . . there are innate, purely grammatical principles" (p. 90).

A specific gene, the FOXP2 gene, has been identified in all the affected KE family members (Lai et al., 2001). This gene is a regulatory gene, meaning it can exert widespread effects on other genes. But while Gopnik and her colleagues' initial emphasis was on the family's grammatical deficits, it was clear from the beginning (e.g., Hurst et al., 1990) that "Speech in the affected individuals is effortful, distorted, and often unintelligible" (Harasty and Hodges, 2002, p. 449). In a comprehensive study of affected family members, Vargha-Khadem et al. (1995) concluded that "the inherited behavior has a broad phenotype which transcends impaired generation of syntactical rules and includes a striking articulatory impairment as well as deficits in intellectual, linguistic, and orofacial praxic [motor skill] functions generally" (p. 930). Subsequent work led to the conclusion that "the verbal and non-verbal deficits arise from a common impairment in the ability to sequence movement or in procedural learning" (Watkins, Dronkers, and Varga-Khadem, 2002, p. 452). ("Procedural learning" is, roughly, motor learning.) These results led Harasty and Hodges (2002) to conclude, in an editorial comment in *Brain* on the paper by Watkins and colleagues, that "The finding of the present study also make[s] untenable the prior claims that the family has a specific deficit in morpho-syntactic rule usage" (p. 450).

More recently, Lai et al. (2003) have studied the expression of the FOXP2 gene in the developing brain of mouse and human. They found similar patterns of gene expression in both taxa, particularly affecting circuits relating the cortex and the basal ganglia, and circuits linking the cerebellum and the inferior olivary nuclei, circuits known to be involved in basic motor control. The basal ganglia and the cerebellum are in fact the two main subcortical motor-control centers. The results led the authors to conclude that "FOXP2 might be generally implicated in aspects of motor control in mammalian species, and was already playing a role in the development of motor-related brain regions *in the human–mouse common ancestor*" (p. 2461, italics added). They interpreted their results as supporting the earlier suggestion that "impairments in sequencing of movement and procedural learning might be central to the FOXP2-related speech and language disorders" (Watkins, Dronkers, and Varga-Khadem, 2002, p. 452). Thus the FOXP2 gene is implicated in fundamental aspects of movement control, and both the speech disorders and the language disorders in the KE family are presumably indirect consequences of the motor disorders attendant on a mutation in this gene. Impairments have even been observed in manual function (Alcock et al., 2000).

In conclusion, *there is currently no validity to the claim that UG has a specific genetic basis*, given what we now know about how genes affect nervous-system structure (see Chapter 2) and also given our present understanding of the effects of the FOXP2 gene in particular. A similar conclusion, namely, that basic motor control is involved, comes from consideration of *another* supposedly linguistic developmental syndrome—"Specific Language Impairment" (Bishop, 2002).

This being said, there is some evidence that the FOXP2 gene does something different for humans than for other species. In hominids there have been two changes in the gene that altered its protein product. These changes apparently happened in the past 200,000 years and gave rise to what Ridley calls a "selective sweep"—"a technical term for elbowing all other versions of the gene aside in short order" (Ridley, 2003, p. 215). These changes have become universally fixed in the population. Ridley comes to the rather cosmic conclusion that the resultant change was "so successful in helping its owner reproduce that his or her descendents now dominate the species to the utter exclusion of all previous versions of the genes" (ibid.).

Ridley offers a guess about how this gene "enables people to speak." His guess is tied up with his notion that gestural language preceded spoken language:

I suspect that in chimpanzees the gene helps to connect the part of the brain responsible for fine control of the hand to various perceptual parts of the brain. In human beings, its extra (longer?) period of activity enables it to connect to other parts of the brain including the region responsible for motor control of the mouth and larynx. (p. 215)

Even if true, and even if an earlier manual language provided a substrate for spoken language, this proposal doesn't get us far toward understanding what the gene actually does for us. And one wonders why the perceptual linkages for speech, which are necessary for learning it with or without genetics, are omitted from the scenario while the perceptual linkages for manual function are not. Presumably it was not intentional.

Thus we are presently at the point that we can make linkages between aspects of the genes and aspects of language. But we haven't yet found any genetic effects that are specific to language, although *language-specific* genetic effects are essential to the nativistic stance of the generativists. We seem to have not progressed from the stage we were at in 1990, when George Miller concluded that "genetic explanations of cognitive phenomena are still pie in the sky" (Miller, 1990, p. 321).

14.3 Vocal learnability in vertebrates: birdsong

Let's now reverse our focus and ask about the *learnability* of speech. We don't stand alone in the animal kingdom in our ability to learn communicative patterns. Another major vertebrate taxonomic group—birds—can also do this. Indeed, thousands of bird species can learn to sing. Is there anything to be gained in our understanding of the origins of speech from looking at birdsong? I think so.

From the ultimate-causes perspective, the same basic question that arises for speech arises for birdsong: *To what extent is there an innate basis for song, and to what extent is it based on learning?* But here students of birdsong have an important methodological advantage. In the case of birds, both availability and type of input can be experimentally manipulated, while in humans we are dependent on the vagaries of experiments of nature, such as various degrees of deafness and social deprivation. In addition, birds can be subject to invasive neural manipulations in a way that humans cannot. Consequently, birdsong can give us a perspective on the scope and limits of our attempts to interpret the effects of abnormal experience, and on the nature of the neural mechanisms underlying vocalization.

Birds can be deafened at any time since birth. They can also be reared in isolation from songs of their conspecifics. The important difference between these two conditions is that in the former condition they can hear neither themselves nor their peers, while in the latter condition they *can* hear themselves. In addition, birds can be exposed to various substitute input patterns such as songs of birds of other species or synthetically constructed acoustic inputs.

The smallest elements of birdsong are called notes, "defined by a continuous marking on a sound spectrogram" (Doupe and Kuhl, 1999, p. 572). Notes are combined to form syllables, which are clustered into phrases. Doupe and Kuhl provide us with two examples of songs, the first simple and the second more complex (Fig. 14.1). In the figure, A is a sound spectrogram of the song of a white-crowned sparrow: "White crowned sparrow songs typically begin with (a) a long whistle followed by (b, c) trills and (d) buzzes" (Doupe and Kuhl, 1999, p. 571). B is a sound spectrogram of a Zebra finch song:

Zebra finch songs start with a number of introductory syllables (marked with i), followed by a sequence of syllables (lower case letters), that can be either simple or

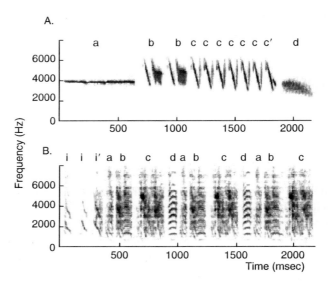

FIG. 14.1   Illustrations of birdsongs. (From Doupe and Kuhl, 1999, Fig. 2)

more complex, with multiple notes (e.g., b, c). Particular sequences of syllables are organized into phrases called motifs (e.g., a–d), which are repeated. (Doupe and Kuhl, 1999, p. 567)

One important aspect of birdsong should be stated at the outset. Young birds go through an initial period when they do not produce song. But it has been shown that if they are exposed to adult song only as long as they are not producing any, they will nevertheless eventually produce song. So there must be a means of storing the acoustic information in a form that can only later be transformed into movement patterns that recreate the song characteristics without there being output practice at the time of exposure. Human infants also go through a six-month prebabbling (prespeech) period, but we are unable to subsequently deprive them of input and see whether the earlier experience was crucial to the production of babbling.

One important similarity between birdsong and speech is that prior to the production of mature song, birds go through a period of *subsong*. It consists of a relatively primitive set of output patterns somewhat analogous to babbling, though to my knowledge no detailed comparison of the two kinds of patterns has been made.

There is definitely some innate basis for the production of birdsong. For example, in the canary, as Gardner, Naef, and Nottebohm (2005) describe it, "canary-like syllables and phrase structure also develop in the absence of imitation, and even in the absence of hearing although under these conditions the repertoire of syllables is uncommonly small" (p. 1046). The songs of deafened birds are much less song-like than isolate songs (Doupe and Kuhl, 1999). Thus, hearing one's own vocalizations makes a contribution to learning.

There is also evidence of an innate perceptual capacity. According to Doupe and Kuhl (1999), when songbirds are given a choice between a conspecific tutor and a tutor of another species, they prefer to copy the conspecific tutor, do it more accurately, and learn the song more quickly. Unfortunately this is a paradigm that cannot be used on human infants because they are all members of the same species.

There is a further finding that seems to require innateness in both production and perception. Mundinger (1995) has shown that roller and border strands of canaries don't learn the note types of the other strand. But hybrid offspring of the two strands readily learn both sets of note types, suggesting a genetic basis for song-learning capabilities.

What about innateness in the development of speech production and perception? As to production, you will remember that infant vocalization during the first six months is not really speech-like, and only becomes so at the beginning of babbling. (My criterion for speechlikeness is the appearance of rhythmic frames.) There are three prebabbling stages (Oller, 2000, pp. 63–64). The first is a "phonation stage" of relatively steady-state vowel-like phonation (without substantial articulatory movements) from birth through two months. The second is a "primitive articulation stage," from one to four months. Vocalizations are still primarily vowel-like, but feature more versatile articulatory use, and include "gooing," which is phonation with the tongue elevated into the velar region. The third is an "expansion stage" from three to eight months, which appears to involve systematic exploration of the phonatory component (e.g., squeals, growls) and the articulatory component (e.g., clicks, and trills or raspberries). Oller and Griebel (2008) have argued that the emergence of the decoupling of these infant hominid vocalizations from specific inciting stimuli, with the result that they can be produced voluntarily, represents an important hominid development with socialization-related survival value. If these three stages were found to be present in profoundly deaf infants that would seem to be satisfactory evidence of their innateness.

But what about babbling itself? Lenneberg (1967) concluded that it was innate. But he was wrong about the data. Oller and Eilers (1988) showed that deaf infants don't begin babbling until several months after normal babies begin, and that the babbling doesn't have a normal pattern. An important test case was presented by Lynch, Oller, and Steffens (1989). They studied an infant born without cochleas and therefore totally deaf. This child produced few sounds and no babbling in the two years or so before the diagnosis was made. But after several months of training in lip-reading and the use of a tactile aid, a considerable amount of babbling was produced. Oller and Griebel (2008) attribute this eventual outcome to the training procedures, and this interpretation cannot be ruled out.

My own conclusion is that if we use the demanding criterion of *independence from experience*, non-cry prebabbling vocalization, which isn't speech-like, may be innate, though we don't yet know about this, but babbling, though speech-like, doesn't have a speech-specific innateness. It does not naturally occur in the absence of hearing but instead needs to be mimetically induced. But its frame property is obviously not directly derived from the input in language environments like that of English which has a complex array of different syllable types. And so far no differences have been reported between babbling in an English environment and in that of languages (e.g., Japanese) that are dominated by the CV form. Couldn't one say, in the manner of Chomsky, that this rhythmic syllabicity is innate but just needs triggering and shaping? Perhaps so, but what I am saying is that what we see today as babbling patterns, evolved for the prespeech function of vocal grooming, and they have deep phylogenetic roots that far transcend hominid evolution. If one wants to label these roots as innate, that is probably appropriate. But this would provide no solace for generative linguists for whom the only "interesting" kind of innateness is "linguistic."

There is also no current evidence that demands the conclusion that humans have an innate speech-specific *perceptual* capacity. When, in 1971, Eimas and his colleagues found that one-month-old infants could distinguish between [p] and [ph] on the basis of their different voice onset times, it was thought that humans *may* have an innate ability to perceive speech. Although subsequent to that it was found that infants had a capacity to distinguish between practically any pair of perceptually adjacent speech sounds, it also became more likely that this indicated a general auditory capacity rather than some speech-specific ability. This conclusion was encouraged by numerous findings that other vertebrates had similar capacities.

A difficulty here is that it's not possible to test the speech perception of infants in the absence of perceptual experience. Infants begin hearing sounds in the womb and by birth have considerable perceptual experience of conspecific vocalizations, and noises in general. The difficulty is illustrated by a recent attempt by Pinker and Jackendoff (2005) to include speech perception among the many things that they considered to be "special" about language, the implication being that these things are innate. They review a number of differences between humans and monkeys in perceiving speech sounds with the intention of showing that the human speech-perception capacity is special. But they then state that "These findings must be qualified by the fact that human speech perception necessarily reflects the effects of experience listening to a specific language, and it is difficult to equate such experience between humans and other animals" (p. 208). They are only able to conclude that "if findings of similarities between humans and other animals trained on human speech contrasts are taken as evidence that primate audition is a sufficient basis for human speech perception, findings of differences following such training must be taken as weakening such a conclusion" (p. 208).

Birds and humans may then be different in terms of the contribution of innateness to subsequent output. Birds seem to have song-specific innateness, but humans may not have speech-specific innateness. But while there may not be any innateness for speech, there is evidence for innateness in visuofacial linkages. Since the initial demonstration of Meltzoff and Moore (1977) it has repeatedly been found that infants imitate human facial expressions (such as putting the tongue out) almost literally from birth. This has been interpreted as providing an initial basis for parent–infant communication (Meltzoff and Decety, 2003). Some tendency to vocally imitate vowel qualities has been found in infants but only at the age of 4 months (Kuhl and Meltzoff, 1996), which allows a good deal of time for the effects of experience to accumulate.

While speech and birdsong may differ in terms of their innate basis, when one comes to comparing their serial organization—and here I am going out on a limb—there may be one remarkable similarity: *birdsong also has a frame/content mode of organization!*

The concept of syllable—for me, the frame—has been used for a long time in birdsong by analogy with speech. But it has been defined at the acoustic level, not at the production level. For example, Doupe and Kuhl (1999) define "syllables" as "units of sound separated by silent intervals"

(p. 572), though they don't say whether the silent interval between syllables is obligatory. These units are superordinate to the most basic temporal unit, the note. A syllable can contain more than one note. But what are birdsong syllables from the production standpoint? First, the silent intervals are taken up with brief inspirations, unlike in speech where it's typical to produce a string of syllables on a single expiratory phase. But secondly, and more importantly, syllables are apparently accompanied by a beak open–close cycle that I will call a "BOCC." And in simple cases, as in the trills of the white-crowned sparrow in Fig. 14 .1, the BOCCs can be extraordinarily rhythmic, just as infant babbling can.

Up until fairly recently, in the study of production of song, most attention has been given to the syrinx, a sound-generation apparatus analogous in some ways to the larynx but situated at the outlet from the lungs at the base of the trachea rather than at its apex. So it seemed reasonable to conclude that the syllable was some kind of time-domain-based syringeal phenomenon. But more recently it has been found that the beak is analogous with the mouth in opening and closing during vocalizations (Nowicki, 1987). (The amount of opening is called "beak gape.") And in many instances there is a one-to-one relation between syllables and occurrences of a beak opening/closing cycle. For an example, we can return to the scene responsible for Darwin's most basic insight. Podos, Southall, and Rossi-Santos (2004) state quite unequivocally that "Darwin's finches on the Galapagos Islands cycle their beak gapes in accordance with syllable production (*one syllable per cycle*)" (p. 607, italics added).

I actually observed this one-to-one relation in a canyon wren singing outside my window while I was working on this book, and that is what made me look into the relationship. In one type of call there was a rhythmic sequence of what my bird book calls "tee's" or "tew's" followed in one call variant by what I will call "screeches." The brief tee's or tew's were each accompanied by a short BOCC and the longer screeches by longer-duration BOCCs. So we have a useful mnemonic here: BOCCs in birdsong are analogous to MOCCs (mouth open–close cycles) in mammals.

I don't profess to know whether there is a one-to-one relation between syllables and BOCCs across the world of birdsong as there is, with minor exceptions, between frames and syllables in speech. Probably nobody else does either, because the syllable may not be defined in such a way as to be automatically identifiable in all cases from the acoustic record, and BOCC data is probably only available for a small number of species. But even if the relationship is not uniformly one-to-one, I think we can safely assume that it is characteristic.

So much for frames. What about content? Just as MOCCs in mammals are accompanied by laryngeal activity, BOCCS are accompanied by syringeal activity. Thus both have a sound source below the head. But while changes in mouth configuration are responsible for most variation in speech, changes in the source (syringeal) function are responsible for most variation in birdsong. At least two modes of source variation are identifiable from Fig. 14.1. In simple rhythmic trills, as in Fig. 14.1A, syllable type c, the syrinx provides the frequency glissandos—briefly upward, then downward, then upward. And in more complex syllable types, as in Fig 14.1B, syllable types a, b, and c, the syrinx provides a noise source somewhat analogous to aspiration in speech.

In addition to this, the beak acts as a variable resonator, just as the mouth does in speech. A basic role of the beak seems to be to track the syringeal frequency, thus increasing its amplitude. The resonant frequency of the mouth cavity in birds is directly proportional to the amount of beak gape. (The cavity gets shorter from the acoustical perspective as the mouth opens more widely.) So the way beak action tracks frequency is by greater beak gape for higher source frequencies and vice versa (Podos, Southall, and Rossi-Santos, 2004).

Thus while birdsong has both frames and content, the way content is provided differs from speech. In speech, segments are programmed into syllables. In birdsong, source (syringeal) variations are the main contributor to the content of syllables, with the assistance of resonance effects of frame variation, particularly when there is tonal input. The way frame and content interact online in birds could perhaps be determined, again by analogy with speech, by studies of birdsong errors. The very idea of birdsong errors may be astonishing to most people, but in fact Thorpe and Hall-Craggs (1976) studied this question, generating in their field notes such phrases as "Bird getting in a muddle" (p. 187). One question is whether it is content elements rather than frames that move around, as is the case in speech. Another is whether there can be serial-ordering errors at the phrasal level. Another is whether the subsong phase of birdsong is characterized primarily as a matter of frames alone, as babbling is.

There is an additional similarity between speech and birdsong, one that is phylogenetically significant. In all probability, frames preceded content in birdsong just as they did in speech. The most basic vocalization in both birds and mammals is a call consisting of a single mouth opening accompanied by a relatively undifferentiated source activation, as observed in young chickens and other farm animals. All birds and mammals have this capability. Obviously mouth opening for ingestive purposes preceded vocal communication in vertebrate evolution. Presumably in the evolution of vocal communication, which must have happened separately in avian and mammalian phylogeny, mouth opening accompanied source activation from the very beginning because mouth opening aids sound transmission. I have argued that the initial mechanism behind the evolution of rhythmic series of mouth openings in speech was the one responsible for ingestive cyclicities. But birds don't chew, suck, or lick. So how did *they* evolve multicycle vocalizations? The fact that they did calls into question whether ingestive cyclicities were a necessary precursor of lipsmacks and syllables in mammalian forms ancestral to us. Andrew (1998) has argued that it is a minor step in a control mechanism to go from a single-cycle action to a multicycle one, and adds that "Viewed this way, the rapid repetition of syllable frames could represent repetitions of the coordinations of a single call within one expiration" (p. 514). He adds, relevantly, "Such repetition is a common way of generating rapid call sequences in birds" (p. 514).

However they evolved, the presence of multicyclical frames in the two main instances of evolution of vocal learnability in vertebrates seems to provide an important part of the answer to Lashley's question regarding the nature of serial order in behavior for the domain of learnable vocalizations for vertebrates in general. And it is an answer that he anticipated when he pointed out the possible importance of rhythm generators for control of serial order in behavior in general. Both systems are organized around a rhythmic biphasic oral open–close cycle.

Why should there be this rather spectacular organizational similarity between these two rather distantly related vertebrate taxa? Obviously speech did not evolve from birdsong or vice versa. So this seems to be an example of a homoplasy. As Hauser (1996) states, "in brief, homoplasies represent traits that are similar and have evolved independently in two distantly related taxonomic groups. Homoplasies commonly arise from convergent evolution, a process that results from the fact that when two species confront similar ecological problems, selection typically provides similar solutions" (p. 5). The ecological problem in both cases was to produce serially organized output that was time-extended. The functions involved are of course different. While birdsong apparently evolved primarily to convey territorial and fitness information (Stap, 2005), human vocal output in my opinion served two successive social purposes—vocal grooming, then linguistic information transmission.

Here is a possible rationale as to why similar solutions were chosen. The dominant vocalization mode preceding both birdsong and speech was one based on a single transient mouth opening. Some birds, such as owls, and some mammals, such as wolves, have evolved a time-extended variant of this form by prolonging a single mouth opening. But rhythmically repeated mouth openings were chosen for the two most momentous instances of vocal learnability—songbirds and hominids. This seems to provide the possibility for both greater complexity and greater variety of output than source modulations accompanying a single mouth opening. Complexity and variety would be selected for different reasons. In birdsong, greater complexity/variety could be an indicant of greater fitness either to other males seeking territory or to females seeking mates. In speech, complexity/variety was perhaps selected to some degree because of its efficacy in social grooming. But following the origin of speech it was also selected in order to increase the size of the message set. The cyclical nature of the control also offered a convenient means of controlling the amount of time-extension of output chunks by control of the number of cycles produced. And lying behind this is the fact, cited in Chapter 4, that biphasic cycles are the main way in which vertebrates get work done in the time domain.

The fact that the organization of speech is so much like that of birdsong has made us look for common evolutionary factors underlying the nature of vocal learnability in general. But it should also dissuade us from suggesting that some unique linguistic mutation was responsible for the basic nature of serial organization of speech. In fact, the greater similarity in serial organization between speech and birdsong than between speech and sign language should also be a sobering thought for those who want to insist that there is a single amodal phonological organization in speech and sign language. It's more likely that the serial nature of the auditory modality is a major factor underlying the design of both speech and birdsong, and that, conversely, the nonserial nature of the visual modality is a major factor underlying the design of sign language.

Finally, there seems to be one further important similarity between speech and birdsong, this time at the level of neural organization. I have argued that the human SMA is implicated in the generation of rhythmic frames for speech. Work on the neural control of birdsong shows that a similar rhythmic control mechanism exists in this taxon.

Vicario and Simpson (1995) have shown that high-frequency electrical stimulation of centers involved in birdsong in both the midbrain and the telencephalon in zebra finches and canaries results in rhythmic syllabic vocal output similar to that in the birds' normal songs. The vocalizations were simpler and more rhythmic when the midbrain was stimulated. Telencephalic stimuli in two centers, the nucleus robustus archistriatalis (RC) and the higher vocal center (HVC), produced more complex responses "with features specific not only to the species but to the individual bird's own learned song" (p. 2602).

Most recently, Solis and Perkell (2005) have induced, by means of high-frequency electrical stimulation, a rhythmic discharge pattern in the nucleus HVC of the zebra finch in vitro—that is, with the nucleus metaphorically sitting in a petri dish! They describe HVC as "a telencephalic song system nucleus that is essential for song production" (p. 2811). The frequency of the response they induced was *similar to the syllable production rate in the naturally occurring vocalizations of the bird.* They attribute the response to a central pattern generator (CPG) in HVC underlying normal syllable sequences. They pointed out that CPGs have been implicated in unlearned vocalizations in, for example, frogs and quail, but these have been in the brainstem. But their work, together with the work of Vicario and Simpson, suggests the presence in these cases of a CPG in the telencephalon implicated in learned vocalizations in birds. Evidence regarding SMA function in humans suggests the presence of a telencephalic CPG for the learned behavior of speech as well.

Again, the similarity between speech and birdsong in the context of the dissimilarity between speech and sign language, this time at the neural level, may have a moral for us. We would not expect to find a rhythm generator for sign production in the brain because there is no peripheral organ in the manual system that continually produces a biphasic movement. Why not? Perhaps because there could be no manual analog to the mouth in sign language in the form of a single biphasic action that facilitates (amplifies) signal transmission during its opening phase, and produces by means of its closing phase such a well-defined parsing of output elements.

While there seems to be an important similarity in the form of output organization in humans and songbirds, there are two important differences in what is learned. The first is of course that there is an elaborate linguistic superstructure lying behind speech, while in birdsong the output sequence may be directly from intention to song. The second is that while vocal learnability in speech is only one aspect of a general-purpose mimetic capability, songbirds to my knowledge do not imitate anything else except song.

In summary, the phenomenon of birdsong has much to tell us about speech, particularly at the level of action. Two contributions are of special interest. First, by comparing the methodology used to evaluate the nature/nurture question in the two domains, it's possible to see that in contrast to birdsong there is not sufficient evidence for domain-specific innateness for speech—either its production or its perception. But when comparing serial-organization patterns in the two domains it can be seen that birdsong, like speech, has a frame/content mode of organization, and that a separate contribution of the frame component can be located at the neural level. This convergent evolution at the output level suggests that biphasic rhythm generation may be an evolutionary imperative for the two main instances of vertebrate vocal learnability.

The greater organizational similarity between speech and birdsong than between speech and sign language, resulting from the common use in the former pair of an oral biphasic rhythm generator, calls further into question the contention that speech and sign share a single amodal phonological component. But speech and sign do share some properties of language not shared by birdsong, indicating that the overall evolutionary trajectories of speech and birdsong were very different. A big difference seems to be that while language output has been dependent on the evolution of general-purpose mimesis in entire human populations, birdsong is an instance of special-purpose mimesis in males only.

14.4 Sociocultural causality in speech: memes

I have said that once modifications started to be made in basic frame types to create new sound packages, each symbolizing a new concept to form a new word, a vocal learning capacity was needed to allow these new concept–symbol packages to propagate through the population. I have said that mirror neurons may have provided a phylogenetic underpinning for the evolution of this capacity, and allied myself with Donald in suggesting that this vocal learning capacity evolved as part of a more general mimetic capacity. An additional suggestion with wide-ranging consequences should be considered, however. It's possible that the new

capacity for imitation came with a radically new mechanism of evolutionary change similar to, but separate from, the genes, namely, "memes."

The *Oxford English Dictionary* defines "meme" as "an element of culture
that can be considered to be passed on by nongenetic means esp. imitation."
Webster's Collegiate, eleventh edition, is a bit more specific: "an idea,
behavior, style, or usage that spreads from person to person within a
culture." The background to this concept is Dawkins' idea of the "selfish
gene" (Dawkins, 1976). He noted that the prime function of genes, or more
specifically the DNA in them, is replication—making copies of themselves.
They are "selfish" in the sense that they devote themselves solely to the goal
of replication. He argued that three properties distinguish successful replicators: fidelity, fecundity, and longevity. As Blackmore (1999) puts it in her
book *The Meme Machine*, "This means that a replicator has to be copied
accurately, many copies must be made, and the copies must last a long time"
(p. 58). But as Dawkins clarifies in a foreword to Blackmore's book, his real
intention in *The Selfish Gene* was not to focus on genes and DNA so much
as on the notion of a replicator as a powerful force in selection. And to
illustrate that genes were only a single example, he offered the meme as one
alternative. He even used the intergeneration of learned patterns of birdsongs as an example of the operation of memes.

The crucial point here is that a meme is considered to be a replicator in its
own right. While what memes get replicated is constrained to some degree by
biology, it is not totally determined by it. Thus the meme can mediate
evolution somewhat independently of the gene, and the results of the cultural
selection in which it participates can be either beneficial to survival or not.
Dawkins was in effect saying something extremely profound: "The genetic
natural selection identified by Neodarwinism as the driving force of evolution
on this planet was only a special case of a more general process that I came to
dub 'Universal Darwinism' " (in Blackmore, 1999, p. xvi). Blackmore (1999)
goes so far as to say that the capacity for imitation that enables memes is what
makes humans different from any other species; moreover, she contends, it is
what led to the evolution of the big brains of humans and, indeed, along with
the genes, to the evolution of language. So we have another cosmic claim here,
in effect opposite to Ridley's claim for the FOXP2 gene.

Leaving aside these two huge claims for the moment, the important
thing about the concept of memes from the present point of view is that
languages can be seen primarily as bodies of memetic material. Each infant
must learn the words of its native language by *imitation*. And, as Blackmore

points out, languages qualify as "memeplexes" (related collections of memes) in terms of the three criterial properties of fidelity, fecundity, and longevity. As to fidelity, you have to be able to speak a language properly in order to fully participate in the culture, and, as we have seen, the necessity of maintaining a language's sound contrasts is very demanding. As to fecundity, most of us talk a lot. And when we do, and when our language is broadcast by various media, including the written one, we are usually communicating with a lot of potential replicators. As to longevity, a language itself never dies out unless its speakers are killed or marginalized, and for an infant it is typically a lifelong possession.

I see the meme as a plausible concept for explaining the second, frame/content stage of evolution of speech—the stage in which imitation became a factor. In my scenario for evolution of the first words, imitation became necessary when phonetic packages that were not already in the repertoire were systematically linked with concepts. What was in the repertoire? The frame stage, presumably made available phylogenetically to all users, consisted of CV forms—motor frames that could be reiterated (reduplicated) with the tongue either at rest or in some readily available nonresting position, and with the soft palate either up or down.

Specifically, I am guessing that when a word with intersyllabic variegation was first assigned to a concept—probably a word with a labial consonant–vowel–coronal consonant (LC) sequence in it, according to the theory—an imitation capacity was needed for people to use that word. Converting earlier discussion into memetic terms, the sound memes with the greatest replicative power would have been the ones that are both distinctive and easy to produce, and according to the theory, words with an LC sequence would have qualified.

At this early stage, to repeat previous discussion, distinctiveness was not a problem because there were so few words to decide between. But as the sound system increased in size, it had to avoid putting other sounds too close to an easy one so that they'd both remain consistently selectable as memes. On the other hand, if a new sound was adopted that was highly contrastive to the others in the system, it would tend to be favored even if it wasn't that easy to produce. The [s] sound seems to fall in that category. It's almost universal in languages. In Maddieson's count of 317 languages, some kind of [s] is present in 83.0 percent of them. But it takes children a few years to get it right, if they ever do. Sounds that were neither distinctive nor easy to produce did not stay around much. They had a big fidelity problem as replicators.

14.5 Gene–meme coevolution

It has been pointed out that once culture got going, and aspects of it had survival value even though they were not genetically driven, it could become responsible for genetic selection by favoring the genes of the culturally adroit. Durham, Boyd, and Richerson (1997) assert that "It is a basic assumption of the Darwinian theory of culture that long-lived cultural traditions should cause a co-evolutionary response on the part of the genes, as well as vice versa" (p. 344). So we could perhaps have had *gene–meme coevolution* in the progression toward modern speech. Ridley (2000) does not approve of this hypothesis: "Yet even bad ideas take a lot of killing, and the notion that language is a form of culture that can shape the brain rather than vice-versa has been an inordinate time a-dying" (p. 96). Perhaps the idea stays with us because there is more than a grain of truth in it, though for it to be true in this case, language must have been around for a long time. And, frankly, I am unwilling to make a guess as to how long it has been since the first words were coined.

One mental property of humans that, given time, might have been driven in the way Durham and his colleagues suggest is "working memory," aka "short-term memory." A key finding of cognitive neuroscience is that we possess a "phonological loop" in short-term memory in which organization of both linguistic input and output occurs. As I noted in Chapter 9, Baddeley (e.g., Baddeley, 1986), the leading figure in the development of the concept of working memory, believes that the phonological loop evolved in order for language to be learned. Working memory is of course the site of the serial-ordering errors of speech that have been such an important part of our story. It's hard to imagine that we had a working memory which could handle individual units approaching the present "magical number seven" (Miller, 1956) at the initial frame stage of speech evolution, when we wouldn't have needed it. In fact, it would have scarcely been needed until we had syntax.

So the general idea here is that we can perhaps wed some aspects of phonetics and therefore phonology to memetics, and talk about meme propagation in terms of the well-accepted phonetic framework of a trade-off between articulatory ease and perceptual distinctiveness. The generalized genetic underpinnings of phonetics/phonology must have provided some constraint on how memetics would get along with it in marriage.

But if memes can indeed act back on genes, biological offspring of the marriage would benefit from a memetic contribution to the genes as well as a simple intergenerational contribution from memes in the adult language of the new listener. Thus there could be some genetic basis for working memory, with some cultural determination, but it would be idle to speculate further about this at the present stage of our knowledge.

Finally, with the meme concept in mind, let's reconsider the hypothesis of Chapter 7 that the first words were created in a baby-talk context. Judging by the evidence from historical linguistics these words may have come and gone in the history of languages, but a restricted pair of forms keeps popping up with a characteristic sound/meaning relationship—a nasal/nonnasal dichotomy signaling the gender (maternal/paternal) dichotomy. From the point of view of Dawkins' three properties of replicators, these terms qualify most in terms of *fecundity*, apparently remaining productive in a similar way over a long period of time. In terms of *fidelity* they tend to succumb to the characteristic historical pressures for sound change, although perhaps to a lesser extent than other words. Nevertheless they tend to reconverge on the original forms. They have some vulnerability on the *longevity* score, periodically dropping out, and then reappearing, due to the fecundity of the mechanism.

Here, then, is my fundamental claim about how speech itself evolved to serve language. The parental terms of baby talk are *living fossils*. They are like, for example, the coelacanth, a deep-sea fish of ancient origin which nevertheless continues to occasionally appear today, as a result of continued high-fidelity replication, in close to its ancestral form. Darwin coined the term *living fossil* for instances of preservation of ancestral bodily form across long periods of time. But unlike the case of the coelacanth, where the mechanism of replication is basically genetic, the replication process for parental terms results from a marriage of genetic and memetic factors, arising from a complex matrix of parent–infant *biosocial dynamics* important enough to have been continually selected for over a substantial stretch of hominid history. And then, in each instance, once initially coined, the contrastive pair spread through the ambient culture, thus going from being an instance of biosocial dynamics to becoming one of *biocultural* dynamics.

What I am also suggesting here is that parental baby-talk terms are the *missing link* between the prelinguistic era of hominids and the linguistic era. With the coining of these terms, hominids began to produce phonetically contrastive words with the phonetic substrate necessary for the subsequent combinatorial level of phonological organization of language—the frame.

But instead of being, as in the usual case of missing links in evolutionary biology, a *structural* link in terms of an intermediate bodily form filling in a gap in a family tree, these parental terms were a *functional* link, setting the stage for subsequent creation of other words—more memetic units, with similar phonetic forms but different meanings.

14.6 Cultural elaboration of speech: the cross as a metaphor for the syllable

We need a metaphor to help us not only understand how memetic culture works but also gain a better perspective on what happens in speech. I suggest the religious symbol of the cross as a metaphor for the syllable, in terms of its sociocultural history. Most importantly, the *explosion of cultural elaboration* that we see in the history of the cross has parallels with the cultural elaboration that must have occurred in syllable structure and content.

The form of the cross that we are perhaps most familiar with is the one consisting of a vertical bar intersected by a symmetrical shorter horizontal bar, more than halfway up. Before talking about the cultural elaboration of this form, let's briefly consider its origin. Most Westerners probably think that it originated in the wooden cross on which Jesus was crucified. But there are numerous examples of it predating the origin of Christianity.

Although this is necessarily speculative, I am assuming that the cross originated as an abstract representation of a standing human-like figure with arms outstretched horizontally. Consider, for example, Fig. 14.2, a photograph of a small stone Cypriot figure, thought to be the goddess Aphrodite from the third millenium BC wearing a cross-like form as a pendant (Webb, 2003, Fig. 2). The human-like form on which it hangs is also relatively cross-like. It is a minimally differentiated, standing human form with arms outstretched. The vertical component has a lower fissure dividing two legs, topped by rudimentary hips. There is a primitive circular head at the top, a bit wider than the trunk, with only eyes, nose, and forehead. The arms are two truncated horizontal stubs. The pendant also seems to have similar rudimentary human-like properties, though with even less detail. It is a small step from such forms to crosses without the human rudiments.

What exactly was involved in the original event? There is presumably an analogy with the origin of the first word in that *someone took a naturally occurring form and endowed it with symbolic significance*. The difference is

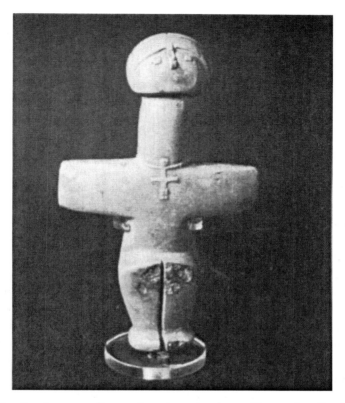

FIG. 14.2   Cypriot stone figure, thought to be the goddess Aphrodite from the 3rd millennium BC. (From Webb, 2003)

that the speaker took a pre-existing form, while the sculptor made a new form in the image of a pre-existing one. For the first word, a mother took [mama] and decided that "It stands for me." For the first cross, the artist constructed a simplified representation of the observable human form to literally and figuratively stand for "human." Conceptualizing the vertical part was easy: it fell out of humans' distinctive bipedal posture. But, on its own, it might not have been distinguishable from "tree." Some apical facial features would have helped here. But a human-like figure without limbs may have been a little too abstract as an initial form. So the horizontal component was added. Of course we don't go around with our arms extended horizontally. However, given that "horizontal" must have been a rather fundamental notion for people who walked around on a flat savanna with a flat horizon, it might have come readily to mind as a way of configuring the two arms, realistically placed more than halfway up the vertical component, in order to make the outline of the form more convincingly human.

I am taking the cross to be an analog of the syllable. The single vertical form is analogous to the vowel. One (nuclear) vowel per syllable, and one vertical form per cross, is the mode. The horizontal form or forms are analogous to consonants. The syllable seems a little more unconstrained than the cross in that there can be single consonants as syllables and single vowels as syllables, though they are not that common. Of course, both the frame underlying the syllable and the human form being simulated by the artist evolved by natural selection. Then both were culturally selected as symbols.

My contention is that both the CV protosyllable and the earliest crosses can be regarded as laying out a problem space for subsequent elaboration in the sense that they afforded some developments and not others. We know that in general the problem space for speech allowed sounds that were producible, within the time-domain boundaries of the frame, having per-haps a graded continuum of production ease, and such sounds, if they were to survive, must have reliably made a perceptual contrast with other sounds. Analogously, the problem space for the cross seems to have a wide range of form affordances consistent with it and also a large number of decorative affordances consistent with its still being seen as a cross. In the context of Western religion there is a huge range of affordances, but with a constraint against sacrilegious forms. To my knowledge, the devil does not get onto the cross. As to form affordances, *Merriam-Webster's Collegiate Dictionary*, tenth edition, (p. 276) shows twenty relatively well-known forms of the cross, including the Calvary cross, the Latin cross, the patriarchal cross, the papal cross, the Lorraine cross, the Greek cross, the Celtic cross, the Maltese cross, the St. Andrew's cross, the Tau cross, etc. Apparently there has been a strong force toward cultural differentiation operating, just as there is for syllables in languages. In the forms pictured, at least, a force toward lateral symmetry, perhaps derived from the origin of the symbol in the human body, can be observed. But variants have evolved that seem to tax any imaginable structural definition of the form. For example, the Tau cross has no vertical component above the crossbar, and there are forms of it that are laterally asymmetrical. In addition, the swastika qualifies as a cross on formal grounds despite its having eventually achieved abhorrent cultural connotations. It was apparently once a good-luck symbol!

Permitted elaborations of crosses include things like embedded precious or semiprecious stones, and flowers and vines, though to my knowledge no fruits or vegetables. Interestingly, in light of its exalted status in language, recursion—crosses within crosses—is not uncommon. And having the four evangelists in the four terminations of the cross is a common variant. Sometimes God the Father looks down from the top extremity. In the extreme, Ethiopean crosses have an extraordinary proliferation of detailed openwork design features on a single metal plate that have expanded to fill, or almost fill, the four right-angled interstices of the basic form. This is a result of the merging of the basic Byzantine iconography of the cross with the more filigree decorative mode of Islam. Perhaps analogous things can happen when languages come into contact with each other.

Crosses, like syllables, have some physical constraints. The precise form of crosses depends on how they are situated in the world. Pendant crosses have a structure at the top that allows an antigravity support to be attached, and, if worn, must conform to a narrow range of sizes. Crosses that are set in the ground must be designed for that interface, which often means that the bottom of the vertical component is designed differently than the three other extremities. One response to this constraint is symbolized in the Calvary cross.

The details of this comparison don't particularly matter. What matters is that *in both cases a single naturally selected form with two basic components has been accorded symbolic status and then subjected to an extraordinary process of cultural elaboration subject to the constraints and affordances of the problem space.* While the constraints and affordances are different in the two cases, the processes of elaboration seem analogous. The propensity for elaboration exists, as far as I can see, for virtually all artifacts of material culture in which the problem space allows decoration. To pick a few at random: women's fashions, tableware, lamps, shoes, suits of armor, trinket boxes, furniture, hats, automobiles, dog collars, handbags and wallets, clothes, guns, decorative tiles, textiles, brass doorknobs, etc. Much of this elaboration is culture-specific, just as the form of language is culture-specific. But the fact of elaboration seems to be a general cultural imperative, though it is totally irrelevant from an essentialistic perspective.

Thus the syllable is behaving as if it is a cultural artifact, as it should if it is indeed a cultural artifact. It has a basic form with a functional origin. Beyond that, it has a problem space defined by its culturally invented communicative role in which there is a family of affordances and constraints, and these, working together, result in the diverse array of observable forms of the entity.

In denying a current specific genetic basis for speech itself, and according a huge role to the alternative cultural unit, the meme, am I backing off from my original contention that a basis for speech can be found within a Neodarwinian framework? Not in the least. I have asserted that there is an orthodox Neodarwinian descent-with-modification scenario for phonation and for the syllable-related frames that presumably formed the initial superstructure for speech. I have also argued that vocal volubility was naturally selected for in the general context of Dunbar's vocal-grooming scenario, though it perhaps didn't reach the stage of gossip. (That would have taken words, and Dunbar does not get us to words.) Falk's "putting the baby down" scenario (2004) would also have contributed to volubility for both infant and parent, and set the stage for word invention. I also assume that natural selection for vocal learnability, in the context of action learnability in general, may have occurred in the form of evolution of mirror neurons, and blossomed, as an additional effect of natural selection, into the general-purpose mimetic capacity noted by Donald.

But from then on the selection for speech was primarily cultural, and the new equivalent to the gene was the meme. The pairing of meanings with sounds to form the first words was a cultural invention, as was the subsequent word explosion. In fact the *mama/papa* words which in their initial incarnation may have been the first words (see Chapter 7) are apparently prime examples of memetic transmission. Judging by their persistence in recorded history, even though it may have often been intermittent, they are the results of a memorable association of nasalized vocalizations of the infant with the female parent, and a contrastive but also memorable association of oral forms with the male parent. But because they originated as naturally selected vocalizations before being momentously put to further use as signals for concepts, their overall history can be considered roughly as a journey from gene to meme.

The subsequent cultural stage I have been discussing was channeled, to be sure, by biological constraints on production capabilities and the communication-based demand for perceptual distinctiveness. But, in my opinion, the only possible *major* candidate for speech-related selection beyond the point of invention of the word is an increase in working-memory capacity, and it could have been motivated by a culturally mediated explosion of linguistic forms. Minor candidates, presumably selected for in a similar way, include the two-tubed vocal tract of Lieberman and increased neural capabilities for breath control, as suggested by McLarnon and Hewitt (1999). I see no reason to posit a speech-related increase in auditory discrimination capacity, though I currently have no reason to deny it either.

In summary, in terms of ultimate causes, the full scenario for the evolution of speech, while containing an essential initial foundational core of orthodox Neodarwinism, ends up, because of its huge memetic overlay, being a proposal in the realm of Universal Darwinism. It is a hybrid of biological and cultural replication processes, much like the modern human mind in general, according to Donald (2001, p. xiii).

15   Conclusions

15.1   Neodarwinism: where did we get to?

I believe I have delivered on my promise that if we take the question of action seriously we will understand something important about the evolution of speech by natural selection. Most basically, my approach has been an ethological one—a study of naturally occurring animal behavior. I have taken a large family of action macropatterns, occurring naturally in the prespeech and speech of infants and in the speech patterns of languages, and asked why they are the same in some cases and different in others.

Prominent among these macropatterns were the following: the universal CV syllable; the three CV co-occurrence patterns, probably universal in infants and near-universal in languages; the three VC co-occurrence patterns, probably universal in infants but reduced or absent in adults; syllable reduplication in infants but syllable variegation in languages; and various striking inabilities in infants, such as fricative and liquid production, and production of final consonants in CVC words.

I came to three major conclusions with respect to these patterns. First, the only unequivocal universal in both infants and languages—the CV form—was the original basis for speech as an action. It constituted what I called the "frame." Second, the patterns that are universal in infants but not in languages—CV and VC co-occurrence patterns, syllabic reduplication, restrictions on fricatives and liquids and on utterance-final consonants—stem from our basic hominid speech capacity, and were present in the first words. Third, the patterns that are universal in languages but not in infants—syllabic variegation and (the related) restrictions on VC co-occurrences—stem from the increasing pressures on speech systems to expand the size of their message sets.

The result of all this was an orthodox Neodarwinian descent-with-modification theory of evolution of speech that fits the normal intuition that speech evolved from simple to more complex rather than instantaneously evolving the mental form that underlies it today.

Let me briefly recapitulate the phylogenetic aspect of the argument. From the action perspective, what our ancestors had to do was to somehow superimpose speech on a movement-control assemblage that didn't previously have it. It did have, of course, some movement capabilities for other purposes, and, like any other biomechanical system, it was subject to inertia.

What were these capabilities? I contend that ancestral forms had available to them three sets of usable movement capabilities—available since the earliest mammals, circa 200 mya—and combined them to form protosyllables.

The *respiratory* system provided the power source for the *phonatory* system, a communicative system which supplied voicing. These systems had been effectively combined since the earliest mammals. The third system was the *articulatory* one, the one controlling the mandible, specifically its cyclical capability. This system was as old as the phonatory system but it didn't take on communicative significance until our primate ancestors started using it for visuofacial communication, primarily in the form of smacks. The first specifically speech-related achievement was to put the articulatory system together with the other two systems to get protosyllables.

The cycle was valuable because it was a *carrier* for speech. The basis for the subsequent complex coding system could be *extended in time* simply by reiteration—yet another way to use biphasic cycles to get work done in the animal kingdom. And the cycle contained the seeds of its own segmentation—an alternation between low-amplitude constrictive phases and high-amplitude unconstricted phases. This cycle is now ubiquitous in speech. Its canonical form, the simple CV alternation, is present in all languages and dominates the speech-acquisition process from the moment it first appears.

What Davis and I discovered was that by looking at speech acquisition we could learn more about the phylogeny of the mandibular cycle. We found that in infants, the cycle operated in the context of inertia in the other articulators, most importantly the tongue. As we also found traces of this inertia were similarly present in sound patterns of modern languages, and as inertia is such a basic property of movement-control systems, we concluded that the inertia-based patterns were probably present in the first words.

The identification of inertia brought into focus the issue of *overcoming* it, something that had to occur if speech was to convey a large set of messages. As inertia was presumably first "tolerated" and then overcome in phylogeny, just as it is in ontogeny, we suggested a two-stage model for phylogeny and ontogeny of speech: the *frame stage* and the *frame/content stage*. As to how we got/get from one stage to another, we suggested a self-organizational model for the first main step in that direction in ontogeny (and possibly phylogeny): the achievement of the trend toward CVC sequences of the labial–vowel–coronal form in particular. Despite working on this question for about twenty years, Davis and I haven't yet got too much to say about what happens in ontogeny after that. It turns out to be a hard question. Hopefully, work on early "accidental" or one-time speech errors, of the kind done by Jaeger (e.g., Jaeger, 2005), will help us to learn more about this development in ontogeny at least.

What I have suggested for the beginnings of speech—the *frame stage*—fits perfectly with Jacob's tinkering metaphor for the process of natural selection (Jacob, 1977). Jacob suggests two main ways in which tinkering can occur—transformation and combination. In the phylogeny of speech, a cyclicity, perhaps originally evolving for ingestion, may have been exapted for the smacks of visuofacial communication (smacks)—"transformation," in Jacob's terms; and then it got put together with respiration/phonation—"combination," in Jacob's terms—to get protosyllables. Alternatively, as suggested by the phylogeny of birdsong, which was not preceded by ingestive cyclicities, cyclical reiteration may have evolved directly for visuofacial communication. In any event, we eventually became able to combine phonation and mandibular cyclicities in order to produce strings of protosyllables, presumably for the purposes of vocal grooming, as suggested by Dunbar (1996). This capability was also to some degree learnable as it was one aspect of the general-purpose mimetic ability postulated by Donald (1991). So, as in the case of birdsong, there might have been some latitude for different dialects and for individual differences.

However, from the time that frames were first paired with concepts to get words (a social invention), the sequence of events went beyond biological evolution as a combinatorial phonological system was gradually built under sociocultural pressures to develop a larger message set. While genes lay, though very indirectly, behind the frame stage before the first words were invented, memes came to be the major force as speech proceeded from the frame stage to the frame/content stage.

15.1.1 *Lashley's problem of serial order*

The focus on serial organization, induced by the work of Lashley, proved a valuable one because it forced us to begin with a realistic conception of what speech and signing are actually like (rather than from assumed abstract structures) and to develop ontogenetic and phylogenetic conceptions based on real-time events.

The solution of the problem for speech—the answer to Tinbergen's "How does it work?" question—is that modern serial organization of speech is a result of the two-step evolutionary process just described, resulting in the capacity to program cognitive-motor frames with content elements.

Considerations of serial organization, including analyses of serial-ordering errors, were also crucial in deciding that signed language had a very different organization from speech. It was clear from this perspective, for example, that the individual sign was not equivalent to the spoken syllable. Perhaps most importantly, serial-ordering errors involved components that for the most part spread throughout the sign (handshapes, locations, or movements) while serial-ordering errors of speech involved either beginnings (onsets), middles (nuclei), or ends (codas) of syllables. And, of course, I argue that the subsyllabic fractionation of speech is inherent in the process of evolving frames and then programming them to make speech what it is. So it's certainly not a superficial aspect of speech.

In contrast, we have seen that the elements of a sign—location, handshape, movement—can be regarded as present simultaneously throughout the sign. However, as indicated by Sandler and Lillo-Martin (2006), spoken syllables and signs, even though sequential and simultaneous, respectively, did seem to have in common the status of rhythmic units.

So even here, as in speech and birdsong, Lashley was on target in pointing to the possible significance of rhythm generators in the serial-ordering process. But birdsong clusters with speech in using an already available cycle, the mouth/beak close–open cycle, as the articulatory basis of rhythmicity, while sign language calls for some kind of synthetic process for creating rhythmic organization at the intrasign and intersign levels.

15.1.2 *Sperry: movements to mind*

The most important response to Sperry's advocacy—that we should derive mind from movements—was the postulation of the cognitive-motor frame underlying speech production. I argued that this frame developed phylo-genetically as part of the apparatus allowing the programming of syllable-sized units. It also develops ontogenetically in modern infants. I saw no need to call this aspect of the mental representation of speech innate. I imagine that it began to be a part of hominid minds when the language that the infant hominid had to learn reached a certain stage on the route from frame to frame/content organization. And I imagine it develops in infants when they reach a certain stage in their attempt to learn speech. In both cases, I believe that this can occur via self-organization.

Notice here that existence of the cognitive-motor frame in the form of a rhythmical frame-reiteration device in the brain doesn't necessarily follow from the existence of a frame/content mode of organization, as revealed by segmental speech errors. Discovery of this device is a "lucky" accident of neuropathology. Without patients' involuntary productions of rhythmical sequences of the same CV syllable, we would never know that this form exists. But note that speech errors also tell us that we have mental units of *segment* size with which we program these frames. They also tell us that consonants and vowels play different roles in the overall generation process because vowels but not consonants are restricted in the kinds of errors they can participate in. Sperry's advocacy is also important in the understanding of birdsong, if we assume birds have minds.

The most spectacular recent vindication of Sperry's proposal that we work from the body to discover the mind comes from the work of Rizzolatti and his colleagues on mirror neurons. Their original intention in recording single neurons in ventral premotor cortex was to better understand the control of characteristic manual movements. But in the course of doing that they found evidence for a body–mind relationship that requires us to radically revise our classical conception of the evolution of the mind, which was hitherto based on innate knowledge and input but not output. In the words of Stamenov and Gallese, "It is hard to overesti-mate the importance of this discovery" (2002, p. 1). In the history of zoological forms the most basic role of the nervous system is to receive input and use it first directly, and then in higher forms, more indirectly, in the service of adaptive output. In animals that evolved to move in order to acquire food, independence of direct stimulus-response relationships de-velops, but even here the causal sequence input-to-output remains im-portant. But mirror neurons have enabled a radical reversal of this causal sequence, a development which can hardly be overemphasized. Now the organism's reflexive (turned back on itself) use of its own output representation capabilities serves as a guide for more highly adaptive processing of input. Speech learnability is only one of a panoply of important emergent functions that this evolutionary development allows.

15.1.3 Consequences for the embodiment perspective

The frame/content theory is a theory about the body's influence on the mind. If it is a correct conception about how speech evolved, it provides much new evidence for the power of the embodiment perspective in understanding the human mind. In my view, speaking was the result of a series of processes of selection of action capabilities of the body. The basic point here is that there is no evidence that basic units such as the syllable and the segment were somehow imposed on speech from above by some kind of mental imperative. They arose out of the constraints of bodily operation.

The power of the body can also be seen in the fact that sign languages are organized differently than spoken languages but are equally expressive and apparently learned as easily. Much of this achievement is presumably a result of the evolution of a general-purpose mimetic capacity, as postulated by Donald. Lying behind the choice of the three main body parameters used in signed languages—handshape, location, and movement—there must be mental representations analogous in function to those that lie behind speech but dependent on the bodily parameters that they represent, and therefore not amodal in nature.

Input systems are also part of the body. I have argued that auditory perceptual capabilities were not very important in the earliest stages of the evolution of speech because the task of discriminating between a small number of message possibilities was not very demanding. But once the system started to get larger, the capabilities of—and constraints on—the auditory system must have become increasingly important, although the old idea that there is a special speech mode of perception seems to no longer be viable (Hauser, Chomsky, and Fitch, 2002), the arguments of Pinker and Jackendoff (2005) notwithstanding. The capability of the visual system for making distinctions between signs of signed languages must also be influential in the design of sign systems.

The discovery of mirror neurons has had more important consequences for the embodiment perspective than any other event in contemporary cognitive neuroscience. These neurons presumably underlie Donald's general-purpose hominid mimetic capability, a capability that makes the learning of both speech and sign-language production possible. The ability of neonatal infants to imitate adult tongue movements, first noted by Meltzoff and Moore (1977), shows the fundamental nature of this imitative capacity in humans. Apropos the work of Rizzolatti and his colleagues, Blakeslee (2006) points out that "The human brain has multiple mirror neuron systems that specialize in carrying out not just the actions of others but their intentions, the social meaning of their behavior and their emotions." They provide an alternative to the disembodied cognition that underlies not only UG but much of current cognitive science. As Rizzolatti (cited by Blakeslee, 2006) notes, "Mirror neurons allow us to grasp the minds of others, not through conceptual reasoning but through direct simulation. By feeling not by thinking." For language in particular, mirror neurons provide the foundation for a more encompassing embodiment-based neurocognitive alternative to UG, one that goes beyond the mechanisms that lie between meaning and sound, considered separately, by including meaning and sound in the same picture, and giving us a better basis for their relationship.

The embodiment perspective was primary in my attempt to say how the first words were made. I suggested that the phonetic structure of the first words resulted from the cognitive pairing of an observed *action*—the infant distress cry—with a concept, namely, "This sound stands for me" by the presumably maternal caregiver. An important point here is that the current widespread conclusion that the relation between sounds and meanings now appears to be arbitrary provides an excuse for not dealing with the certainty that such pairings could not have *begun* by being arbitrary. We have never possessed a random sound/meaning pairing device. The body must have been involved in the initial equation in a naturally occurring way.

15.1.4 Evolution of brain organization for speech

In the age of cognitive neuroscience, any theory of origin of a human mental function ought to have something to say about how the brain organization underlying it evolved. The only other view of the evolution of speech that is accompanied by a scenario for brain organization is that of Lieberman. In a monograph entitled *Human Language and our*

Reptilian Brain (2000) he asserts that the neural basis of speech, and in fact grammar in general, is to be found almost exclusively in the basal ganglia's ability to sequence movements. However, in discussing speech production he only considers the question of the relative timing of release of occlusion and voice onset in stop consonants rather than sequencing of successive consonants and vowels. He does not touch on the most fundamental question of speech sequencing—that of syllabic organization.

In his exclusive attribution of sequencing to the subcortical structures of the basal ganglia, Lieberman is out of tune with the zeitgeist. In their introductory textbook in cognitive neuroscience, Gazzaniga, Ivry, and Mangun (1998) state that "Whether or not the basal ganglia are central to generating movement sequences is a debatable issue" (p. 417). And we have seen that *damage* to the basal ganglia in global aphasics seems to have a disinhibiting effect on speech resulting, paradoxically for Lieberman, in the basic rhythmic syllabic *sequencing* of NMRUs. Most fundamentally, no view of the evolution of brain organization for speech which does not focus primarily on the cerebral cortex will ever attain overall importance.

The view of brain evolution that I have presented allows us to better understand the significance of the main cortical site of action control for speech—Broca's area. It does this by recognizing that it and its immediately surrounding areas constitute the main cortical region for the evolution of control of ingestive functions, and probably for visuofacial communicative cyclicities, too.

An important perspective on the joint role of Broca's area for vocal and manual function, revealed most clearly by the presence of mirror neurons associated with both functions in monkeys, is provided by Wise (2007) in a review of the evolution of ventral premotor cortex (in his terms, "PMv"), widely considered a precursor of Broca's area. In the process he brings together implications of my two theories of evolution of speech, the frame/content theory and the postural origins theory.

He notes evidence that ventral premotor cortex first evolved in primates, and is considered to be an adaptation to the arboreal lifestyle initiated by prosimians. Associated with the new functional role of this region is the fact that it has direct subcortical projections to spinal and brainstem motor centers, thus bypassing primary motor cortex. The spinal projections seem to mediate four principal functions: "control of head orientation by neck muscles, control of the shoulder girdle, regulation of inspiration, and tongue stabilization." The brainstem projections include those associated with control of the lip and the jaw. Wise concludes that ventral premotor cortex "evolved to coordinate head, mouth, and limb movements during unimanual feeding." As evidence for the highly specialized nature of this emergent adaptation, he cites the conclusion of the postural origins theory that left-hand preferences for prehension evolved in prosimians (see Chapter 10).

Wise also notes that "the capability for enhanced control of the head and orofacial musculature might also have served social signaling." Referring to the implications of the frame/content theory for the evolution of motor organization in Broca's area he suggests that "PMv's projection to the motor nuclei for controlling the lips and jaw accord with MacNeilage's idea."

Wise's proposals also have implications for the broader picture of relationships between vocal and manual function in the evolution of communication. He argues that PMv may have played an important role in the evolution of the basis of "the primate way of reaching" as it "computes the difference between hand position and target location in a coordinate frame based on vision, and similar computations could support visually guided reaching and pointing generally, as well as the orientation of the head during social signaling."

With Wise's work, we begin to see the promise of an evolutionary cognitive neuroscientific basis for the young child's triadic declarative pointing acts, in which she *points* at an object (typically with the right hand) while *looking* at the parent, and simultaneously *vocalizing*. In this context it is of interest to note that Abry et al. (2008) make an evolutionary argument for a fundamental semantics/action coupling based on the the fact that an infant's pointing movement takes about the same amount of time that it takes to produce two syllables (about two-thirds of a second). It's also interesting to note, in the light of the depth of the evolutionary perspective provided by Wise, that Lashley (1951) suggested that our understanding of reaching and grasping might eventually make a contribution to the physiology of logic—a far cry indeed from Descartes' position.

An important point in the present context is that we can identify, here and elsewhere, a heuristic role of both the frame/content theory and the postural origins theory in contemporary cognitive neuroscience. But notwithstanding the importance of Broca's area for the neurobiology of both speech and manual function, I hope that *my* most important neuroscientific contribution to the understanding of speech in this book will be to draw attention to the evidence from neuropathology that frames have a neurological reality, and that it might be a neurological reality shared by birdsong. To me there is something very compelling about the combination of the high level of organization of Non-Meaningful Recurrent Utterances (NMRUs) and the fact that they do not occur as part of normal speech. Why are they so organized when they are not normally used as such? In all likelihood, it's because they reveal a basis for normal speech that is masked by the elaborations it undergoes in ordinary speech output, but revealed to us in pathology. I hope that in addition to the realization of the importance of this phenomenon there will be a realization of the importance of the intrinsic motor subsystem that mediates it, a subsystem that is currently upstaged by the extrinsic subsystem that has Broca's area with its mirror neuron capability as a component.

The postural origins theory has received sufficient confirmation in many of its details to make it a useful continued basis for study of the evolution of cerebral hemispheric specializations in vertebrates in general. Now that the claim that nonhuman primate right-handedness is an artifact of captivity has been disproved, we can look forward to a much increased understanding of the evolution of right-handedness in primates, including ourselves, and a better understanding of how the right-hand specialization relates to the speech specialization. Consequently, we should gain more freedom from the solipsistic consequences of a purely anthropocentric approach to this question. Perhaps Geschwind was right when he said in 1985 that "the recognition of asymmetry in the nonhuman nervous system is likely to lead to major conceptual advances in fields as widely disparate as human evolution, linguistics, psychology and psychiatry. If these suppositions are correct, it will also have major philosophical repercussions" (Geschwind, 1985, p. 268).

Finally, note that the postural origins theory is another contribution to the embodiment perspective. The left hemisphere is specialized for routine *actions*, and the right hemisphere is specialized for emergency *reactions*.

15.2 Classicism/generativism: how did it fare?

In Chapter 2, I concurred with Hauser in asserting that answering Tinbergen's four questions was necessary for a "fully encompassing and explanatory approach" (Hauser, 1996, p. 2) to speech. The questions were mechanistic (*How does it work?*), functional (*What does it do for the organism?*), ontogenetic

(*How does it get that way in development?*), and phylogenetic (*How did it get that way in evolution?*). We have found that the classical/generative approach doesn't provide an answer to any of these questions. Let us consider this point a little further.

Consideration of the mechanism of real-time action, required in order to answer Tinbergen's first question, is ruled out of court by Chomsky's Cartesian competence/performance distinction. Actual performance is regarded as something that has to be factored out in order to apprehend competence. And it should be emphasized that although what is talked about in this context is performance today, what is being ruled out is the entire history of performance. So while modern performance is what we evolved to do, the history of action including the question of what hurdles the action component needed to clear to achieve its present, in my view miraculous, status, is not part of the story. More generally we saw the adoption of a double standard with regard to performance, in which on the one hand obviously performance-related facts were deemed aspects of competence when they facilitated generalizations about the nature of sounds and sound patterns, but declared irrelevant when they gave no such assistance. This latter stance led to the bizarre situation (Chapter 12) in which Blevins (2004) regarded the same favored CV co-occurrence pattern of an infant as part of competence if it is correct, but part of performance if it is wrong.

After abstracting away performance-related aspects of phonological structure, such as perceptually based sonority and an articulatorily based conception of distinctive features, we were not able to discern what the actual nature of phonological competence as a purely mental phenomenon was deemed to be. We found, for example, that Anderson (1985) and Blevins (2004) characterized phonology in terms of what was left when other properties were excluded rather than in terms of what it actually is. And when one adds the fact that we did not find even indirect evidence that the phonological component of language is amodal, as claimed, the absence of a mental structure puts the generativists even further away from their target. Note, though, a problem that arises here. The more one incorporates performance aspects of speech into the phonology, the more difficult it is to make the claim that phonology is amodal.

But even if a specific mental phonology had been proposed, it would not have necessarily had implications for function. The approach to this question has remained in the pre-Chomskyan structuralist perspective.

Ingold (1993) nicely captures the structuralist approach to language by describing it as "an invention of linguists who have sought to model the activities of speaking as the application of a coherent system of syntactic and semantic rules, [and, I would add, phonological rules] derived by abstraction from observed behavior" (p. 457). He continues:

they have gone on to transfer, onto the speakers themselves, their own external relationship to the object of study, imagining the abstractions derived from this "view from the outside" to be implanted within the speakers' minds and to constitute the essence of their competence. Hence speaking is seen to consist in the implementation of linguistic rules. Inside the head of every speaker there appears a miniature linguist. (p. 457)

The prime example of this that we have considered is the attempt to transfer the concept of distinctive features, an artifact of linguistic analysis, into the minds of speakers. Chomsky and Halle's 1968 attempt to construct a purely formal conception of phonology along the lines of Russell and Whitehead's *Principia Mathematica* was a failure. The currently favored conception of phonology, optimality theory, while deemed a major advance, basically gives up the attempt at a uniform universal phonology by conceding that individual languages have the power to rank a set of universal constraints in whichever way they please.

Because the generative perspective is non-evolutionary, practitioners have not addressed the second, functional question of Tinbergen, the question of why speech was naturally selected for. In Chomsky's conception, speech was not naturally selected for at all. It just happened to originate with the syntactic component of UG, even though UG is considered to have been an initial aid to thought, and the existence of phonology only makes sense in the context of communication. And apart from saying that the sensorimotor component may have had to adapt to the phonology, he says nothing about the communicative contingencies that would impinge on the phonology. As I said in Chapter 2, the likelihood that an earlier evolving mental phonological component would happen to be able to subsequently interface smoothly with the action component (and the perceptual component) for its new communicative purpose would seem to be extremely slim. We are at a disadvantage here because we don't even know what the putative mental phonology is like now.

As Braine (1994) pointed out, the nativistic approach to linguistics doesn't include a theory of development, which is required for answering

Tinbergen's third question, the ontogenetic one. As we don't have a conception of what the innate phonology is, we can't say in advance what should manifest itself. Even if we could say that, nothing in the generativist conception would tell us the order in which things would develop. There seems to be agreement that the generativist conception of development is one of continuity because the necessary innate structure just needs to manifest itself across the time domain. But we found that Chomsky's organ-growth metaphors presented in support of this conception were too nativistic, too unidirectional (only genes to behavior), and too simple to fit the case. In short, choosing the heart as a metaphor for UG doesn't work because hearts don't have culture to contend with.

We also found that in a general perspective, the course of events in speech development is better described in terms of discontinuity than continuity. Infants go from reduplicating syllables to the reverse—variegating them, as all languages require. This has in fact been a long-standing problem for developmental phonology. It is specifically a problem for the concept of markedness. This concept, ineffective from the beginning onward because of the circular reasoning it involves, was conceived as a means of addressing preferences in sounds and sound patterns of languages. These are required to be similar across different domains but are often different in infant speech than they are in languages.

In detail, in considering generativist conceptions of the three central developmental phenomena of F/C theory—the CV syllable (frame), the consonant–vowel co-occurrence constraints, and the labial–coronal effect—we encountered a set of diverse characterizations (e.g., phonologically placeless vowels, underspecification, left-edge effects, consonantal harmony, and melody templates) that were ad hoc rather than encompassed by a central theoretical conception. These were uniformly non-explanatory, as would be expected from the structuralist tradition from which they arose.

A treatment in terms of descent with modification is necessary to address Tinbergen's fourth question, the evolutionary one. But as even the generativist Newmeyer (2002) notes, Chomsky's perspective is a uniformitarian one, lacking a progression. And here we need to again heed Lakoff's reminder that "philosophy matters" (1987, p. 157). The physicalistic origins scenarios that Chomsky has presented featuring such things as a cosmic-ray shower and physical pressure on an enlarging brain, tend to mask the fact that the forms of generative linguistics are in the philosophical tradition of Platonic essentialism. In effect, the forms are treated as being "just there." Even if we took these physicalistic scenarios seriously, they would still be problematical. As Jacob (1977) has pointed out when discussing ultimate causes, "Simple objects are more dependent on [physical] constraints than on history. As complexity increases, history plays the greater part" (p. 1163). Phonology is a complex form par excellence. But there is no history in the generative conception of phonology. There is no progression, beyond the written history of historical linguistics, though such a progression would be expected, not only from Jacob's dictum but simply from common sense.

Finally, a related point. Many scientists have commented on the unlikelihood of the kind of unicausal or "magic bullet" approaches to the explanation of complex biological phenomena that the generativists either espouse or tacitly assume. From the domain of artificial intelligence, Resnik (1994) notes that "people tend to look for *the* cause, *the* reason, *the* driving force, *the* deciding factor" (p. 120). From evolutionary neurobiology, Allman (1999), in the context of evolution of constant body temperature in mammals (homeostasis), credits T.S. Kemp (1982) with the observation that "only small changes in any one system could occur without changes in related systems to support it" (p. 105). He goes on to say that "It is precisely this interdependence of adaptations that makes the study of evolution such a difficult intellectual challenge. One cannot isolate any single factor and declare it to be the 'cause' responsible for the evolution of temperature homeostasis or any other adaptive complex" (pp. 105–106). Allman then lists no fewer than twenty-five variables relevant to homeostasis. The developmental psychologists Thelen and Smith (1994) most directly address the generative approach, noting that "The problem with the competence–performance distinction is...the fallacy of single causation" (p. 26).

15.3 Coda

Many years ago, the evolutionary biologist E. O. Wilson (1975, p. 559) noted some problems of the structuralist approach to language, embraced by the generativists and centered on the concept of universal grammar. He observed that "Students of the subject seldom confront the problem as if it were genuinely scientific, in a way that would reveal how concrete and soluble it might be." He saw the analysis as "nontheoretical in the sense that it fails to argue from postulates that can be tested and extended empirically." He concluded that

Like poet naturalists, the structuralists celebrate idiosyncratic personal visions. They argue from hidden premises; relying largely on metaphor and exemplification, and with little regard for the method of competing hypotheses. Clearly this discipline, one of the most important in all of science, is ripe for the application of rigorous theory and properly meshed experimental investigation. (p. 560)

In the light of Wilson's comments, it's not surprising to find that phonology is an intellectually isolated subdiscipline, cut off from the mainstream of modern cognitive science. In the context of evolutionary biology, it is perhaps best characterized as being at a Linnaean stage because of its basically essentialistic stance (see Mayr, 1982, for a historical perspective). Apart from the paper by Prince and Smolensky (1997), articles with a focus on generative phonology have not appeared in flagship journals including cognitive science in general such as *Science, Nature,* and *Behavioral and Brain Sciences* in recent years. Neither is phonology typically found in major general reference sources in cognitive science (e.g., *The Oxford Companion to the Mind* [Gregory, 1989]; *The Science of Mind* [Klivington, 1989]; *Foundations of Cognitive Science* [Posner, 1989]; *The Cognitive Neurosciences* [Gazzaniga, 1995]; *The Blackwell Companion to Cognitive Science* [Bechtel and Graham, 1999]); *The New Cognitive Neurosciences* [Gazzaniga, 2000]. I hope that the Darwinian approach to the evolution of speech I have presented here will become part of a framework enabling the phonological component of speech to enter the mainstream of modern science where it deserves to be, considering its importance in getting us to be who we are.

References

Abbs, J. H., and DePaul, R. (1998). 'Motor cortex fields and speech movements: Simple dual control is implausible.' *Behavioral and Brain Sciences, 21*, 511–512.

Abler, W. (1989). 'On the particulate principle of self-diversifying systems.' *Journal of Social and Biological Structures, 12*, 1–13.

Abry, C., Boë, L. J., Laboissière, R., and Schwartz, J. L. (1998). 'A new puzzle for the evolution of speech.' *Behavioral and Brain Sciences, 21*, 512–513.

——, Stefanuto, M., Villain, A., and Laboissière, R. (2002). 'What can the utterance "tan, tan" of Broca's patient Leborgne tell us about the hypothesis of an emergent "babble-syllable" downloaded by SMA?' In J. Durand and B. Laks (eds.), *Phonetics to Cognition*. Oxford: Oxford University Press, 432–468.

——, Ducey, V., Vilain, A., and Lalevée, C. (2008). "When the babble-syllable feeds the foot." In B. L. Davis and K. Zajdö (eds.), *The Development of the Syllable*. Mahwah, NJ: Erlbaum, 409–428.

Aich, H., Moos-Heilen, R., and Zimmermann, E. (1990). 'Vocalizations of adult gelada baboons (*Theropithecus gelada*): Acoustic structure and behavioural context.' *Folia Primatologica, 55*, 109–132.

Alcock, K. J., Passingham, R. E., Watkins, K. E., and Vargha-Khadem, F. (2000). 'Oral dyspraxia in inherited speech and language impairment and acquired dysphasia.' *Brain and Language, 75*, 17–33.

Allman, J. (1999). *Evolving Brains*. New York: Scientific American Library.

Allman, W. F. (1990). 'Mother tongue.' *U.S. News & World Report*, November 5, 60–70.

Anderson, S. R. (1981). 'Why phonology isn't natural.' *Linguistic Inquiry, 12*, 493–539.

—— (1985). *Phonology in the Twentieth Century*. Chicago: University of Chicago Press.

Andrew, R. J. (1976). 'Use of formants in the grunts of baboons and other nonhuman primates.' *Annals of the New York Academy of Sciences, 280*, 673–693.

—— (1998). 'Cyclicity in speech derived from call repetition rather than from intrinsic cyclicity of ingestion.' *Behavioral and Brain Sciences, 21*, 513–514.

—— Tommasi, L., and Ford, N. (2000). 'Motor control by vision and the evolution of cerebral lateralization.' *Brain and Language, 73*, 220–235.

Annett, M. (2002). *Handedness and Brain Asymmetry*. New York: Taylor and Francis.

Arai, T., and Greenberg, S. (1997). *The temporal properties of spoken Japanese are similar to those of English.* Paper presented at the Eurospeech Meeting, Rhodes, Greece.

Arbib, M. A. (2005). 'From monkey-like action recognition to human language: An evolutionary framework for neurolinguistics.' *Behavioral and Brain Sciences*, *28*, 105–167.

Arboitiz, F., and García, R. V. (1997). 'The evolutionary origin of the language areas in the human brain: A neuroanatomical perspective.' *Brain Research Reviews*, *25*, 381–396.

Archangeli, D. B. (1997). 'Optimality Theory: An introduction to linguistics in the 1990's.' In D. B. Archangeli and D. C. Pulleyblank (eds.), *Optimality Theory: An Overview*. Malden, MA: Blackwell 1–32.

Aron, A. R., Robins, T. W., and Poldrack, R. A. (2004). 'Inhibition and the right frontal cortex.' *Trends in Cognitive Science*, *8*, 170–177.

Baddeley, A. D. (1986). *Working Memory*. London: Clarendon Press.

—— (1995). 'Working memory.' In M. S. Gazzaniga (ed.), *The Cognitive Neurosciences*. Cambridge, MA: MIT Press, 755–764.

—— and Hitch, G. (1974). 'Working memory.' In E. D. Bower (ed.), *The Psychology of Learning and Motivation*. New York: Academic Press, 47–89.

Bard, K., Hopkins, W. D., and Fort, C. L. (1990). 'Lateral bias in infant chimpanzees (*Pan troglodytes*).' *Journal of Comparative Psychology*, *104*, 309–321.

Bauer, R. H. (1993). 'Lateralization of neural control for vocalization by the frog (*Rana pipiens*).' *Psychobiology*, *21*, 243–248.

Bechtel, W., and Graham, G. (eds.) (1999). *Companion to Cognitive Science* (*Blackwell Companions to Philosophy*). Malden, MA: Bleckwell.

Bellugi, U., and Fischer, S. (1972). 'A comparison of sign language and spoken language: Rate and grammatical mechanisms.' *Cognition*, *1*, 173–200.

Bengtson, J. D., and Ruhlen, M. (1994). 'Global etymologies.' In M. Ruhlen, *On the Origin of Languages*. Stanford: Stanford University Press, 277–336.

Bianki, V. L. (1988). *The Right and Left Hemispheres of the Animal Brain*. New York: Gordon and Breach.

Bickerton, D. (1990). *Language and Species*. Chicago: University of Chicago Press.

Bishop, D. V. M. (2002). 'Motor immaturity and specific speech and language impairment. Evidence for a common genetic basis.' *American Journal of Medical Genetics (Neuropsychiatric Genetics)*, *114*, 56–63.

Blackmore, S. (1999). *The Meme Machine*. Oxford: Oxford University Press.

Blakeslee, S. (2006). 'Cells that read minds.' *New York Times Science section*, Jan. 10.

Blanken, G., Wallesch, C-W., and Papagno, C. (1990). 'Dissociations of language functions in aphasics with speech automatisms (recurring utterances).' *Cortex*, *26*, 41–63.

Bleile, K. M., Stark, R. E., and McGowan, J. S. (1993). 'Speech development in a child after decannulation: Further evidence that babbling facilitates later speech development.' *Clinical Linguistics & Phonetics, 7*, 319–337.

Blevins, J. (1995). 'The syllable in phonological theory.' In J. Goldsmith (ed.), *Handbook of Phonological Theory*. Oxford: Blackwell, 206–244.

—— (2004). *Evolutionary Phonology: The Emergence of Sound Patterns*. Cambridge: Cambridge University Press.

Bloch, J. I., and Boyer, D. M. (2002). 'Grasping primate origins.' *Science, 298*, 1606–1610.

Boë, L. J., Bessière, P., Ladjili, N., and Audibert, N. (2008). 'Simple combinatorial considerations challenge Ruhlen's mother tongue theory.' In B. L. Davis and K. Zajdö (eds.), *The Development of the Syllable*. Mahwah, NJ: Erlbaum, 63–92.

Boer, B. de (2001). *The Origins of Vowel Systems*. Oxford: Oxford University Press.

Boye, M., Güntürkün, O., and Vauclair, J. (2005). 'Right ear advantage for conspecific calls in adults and subadults, but not infant California sea lions (*Zalophus californianus*): Hemispheric specialization for communication?' *European Journal of Neuroscience, 21*, 1727–1732.

Boysson-Bardies, B. de (1993). 'Ontogeny of language-specific syllabic productions.' In B. de Boysson-Bardies, S. de Schonen, P. Jusczyk, P. F. MacNeilage, and J. Morton (eds.), *Developmental Neurocognition: Speech and Face Processing in the First Year of Life*. Dordrecht: Kluwer, 353–363.

—— Vihman, M., Roug-Hellichius, L., Durand, C., Landberg, I., and Arao, F. (1992). 'Material evidence of infant selection from the target language.' In C. Ferguson, L. Menn, and C. Stoel-Gammon (eds.), *Phonological Development*. Timonium, MD: York Press, 369–392.

Braine, M. D. (1994). 'Is nativism sufficient?' *Journal of Child Language, 21*, 9–31.

Brentari, D. (2002). 'Modality differences in sign language phonology and morphophonemics.' In R. P. Meier, K. Cormier, and D. Quinto-Pozos (eds.), *Modality and Structure in Signed and Spoken Languages*. Cambridge: Cambridge University Press, 35–64.

—— and Poizner, H. (1994). 'A phonological analysis of a deaf Parkinsonian signer.' *Language and Cognitive Processes, 9*, 69–99.

Brickner, R. M. (1940). 'A human cortical area producing repetitive phenomena when stimulated.' *Journal of Neurophysiology, 3*, 128–130.

Broca, P. (1861). 'Remarques sur la siege de la faculté du langage articule, suivies d'une observation d'aphemie.' *Bulletin de la Société anatomique de Paris, 2*, 330–357.

Brock, W. H. (1993). *The Norton History of Chemistry*. New York: Norton.

Brodmann, K. (1909). *Vergleichende Lokalisationslehre der Grosshirnrinde in ihren Prinzipien dargestellt auf Grund des Zellenbaues*. Leipzig: Barth.

Browman, C. P., and Goldstein, L. (1986). 'Towards an articulatory phonology.' *Phonology Yearbook, 3*, 219–252.

Bruce, D. (1994). 'Lashley and the problem of serial order.' *American Psychologist*, 49, 93–105.

Brunner, R. J., Kornhuber, H. H., Seemuller, E., Suger, G., and Wallesch, C-W. (1982). 'Basal ganglia participation in language pathology.' *Brain and Language*, 16, 281–299.

Buss, D. (ed.) (2005). *Handbook of Evolutionary Psychology*. New York: Wiley.

Byrne, R. W. (2000). 'The evolution of primate cognition.' *Cognitive Science*, 24, 543–570.

—— and Byrne, J. E. (1991). 'Hand preferences in the skilled gathering tasks of mountain gorillas (*Gorilla g. beringei*).' *Cortex*, 27, 521–546.

Calvin, W. H., and Bickerton, D. (2000). *Lingua Ex Machina: Reconciling Darwin and Chomsky with the Human Brain*. Cambridge, MA: MIT Press.

Caplan, D. (1994). 'Language and the brain.' In M. A. Gernsbacher (ed.), *Handbook of Psycholinguistics*. New York: Academic Press, 1023–1054.

Carson, R. G., Chua, R., Goodman, D., and Byblow, W. D. (1995). 'The preparation of aiming movements.' *Brain and Cognition*, 28, 133–154.

Carstairs-McCarthy, A. (1999). *The Origins of Complex Language: An Inquiry into the Evolutionary Beginnings of Sentences, Syllables, and Truth*. Oxford: Oxford University Press.

Cartmill, M., Pilbeam, D., and Isaac, G. (1986). 'One hundred years of paleoanthropology.' *American Scientist*, 74, 410–420.

Catani, M. C., Jones, D. K., and ffytche, D. H. (2005). 'Perisylvian networks of the human brain.' *Annals of Neurology*, 57, 8–16.

Catrin Blank, C., Scott, S. K., Murphy, K., Warburton, E., and Wise, R. J. (2002). 'Speech production: Wernicke, Broca and beyond.' *Brain*, 125, 1829–1838.

Cavada, C., and Goldman-Rakic, P. (1989) 'Posterior parietal cortex in rhesus monkeys: I. Parcellation of areas based on distinctive limbic and sensory cortico-cortical connections.' *Journal of Comparative Neurology*, 287, 393–421.

Chomsky, N. (1957). *Syntactic Structures*. The Hague: Mouton.

—— (1964). *Current Issues in Linguistic Theory*. The Hague: Mouton.

—— (1965). *Aspects of the Theory of Syntax*. Cambridge, MA: MIT Press.

—— (1966). *Cartesian Linguistics*. New York: Harper & Row.

—— (1968). *Language and Mind*. New York: Harcourt Brace Jovanovich.

—— (1976) Discussion of Chomsky, N. "On the Nature of Language." In S. Harnad, H. D. Steklis, and J. Lancaster (eds.), *Origins and Evolution of Language and Speech*. New York: New York Academy of Sciences, 57.

—— (1986). *Knowledge of Language: Its Nature, Origin, and Use*. New York: Praeger.

—— (1988). *Language and Problems of Knowledge: The Managua Lectures*. Cambridge, MA: MIT Press.

—— (2000). *The Architecture of Language*. Oxford: Oxford University Press.

—— (2006). 'Some simple evo-devo theses: How true might they be for language.' http://www.derekbickerton.com/blog/_archives/2005/10/24/1320752.html

—— and Halle, M. (1968). *The Sound Pattern of English.* New York: Harper & Row.

Clark, A. (1997). *Being There: Putting Brain, Body and World Together Again.* Cambridge, MA: MIT Press.

Clements, G. N., and Hume, E. V. (1995). 'The Internal Organization of Speech Sounds.' In J. A. Goldsmith (ed.), *The Handbook of Phonological Theory.* Oxford: Blackwell Publishing, 245–306.

Code, C. (1982). 'Neurolinguistic analysis of recurrent utterances in aphasia.' *Cortex, 18*, 141–152.

—— (1994). 'Speech automatism production in aphasia.' *Journal of Neurolinguistics, 8*, 149–156.

—— (2002). 'Are syllables hard-wired? Evidence from brain damage.' In R. J. Hartsuiker, R. Bastiaanse, A. Postma, and F. N. K. Wijnen (eds.), *Phonological Encoding and Monitoring in Normal and Pathological Speech.* Hove, Sussex, England: Psychology Press, 312–321.

Cohen, A. H. (1988). 'Evolution of the vertebrate central pattern generator for locomotion.' In A. Cohen, S. Rossignol, and S. Grillner (eds.), *Neural Control of Rhythmic Movements.* New York: John Wiley & Sons, 129–166.

Conrad, R., and Hull, A. J. (1964). 'Information, acoustic confusion and memory span.' *British Journal of Psychology, 55*, 429–432.

Corballis, M. C. (1991). *The Lopsided Ape: Evolution of the Generative Mind.* Oxford: Oxford University Press.

—— (2003). 'From mouth to hand: Gesture, speech and the evolution of right handedness.' *Behavioral and Brain Sciences, 26*, 199–260.

Corbetta, M., and Shulman, G. L. (2002). 'Control of goal-directed and stimulus-driven attention in the brain.' *Nature Reviews: Neuroscience, 3*, 201–215.

Crick, F. (1988). *What Mad Pursuit: A Personal View of Scientific Discovery.* New York: Basic Books.

Crow, T. J. (2004). 'Directional asymmetry is the key to the origin of modern Homo sapiens (the Broca-Annett axiom): A reply to Rogers' review of The Speciation of modern Homo sapiens.' *Laterality, 9*, 233–242.

Crystal, T., and House, A. (1982). 'Segmental durations in connected speech signals: Preliminary results.' *Journal of the Acoustical Society of America, 72*, 705–716.

Damasio, A. (1994). *Descartes' Error: Emotion, Reason, and the Human Brain.* New York: Gosset/Putnam.

—— and Damasio, H. (1994). 'Cortical systems for retrieval of concrete knowledge: The convergence zone framework.' In C. Koch and J. L. Davis (eds.), *Large-Scale Neuronal Theories of the Brain.* Cambridge, MA: MIT Press, 61–75.

Darwin, C. (1859). *On the Origin of Species by Means of Natural Selection or the Preservation of Favored Races in the Struggle for Life.* London: Murray. Reprinted (1952) as *The Origin of Species by Means of Natural Selection.* (Great Books) Encyclopedia Brittanica.

Darwin, C. (1871). *The Descent of Man*. Chicago: (Great Books) Encyclopedia Brittanica (1952).

Davidson, R. J. (1995). 'Cerebral asymmetry, emotion and affective style.' In R. J. Davidson and K. Hugdahl (eds.), *Brain Asymmetry*. Cambridge, MA: MIT Press, 361–388.

Davies, R. (1985). *What's Bred in the Bone*. New York: Viking.

Davis, B. L., and MacNeilage, P. F. (1990). 'The acquisition of correct vowel production: A quantitative case study.' *Journal of Speech and Hearing Research, 33*, 16–27.

—— —— (1995). 'The articulatory basis of babbling.' *Journal of Speech and Hearing Research, 38*, 1199–1211.

—— —— (2000). 'An embodiment perspective on the acquisition of speech perception.' *Phonetica, 57*, 229–241.

—— —— (2002). 'The internal structure of the syllable.' In T. Givón and B. F. Malle (eds.), *The Evolution of Language out of Prelanguage*. Amsterdam: John Benjamins, 135–154.

—— —— and Matyear, C. L. (2002). 'Acquisition of serial complexity in speech production: A comparison of phonetic and phonological approaches.' *Phonetica, 59*, 75–107.

—— —— —— (2005). 'The relationship of early accuracy patterns to the phonetic substrate in the single word period.' Paper presented at the Child Phonology Conference, Vancouver, Canada, June 2005.

Davis, B. P., and Hersch, R. (1986). *Descartes' Dream: The World According to Mathematics*. Sussex: Harvester Press.

Dawkins, R. (1976). *The Selfish Gene*. Oxford: Oxford University Press.

—— (1986). *The Blind Watchmaker*. New York: Norton.

Day, E., and MacNeilage, P. F. (1996). 'Postural asymmetries and language lateralization in humans (Homo sapiens).' *Journal of Comparative Psychology, 110*, 88–96.

Deacon, T. W. (1997). *The Symbolic Species: The Co-evolution of Language and the Brain*. New York: Norton.

DeBleser, R., and Poeck, K. (1985). 'Analysis of prosody in the spontaneous speech of patients with CV-recurring utterances.' *Cortex, 21*, 405–416.

Delis, D., Robertson, L., and Effron, R. (1986). 'Hemispheric specialization of memory for visual hierarchical stimuli.' *Neuropsychologia, 24*: 205–214.

Dennett, D. C. (1995). *Darwin's Dangerous Idea: Evolution and the Meanings of Life*. New York: Simon & Schuster.

DeRenzi, E. (1982). *Disorders of Space Exploration and Cognition*. New York: Wiley.

Descartes, R. (1637). *Discours de la Méthode*.

Dinner, D. S., and Lüders, H. O. (1995). 'Human supplementary sensorimotor area: Electrical stimulation and movement-related potential studies.' In H. H. Jasper, S. Riggio, and P. S. Goldman-Rakic (eds.), *Epilepsy and the Functional Anatomy of the Frontal Lobe*. New York: Raven Press, 261–270.

Dixon, R. (1997). *The Rise and Fall of Languages.* Cambridge: Cambridge University Press.

Dolata, J., Davis, B. L., and MacNeilage, P. F. (2008). 'Characteristics of the rhythmic organization of babbling: Implications for an amodal linguistic rhythm.' Submitted to *Infant Behavior and Development, 31*, 422–431.

Domelöff, E., Rönnqvist, L., and Hopkins, B. (2007). 'Functional asymmetries in the stepping response of the human newborn: A kinematic approach.' *Experimental Brain Research, 177*, 324–335.

Donald, M. (1991). *Origins of the Modern Mind.* Cambridge, MA: Harvard University Press.

—— (1999). 'Preconditions for the evolution of protolanguages.' In M. C. Corballis and S. E. G. Lea (eds.), *The Descent of Mind: Psychological Perspectives on Hominid Evolution.* Oxford: Oxford University Press, 138–154.

—— (2001). *A Mind So Rare.* New York: Norton.

Donegan, P., and Stampe, D. (1979). 'The study of Natural Phonology.' In D. Dinnsen (ed.), *Current Approaches to Phonological Theory.* Bloomington, IN: Indiana University Press, 126–173.

Doupe, A. J., and Kuhl, P. K. (1999). 'Birdsong and human speech: Common themes and mechanisms.' *Annual Review of Neuroscience, 22*, 567–631.

Drachman, G. (1976). 'Child language and language change: A conjecture and some refutations.' In J. Fisiak (ed.), *Recent Developments in Historical Phonology.* The Hague: Mouton, 123–144.

Dunbar, R. I. M. (1996). *Grooming, Gossip and the Evolution of Language.* Cambridge, MA: Harvard University Press.

—— and Dunbar, P. (1975). *Social Dynamics of Gelada Baboons.* Basel: Karger.

Durham, W. H., Boyd, R., and Richerson, P. J. (1997). 'Models and forces of cultural evolution.' In P. Weingart, P. J. Richerson, S. D. Mitchell, and S. Maasen (eds.), *Human by Nature: Between Biology and the Social Sciences.* Mahwah, NJ: Erlbaum, 327–353.

Eccles, J. C. (1982). 'The initiation of voluntary movements by the supplementary motor area.' *Archiv für Psychiatrie Nervenkrankheiten, 231*, 423–441.

—— (1989). *Evolution of the Brain: Creation of the Self.* New York: Routledge.

Edelman, G. M. (1992). *Bright Air, Brilliant Fire: On the Matter of the Mind.* New York: Basic Books.

Ehret, G. (1987). 'Left hemisphere advantage in the mouse brain for recognizing ultrasonic communication calls.' *Nature, 325*, 249–251.

Eimas, P. D., Siqueland, E. R., Jusczyk, P., and Vigorito, J. (1971). 'Speech perception in infants.' *Science, 171*, 303–306.

Elias, L. J., and Bryden, M. P. (1998). 'Footedness is a better predictor of language lateralization than handedness.' *Laterality, 3*, 41–52.

—— —— and Bulman-Fleming, M. B. (1998). 'Footedness is a better predictor than is handedness of emotional lateralization.' *Neuropsychologia, 36*, 37–43.

Elman, J. L., Bates, E. A., Johnson, M. H., Karmiloff-Smith, A., Parisi, D., and Plunkett, K. (1996). *Rethinking Innateness: A Connectionist Perspective on Development.* Cambridge, MA: MIT Press.

Fagot, J., and Bard, K. A. (1995). 'Asymmetric grasping response in neonate chimpanzees (*Pan troglodytes*).' *Infant Behavior and Development*, 18, 253–255.

Falk, D. (2004). 'Prelinguistic evolution in early hominids: Whence motherese.' *Behavioral and Brain Sciences*, 27, 491–503.

Fecteau, S., Armony, J. L., Joanette, Y., and Belin, P. (2005). 'Sensitivity to voice in human prefrontal cortex.' *Journal of Neurophysiology*, 94, 2251–2254.

Ferguson, C. A. (1964). 'Baby talk in 6 languages.' *American Anthropologist*, 66, 103–114.

Fernandes, E. B. M. (1991). 'Tool use and predation of oysters (*Crassostrea rhizophorae*) by the tufted capuchin, *Cebus apella apella*, in brackish water mangrove swamp.' *Primates*, 32, 529–531.

Ferrari, P. F., Gallese, P., Rizzolatti, G., and Fogassi, L. (2003). 'Mirror neurons responding to the observation of ingestive and communicative mouth movements in the monkey ventral premotor cortex.' *European Journal of Neuroscience*, 17, 1703–1714.

Fine, M. L., McElroy, D., Rafi, J., King, C. B., Loesser, K. B., and Newton, S. (1996). 'Lateralization of pectoral stridulation sound production in the channel catfish.' *Physiology and Behavior*, 60, 753–757.

Foerster, O. (1936). 'The motor cortex in man in the light of Hughlings Jackson's doctrines.' *Brain*, 59, 135–159.

Fox, M. D., Corbetta, M., Snyder, A. Z., Vincent, J. L., and Raichle, M. E. (2006). 'Spontaneous neural activity distinguishes human dorsal and ventral attention systems.' *Proceedings of the National Academy of Sciences*, 103, 10046–10051.

Freedman, M., Alexander, M. P., and Naeser, M. A. (1984). 'Anatomic basis of transcortical motor aphasia.' *Neurology*, 34, 409–417.

Fromkin, V. A. (1973). *Speech Errors as Linguistic Evidence.* The Hague: Mouton.

Gardner, R. A., and Gardner, B. T. (1969). 'Teaching language to a great ape.' *Science*, 165, 664–672.

Gardner, T. J., Naef, F., and Nottebohm, F. (2005). 'Freedom and rules: The acquisition and reprogramming of a bird's learned song.' *Science*, 308, 1046–1049.

Garrett, M. F. (1988). 'Processes in language production.' In F. J. Newmeyer (ed.), *Language: Psychological and Biological Aspects.* New York: Cambridge University Press, 69–96.

Gazzaniga, M. S. (ed.) (1995). *The Cognitive Neurosciences.* Cambridge, MA: MIT Press.

—— (ed.) (2000). *The New Cognitive Neurosciences* (2nd edition) Cambridge, MA: MIT Press.

—— and Heatherton, T. F. (2003). *Psychological Science.* New Haven, CT: Yale University Press.

—— Ivry, R., and Mangun, R. (1998). *Cognitive Neuroscience.* New York: Norton.

—— —— —— (2001). *Cognitive Neuroscience* 2nd edition). New York: Norton.

Gentilucci, M., Fogassi, L., Luppino, G., Matelli, M., Camarda, R., and Rizzolatti, G. (1988). 'Functional organization of inferior area 6 in the macaque monkey: 1. Somatotopy and control of proximal movements.' *Experimental Brain Research,* 71, 475–490.

Gernsbacher, M. A. (1994). *Handbook of Psycholinguistics.* New York: Academic Press.

Geschwind, N. (1985). 'Implications for evolution, genetics and clinical syndromes.' In S. D. Glick (ed.), *Cerebral Lateralization in Nonhuman Species.* Orlando: Academic Press, 267–278.

—— Quadfasel, F. A., and Segarra, J. M. (1968). 'Isolation of the speech area.' *Neuropsychologia,* 6, 327–340.

Gibson, J. J. (1977). 'The theory of affordances.' In R. Shaw and J. Bransford (eds.), *Perceiving, Acting and Knowing.* Hillsdale, NJ: Erlbaum, 67–82.

Gibson, K. R. (2002). 'Customs and cultures in animals and humans.' *Anthropological Theory,* 2, 323–339.

Gil-da-Costa, R., Martin, A., Lopes, M. A., Munoz, M., Fritz, J. B., and Braun, A. R. (2006). 'Species-specific calls activate homologs of Broca's and Wernicke's areas in the macaque.' *Nature Neuroscience,* 9, 1064–1070.

Gildersleeve-Neumann, C. E. (2000). 'Production versus ambient language influences on speech development in Quichua.' Unpublished Ph.D. dissertation, University of Texas at Austin.

—— Davis, B. L., and MacNeilage, P. F. (2000). 'Contingencies governing the production of fricatives, affricates, and liquids in babbling.' *Applied Psycholinguistics,* 21, 341–363.

Goldberg, G. (1985). 'Supplementary motor area structure and function: Review and hypothesis.' *Behavioral and Brain Sciences,* 8, 567–616.

Goldin-Meadow, S., and McNeill, D. (1999). 'The role of gesture and mimetic representation in making language the province of speech.' In M. C. Corballis and S. Lea (eds.), *The Descent of Mind: Psychological Perspectives on Hominid Evolution.* Oxford: Oxford University Press, 155–172.

Goldman, H. I. (2001). 'Parental reports of "MAMA" sounds in infants: An exploratory study.' *Journal of Child Language,* 28, 497–506.

Goldschmidt, R. (1940). *The Material Basis of Evolution.* New Haven, CT: Yale University Press.

Goldsmith, J. A. (ed.) (1995). *A Handbook of Phonological Theory.* Oxford: Blackwell.

Gopnik, M., and Crago, M. B. (1991). 'Familial aggregation of a developmental language disorder.' *Cognition,* 39, 1–50.

Gould, S. J. (1977). *Ontogeny and Phylogeny.* Cambridge, MA: Belknap.

Gould, S. J., and Vrba, E. S. (1982). 'Exaptation—a missing term in the science of form.' *Paleobiology, 8,* 4–15.

Grant, P. R. (1986). *Ecology and Evolution of Darwin's Finches.* Chicago: University of Chicago Press.

Green, E., and Howes, D. H. (1977). 'The nature of conduction aphasia: A study of anatomic and clinical features and of underlying mechanisms.' In H. Whitaker and H. A. Whitaker (eds.), *Studies in Neurolinguistics,* Vol. 3. New York: Academic Press, 123–156.

Green, S. (1975). 'Variations of vocal pattern with social situation in the Japanese monkey (*Macaca fuscata*): A field study.' In L. A. Rosenblum (ed.), *Primate Behavior. Vol. 4: Developments in Field and Laboratory Research.* New York: Academic Press, 1–102.

Grégoire, A. (1937). *L'apprentissage du langage. Les deux premières années.* [*The learning of language. The first two years.*] Oxford: Droz.

Gregory, R. L. (ed.) (1989a). *The Oxford Companion to the Mind.* Oxford: Oxford University Press.

—— (1989b). 'Recovery from blindness.' In R. L. Gregory (ed.), *The Oxford Companion to the Mind.* Oxford: Oxford University Press, 94–96.

Grimes, B. (1988). *Ethnologue: Languages of the World* (11th ed.). Dallas, TX: Summer Institute of Linguistics.

Gruber, H. E. (1974). 'Charles Darwin, "M notebook (Jul 1838–Oct 1838)".' In *Darwin on Man: A Psychological Study of Scientific Creativity Together with Darwin's Early and Unpublished Notebooks.* (Paul H. Barrett, transcriber and ed.) New York: Dutton & Co.

Grudin, J. T. (1981) 'The organization of serial order in typing.' Unpublished Ph.D. Dissertation, University of California, San Diego.

Güntürkün, O. (2003). 'Human behavior: Adult persistence of head-turning asymmetry.' *Nature, 421,* 711.

—— and Hoferichter, H. H. (1985). 'Neglect after section of a left telencephalotectal tract in pigeons.' *Behavioral Neuroscience, 18,* 1–9.

Guthrie, E. (1935). *The Psychology of Learning.* New York: Harper.

Guthrie, W. K. C. (1962). *A History of Greek Philosophy.* Cambridge: Cambridge University Press.

Haeckel, E. (1866). *Generelle Morphologie der Organismen.* Berlin: Georg Reimer.

Hage, S. R., and Jürgens, U. (2006). 'On the role of the pontine brain stem in vocal pattern generation: A telemetric single-unit recording study in the squirrel monkey.' *Journal of Neuroscience, 26,* 7105–7115.

Haldane, E. S., and Ross, G. R. T. (1955). *The Philosophical Works of Descartes.* 2 vols. New York: Dover Publications, Inc.

Hale, M., and Reiss, C. (1998). 'Formal and empirical arguments concerning phonological acquisition.' *Linguistic Inquiry, 29,* 656–683.

Halle, M. (1990). 'Phonology.' In D. Osherson and H. Lasnik (eds.), *Invitation to Cognitive Science. Vol. 2: Language.* Cambridge, MA: MIT Press, 43–68.

Hallett, G. L. (1991). *Essentialism: A Wittgensteinian Critique.* Albany: State University of New York Press.

Harasty, J., and Hodges, J. R. (2002). 'Towards the elucidation of the genetic and brain bases of developmental speech and language disorders.' *Brain, 125,* 449–451.

Harrington, A. (1995). 'Unfinished business: Models of laterality in the nineteenth century.' In R. J. Davidson and K. Hugdahl (eds.), *Brain Asymmetry.* Cambridge, MA: MIT Press, 3–28.

Hast, M. H., Fischer, J. M., Wetzel, A. B., and Thompson, V. E. (1974). 'Cortical motor representation of the larynx in *Macaca mullata.*' *Brain Research, 73,* 229–240.

Hauser, M. D. (1996). *The Evolution of Communication.* Cambridge, MA: MIT Press.

—— and Andersson, K. (1994). 'Left hemisphere dominance for processing vocalizations in adult, but not infant, rhesus monkeys: Field experiments.' *Proceedings of the National Academy of Sciences, 91,* 3946–3948.

—— Chomsky, N., and Fitch, W. T. (2002). 'The faculty of language: what is it, who has it, and how did it evolve?' *Science, 298,* 1569–1579.

Hebb, D. O. (1949). *The Organization of Behavior: a Neuropsychological Theory.* New York: John Wiley & Sons.

Heffner, H. E., and Heffner, R. S. (1984). 'Temporal lobe lesions and the perception of species-specific vocalizations by macaques.' *Science, 226,* 75–76.

Hepper, P. G., Wells, D. L., and Lynch, C. (2005). 'Prenatal thumb sucking is related to postnatal handedness.' *Neuropsychologia, 43,* 313–315.

——, Shahidullah, S., and White, R. (1990). 'Origins of fetal handedness.' *Nature, 347,* 431.

Hewes, G. W. (1973). 'Primate communication and the gestural origin of language.' *Current Anthropology, 14,* 5–24.

—— (1996). 'The current status of the gestural theory of language origins.' *Annals of the New York Academy of Sciences, 280,* 482–504.

Hickok, G., Bellugi, U., and Klima, E. S. (1996). 'The neurobiology of sign language and its implications for the neural basis of language.' *Nature, 381,* 699–702.

Hiiemae, K. M., and Palmer, J. B. (2003). 'Tongue movements in feeding and speech.' *Critical Reviews in Oral Biology and Medicine, 14,* 413–429.

Hiscock, M., and Kinsbourne, M. (1995). 'Phylogeny and ontogeny of cerebral lateralization.' In R. J. Davidson and K. Hugdahl (eds.), *Brain Asymmetry.* Cambridge, MA: MIT Press, 535–578.

Hock, H. H. (1986). *Principles of Historical Linguistics.* Berlin: Mouton de Gruyter.

Hockett, C. F. (1955). *A Manual of Phonology.* Baltimore: Waverly Press.

—— (1958). 'In search of Jove's brow.' *American Speech, 34,* 243–313.

Hockett, C. F. (1960). 'The origin of speech.' *Scientific American, 203,* 88–96.

Hohenberger, A., Happ, D., and Leuninger, H. (2002). 'Modality-dependent aspects of sign language production: Evidence from slips of the hands and their repairs in German Sign Language.' In R. P. Meier, K. Cormier, and D. Quinto-Pozos (eds.), *Modality and Structure in Signed and Spoken Languages.* Cambridge: Cambridge University Press, 112–142.

Holman, S. D., and Hutchinson, J. B. (1991). 'Lateralized action of androgen and development of behavior and brain sex differences.' *Brain Research Bulletin, 27,* 261–265.

Hook-Costigan, M. A., and Rogers, L. J. (1996). 'Hand preferences in new world primates.' *International Journal of Comparative Psychology, 9,* 173–207.

—— —— (1998). 'Lateralized use of the mouth in production of vocalizations by marmosets.' *Neuropsychologia, 36,* 1265–1273.

Hopkins, W. D. (1994). 'Hand preferences for bimanual feeding in 140 captive chimpanzees (*Pan troglodytes*): Rearing and ontogenetic determinants.' *Developmental Psychobiology, 27,* 395–407.

—— (1995). 'Hand preferences for a coordinated bimanual task in 110 chimpanzees (*Pan troglodytes*): Cross-sectional analysis.' *Journal of Comparative Psychology, 109,* 291–297.

—— and Bard, K. (1995). 'Asymmetries in spontaneous head turning in infant chimpanzees.' *Behavioral Neuroscience, 109,* 808–812.

—— —— Jones, A., and Bales, S. L. (1993). 'Chimpanzee hand preference in throwing and infant cradling: Implications for the origin of human handedness.' *Current Anthropology, 34,* 786–790.

—— and Cantero, M. (2003). 'From hand to mouth in the evolution of language: The influence of vocal behavior on lateralized hand use in manual gestures by chimpanzees (*Pan troglodytes*).' *Developmental Science, 6,* 55–61.

—— Dahl, J.F., and Pilcher, D. (2001). 'Genetic influence on the expression of hand preferences in chimpanzees (*Pan troglodytes*).' *Psychological Science, 12,* 299–303.

—— and deWaal, F. B. M. (1995). 'Addendum to "Behavioral laterality in captive bonobos (*Pan paniscus*)": Replication and extension.' *International Journal of Primatology, 16,* 261–276.

—— and Leavens, D. A. (1998). 'Hand use and gestural communication in chimpanzees (*Pan troglodytes*).' *Journal of Comparative Psychology, 112,* 95–99.

—— Stoinski, T. S., Lukas, K. E., Ross, S. R., and Wesley, M. J. (2003). 'Comparative assessment of handedness for a coordinated bimanual task in chimpanzees (*Pan troglodytes*), gorillas (*Gorilla gorilla*), and orangutans (*Pongo pygmaeus*).' *Journal of Comparative Psychology, 117,* 302–308.

—— —— —— —— —— (2004). 'Chimpanzees (*Pan troglodytes*) are predominantly right handed: Replication in three populations of apes.' *Behavioral Neuroscience, 118,* 659–663.

—— and Wesley, M. J. (2002). 'Gestural communication in chimpanzees (*Pan troglodytes*): The influence of experimenter position on gesture type and hand preference.' *Laterality, 7,* 19–30.

Humboldt, W. von (1836). *Über die Verschiedenheit des menschlichen Sprachbaus.* Facsimile ed. Bonn: F. Dummlers Verlag, 1960.

Hura, S. L., Lindblom, B., and Diehl, R. L. (1992). 'On the role of perception in shaping phonological assimilation rules.' *Language and Speech, 35,* 59–72.

Hurst, J. A., Baraitser, M., Auger, E., Graham, F., and Norell, S. (1990). 'An extended family with a dominantly inherited speech disorder.' *Developmental Medicine and Child Neurology, 32,* 352–355.

Huxley, T. H. (1863/2005). *Collected Essays of Thomas Huxley: Man's Place in Nature and Other Anthropological Essays.* Whitefish, MT: Kissinger Publishing.

—— (1871). 'On the relations of man to the lower animals.' *Collected Essays, Volume 7.* http://aleph0.clarku.edu/huxley/CE7RelM-L-A.html

Indefrey, P., and Levelt, W. J. M. (2000). 'The neural correlates of language production.' In M. S. Gazzaniga (ed.), *The New Cognitive Neurosciences.* Cambridge, MA: MIT Press, 845–866.

Ingold, T. (1993). 'Tool-use, sociality and intelligence.' In K. R. Gibson and T. Ingold (eds.), *Tools, Language and Cognition in Human Evolution.* Cambridge: Cambridge University Press, 429–472.

Ingram, D. (1974). 'Fronting in infant phonology.' *Journal of Child Language, 1,* 233–241.

Iverson, J., and Fagan, M. K. (2004). 'Infant vocal-motor coordination: Precursor to the Gesture-Speech system?' *Child Development, 75,* 1053–1066.

—— Hall, A. J., Nickel, L., and Wozniak, R. H. (2007). 'The relationship between reduplicated babble onset and laterality biases in infant rhythmic arm movements.' *Brain and Language, 101,* 198–207.

Jackendoff, R. (1988). 'Why are they saying these things about us?' *Linguistic Inquiry, 6,* 435–442.

—— (2002). *Foundations of Language: Brain, Meaning, Grammar, Evolution.* Oxford: Oxford University Press.

Jacob, F. (1977). 'Evolution and tinkering.' *Science, 196,* 1161–1166.

Jaeger, J. J. (1997) 'How to say 'Grandma': The problem of developing phonological representations.' *First Language, 17,* 1–29.

—— (2005). *Kid's Slips: What Young Children's Slips of the Tongue Reveal about Language Development.* Mahwah, NJ: Lawrence Erlbaum Associates.

Jakobson, R. (1960). 'Why "Mama" and "Papa".' In B. Caplan and S. Wapner (eds.), *Essays in Honor of Heinz Werner.* New York: International Universities Press, 124–134.

—— (1967). 'About the relation between visual and auditory signs.' In W. Wathen-Dunn (ed.), *Models for the Perception of Speech and Visual Form.* Cambridge, MA: MIT Press, 1–7.

Jakobson, R. (1968). *Child Language, Aphasia, and Phonological Universals.* The Hague: Mouton.

—— Fant, G., and Halle, M. (1963). *Preliminaries to Speech Analysis.* Cambridge, MA: MIT Press.

—— and Halle, M. (1956). *Fundamentals of Language.* The Hague: Mouton.

Janson, T. (1986). 'Cross-linguistic trends in the frequency of CV sequences.' *Phonology Yearbook, 3,* 179–195.

Jesperson, O. (1922). *Language: its Nature, Development and Origin.* (Reproduced in 1964.) New York: Norton.

Johnson, M. (1987). *The Body in the Mind: The Bodily Basis of Meaning, Imagination, and Reason.* Chicago, IL: University of Chicago Press.

Jonas, S. (1981). 'The supplementary motor region and speech emission.' *Journal of Communication Disorders, 14,* 349–373.

Jordan, M., and Rosenbaum, D. A. (1989). 'Action.' In M. Posner (ed.), *Foundations of Cognitive Science.* Cambridge, MA: MIT Press, 727–768.

Jürgens, U. (1987). 'Primate communication: Signaling, vocalization.' In G. Adelman (ed.), *Encyclopedia of Neuroscience.* Boston: Birkhauser, 976–979.

—— (1998). 'Speech evolved from vocalization, not mastication.' *Behavioral and Brain Sciences, 21,* 519–520.

—— and von Cramon, D. (1982) 'On the role of the anterior cingulate cortex on phonation: A combined case report and experimental monkey study.' *Brain and Language, 15,* 234–248.

—— Kirzinger, A., and von Cramon, D. (1982). 'The effect of deep reaching lesions in the cortical face area on phonation: A combined case report and experimental monkey study.' *Cortex, 18,* 125–140.

Keller, H. (2003). *The Story of My Life.* New York: The Modern Library.

Kemp, T. S. (1982). *Mammal-like Reptiles and the Evolution of Mammals.* London: Academic Press.

Kenstowicz, M. (1994). *Phonology in Generative Grammar.* Oxford: Blackwell Publishing.

Kern, S., and Davis, B. L. (in press). 'Emerging complexity in early vocal acquisition: Cross-linguistic comparison of canonical babbling.' In I. Chirotan, C. Coupé, E. Marsico, and F. Pellegrino (eds.), *Approaches to Phonological Complexity.* Phonology and Phonetics Series, Berlin: Mouton de Gruyter.

Kimura, D. (1979). 'Neuromotor mechanisms in the evolution of human communication.' In H. D. Steklis and M. J. Raleigh (eds.), *Neurobiology of Social Communication in Primates.* New York: Academic Press, 197–220.

King, J. E., and Landau, V. I. (1993). 'Manual preferences in varieties of reaching in squirrel monkeys.' In J. P. Ward and W. D. Hopkins (eds.), *Primate Laterality: Current Evidence of Primate Asymmetries.* New York: Springer-Verlag, 107–124.

Kingston, J. (1990). 'Five exaptations in speech: Reducing the arbitrariness of the constraints on language.' *Behavioral and Brain Sciences, 13*, 738–739.

Klima, E., and Bellugi, U. (1979). *The Signs of Language*. Cambridge, MA: Harvard University Press.

Klivington, K. (ed.) (1989). *The Science of Mind*. Cambridge, MA: MIT Press.

Knight, C., Studdert-Kennedy, M. G., and Hurford, J. R. (2000). 'Language: A Darwinian adaptation.' In Knight, C., Studdert-Kennedy, M. G., and Hurford, J. R., *The Evolutionary Emergence of Language: Social Functions and the Origin of Linguistic Form*. Cambridge: Cambridge University Press, 1–15.

Kozhevnikov, V. A., and Chistovich, L. (1965). *Speech: Articulation and Perception*. Washington: Clearing House for Federal Scientific and Technical Information.

Kuhl, P. K., and Meltzoff, A. N. (1996). 'Infant vocalizations in response to speech: Vocal imitation and developmental change.' *Journal of the Acoustical Society of America, 100*, 2425–2438.

Ladefoged, P. (1993). *A Course in Phonetics*. (3rd ed.). New York: Harcourt Brace Jovanovich.

—— (2006). 'Features and parameters for different purposes.' http://www.linguistics. ucla.edu/people/ladefoge/PLfeaturesParameters.pdf

—— and Maddieson, I. (1996). *The Sounds of the World's Languages*. Oxford: Blackwell.

Lahiri, A., and Evers, V. (eds.) (1991). *Palatalization and Coronality*. San Diego: Academic Press.

Lai, C. S. L., Fisher, S. E., Hurst, J. A., Vargha-Khadem, F., and Monaco, A. P. (2001). 'A forkhead-domain gene is mutated in a severe speech and language disorder.' *Nature, 413*, 519–523.

—— Gerrelli, D., Monaco, A. P., Fisher, S. E., and Copp, A. J. (2003). 'FOXP2 expression during brain development coincides with adult sites of pathology in a severe speech and language disorder.' *Brain, 126*, 2455–2462.

Lakoff, G. (1987). *Women, Fire, and Dangerous Things: What Categories Reveal about the Mind*. Chicago: University of Chicago Press.

—— and Johnson, M. (1980). *Metaphors We Live By*. Chicago: Chicago University Press.

—— —— (1999). *Philosophy in the Flesh*. New York: Basic Books.

Lancaster, J. (1973). *Primate Behavior and the Emergence of Human Culture*. New York: Holt, Rinehart and Winston.

Lashley, K. S. (1942). 'The problem of cerebral organization in vision.' In H Klüver (ed.), 'Visual Mechanisms.' *Biological Symposia, 7*, 301–322.

—— (1951). 'The problem of serial order in behavior.' In L. A. Jeffress (ed.), *Cerebral Mechanisms in Behavior: The Hixon Symposium*. New York: Wiley, 112–136.

Laska, M. (1996). 'Manual laterality in spider monkeys (*Ateles geoffroyi*) solving visually and tactually guided food-reaching tasks.' *Cortex, 32*, 717–726.

Lass, R. (1972). 'How intrinsic is content? Markedness, sound change and "family universals".' In D. Goyvaerts and G. Pullum (eds.), *Essays on the Sound Pattern of English*. Ghent: Story, Scientia, 475–504.

Leben, William (1973). 'Suprasegmental Phonology.' Unpublished Ph.D. dissertation. Bloomington, IN: Indiana University Linguistics Club.

Lee, S., Davis, B. L., and MacNeilage, P. F. (2007). '"Frame Dominance" and the serial organization of babbling and first words in Korean-learning infants.' *Phonetica*. Oxford: Academic Press, 59–92

Lenneberg, E. H. (1967). *Biological Foundations of Language*. New York: John Wiley & Sons.

Levelt, C. (1994). *The Acquisition of Place*. Leiden: Holland Institute of Generative Linguistics.

Levelt, W. J. M. (1989). *Speaking: From Intention to Articulation*. Cambridge, MA: MIT Press.

—— (1992). 'Accessing words in speech production: Stages, processes and representations.' *Cognition, 48*, 1–22.

Levitt, A., and Wang, Q. (1991). 'Evidence for language-specific rhythmic influences in the reduplicative babbling of French- and English-learning infants.' *Language and Speech, 34*, 235–249.

Lieberman, P. (1984). *The Biology and Evolution of Language*. Cambridge, MA: Harvard University Press.

—— (2000). *Human Language and Our Reptilian Brain: The Subcortical Bases of Speech, Syntax and Thought*. Cambridge, MA: Harvard University Press.

Lindblom, B. (1984). 'Can the models of evolutionary biology be applied to phonetic problems?' In M. P. R. Van den Broecke and A. Cohen (eds.), *Proceedings of the 10th International Congress of Phonetic Sciences, Utrecht*. Dordrecht: Foris, 67–81.

—— (1986). 'Phonetic universals in vowel systems.' In J. J. Ohala and J. J. Jaeger (eds.), *Experimental Phonology*. Orlando: Academic Press, 13–44.

—— (1998). 'Systematic constraints and adaptive change in the formation of sound structure.' In J. Hurford, C. Knight, and M. G. Studdert-Kennedy (eds.), *Approaches to the Evolution of Language*. Cambridge: Cambridge University Press, 242–262.

—— and Maddieson, I. (1988). 'Phonetic universals in consonant systems.' In L. Hyman and C. M. Li (eds.), *Language, Speech and Mind*. London & New York: Routledge, 62–78.

Liotti, M., and Tucker, D. M. (1995). 'Emotion in asymmetric corticolimbic networks.' In R. J. Davidson and K. Hugdahl (eds.), *Brain Asymmetry*. Cambridge, MA: MIT Press, 389–424.

Locke, J. L. (1983). *Phonological Acquisition and Change.* New York: Academic Press.

—— and Pearson, D. M. (1990). 'Linguistic significance of babbling: Evidence from a tracheostomized infant.' *Journal of Child Language, 17,* 1–16.

Loeb, G. E. (1987). 'Motor control.' In G. Edelman (ed.), *Encyclopedia of Neuroscience, Volume 2.* Boston: Birkhauser, 690–692.

Lonsdorf, E. V., and Hopkins, W. D. (2005). 'Wild chimpanzees show population-level handedness for tool use.' *Proceedings of the National Academy of Sciences, 102,* 12634–12638.

Lund, J. P. (1998). 'Is speech just chewing the fat?' *Behavioral and Brain Sciences, 21,* 522.

—— and Enomoto, S. (1988). 'The generation of mastication by the central nervous system.' In A. Cohen, S. Rossignol, and S. Grillner (eds.), *Neural Control of Rhythmic Movements.* New York: John Wiley & Sons, 47–72.

—— and Kolta, A. (2006). 'Brainstem circuits that control mastication: Do they have anything to say during speech?' *Journal of Communication Disorders, 39,* 381–390.

—— Sasamoto, K., and Murakami, T. (1984). 'Analysis of rhythmical jaw movements produced by electrical stimulation of motor-sensory cortex of rabbits.' *Journal of Neurophysiology, 52,* 1014–1029.

Luria, A. R. (1970). *Traumatic Aphasia.* The Hague: Mouton.

Luschei, E. S., and Goldberg, L. J. (1981). 'Neural mechanisms of mandibular control: Mastication and voluntary biting.' In V. B. Brooks (ed.), *Handbook of Physiology. Section 1, the Nervous System, vol. ii, Motor Control.* Washington: American Physiological Society, 1237–1274.

Lynch, M. P., Oller, K. D., and Steffens, M. (1989). 'Development of speech-like vocalizations in a child with congenital absence of cochleas: The case of total deafness.' *Applied Psycholinguistics, 10,* 315–333.

Lynch, M. P., Oller, D. K., Steffans, M. L., and Buder, E. H. (1995). 'Phrasing in pre-linguistic vocalizations.' *Developmental Psychobiology, 28,* 3–23.

MacFarquhar, L. (2003). 'The devil's accountant.' *The New Yorker,* March 31, 64–79.

MacKay, D. G. (1987). *The Organization of Perception and Action: A Theory for Language and Other Cognitive Sciences.* New York: Springer Verlag.

Macken, M. (1995). 'Phonological acquisition.' In J. Goldsmith (ed.), *A Handbook of Phonological Theory.* Oxford: Blackwell, 671–696.

Macken, M. A. (1978). 'Permitted complexity in phonological development: One child's acquisition of Spanish consonants.' *Lingua, 44,* 219–253.

MacLean, P. D., and Newman, J. D. (1988). 'The role of midline frontolimbic cortex in production of the isolation call of squirrel monkeys.' *Brain Research, 45,* 111–123.

MacNeilage, P. F. (1964). 'Typing Errors as Clues to Serial Ordering Mechanisms in Language Behaviour.' *Language and Speech*, 7, 144–159.

—— (1970). 'Motor control of serial ordering of speech.' *Psychological Review*, 77, 182–196.

—— (1985). 'Serial ordering errors in speech and typing.' In V. A. Fromkin (ed.), *Phonetic Linguistics*. New York: Academic Press, 193–201.

—— (1998a). 'The frame/content theory of evolution of speech production.' *Behavioral and Brain Sciences*, 21, 499–511.

—— (1998b). 'Towards a unified view of cerebral hemispheric specializations in vertebrates.' In A. D. Milner (ed.), *Comparative Neuropsychology*. Oxford: Oxford University Press, 167–183.

—— (1998c). 'Evolution of the mechanism of language output: Comparative neurobiology of vocal and manual communication.' In J. R. Hurford, M. G. Studdert-Kennedy, and C. Knight (eds.), *Approaches to the Evolution of Language: Social and Cognitive Bases*. Cambridge: Cambridge University Press, 222–241.

—— (2000). 'The explanation of "mama." ' *Behavioral and Brain Sciences*, 23, 440–441.

—— (2003). 'Mouth to hand and back again: Could language have made those journeys?' *Behavioral and Brain Sciences*, 26, 233–234.

—— (2007). 'Present status of the postural origins theory of handedness.' In W. D. Hopkins (ed.), *The Evolution of Hemispheric Specialization in Primates*. Amsterdam: Elsevier. Oxford: Academic Press, 59–92.

—— and Davis, B. L. (1990). 'Acquisition of speech production: The achievement of segmental independence.' In W. J. Hardcastle and A. Marchal (eds.), *Speech Production and Speech Modelling*. Dordrecht: Kluwer, 55–68.

—— —— (1993). 'Motor explanations of babbling and early speech patterns.' In B. de Boysson-Bardies, S. de Schonen, P. W. Jusczyk, P. F. MacNeilage, and J. Morton (eds.), *Developmental Neurocognition: Speech and Face Processing in the First Year of Life*. Dordrecht: Kluwer, 341–352.

—— —— (1999). 'Consonant (vowel) consonant sequences in early words.' *Proceedings of the 14th International Congress of Phonetic Sciences*, Vol. 3. San Francisco: University of California, 2481–2484.

—— —— (2000). 'On the origin of the internal structure of word forms.' *Science*, 288, 527–531.

—— —— (2001). 'Motor mechanisms in speech ontogeny: Phylogenetic, neurobiological and linguistic implications.' *Current Opinion in Neurobiology*, 11, 696–700.

—— —— (2005a). 'Evolution of language.' In D. Buss (ed.), *Handbook of Evolutionary Psychology*. New York: John Wiley & Sons, 698–723.

—— —— (2005b). 'A cognitive-motor frame for speech production: Evidence from neuropathology.' In W. J. Hardcastle and J. M. Beck (eds.), *A Figure of Speech: A Festschrift for John Laver*. Mahwah, NJ: Erlbaum, 130–144.

—— —— (2005c). 'The frame/content theory of evolution of speech: A comparison with a gestural-origins alternative.' *Journal of Interaction Studies*, 6, 173–199.

—— —— (2005d). 'Evolutionary sleight of hand: Then they saw it, now we don't.' *Behavioral and Brain Sciences*, 28, 137–138.

—— —— Kinney, A., and Matyear, C. L. (1999). 'Origin of serial output complexity in speech.' *Psychological Science*, 10, 459–460.

—— —— —— —— (2000). 'The motor core of speech: A comparison of serial organization patterns in infants and languages.' *Child Development*, 71, 153–163.

—— —— and Matyear, C. L. (1997). 'Babbling and first words: Phonetic similarities and differences.' *Speech Communication*, 22, 269–277.

—— and Sholes, G. (1964). 'An electromyographic study of the tongue during vowel production.' *Journal of Speech and Hearing Research*, 7, 209–232.

—— Studdert-Kennedy, M. G., and Lindblom, B. (1987). 'Primate handedness reconsidered.' *Behavioral and Brain Sciences*, 10, 247–303.

Maddieson, I. (1984). *Patterns of Sounds (Cambridge Studies in Speech Science and Communications)*. Cambridge: Cambridge University Press.

—— (1999). 'In search of universals.' *Proceedings of the 14th International Congress of Phonetic Sciences*, Vol. 3. San Francisco: University of California, 2521–2528.

—— and Precoda, K. (1992). 'Syllable structure and phonetic models.' *Phonology*, 9, 45–60.

Maki, S. (1990). 'An experimental approach to the postural origins theory of neurobiological asymmetries in primates.' Unpublished Ph.D. Dissertation, University of Texas at Austin.

Malecot, A., Johnson, R., and Kizziar, P. A. (1972). 'Syllable rate and utterance length in French.' *Phonetica*, 26, 235–251.

Malmberg, B. (1978). 'The linguistic basis of phonetics.' In B. Malmberg (ed.), *Manual of Phonetics*. Amsterdam: North Holland Publishing Company, 1–16.

Marshall, J. C. (1987). 'Introduction.' In H. Poizner, E. S. Klima, and U. Bellugi, *What the Hands Reveal About the Brain*. Cambridge, MA: MIT Press, xiii–xvii.

Martinet, A. (1955) *Economie des changements phonétiques*. Berne: Frank.

Matyear, C. L., MacNeilage, P. F., and Davis, B. L. (1998). 'Nasalization of vowels in nasal environments in babbling: Evidence for frame dominance.' *Phonetica*, 55, 1–17.

Maynard-Smith, J., and Szathmary, E. (1999). *The Origins of Life*. Oxford: Oxford University Press.

Mayr, E. (1982). *The Growth of Biological Thought*. Cambridge, MA: Bellknap.

McCaffrey, H. L., Davis, B. L., and MacNeilage, P. F. (1999). 'Effects of multichannel cochlear implantation on the organization of early speech.' *Volta Review*, 101, 5–28.

McCarthy, R., and Warrington, E. K. (1984). 'A two-route model of speech production. Evidence from aphasia.' *Brain, 107*, 463–485.

McCune, L., Vihman, M. M., and Roug Hellichius, L. (1996). 'Grunt communication in human infants (*Homo sapiens*).' *Journal of Comparative Psychology, 110*, 27–36.

McGrew, W. C., and Marchant, L. F. (1997). 'On the other hand: Current issues in and meta-analysis of the behavioral laterality of hand function in nonhuman primates.' *Yearbook of Physical Anthropology, 40*, 201–232.

McLarnon, A., and Hewitt, G. (1999). 'The evolution of human speech: the role of enhanced breathing control.' *American Journal of Physical Anthropology, 109*, 341–363.

McNeill, D. (1992). *Gesture and Thought.* Chicago: University of Chicago Press.

McShane, J. (1979). 'The development of naming.' *Linguistics, 17*, 879–905.

Medicus, G. (1992). 'On the inapplicability of the biogenetic rule to behavioral development.' *Human Development, 35*, 1–8.

Meguerditchian, A., and Vauclair, J. (2006). 'Baboons communicate with their right hand.' *Behavioral Brain Research, 171*, 170–174.

Meier, R. P. (2002). 'Why different, why the same? Explaining effects and non-effects of modality upon linguistic structure in sign and speech.' In R. P. Meier, K. Cormier, and D. Quinto-Pozos (eds.), *Modality and Structure in Signed and Spoken Languages.* Cambridge: Cambridge University Press, 1–25.

—— Mauk, C. E., Cheek, A., and Moreland, C. J. (in press). 'The form of children's early signs: Iconic or motoric determinants?' *Language and Language Learning.*

—— and Willerman, R. (1995). 'Prelinguistic gesture in deaf and hearing infants.' In K. Emmorey and J. Reilly (eds.), *Language, Gesture and Space.* Hillsdale, NJ: Erlbaum, 391–409.

Meltzoff, A. N., and Decety, J. (2003). 'What imitation tells us about social cognition: a rapprochement between developmental psychology and cognitive neuroscience.' *Philosophical Transactions of the Royal Society of London. Series B. Biological Sciences, 358*, 491–500.

—— and Moore, M. K. (1977). 'Imitation of facial and manual gestures by human neonates.' *Science, 198*, 75–78.

Merriam-Webster's Collegiate Dictionary, Eleventh Edition, 2003.

Michel, G. A. (2002). 'Development of infant handedness.' In D. J. Lewkowics and R. Lickliter (eds.), *Conceptions of Development: Lessons from the Laboratory.* New York: Psychology Press, 165–186.

Mielke, J. (2004). 'The emergence of distinctive features.' Unpublished Ph.D. dissertation, Ohio State University.

Miller, G. A. (1956). 'The magical number seven, plus or minus two: Some limits on our capacity for processing information.' *Psychological Review, 63*, 81–97.

—— (1962). 'Some psychological studies of grammar.' *American Psychologist*, *17*, 748–762.

—— (1990). 'Linguists, psychologists and the cognitive sciences.' *Language*, *66*, 317–322.

Mines, M. A., Hanson, B. F., and Shoup, J. E. (1978). 'Frequency of occurrence of phonemes in conversational English.' *Language and Speech*, *21*, 221–241.

Mitchell, P. R., and Kent, R. D. (1990). 'Phonetic variation in multisyllable babbling.' *Journal of Child Language*, *17*, 247–265.

Moskowitz, B. A. (1991). 'The acquisition of language.' In W. S.-Y. Wang (ed.), *The Emergence of Language: Development and Evolution*. Readings from the Scientific American. New York: W.H. Freeman and Co., 133–149.

Mundinger, P. (1995). 'Behavior-genetic analysis of canary song: Interstrain differences in sensory learning and epigenetic rules.' *Animal Behaviour*, *50*, 1491–1511.

Murdock, G. P. (1959). 'Cross-language parallels in parental kin terms.' *Anthropological Linguistics*, *1*, 1–5.

Murphy, K., Corfield, D. R., Guz, A., Fink, G. R., Wise, R. J., and Harrison, J. (1997). 'Cerebral areas associated with motor control of speech in humans.' *Journal of Applied Physiology*, *83*, 1438–1447.

Myers, R. E. (1976). 'Comparative neurology of vocalization and speech: Proof of a dichotomy.' *Annals of the New York Academy of Sciences*, *280*, 745–757.

Nathani, S., Oller, D. K., and Cobo-Lewis, A. (2003). 'Final syllable lengthening (FSL) in infant vocalizations.' *Journal of Child Language*, *30*, 3–25.

Neville, H. J., Coffey, S. A., Lawson, D., Fischer, A., Emmorey, K., and Bellugi, U. (1997). 'Neural systems mediating American Sign Language: Effects of sensory experience and age of acquisition.' *Brain and Language*, *57*, 285–308.

Newkirk, D., Klima, E. S., Pedersen, C. C., and Bellugi, U. (1980). 'Linguistic evidence from slips of the hand.' In V. Fromkin (ed.), *Errors of Linguistic Performance*. New York: Academic Press, 165–198.

Newman, A. J., Bavelier, D., Corina, D., Jezzard, P., and Neville, H. J. (2002). 'A critical period for right hemisphere recruitment in American Sign Language processing.' *Nature Neuroscience*, *5*, 76–80.

Newmeyer, F. (1998). *Language Form and Language Function*. Cambridge, MA: MIT Press.

—— (2002). 'Uniformitarian assumptions and language evolution research.' In A. Wray (ed.), *The Transition to Language*. Oxford: Oxford University Press, 359–375.

Nowicki, S. (1987). 'Vocal tract resonances in oscine bird sound production: Evidence from birdsongs in a helium atmosphere.' *Nature*, *325*, 53–55.

Ohala, J. J. (1994). 'The frequency code underlies the sound symbolic use of voice pitch.' In L. Hinton, J. Nichols, and J. J. Ohala (eds.), *Sound Symbolism*. Cambridge: Cambridge University Press, 325–347.

Ohala, J. J. (1997). 'The relation between phonetics and phonology.' In W. J. Hardcastle and J. Laver (eds.), *Handbook of Phonetic Sciences*. Oxford: Blackwell Publishing, 674–694.

Ojemann, G. A. (1983). 'Brain organization for language from the perspective of electrical stimulation mapping.' *Behavioral and Brain Sciences*, 6, 189–230.

Oller, D. K. (1980). 'The emergence of speech sounds in infancy.' In G. Yeni-Komshian, J. F. Kavanagh, and G. A. Ferguson (eds.), *Child Phonology, 1. Production*. New York: Academic Press, 93–112.

—— (1986). 'Metaphonology and infant vocalizations.' In B. Lindblom and R. Zetterström (eds.), *Precursors of Early Speech*. New York: Stockton Press, 21–35.

—— (2000). *The Emergence of the Speech Capacity*. Mahwah, NJ: Erlbaum.

—— and Eilers, R. E. (1988). 'The role of audition in infant babbling.' *Child Development*, 59, 441–449.

—— —— and Bassinger, D. (2001). 'Intuitive identification of infant vocal sounds by parents.' *Developmental Science*, 4, 49–60.

—— and Greibel, U. (2008). 'The origins of syllabification in human infancy and in human evolution.' In B. L. Davis and. K. Zajdö (eds.), *The Development of the Syllable*. Mahwah, NJ: Erlbaum, 29–62.

—— and Steffans, M. L. (1994). 'Syllables and segments in infant vocalizations and young child speech.' In M. Yavas (ed.), *First and Second Language Phonology*. San Diego: Singular Publishing Group, 45–61.

Orgogozo, J. M., and Larsen, B. (1979). 'Activation of the supplementary motor area during voluntary movement in man suggests it works as a supramotor area.' *Science*, 206, 847–850.

Oudeyer, P-Y. (2006). *Self-Organization in the Evolution of Speech*. Oxford: Oxford University Press.

Pandya, D. (1987). 'Association cortex.' In G. Adelman (ed.), *The Encyclopedia of Neuroscience*. Boston: Birkhauser, 80–83.

Paradis, C., and Prunet, J.-F. (1991). *The Special Status of Coronals*. San Diego: Academic Press.

Parnell, R. J. (2001). 'Hand preference for food processing in wild western lowland gorillas (*Gorilla gorilla*).' *Journal of Comparative Psychology*, 115, 365–375.

Passingham, R. E. (1987). 'Two cortical systems for directing movement.' In G. Bock, M. O'Connor, and J. Marsh (eds.), *Ciba Foundation Symposium* (Vol. 132). New York: John Wiley & Sons, 151–164.

Pater, J. (1997). 'Minimal violation and phonological development.' *Language Acquisition*, 6, 201–253.

Penfield, W., and Jasper, H. (1954). *Epilepsy and the Functional Anatomy of the Human Brain*. New York: Little Brown.

—— and Roberts, L. (1959). *Speech and Brain Mechanisms*. Princeton, NJ: Princeton University Press.

—— and Welch, K. (1951). 'The supplementary motor area of the cerebral cortex: A clinical and experimental study.' *A.M.A. Archives of Neurology and Psychiatry*, 66, 289–317.

Perkell, J. S., Matthies, M. L., Svirsky, M. A., and Jordan, M. L. (1995). 'Goal-based speech motor control.' *Journal of Phonetics*, 23, 22–25.

Pesetsky, D. (1999). 'Linguistic universals and universal grammar.' In R. A. Wilson and F. Keil (eds.), *The MIT Encyclopedia of the Cognitive Sciences*. Cambridge, MA: MIT Press, 476–478.

Petersen, M., Beecher, B., Zoloth, S., Moody, D., and Stebbins, W. (1978). 'Neural lateralization of species-specific vocalizations by Japanese macaques (*Macaca fuscata*).' *Science*, 202, 324–327.

Pettito, L. A. (1993). 'On the ontogenetic requirements for early language acquisition.' In B. de Boysson-Bardies, S. de Schonen, P. W. Jusczyk, P. F. MacNeilage, and J. Morton (eds.), *Developmental Neurocognition: Speech and Face Processing in the First Year of Life*. Dordrecht: Kluwer, 365–383.

—— Holowka, S., Sergio, L., Levy, B., and Ostry, D. (2004). 'Baby hands that move to the rhythm of language: Hearing babies acquiring sign languages babble silently on the hands.' *Cognition*, 93, 43–73.

—— and Marentette, P. F. (1991). 'Babbling in the manual mode: Evidence for the ontogeny of language.' *Science*, 251, 1493–1496.

Piaget, J. (1954). *The Construction of Reality in the Child*. Oxford, England: Basic Books Press.

Piattelli-Palmarini, M. (1989). 'Evolution, selection, and cognition: From learning to parameter setting in biology and in the study of language.' *Cognition*, 31, 1–44.

Pinker, S. (1994). *The Language Instinct*. New York, NY: William Morrow.

—— and Bloom, P. (1990). 'Natural language and natural selection.' *Behavioral and Brain Sciences*, 13, 707–784.

—— and Jackendoff, R. (2005). 'The faculty of language: What's special about it?' *Cognition*, 95, 201–236.

Plotkin, H. C. (1998). *Evolution in Mind: An Introduction to Evolutionary Psychology*. Cambridge, MA: Cambridge University Press.

Podos, J., Southall, J. A., and Rossi-Santos, M. R. (2004). 'Vocal mechanics in Darwin's finches: Correlation of beak gape and song frequency.' *Journal of Experimental Biology*, 207, 607–619.

Poeck, K., DeBleser, R., and Graf von Keyserlingk, D. (1984). 'The neurolinguistic status and localization of lesion in aphasic patients with exclusively consonant–vowel (CV-) recurrent utterances.' *Brain*, 107, 200–217.

Poizner, H., Klima, E., and Bellugi, U. (1987). *What the Hands Reveal about the Brain*. Cambridge, MA: MIT Press.

Poremba, A., Malloy, M., Saunders, R. C., Carson, R. E., Hersovitch, P., and Mishkin, M. (2004). 'Species-specific calls evoke asymmetric activity in the monkey's temporal poles.' *Nature*, 427, 448–451.

Posner, M. (1989). *Foundations of Cognitive Science.* Cambridge, MA: MIT Press.

Previc, F. H. (1991). 'A general theory concerning the prenatal origins of cerebral lateralization in humans.' *Psychological Review, 98,* 299–334.

Pribram, K. H. (1976). 'hemispheric specialization: Evolution or revolution.' In S. J. Dimond and D. A. Blizzard (eds.), *Evolution and Lateralization of the Brain.* New York: New York Academy of Sciences, 18–22.

Prigogine, I., and Stengers, I. (1984). *Order Out of Chaos.* London: Fontana.

Prince, A., and Smolensky, P. (1997). 'Optimality: From neural networks to universal grammar.' *Science, 275,* 1604–1610.

Purvis, A. (1995). 'A composite estimate of primate phylogeny.' *Philosophical Transactions of the Royal Society of London, Series B., 348,* 405–421.

Quaranta, A., Sinischalchi, M., and Vallortigara, G. (2007). 'Asymmetric tail-wagging responses by dogs to different emotive stimuli.' *Current Biology, 17,* 199–201.

Ramsay, S. C., Adams, L., Murphy, K., Corfield, D. R., Grootoonk, S., and Bailey, D. L. (1993). 'Regional cerebral blood flow during volitional expiration in man: A comparison with volitional inspiration.' *Journal of Physiology (London), 461,* 85–101.

Redford, M. A., MacNeilage, P. F., and Davis, B. L. (1997). 'Production constraints on utterance-final consonant characteristics in babbling.' *Phonetica, 54,* 172–186.

—— and van Donkelaar, P. (2008). 'Jaw cycles and linguistic syllables in adult English.' In B. L. Davis and K. Zajdö (eds.), *The Development of the Syllable.* Mahwah, NJ: Erlbaum, 355–376.

Redican, W. K. (1975). 'Facial expressions in nonhuman primates.' In L. A. Rosenblum (ed.), *Primate Behavior: Developments in Field and Laboratory Research,* Vol. 4. New York: Academic Press, 103–194.

Resnik, M. (1994). *Turtles, Termites and Traffic Jams: Explanations in Massively Parallel Microworlds.* Cambridge, MA: MIT Press.

Ridley, M. (2000). *Genome.* New York: Perennial (HarperCollins).

—— (2003). *Nature Via Nurture: Genes, Experience and What Makes Us Human.* New York: Harper Collins.

Rizzolatti, G., Camarda, R., Fogassi, L., Gentilluci, M., Luppino, G., and Matelli, M. (1988). 'Functional organization of inferior area 6 in the macaque monkey: II. Area F5 and the control of distal movements.' *Experimental Brain Research, 71,* 491–507.

—— Matelli, M., and Pavesi, G. (1983). 'Deficits in attention and movement following the removal of postarcuate (area 6) and prearcuate (area 8) cortex in macaque monkeys.' *Brain, 106,* 655–673.

Robinson, B. W. (1976). 'Limbic influences on human speech.' *Annals of the New York Academy of Sciences, 280,* 761–771.

Robinson, J. G. (1979). 'An analysis of the organization of vocal communication in the titi monkey (*Callicebus moloch*).' *Zeitschrift für Tierpsychologie, 49,* 381–405.

Robinson, R. J., and Downhill, J. E. (1995). 'Lateralization of psychopathology in response to focal brain injury.' In R. J. Davidson and K. Hugdahl (eds.), *Brain Asymmetry.* Cambridge, MA: MIT Press, 693–712.

Rogers, L. J., and Andrew, R. J. (2002). *Comparative Vertebrate Lateralization.* Hove, UK: Psychology Press.

Roland, P. (1993). *Brain Activation.* New York: John Wiley & Sons.

Romanski, L. M., and Goldman-Rakic, P. S. (2002). 'An auditory domain in primate ventrolateral prefrontal cortex.' *Nature Neuroscience, 5,* 15–16.

—— Averbeck, B. B., and Diltz, M. (2005). 'Neural representation of vocalizations in the primate prefrontal cortex.' *Journal of Neurophysiology, 93,* 734–747.

Ronnqvist, L., and von Hofsten, C. (1994). 'Varieties and determinants of finger movements in neonates.' *Early Development and Parenting, 3,* 81–94.

Rosenbaum, D. A. (2005). 'The neglect of motor control in the science of mental life and behavior.' *American Psychologist, 60,* 308–317.

Rossignol, S., Lund, J. P., and Drew, T. (1988). 'The role of sensory inputs in regulating patterns of rhythmical movements in higher vertebrates: A comparison between locomotion, respiration and mastication.' In A. Cohen, S. Rossignol, and S. Grillner (eds.), *Neural Control of Rhythmic Movements in Vertebrates.* New York: John Wiley & Sons, 201–284.

Rousset, I. (2003). 'From lexical to syllabic organization: Favored and disfavored co-occurrences.' *Proceedings of the 15th International Congress of Phonetics.* Barcelona: Autonomous University of Barcelona, 2705–2708.

Rowe, N. (1996). *The Pictorial Guide to Living Primates.* East Hampton, N.Y.: Pegonias Press.

Rubens, A. B. (1975). 'Aphasia with infarction in the territory of the anterior cerebral artery.' *Cortex, 11,* 239–250.

—— (ed.) (1976). *Transcortical Motor Aphasia.* New York: Academic Press.

Ruhlen, M. (1994). *The Origin of Language: Tracing the Evolution of the Mother Tongue.* New York: John Wiley & Sons.

Russell, B. (1945). *History of Western Philosophy.* New York: Touchstone.

Sacks, O. (1995). *An Anthropologist on Mars: Seven Paradoxical Tales.* New York: Vintage.

Salmons, J. C., and Joseph, B. D. (1998). *Nostratic: Sifting the Evidence.* Amsterdam: John Benjamins.

Sandler, W. (2008). 'The syllable in sign language: Considering the other natural language modality.' In B. L. Davis and K. Zajdö (eds.), *The Development of the Syllable.* Mahwah, NJ: Erlbaum, 379–408.

—— and Lillo-Martin, D. (2001). 'Natural sign languages.' In M. Aronoff (ed.), *The Blackwell Handbook of Linguistics.* Oxford: Blackwell, 533–562.

Sandler, W. and Lillo-Martin, D. (2006). *Sign Language and Linguistic Universals.* Cambridge: Cambridge University Press.

Saussure, F. de (1915). *Cours de Linguistique Générale,* ed. C. Bally and A. Sechehaye. English translation: *Course in General Linguistics.* New York: Philosophical Library, 1959.

Seidenberg, M.S. (1997). 'Language acquisition and use: Learning and applying probabilistic constraints.' *Science, 275,* 1599–1603.

Sergent, J. (1982) 'The cerebral balance of power: Confrontation or cooperation.' *Journal of Experimental Psychology: Human Perception and Performance, 8,* 253–272.

Shattuck-Hufnagel, S. (1979). 'Speech errors as evidence for a serial ordering mechanism in speech production.' In W. E. Cooper and E. C. T. Walker (eds.), *Sentence Processing: Psycholinguistic Studies presented to Merrill Garrett.* Hillsdale, NJ: Erlbaum, 295–342.

—— (1980). 'Speech units smaller than the syllable.' *Journal of the Acoustical Society of America, 72,* suppl. 1.

—— and Klatt, D. H. (1979). 'The limited use of distinctive features and markedness in speech production: Evidence from speech error data.' *Journal of Verbal Learning and Verbal Behavior, 18,* 41–55.

Singer, W. (1989). 'The brain: a self-organizing system.' In K. Klivington (ed.), *The Science of Mind.* Cambridge, MA: MIT Press, 174–180.

Smith, B. L., Brown-Sweeney, S., and Stoel-Gammon, C. (1989). 'A quantitative analysis of reduplicated and variegated babbling.' *First Language, 9,* 175–189.

Solis, M. M., and Perkel, D. J. (2005). 'Rhythmic activity in a forebrain vocal control nucleus in vitro.' *Journal of Neuroscience, 25,* 2811–2822.

Sperry, R. (1952). 'Neurology and the mind-brain problem.' *American Scientist, 39,* 291–312.

Spinazzola, L., Cubelli, R., and Della Sala, S. (2003) 'Impairment of trunk lesions following left and right hemisphere lesions: Dissociation between apraxic errors and postural instability.' *Brain, 126,* 2656–2666.

Spinozzi, G., Castorina, M. G., and Truppa, V. (1998). 'Hand preferences in unimanual and coordinated-bimanual tasks by tufted capuchin monkeys (*Cebus apella*).' *Journal of Comparative Psychology, 112,* 183–191.

Stager, C. L., and Werker, J. F. (1997). 'Infants listen for more phonetic detail in speech perception than in word-learning tasks.' *Nature, 388,* 381–382.

Stap, D. (2005). *Birdsong.* New York: Scribner.

Stamenov, M. I., and Gallese, V. (2002). 'Introduction.' In M. I. Stamenov and V. Gallese (eds.), *Mirror Neurons and the Evolution of Brain and Language.* Amsterdam: John Benjamins Publishing Company, 1–10.

Stelt, J. M. van der, and Koopmans-van Beinum, F. J. (1986). 'Early stages in the development of speech movements.' In B. Lindblom and R. Zetterström (eds.), *Precursors of Early Speech.* New York: Stockton Press, 37–50.

Stent, G. S. (1981). 'Strength and weakness of the genetic approach to the development of the nervous system.' *Annual Review of Neuroscience, 4*, 163–194.

Studdert-Kennedy, M. G. (1998). 'The particulate origins of language generativity: From syllable to gesture.' In J. Hurford, C. Knight, and M. G. Studdert-Kennedy (eds.), *Approaches to the Evolution of Language.* Cambridge: Cambridge University Press, 202–221.

—— and Lane, H. (1980). 'Clues from the difference between signed and spoken languages.' In U. Bellugi and M. Studdert-Kennedy (eds.), *Signed and Spoken Language: Biological Constraints on Linguistic Form.* Berlin: Verlag Chemie, 29–40.

Talairach, J., Bancaud, J., Geier, J. S., Bordas-Ferrer, M., Bonis, A., Szikla, G., and Rusu, M. (1973). 'The cingulate gyrus and human behaviour.' *Electroencephalography and Clinical Neurophysiology, 34*, 45–52.

Tanji, J., Shima, Y., Matsuzaka, Y., and Halsband, U. (1995). 'Neuronal activity in the supplementary, presupplementary and premotor cortex of monkey.' In M. Kimura and A. M. Graybiel (eds.), *Functions of the Cortico-Basal Ganglia Loop.* Tokyo: Springer, 154–165.

Teixeira, E. R., and Davis, B. L. (2002). 'Early sound patterns in the speech of two Brazilian Portuguese speakers.' *Language and Speech, 45*, 179–204.

Thelen, E. (1981). 'Rhythmical behavior in infants: An ethological perspective.' *Developmental Psychology, 17*, 237–257.

—— (1995). 'Motor development: A new synthesis.' *American Psychologist, 50*, 79–95.

—— and Smith, L. B. (1994). *A Dynamic Systems Approach to the Development of Cognition and Action.* Cambridge, MA: MIT Press.

Thompson, D. W. (1917). *On Growth and Form.* Cambridge: Cambridge University Press.

Thong, H. S. (1999). *The Golden Serpent. How Humans Learned to Speak and Invent Culture.* Self-published.

Thorpe, W. H., and Hall-Craggs, J. (1976). 'Sound production and perception in birds as related to the general principles of pattern perception.' In P. P. G. Bateson and R. A. Hinde (eds.), *Growing Points in Ethology.* Cambridge: Cambridge University Press, 171–189.

Tinbergen, N. (1952). 'Derived activities: Their causation, biological significance, origin and emancipation during evolution.' *Quarterly Review of Biology, 27*, 1–32.

Tolman, E. C. (1932). *Purposive Behavior in Animals and Men.* London: Century/ Random House UK Ltd.

Tomasello, M. (1998a). 'Introduction: A cognitive-functional-perspective on language structure.' In M. Tomasello (ed.), *The New Psychology of Language: Cognitive and Functional Approaches to Language Structure.* Mahwah, NJ: Erlbaum, vii–xxiii.

—— (ed.) (1998b). *The New Psychology of Language: Cognitive and Functional Approaches to Language Structure.* Mahwah, NJ: Erlbaum.

Tomasello, M. and Camaioni, L. (1997). 'A comparison of the gestural communication of apes and human infants.' *Human Development, 40*, 7–24.

Tooby, J., and Cosmides, L. (1992). 'The psychological foundations of culture.' In J. H. Barkow, L. Cosmides, and J. Tooby (eds.), *The Adapted Mind: Evolutionary Psychology and the Generation of Culture*. New York: Oxford University Press, 19–136.

Toulmin, S. E., and Goodfield, J. (1965). *The Discovery of Time*. New York: Harper and Row.

Trask, L. R. (2003). 'Where do mama/papa words come from?' http://www.sussex.ac.uk/linguistics/documents/where_do_mama2.pdf

Trevarthen, C. (1978) 'Manipulative strategies of baboons and the origins of cerebral asymmetry.' In M. Kinsbourne (ed.), *Asymmetrical Function of the Brain*. Cambridge: Cambridge University Press, 329–389.

Turvey, M. T., and Carello, C. (1995). 'Some dynamical themes in perception and action.' In R. F. Port and T. van Gelder (eds.), *Mind as Motion: Explorations in the Dynamics of Cognition*. Cambridge, MA: MIT Press, 373–401.

Tyler, A. A., and Langsdale, T. E. (1996). 'Consonant–vowel interaction in early phonological development.' *First Language, 16*, 159–191.

Vaivre-Douret, L., Le Normand, M. T., and Wood, C. (1995). 'Developmental outcome in a tracheostomized child: A case study.' *Early Child Development and Care, 112*, 13–26.

Vallortigara, G., and Rogers, L. J. (2005). 'Survival with an asymmetrical brain: Advantages and disadvantages of cerebral lateralization.' *Behavioral and Brain Sciences, 28*, 575–589.

Varela, F. J., Thompson, E., and Rosch, E. (1991). *The Embodied Mind: Cognitive Science and Human Experience*. Cambridge, MA: MIT Press.

Vargha-Khadem, F., Watkins, K., Alcock, K., Fletcher, P., and Passingham, R. (1995). 'Praxic and nonverbal cognitive deficits in a large family with a genetically transmitted speech and language disorder.' *Proceedings of the National Academy of Sciences, USA, 92*, 930–933.

Vauclair, J., Meguerditchian, A., and Hopkins, W. D. (2005). 'Hand preferences for unimanual and coordinated bimanual tasks in baboons (*Papio anubis*).' *Cognitive Brain Research, 25*, 210–216.

Vicario, D. S., and Simpson, H. B. (1995). 'Electrical stimulation in forebrain nuclei elicits learned vocal patterns in songbirds.' *Journal of Neurophysiology, 73*, 2602–2607.

Vihman, M. (1992). 'Early syllables and the construction of phonology.' In C. A. Ferguson, L. Menn, and C. Stoel-Gammon (eds.), *Phonological Development: Models, Research, Implications*. Timonium, MD: York Press, 393–422.

Visalberghi, E., and Fragaszy, D. (2002). ' "Do monkeys ape?"—Ten years after.' In K. Dautenhahn and K. Nehaniv (eds.), *Imitation in Animals and Artifacts*. Cambridge, MA: MIT Press, 471–500.

Walker, A., and Shipman, P. (1996). *The Wisdom of Bones*. London: Wiedenfeld and Nicolson.

Wallesch, C–W. (1990). 'Repetitive verbal behavior: Functional and neurological considerations.' *Aphasiology*, 4, 133–154.

Ward, J. P., Milliken, G. K., and Stafford, D. K. (1993). 'Patterns of lateralized behavior in prosimians.' In J. P. Ward and W. D. Hopkins (eds.), *Primate Laterality: Current Evidence of Primate Asymmetries*. New York: Springer-Verlag, 43–74.

Warren, J. M. (1980). 'Handedness and laterality in humans and other animals.' *Physiological Psychology*, 8, 351–359.

Watanabe, K., and Kawai, M. (1993). 'Lateralized hand use in the precultural behavior of the koshima monkeys (*Macaca fuscata*).' In W. D. Hopkins and J. P. Ward (eds.), *Primate Laterality: Current Behavioral Evidence of Primate Asymmetries*. New York: Springer-Verlag, 183–192.

Watkins, K. E., Dronkers, N. F., and Vargha-Khadem, F. (2002). 'Behavioral analysis of an inherited speech and language disorder: Comparison with acquired aphasia.' *Brain*, 125, 452–464.

Watson, J. B. (1913). 'Psychology as the behaviorist views it.' *Psychological Review*, 20, 158–177.

—— (1920). 'Is thinking merely the action of the language mechanisms?' *British Journal of Psychology*, 11, 86–104.

Watson, R. T., Fleet, W. S., Gonzales-Rothi, L., and Heilman, K. M. (1986). 'Apraxia and the supplementary motor area.' *Archives of Neurology*, 43, 787–792.

Webb, J. (2003). 'From Ishtar to Aphrodite: The transformation of a goddess.' In S. Hadjisävväs (ed.), *From Ishtar to Aphrodite: 3200 years of Cypriot Hellenism. Treasures from the Museums of Cyprus*. New York: Alexander S. Onassis Public Benefit Foundation, 15–20.

Weiner, J. (1994a). 'The handy-dandy evolution prover.' *New York Times*, May 8.

—— (1994b). *The Beak of the Finch*. New York: Alfred A. Knopf, Inc.

Wernicke, C. (1874) *Der Aphasische Symptomenkomplex*. Breslau: Max Cohn and Weigert.

Westergaard, G. C., Kuhn, H. E., and Suomi, S. J. (1998). 'Bipedal posture and hand preference in humans and other primates.' *Journal of Comparative Psychology*, 112, 55–64.

—— and Suomi, S. J. (1996). 'Hand preference for a bimanual task in tufted capuchins (*Cebus apella*) and rhesus macaques (*Macaca mulatta*).' *Journal of Comparative Psychology*, 110, 406–411.

Whitehead, A. N., and Russell, B. (1910). *Principia Mathematica* (2nd ed. Vol. 1–3). Cambridge: Cambridge University Press.

Whittemore, G. (1987). 'The production of ASL signs.' Unpublished Ph.D. dissertation, University of Texas at Austin.

Williams, H. W. (1971). *Dictionary of the Maori Language* (7th ed.). Wellington, New Zealand: A. H. & A.W. Reed.

Wilson, E. O. (1975). *Sociobiology: The New Synthesis*. Cambridge, MA: Harvard University Press.

Wilson, F. R. (1998). *The Hand: How its Use Shapes the Brain, Language and Human Culture*. New York: Pantheon Books.

Wise, S. P. (1984). 'Nonprimary motor cortex and its role in the cerebral control of movement.' In G. Edelman, W. E. Gall, and W. M. Cowans (eds.), *Dynamic Aspects of Neocortical Function*. New York: John Wiley & Sons, 525–555.

—— (2007). 'The Evolution of Primate Nervous Systems.' In L. H. Krubitzer & J. H. Kass (eds.), *Evolution of Nervous Systems, Vol. 4: Evolution of Nervous Systems in Mammals*. Amsterdam: Elsevier, 157–166.

Wittling, W. (1995). 'Brain asymmetry in the control of autonomic-physiologic activity.' In R. J. Davidson and K. Hugdahl (eds.), *Brain Asymmetry*. Cambridge, MA: MIT Press, 305–308.

Woll, B., and Sieratzki, J. S. (1998). 'Echo phonology: Signs of a link between gesture and speech.' *Behavioral and Brain Sciences*, *21*, 531–532.

Woolsey, C. N. (1958). 'Organization of somatic sensory and motor areas of the cerebral cortex.' In H. F. Harlow and C. N. Woolsey (eds.), *Biological and Biochemical Bases of Behavior*. Madison: University of Wisconsin Press, 61–74.

Wright, J. T. (1986). 'The behavior of nasalized vowels in the perceptual vowel space.' In J. J. Ohala and J. J. Jaeger (eds.), *Experimental Phonology*. New York: Academic Press, 45–67.

Ziegler, W., Kilian, B., and Deger, K. (1997). 'The role of left mesial frontal cortex in fluent speech: Evidence from a case of left supplementary motor area hemorrhage.' *Neuropsychologia*, *35*, 1197–1208.

Zmarich, C., and Lanni, R. (1999). 'A phonetic and acoustic study of the babbling of an Italian child.' *Proceedings of the 5th International Conference on Spoken Language Processing*. Sydney, Australia, 2703–2706.

Index

a priori form
  classical (Platonic/Cartesian)
    view 9–10
  language 5, 27–8, 52–3, 132,
    166
Abler, W. 97
Abry, C. 187, 328
acoustics of speech 78–9, 245
action/s
  adaptations 12
  and hemispheric
    specializations 210–14
  and iconicity 138
  and kinematic imagination 100
  as primary focus 4–9, 12
  biphasic cycle as main basis 90
  birdsong 305–8, 330–1
  brain control dichotomy for 163,
    167–71
  chewing 91
  conclusions re 320–2, 326
  Donald on mimesis 98–102
  elaboration in humans 173
  frame as speech basis 105
  "great end of life" 218
  human, monkey precursors 198–9
  initiation 180
  Lashley on serial order 34–8
  neglect in epistemology 10–11
  not de novo 89
  rehearsal loop; e.g., babbling 99
  role of frame 105
  role of, vis a vis perception 11

speech as 81, 248
typing 86
vocal learnability 60
see also extrinsic system; intrinsic
  system
adamic language 137
adaptation/s 6, 39
  and language 17
  arboreal, in prosimians 327
  definition 12
  Jacob on 15
  reaching, in primates 213
  speech as 57
  Tinbergen and 34, 38
  tool use 200–2
affordance, defined 132
airstream mechanisms 72–3
Alexander, M. 195
Allman, J. 333
amodal language capacity
  and first language 284
  brain organization and 281–3
  phonological structure and 274–7,
    288
  phonology, lack of evidence 60, 325,
    330
  sign babbling and 277–81
  sign language action and 275–6,
    280, 307, 309
  versus embodied capacities 273
Anderson, S. 228–30, 236–9, 261, 267,
  330
Andrew, R. 94, 201, 306

first words (hominids) (*cont.*)
LC preferences as self-
organizational 130
monogenesis versus
polygenesis 153–4
nasal demand cry and 149–50
nasal/oral contrast in 150–1
no generative approach 158–9
no separate syllables 125–6
nominal insight and 151–2, 157
nouns favored 157
onomatopoeia 154–5
size principle 155
summary 158
when? 312
see also parental terms
Fischer, S. 280
Fitch, W. 42
Foerster, O. 176
footedness
and hemispheric
specialization 210–11
coordination asymmetry,
neonates 214
formalism 20
formalism in phonology
and Saussure 28
The Sound Pattern of English 236–9
formant/s 68
for vowels 78–9
Fort, C. 214
Fox, M. 215
frame/content (F/C) theory 57, 60, 86,
135
and primate handedness 203
frame stage 59, 105–20, 197
frame/content stage 59, 131, 197, 322
F/C mode as evolutionary target 87,
102
heuristic role 328
no speech-specific innateness 132

speech from bimanual
coordination 203
see also content; frames
frames 57, 121, 133, 322
and learnable vocalization 306–7
and syllable structure 84
as carrier 105, 321
cognitive/cognitive-motor 60, 107,
188–9, 324
cyclicity not de novo 89
fronted, and backed 113
high amplitude in babbling 122
in birdsong 304–6
in hominids' first words 320
mental 58
motor 58, 89, 95–6, 102, 107, 117,
188, 311
not simply endogenous 108
premotor frame 188
programming of 89, 163, 170, 199,
323–4
pure 113, 126–7, 25
rhythmicity of 108
then content 58, 106
to frame/content mode 102, 105
Freedman, M. 195
Fromkin, V. 83
frontal lobe 164–5, 175, 177, 28
functionalists 53

Gallese, P. 324
García, R. 191–3
Gardner, B. 285
Gardner, R. 285
Gardner, T. 301
Garrett, M. 85
Gazzaniga, M. 170, 212, 327
generative/generativist (use of
terms) 52–3
generative grammar
closed mathematical system 31

Oxford Studies in the Evolution of Language

General Editors
Kathleen R. Gibson, *University of Texas at Houston,* and James R. Hurford, *University of Edinburgh*

In Preparation

Darwinian Linguistics
Evolution and the Logic of Linguistic Theory
Stephen R. Anderson

The Evolution of Linguistic Form
Language in the Light of Evolution 2
James R. Hurford

To be Published in Association with the Series

The Oxford Handbook of Language Evolution
edited by Maggie Tallerman and Kathleen R. Gibson

Published in Association with the Series

Language Diversity
Daniel Nettle

Function, Selection, and Innateness
The Emergence of Language Universals
Simon Kirby

The Origins of Complex Language
An Inquiry into the Evolutionary Beginnings of Sentences, Syllables, and Truth
Andrew Carstairs McCarthy